CW01302806

The Townshends of Raynham

Courtesy, The National Museum of Wales, Cardiff

Courtesy, National Portrait Gallery, London

Horatio Townshend (right) and Charles Townshend (left), oil portraits respectively by P. Lely and G. Kneller.

James M. Rosenheim

The Townshends of Raynham

*Nobility in Transition in Restoration
and Early Hanoverian England*

Wesleyan University Press
Middletown, Connecticut

Copyright © 1989 by James M. Rosenheim
All rights reserved

All inquiries and permissions requests should be addressed to the Publisher, Wesleyan University Press, 110 Mt. Vernon Street, Middletown, Connecticut 06457.

Library of Congress Cataloging-in-Publication Data
Rosenheim, James M.
The Townshends of Raynham : nobility in transition in Restoration and early Hanoverian England / James M. Rosenheim—1st ed.
   p. cm.
Bibliography: p.
Includes index.
ISBN 0-8195-5217-8
1. Townshend, Charles Townshend, Viscount, 1674–1738.
2. Townshend, Horatio Townshend, Viscount, 1630–1687. 3. Statesmen—Great Britain—Biography. 4. Agriculturists—England—Biography.
5. England—Nobility—History—18th century. 6. England—Nobility—History—17th century. 7. Norfolk (England)—Biography.
8. Raynham Hall (England)   I. Title.
       DA501.T72R68   1989
     941.06'092—dc20   89-31140
                             CIP

Manufactured in the United States of America

First Edition

to the memory of Ann Marchioness Townshend

❋ Contents ❋

Tables ix
Figures and Maps xi
Preface and Acknowledgments xiii
Abbreviations xix
A Note on Style xxi

Introduction
3

Chapter 1
The Failed Politician
Horatio First Viscount Townshend
13

Chapter 2
Horatio Townshend
From Spendthrift to Patriarch
64

Chapter 3
A Time of Transition, 1687–1709
105

Chapter 4
Getting and Spending
The Second Viscount as Landlord
132

Chapter 5
The Renovation of Raynham Hall
A Study in Cultural Change

167

Chapter 6
Charles Townshend
National Reputation and Local Politics

190

Conclusion

242

Selected Bibliography 247
Index 257

❋ Tables ❋

2.1	Rentals, 1655–1684	69
2.2	Average Annual Raynham Household Expenses	74
2.3	Lord Townshend's Estimate of Annual Expenses, 1685	77
2.4	Mortgages of the First Viscount Townshend	88
2.5	Rents and Arrears, 1679	99
4.1	Norfolk Rentals, 1701–1737	137
4.2	Rent Outstanding One Year after Due, 1732–1738	138
4.3	Farm Rents and Tenant Allowances, 1701–1738	139
4.4	Sources of Increase in Rental Value on Norfolk Bailiwicks, 1701–1737	142
4.5	Monthly Rates of Household Expenditure, 1704–1724	161
4.6	London and Related Expenses, 1724–1730	162
4.7	Raynham Household Expenditures, 1730–1736	163
5.1	Thomas Ripley's Bills for Work at Raynham, 1724–1732	186
5.2	Expenditures on Raynham Renovations, 1724–1731	188

Figures and Maps

Figures

2.1	Horatio Townshend's Known Debt, 1651–1687	83
5.1	East façade of Raynham Hall, c. 1671	178
5.2	West façade of Raynham Hall, c. 1671	178
5.3	East façade at present	179
5.4	West façade at present	179
5.5	Ground-floor plan of Raynham Hall, c. 1671	180
5.6	Ground-floor plan of Raynham Hall at present	181
5.7	First-story plan of Raynham Hall, c. 1671	182
5.8	First-story plan of Raynham Hall at present	183

Maps

Southeastern England in 1680, showing London and the county of Norfolk	28
Detail of Emanuel Bowen's 1749 map of Norfolk, showing "Rainham Hall" and "King's Linn"	29
"The Roads from London to Wells in Norfolk and St. Edmonsbury in Suffolk," an engraved strip road map from John Ogilby's Britannia	114

Preface and Acknowledgments

My interest in the lives of the first and second viscounts Townshend grows from my concern to explain how England's ruling elite, which underwent a crisis of confidence during the first half of the seventeenth century, regained assurance in, and extended its control over, the structures of society in the century after the civil wars and revolution of the 1640s and 1650s. I first came upon the Townshends, father and son, during research for a doctoral dissertation on the Norfolk gentry after the Restoration, work which focused on elite county society and sought to explain the growing influence of national issues and central government agencies on the provincial community. The current book tells part of that story by examining the fortunes of two generations of an aristocratic family between 1650 and 1740, fortunes which illustrate the transformation of England's provincial elites into a truly national ruling class, a development essential for the emergence of modern English society. In this sense, the book is part of the continuing reassessment and redating of the growth of oligarchic government in England, a scholarly interest that once focused on London after the first third of the eighteenth century and that has now pushed back into the late seventeenth century and into the provinces as well.

Because much of the elite's transformation occurred as a result of specific political (and often electoral) crises, and in tandem with the acceptance of the legitimacy of political partisanship, I have focused extensively on the Townshends' lives as political actors, on both the local and the national stages. Their other affairs, however, also warrant substantial treatment, for in their expenditures and their domestic architecture, in their estate management and their strategies as landowners, the two men also reveal the increasing influence of national markets, metropolitan culture, and modern business attitudes on the lives of England's aristocracy. As a result, this is neither purely political biography nor a strictly socioeconomic study, but a combination of the two. Such an offering risks leaving readers with too little of one ingredient and an unappetizing surfeit of another, which is perhaps why studies like this are few; yet I like to believe that the components are combined here to produce digestible and even nourishing fare. This book, insofar as the sources allow, seeks to present each of the viscounts in a variety of identities: as husband and father, landlord and landowner, profligate and planner, saver and spender, politician and patron.

One who has confronted the chaos of early modern estate papers can easily understand why scholars have tended to focus on those elements of a life or a household that are illuminated by correspondence rather than by farm accounts, estate vouchers, and bills rendered. But this kind of documentation, upon which my study heavily relies, reveals new patterns of life in seemingly obscure avenues, and suggests that more was involved in making what John Cannon has called the "aristocratic century" than political oligarchy alone. Archives like that of the Townshend family are not entirely rare, and surely survive in greater number than is recognized, yet they have been exploited fitfully and often partially. That two recent surveys of the aristocracy, by Cannon and J. V. Beckett, had to rely on a decidedly limited number of modern case histories underscores the need for further research into the nature of the ruling elite in the century before 1750.

The partial dispersal of the Townshend family papers in the nineteenth and twentieth centuries made visits to diverse repositories necessary in order to obtain documentation for this book, but the manuscripts at Raynham Hall in Norfolk provided the core of sources. In fact, the bulk of my research was comfortably conducted on a convenient table in a niche under the "Kent" staircase, although my first exposure to the archive at Raynham on an icy February morning in 1983 was more daunting than that would suggest. This was so not just because two walk-in cupboards in the library contained over 120 drawers full of papers, but also because, in the unheated attics, some thirty large chests and tin boxes and over a hundred shelved box files were all full of manuscripts. Much of this material, which ranged from the fourteenth to the nineteenth centuries, had little interest for me, and happily my initial way was eased by the curatorial efforts of others. Much correspondence had been extracted from the attic trunks by the late honorary archivist T. S. Blakeney and sorted by him into the box files. These files, chronologically arranged and provided with general labels, hold scores of pieces each, and some are rather ill-sorted miscellanies. Additional manuscripts from the attic chests, extracted in 1982–83 by Paul Rutledge of the Norfolk Record Office, were first made available to me at that office, and I worked with them later at Raynham Hall when they were returned there in cartons. After I had been at work for some months, an array of volumes in damp condition were found in a cupboard off the state bedroom (where they had been stored to protect them from leaks in the attic); when dried and fumigated, they proved important objects for study. In 1988, at a late stage in the preparation of my manuscript, a trunk in the basement of Raynham Hall yielded further manuscripts, and it is not unlikely that more papers will turn up in another obscure corner someday.

While writing this book, in which the matters of indebtedness and obligation recur, I have incurred my own volume of debt; unlike the Lords Townshend with theirs, I am unable to work mine off in any way except by acknowledging it with heartfelt gratitude. During the course of my dissertation defense, John Murrin pointed out the feasibility and potential merit of a study such as this, yet the venture proceeded no further until I received a Fellowship for College Teachers from the National Endowment for the Humanities. The Endowment's support, for which I am most appreciative, enabled me to begin research in England in 1983, when the Marquess Townshend gave me unreserved access to the papers at Raynham Hall, from basement to attic. Then and during recurrent visits in succeeding years, I, like Roger Gale (who visited Raynham in 1730), received the "kindest entertainment" in that "delightfullest place," and I hope this book in some way indicates my profound gratitude for the vast and unfailing hospitality, kindness, and friendship Lord and Lady Townshend have always extended to me. I am deeply saddened that Lady Townshend did not live to see in its final form this work dedicated to her memory.

Lawrence Stone, my dissertation advisor, and Anthony Fletcher have particularly guided me in shaping this study, the one with his unparalleled insight into aristocratic life, the other with his keen perceptions about the relations between province and center. More generally, participants at a seminar of the Center for East Anglian Studies at the University of East Anglia helped me clarify my ideas at a preliminary stage. I also benefited from comments on portions of the manuscript by participants at the Western Conference on British Studies in 1982, 1983, and 1986, and from further comments by those at a postgraduate seminar in the Department of History at the University of Sheffield in 1986. Cynthia Herrup courageously read the entire typescript at an early stage and offered invaluable and cheering advice; Henry Horwitz, John Miller, and Lois Schwoerer all generously went over a later redaction and provided careful and helpful comments. Robert Ashton, David Cannadine, Linda Campbell, Linda Colley, John Harris, James Jones, Mark Kishlansky, Chuck Middleton, Victor Morgan, Pat Murrell, Hassell Smith, Joan Thirsk, and Tom Williamson have combined to keep me from graver errors of interpretation and emphasis than those into which I have surely fallen. Andrew Rosenheim performed timely, generous, and sometimes radical surgery on my prose, upon which Edward Rosenheim later bestowed his expert editorial skills—both, I believe, to much good effect. To all these people I am profoundly grateful, but none bears any responsibility for shortcomings that remain.

My research at Raynham Hall was particularly brightened and abetted by Jane Kilvert, who has come to know the Townshend manuscripts better than she might have wished. Arthur Bell, Valerie King, Tom and Mary Marshall, Trudy Szczepanski, and the rest of the staff added to the comfort and productivity of my stays at Raynham Hall. Many others provided me with hospitality and succor in England, above all the Wingate family, Richard De Luchi, Sue Jenkins, Claire Preston, and Andrew Rosenheim. The Evans-Lombe family, with patience and open arms, have now seen me through two research projects.

Those who work in the Norfolk Record Office, and especially Jean Kennedy and Paul Rutledge, have given me extraordinary welcome since I first began research into Norfolk matters. Their unfailing cooperation and assistance, especially in allowing me access to the Townshend manuscripts temporarily in their care, were instrumental in helping me complete this book. I am also grateful to the staffs of the British Library, the Public Record Office, the Cambridge University Library, the Bodleian Library, the Folger Shakespeare Library, the Spencer Library at the University of Kansas, the Clements Library at the University of Michigan, the Beinecke Library at Yale University, and the libraries of the University of Chicago, Harvard University, and the University of Texas at Austin. The staff of Sterling C. Evans Library at Texas A&M University, especially those who work in Interlibrary Services, have notably eased my way. Permission was granted by the Clements Library at the University of Michigan to cite from papers in their possession. Acknowledgment is further due to the following for permission to reproduce works they possess: the British Architectural Library of the Royal Institute of British Architects; the National Portrait Gallery, London; and the National Museum of Wales, Cardiff. Brad Nass of the Department of Architecture, Texas A&M University, rendered the drawings that appear as Figs. 5.6 and 5.8 from architectural plans in Lord Townshend's possession. Texas A&M University granted me a leave of absence for the calendar year 1983 and awarded funding through a University Mini-Grant and two International Enhancement Grants. The College of Liberal Arts gave me a course release in spring 1985, and both the College and the Department of History generously provided subvention for the plates reproduced here. I have also been assisted in this work by funds

Preface and Acknowledgments xvii

from the Kellogg Foundation, made available through Texas A&M University's Agriculture in the Liberal Arts Project.

Much is due to my former and current colleagues in the Department of History at Texas A&M University—notably to Quince Adams, Dale Baum, Larry Cress, Dale Knobel, and Bruce Seely—who patiently bore my odd questions and odder speculations. Patty Stranahan particularly encouraged me in the early going. Larry Yarak, my office neighbor, has been especially supportive and long suffering. The late Carole Knapp transferred most of my typescript into a word processor, and Nelda Bravo and Jude Swank helped me produce the final version. Brian Stagner knows the significance of his assistance, even if he would insist it was indirect. Ann Baum has been an indispensable friend and neighbor. And Lester Brown, whose patience and companionship have sustained me throughout, has endured more—and with better grace—than anyone should have to do; my debt to him is immeasurable.

December 1988
College Station, Texas

❋ Abbreviations ❋

Add.	BL, Additional manuscripts
AHEW, V	J. Thirsk, ed., *The Agrarian History of England and Wales*, vol. 5: *1640–1750*, pt. 1 (Cambridge, 1984); pt. 2 (Cambridge, 1985).
Beckett, *Aristocracy*	J. V. Beckett, *The Artistocracy in England, 1660–1914* (Oxford, 1986).
BL	British Library
Bodl.	Bodleian Library
CJ	House of Commons *Journals*
C (H) corr.	Cholmondeley (Houghton) correspondence
CSPD	*Calendar of State Papers, Domestic Series*
CT	Charles, 2nd Viscount Townshend
CUL	Cambridge University Library
DNB	*Dictionary of National Biography*
GEC, *Peerage*	G.E.C., *The Complete Peerage . . .* , new ed., 12 vols. (London, 1910–59).
HMC	Historical Manuscripts Commission
HP 1660–90	B. D. Henning, *The History of Parliament: The House of Commons, 1660–90*, 3 vols. (London, 1983).
HP 1715–54	R. Sedgwick, *The History of Parliament: The House of Commons, 1715–1754*, 2 vols. (London, 1970).
HT	Horatio, 1st Viscount Townshend
Le Strange, *Lists*	H. Le Strange, *Norfolk Official Lists* (Norwich, 1890).
LJ	House of Lords *Journals*
NLJ	Norfolk Lieutenancy Journal
NLJ 1660–76	*Norfolk Lieutenancy Journal, 1660–1676*, ed. R. M. Dunn, Norfolk Record Society, vol. 45 (1977).
NLJ 1676–1701	*Norfolk Lieutenancy Journal, 1676–1701*, ed. B. Cozens-Hardy, Norfolk Record Society, vol. 30 (1961).
NRO	Norfolk Record Office
Paston letters	"Historical Original State Letters," vols. 1 and 2, NRO, Bradfer-Lawrence, I c.

Plumb, *Walpole*	J. H. Plumb, *Sir Robert Walpole*, vol. 1, *The Making of a Statesman,* and vol. 2, *The King's Minister* (London, 1972).
Prideaux letters	*Letters of Humphrey Prideaux . . . to John Ellis . . . 1674–1722,* ed. E. M. Thompson, Camden Society, n.s., vol. 15 (1875).
PRO	Public Record Office
R	Raynham Hall manuscripts (see bibliography for a full list of abbreviations).
Rosenheim, "Oligarchy"	J. M. Rosenheim, "An Examination of Oligarchy: The Gentry of Restoration Norfolk, 1660–1720," Ph.D. diss., Princeton University, 1981.
TF	Timothy Felton, auditor, 1644–82
TW	Thomas Warde, bailiff and steward, 1686–1710

A Note on Style

Dates are in Old Style, except as indicated, but the year is taken to begin on 1 January. In quotations, original spelling has been retained, but punctuation and capitalization have been modernized and common contractions and abbreviations have been silently expanded.

The Townshends of Raynham

Introduction

I

This book began as an effort to shed some light on the nature of the English landed elite in a period that still claims less attention from historians than is its due. If the behavior of local elites is central to an explanation of the events of the first half of the seventeenth century, it is no less so for the years after the Restoration, yet only recently have studies begun to emerge which explore provincial landed society and its relations with central government in the years after 1660.[1] Recent work has made it impossible to sustain the picture of eighteenth-century society as that of an ascendant oligarchy in a one-party world, and there is no effort to underwrite such an image here.[2] At the same time, the view which sees 1660 or 1688 as beginning an "ancien régime" in England, marked by Anglican, aristocratic, and monarchical values,[3] is also an unduly restrictive one, for it would read out of court the kind of historical developments that made this study of two English noblemen appear worthwhile. While the aristocratic domination of society in the period under study cannot be denied,[4] the premise of

---

1. See P. Jenkins, *The Making of a Ruling Class: The Glamorgan Gentry, 1640–1790* (Cambridge, 1983); A. M. Coleby, *Central Government and the Localities: Hampshire, 1649–1689* (Cambridge, 1987).

2. See L. Colley, *In Defiance of Oligarchy: The Tory Party, 1714–60* (Cambridge, 1982); G. Holmes, "The Achievement of Stability: The Social Context of Politics from the 1680s to the Age of Walpole," in J. Cannon, ed., *The Whig Ascendancy: Colloquies on Hanoverian England* (London, 1981), 1–27.

3. See J. C. D. Clark, *English Society, 1688–1832: Ideology, Social Structure and Political Practice during the Ancien Regime* (Cambridge, 1985).

4. On this domination and the character of the nobility, see J. Cannon, *Aristocratic Century: The Peerage of Eighteenth-Century England* (Cambridge, 1984).

this book quite simply is that between the mid-seventeenth and mid-eighteenth centuries English aristocratic life altered profoundly.

Without denying historical continuities or asserting that change constitutes revolution, it is nonetheless clear that the gap separating the active political life of Horatio first Viscount Townshend (1630–87) from his son Charles (1675–1738) is characterized by both subtle and arresting alterations in the structures and values of life. Somewhere in a watershed toward the end of the seventeenth century, a striking series of developments began to redefine what it meant to be an aristocrat. These were not without antecedents, and they did not mark unrecognizable or even irreversible change, but they were extensive all the same. The changes took place at different rates and with varying impact on English society, and this book tells part of the story of England's reshaping by examining the process at work in a single family whose experience is emblematic of the alterations in national patterns of life: the pull of the metropolis, changes in agriculture, the growth of adversarial party politics, and the reshaping of social relations in national, county, and local community.

To begin with politics, the regular elections to a parliament that met annually after 1689 (even if ill attended by members often selected in traditional fashion) created a permanent political world of party that had existed only fitfully before. The struggles to the death that had animated Tudor Norfolk and other counties, when appointment to and precedence on the commission of the peace could stain one's honor and make or mar reputations,[5] became tamer by 1700. In electoral politics, a renewed emphasis on ideology at the end of the seventeenth century apparently lessened (but did not remove) the impact of custom, hierarchy, and even personality in determining parliamentary choices, and overt partisan competition became legitimate within a pattern of "participatory deference."[6] On different ground, the strategic imperatives of William III dramatically furthered the emergence of an increasingly worldly and professional state bureaucracy that extended its influence deeply into everyday life, affecting the exercise of aristocratic power in the countryside and

---

5. See A. H. Smith, *County and Court: Government and Politics in Norfolk, 1558–1603* (Oxford, 1974); A. J. Fletcher, "Honour, Reputation and Local Officeholding in Elizabethan and Stuart England," in A. Fletcher and J. Stevenson, eds., *Order and Disorder in Early Modern England* (Cambridge, 1985), 92–115.

6. The phrase is from N. Landau, who notes "the extent to which the [eighteenth-century] politics of party ... was structured by the behaviour of England's elite": "Independence, Deference, and Voter Participation: The Behavior of the Electorate in Early-Eighteenth-Century Kent," *Historical Journal* 22 (1979), 562. M. Kishlansky, *Parliamentary Selection: Social and Political Choice in Early Modern England* (Cambridge, 1986), 192–93, suggests that choices became "depersonalized."

enhancing the opportunities for patronage.[7] In the agricultural realm, the accelerated adoption of new practices made more businesslike the relationship between landlord, tenant, and laborer, and such practices spurred an increasingly professional attitude toward estate management. In finance, the demands of government spending and the expansion of overseas trade changed the markets for credit and spawned sophisticated financial institutions. And the impact of "metropolitan standards" among the elite,[8] which coincided with a distancing of patrician from plebeian, began to give national coherence to aristocratic culture.

Focusing on members of an elite family to illuminate these processes requires little justification. The role of the landed order as both an engine of change and an anchor of stability in a fundamentally agrarian, hierarchical, and personalized society cannot be ignored. Early modern English landowners have been studied in a number of ways, and ambitious national studies, county profiles, and biographies have all made their mark. Yet the peerage has been neglected in favor of the gentry, and multigenerational studies are rare for either group.[9] Profiles over time, however, provide what none of the other approaches do, an occasion to examine individual motives and the particular circumstances in which actions were taken, as well as an opportunity to pursue the consequences of actions into later generations.

Horatio and Charles, first and second viscounts Townshend, present particularly apt subjects for study, for their lives lie across a kind of early modern divide. Horatio Townshend was a figure clearly more at home in the traditional and consensual political world associated with the early seventeenth century; Charles Townshend's embrace and mastery of a party-based political culture marks him as the product of another era. The distinction elucidated by Norma Landau between "patriarchal" and "patrician" values among the elite is clear in the life of the two Townshends, the first a product of what was still very much a provincially oriented society, the second defining himself in more nationally oriented terms.[10] Without claiming the son for the modern

---

7. G. Holmes, *Augustan England: Professions, State and Society, 1680–1730* (London, 1982).
8. Jenkins, *The Making of a Ruling Class*, chap. 9.
9. But see J. H. Plumb, "The Walpoles: Father and Son," in J. H. Plumb, ed., *Studies in Social History* (London, 1955), 179–207; L. Stone, *Family and Fortune: Studies in Aristocratic Finance in the Sixteenth and Seventeenth Centuries* (Oxford, 1973); R. A. C. Parker, *Coke of Norfolk: A Financial and Agricultural Study, 1707–1842* (Oxford, 1975); J. V. Beckett, *Coal and Tobacco: The Lowthers and the Economic Development of West Cumberland, 1660–1760* (Cambridge, 1981); J. R. Wordie, *Estate Management in Eighteenth-Century England: The Building of the Leveson-Gower Fortune* (London, 1982); B. Coward, *The Stanleys, Lords Stanley and Earls of Derby*, Chetham Society, 3rd ser., 30 (1983).
10. N. Landau, *The Justices of the Peace, 1679–1760* (Berkeley, 1984), 3–5, 359–62.

world and implicitly relegating the father to near-medievalism, this study will prove in many ways to be a study in contrasts.

II

Horatio Townshend was born in 1630, the second son of a prominent Norfolk landowner. His father lived only until Horatio was seven; when his elder brother died in 1648, Townshend inherited the family estate and shortly thereafter married Mary Lewkenor, sole heir of Edward Lewkenor of Denham, Suffolk. Theirs was a childless marriage that lasted until her death in 1673. Elected to parliament in the 1650s, Townshend was active in public life late in the decade, when he provided a guiding energy for Norfolk royalists aiming at a restoration of the Stuarts. As reward for his efforts on behalf of Charles II, Townshend was elevated to the peerage in 1661 as Baron Townshend of Lynn Regis and three years later received a royal grant worth over £2,000 a year.

Townshend was fully occupied in the 1650s and 1660s with the completion of the country house left unfinished at his father's death, with the search for matches for three of his four sisters, and with financial worries increased by his own generous spending and by the constraints placed on his income by jointure claims and dowry payments. Beyond these domestic activities, Townshend nonetheless worked to make a place for himself both in the county and in the larger arena of national politics, succeeding far better in the former than the latter. Armed with his peerage and his appointment as Norfolk's lord lieutenant in 1661, he was especially active in the county, curbing its sometimes wayward boroughs, and marshaling its militia during the second and third Dutch wars. In the final analysis, however, Townshend's leadership generated resentment in Norfolk, a county which had shown no easy acceptance of any lord lieutenant's dominance since the execution of the fourth Duke of Norfolk in 1572.[11] In the early 1670s, when Townshend became disgruntled with his failure to procure the further royal favor he thought he deserved, his disenchantment with the government at Whitehall (and its with him) encouraged his enemies, inside the county and outside, to challenge his claim to local leadership.

Because deep and long-standing rifts in county politics undercut his own schemes, Townshend failed to meet this challenge and lost his place as lord lieutenant in 1676. He subsequently tried to mediate between newly organized Whigs and Tories in Norfolk but could not

11. Smith, *County and Court*, chap. 2.

fully regain royal favor (although he received a viscountcy in 1682 as a sop); instead, he lost any remaining local influence and stature he possessed. The precociously fevered character of Norfolk political life, along with Townshend's impolitic trimming of position, his inability to secure effective county allies, his overall political ineptitude, and finally his ill health—all combined to thwart his ambitions. By the time he died in 1687, however, he had apparently become reconciled to his political failures. A second marriage in 1673 to twenty-year-old Mary Ashe of Twickenham, Middlesex (who died in 1685) produced three boys, a great consolation for his public losses. The responsibilities of fatherhood spurred Townshend at last to put his financial affairs on a more solvent basis.

As a consequence, the orphaned twelve-year-old Charles Townshend inherited a bright future in 1687. Thanks to honest estate management in his minority, based on lines his father had established, he took over a thriving landed estate when he came of age. The deaths of the first generation of Norfolk Tories and Whigs—and of the last survivors from Civil War days—left something of a political vacuum in the county, into which Charles Townshend slipped with little opposition. He became lord lieutenant in 1701, aged twenty-six, and soon assumed an active part in county elections. His forays were generally, if not totally, successful, enjoying the support of Norfolk Whig allies for whom he provided access to the avenues of central power. His own access there was facilitated by his marriage in 1698 to Elizabeth Pelham, who brought him not only a dowry of £30,000 but the assistance of her politically influential father, Thomas Pelham of Laughton, Sussex, later first Baron Pelham. Largely undistracted by local disputes, and undeterred by the need to seek remunerative government favor, the second viscount took advantage of the opportunity afforded in an era of regular parliamentary sessions to advance local interest at the center of politics. He rose in stature both locally and nationally, without having to devote his time to cultivating the secure provincial political base his father found so requisite—and so elusive.

The perspicacity and willingness to work which the son displayed in the capital brought him before long the kind of reward his father never attained. In 1706 the Whig Townshend was named one of the commissioners to negotiate the union with Scotland; made privy councillor in 1707, two years later he became ambassador plenipotentiary in diplomatic negotiations with the Dutch. Revulsion against the Barrier Treaty that Townshend concluded with the States led in 1712 to his temporary political eclipse (including censure by the House of Commons) and to the reinvigoration of the Tory interest across the country, but Townshend rose to greater heights than ever before with his appointment as secretary of state in 1714. Despite a period out of office in 1717–20, for the next decade and a half, the rhythms of parliament and metropolitan life, royal visits to Hanover, and attendance at Hampton Court or Windsor dominated Townshend's life. He received a Garter and could have had an earldom.

This worldly success and access to power were nonetheless qualified by personal loss. Elizabeth Townshend died in 1711, predeceased by three of the nine children she had borne in thirteen years of apparently close and affectionate marriage. Two years later Townshend and his old friend Dorothy Walpole, the sister of his political colleague Robert Walpole, were married, but this match was also broken after thirteen years, when Dorothy died in 1726. She too suffered the loss of children in her lifetime—four of the eleven she bore, and when she died, she was followed shortly by yet another of her children. In May 1730 public loss was added to private ones as Townshend, losing influence with George II, submitted his resignation. Although he had remained a figure to reckon with through the 1720s (even as dominance in the Townshend-Walpole partnership shifted from his into Sir Robert's hands), various circumstances—the death of George I, the mixed relations Townshend enjoyed with George II, and Walpole's growing role in foreign policy—all conspired to frustrate Townshend's hopes of speaking with the only voice in foreign policy. All the same, when he departed he left office with honor and voluntarily, perhaps worn down with ill health as much as anything. That he survived for eight more years in retirement at Raynham is a testimony to the reinvigoration he experienced there.

III

The nature of surviving sources has largely dictated the shape of this book, which is not formally a biography, in that it does not fully chart every significant event in the lives of its two subjects. Nor is this strictly speaking a family study, for the women in the Townshend family have remained cloudy figures. Townshend women of earlier generations had a dramatic impact on the family's history.[12] Jane Lady Berkeley, Horatio Townshend's great-grandmother, left her mark indelibly, partly because she expended some £24,000 on the family's behalf,[13] but also because she was a shrewd and determined woman

12. I owe my insights into the early generations of Townshend women to discussions with Linda Campbell and to her unpublished paper, "Women of Raynham," which she kindly allowed me to consult.
13. "Particulars of moneys paid by Jane Lady Berkeley," RUF/P [NRO]. Linda Campbell suggests that the survival of multiple copies of this paper shows Lady Berkeley's desire to inform her descendants of her contributions to the family.

devoted to her family's welfare. Anne Townshend, Horatio's grandmother, herself the object of rough treatment at the hands of Lady Berkeley, was nonetheless an independent and strong-minded woman whose religious convictions, if nothing more, had a profound influence on her son, Sir Roger.[14]

Unfortunately, where the female forebears of the first two viscounts Townshend emerge as women of great capacity, far from powerless or unthinkingly subordinate to the family's men, the viscounts' wives (and the second viscount's daughters) have left very little data by which we can assess them.[15] In the days of the first Viscount Townshend, it was the husband who "perused," verified, and signed the weekly household accounts, although this may say more about his obsession for close control than about his wives' capabilities.[16] In the second viscount's time his second wife, Dorothy Townshend, had a direct role in household management, but its profile is discernible only in the minimally revealing pages of account books. Beyond the evidence of this activity in a traditional domestic sphere, no sign survives that the Townshend women partook of the vibrant intellectual life which Margaret Ezell has shown "the patriarch's wife" could make for herself; nor, it seems, is there among the four Townshend wives a woman who, like Lady Rachel Russell, served as her husband's political advisor and ultimately as family matriarch.[17] In part, the paucity of direct evidence results from the frequency with which the husbands and wives of these two generations of Townshends remained together in the country, in London, and even abroad. Insofar as separations did take place, however, and letters evidently were exchanged, one wonders whether the women's correspondence (perhaps less valued than that of men, perhaps too personal to preserve) may have been destroyed.[18] In any event, the lack of raw material about the Townshend

14. See A. Townshend to Sir Roger, n.d. and 29 November 1619, Add. 63081, ff. 83, 89, 91; C. H. Townshend, *The Townshend Family of Lynn, in Old and New England . . .*, 4th ed. (New Haven, 1884), 19–20.

15. The entire correspondence between the viscounts and their wives that has emerged in the course of this study is a batch of five letters over a two-week period from Elizabeth Townshend to CT. Beyond this, I have found almost no other letters written by Townshend women and only a few handfuls of letters to them.

16. See household a/cs, 1659–70, 1671–86, RUBV. HT's second wife did apparently receive the dairy a/cs: TF to HT, 27 March 1679, RBF/HT Felton, and P. Lowke to Lady Townshend, 27 February 1682, RUEM/HT.

17. See M. J. M. Ezell, *The Patriarch's Wife: Literary Evidence and the History of the Family* (Chapel Hill, 1987); L. G. Schwoerer, *Lady Rachel Russell, "One of the Best of Women"* (Baltimore, 1988).

18. That CT corresponded regularly with his second wife when he was in Hanover is clear from his secretary's explanation that CT was awaiting a tardy messenger from England before writing, which "my Lady should know, if she is inquisitive after letters every post": G. Tilson to C. Delafaye, 13/24 August 1723, PRO, SP 43/4.

women makes impossible any presentation of the "doubled" view of the social order which feminist theorist Joan Kelly urges scholars to employ, a vision which is meant to clarify our understanding of society by seeing together the sociosexual spheres of women and men.[19] It is a sore loss.

The infrequent discussion of Townshend women is thus explained by their relatively rare appearance in existing sources, but in one area of voluminous manuscript survivals—diplomacy—I have consciously foregone any attempt to assess the second Viscount Townshend's role as statesman, although he warrants a statesman's biography.[20] My story is that of the interplay between province and center, between centripetal and centrifugal forces in shaping these two elite careers. It is the fact that Charles Townshend possessed office, rather than what he did in it, that most matters in gauging the gap between the environment he lived in and that of his Restoration father.

The differences are shown here in several ways. By exploring the role of each man in Norfolk politics, one discerns how local constraints impinged on freedom of activity in London, and how connection and office in central government shaped life in the county community.[21] Whereas the century and a half before 1640 saw the vitality and cohesion of English counties grow at the expense of other local groups and the state,[22] this book documents the challenges presented to county cohesion after 1660, and especially after 1690, by the explosion of the state. Furthermore, beyond the sphere of politics, the two Townshends reveal the evolution of elite values and behavior, and the sometimes jarring economic demands of metropolitan and provincial life in the late-seventeenth and early-eighteenth centuries. In this way, what follows provides a view of the aristocracy in transition, adjusting itself, as it would do with enormous success, so as to take advantage of the new investment opportunities, career choices, and even social alliances in Hanoverian England.

Analysis of estate management and agricultural practices constitutes another essential component of the comparison between father and

---

19. J. Kelly, "The Doubled Vision of Feminist Theory," in *Women, History & Theory: The Essays of Joan Kelly* (Chicago, 1984), 51–64. My attention was drawn to this work by a reference in Schwoerer, *Lady Rachel Russell*, xviii.

20. While recognizing the importance of foreign affairs, I have shied away from what A. S. Turberville called "the complicated and ... not particularly absorbing story of British foreign policy from 1714 to 1737": *The House of Lords in the XVIIIth Century* (Oxford, 1927; reprinted Westport, Conn., 1970), 221.

21. See especially Fletcher, "Honour, Reputation and Local Officeholding."

22. D. Underdown, "Community and Class: Theories of Local Politics in the English Revolution," in B. C. Malament, ed., *After the Reformation: Essays in Honor of J. H. Hexter* (Philadelphia, 1980), 147–62, especially 147–54.

son. The papers remaining hitherto unexplored in the Raynham Hall attics, including as they do extensive runs of household and farm accounts (as well as estate correspondence), permit careful appraisal of the Townshends' posture as landowners and financial strategists. These documents themselves change over time. The retirement of "Turnip" Townshend, the second viscount, to Raynham Hall in 1730 brought the need for estate correspondence to a virtual end until his death. Yet from the 1720s, a growing rationalization and routinization in taking accounts generated increasingly formal and formulaic records, although accompanied by such staggering amounts of tenant vouchers as nearly to defy analysis. The years of Charles Townshend's closest control in shaping agricultural policy and in overseeing tenants and employees are thus those most difficult to reconstruct. Yet it is clear that the mechanisms he used after 1730 were in place beforehand and even derived from practices employed in his father's day. For this reason, the history of estate management under the first viscount and until his son's retirement is most important in explaining the dynamics of improvement on their estates. The interplay found here between particular, personalized factors (inept or good employees; an heir who was a minor), secular trends (low grain prices in the 1670s and 1680s and after 1710), and new methods and attitudes (capital improvement of land; careful leasing policy; use of innovative crops) has not been much explored by agricultural historians painting the broader picture of agrarian change. There are exceptions, like R. A. C. Parker's study of the Cokes of Norfolk, although that work focuses on the eighteenth and nineteenth centuries exclusively. An examination of the Leveson-Gowers and eighteenth-century estate management likewise has little to say about the seventeenth century;[23] if that family typifies Midlands landowners who built fortunes on a combination of agricultural profits and the development of mineral resources, the Townshends are probably more typical of the majority of landlords who enjoyed no such mineral windfall.

Thus this book provides a multifaceted view of the English aristocracy at a critical point in its history when it recovered, consolidated, and strengthened its position of dominance in society.[24] This view above all lays open the shifting balance for the elite of the demands and rewards of province and center. It sheds new light on the sophistication of agricultural improvers in the eighty years after 1660, revealing a well-developed leasing policy on the Townshend lands that pre-

23. Wordie, *Estate Management*.
24. J. Cannon is illuminating on the extent and result of this consolidation in the eighteenth century: Cannon, *Aristocratic Century*, chaps. 4 and 6.

dates such practices elsewhere and may go far to account for Charles Townshend's agricultural success and reputation. Indeed, for the first time "Turnip" Townshend's career as an agriculturalist is laid open to view.

What follows also examines the route by which politicians made their way locally and nationally before, during, and after the first age of party. It confirms the uneven spread of political awareness and political machinations throughout the country and makes a strong case for Norfolk's priority and precocity in early party development and later party manipulation. It also reveals the continuing patterns of deference that characterized early-eighteenth-century politics.[25] It presents in its subjects, finally, two types. The first is a disgruntled royalist whose growing unhappiness with his monarch and the government helps explain the genesis of the first Whig party and identify the sources of its support. The second is a party man who embraced the party organism and partisan politics as instruments to gain power, and whose career helps explain much of the success of the Hanoverian Whigs. Together, the two men reveal many of the changing forces that helped determine England's evolution into a modern society.

25. On the persistence of deference, see J. Broad, "Sir John Verney and Buckinghamshire Elections, 1696–1715," *Bulletin of the Institute for Historical Research* 56 (1983): 195–204; N. Landau, "Independence, Deference, and Voter Participation."

✶ *Chapter 1* ✶

The Failed Politician
Horatio First Viscount Townshend

ʃɑ ᴅʒ✻ʃɑ ᴅʒ✻ʃɑ ᴅʒ✻ʃɑ ᴅʒ✻ʃɑ ᴅʒ

Early Life and Royalist Activity

The first record of the Townshends at Raynham dates from the late fourteenth century. In the sixteenth century Townshend men practiced law or went to sea, served the county as justices of the peace and the nation as members of parliament, and became substantial landowners in northwestern Norfolk. Sir Roger Townshend (c. 1543–90) acquired land in Middlesex and Essex, and his widow secured the family's position further by purchasing a baronetcy in 1617 for her twenty-two-year-old grandson Roger, Horatio Townshend's father.[1] Sir Roger the younger had by this time begun to carve a place in Norfolk under the careful eye of his grandfather, Sir Nathaniel Bacon of Stiffkey; then, through his mother, Townshend inherited Stiffkey Hall and much of the Bacon property when she and her father both died in 1622.[2] Under the influence of his pious grandfather Bacon and his equally devout mother, Sir Roger became a dedicated Puritan and an energetic Norfolk landowner: in Thomas Fuller's eyes he was "a religious gentleman, expending his soul in piety and charity; a lover

---

1. J. Durham, *The Townshends of Raynham, Part I: 1398–1600* (Cambridge, 1922); C. H. Townshend, *The Townshend Family of Lynn, in Old and New England* . . . 4th ed. (New Haven, 1884), 18; *DNB*, "Sir Roger Townshend"; "particulars of money paid by Jane Lady Berkeley," n.d., RUFP [NRO].

2. A. H. Smith, *County and Court: Government and Politics in Norfolk, 1558–1603* (Oxford, 1974), 173. For Bacon see A. H. Smith, ed., *The Papers of Nathaniel Bacon of Stiffkey*, vol. 1, *1556–1577*, and vol. 2, *1577–1585*, Norfolk Record Society 46 (1978–79) and 49 (1982–83); H. W. Saunders, ed., *The Official Papers of Sir Nathaniel Bacon of Stiffkey . . . 1580–1620*, Camden Society, 3rd ser., 26 (1915).

of God, his service, and servants."[3] His tenure as JP from 1625 to his death, and as deputy lieutenant probably for the same period, demonstrates his political activity. He was also sheriff in 1629–30 and a unanimous choice as knight of the shire in 1627. With others, he stood up against Privy Council interference in the county during the 1620s and 1630s, and from 1632 until his death he was the predominant officer in the lieutenancy, providing the regular link between the lord lieutenant and other deputies. He was a man of much account.[4]

Testimony to Sir Roger's stature lay in the new house he began to build at Raynham in 1619. Influenced by Inigo Jones but probably designed by Sir Roger, Raynham Hall was structurally completed by 1632, although the inside was left unfinished.[5] As important as the house was as a symbol of gentry power, Sir Roger's mother worried that his determination to build at Raynham distracted him from the need to lay a domestic foundation for his life.[6] He did not marry until after her death, however, and then, for all his Norfolk ties, he looked outside the county, although not far beyond the region.[7] His wife was Mary, the daughter and coheiress of Horace Lord Vere, Baron of Tilbury, Essex, and the couple bestowed his name on their second son, baptized Horatio on 16 December 1630.[8] It was a name to live up to. Vere, who died in 1635, was a distinguished military commander and staunch advocate of English intervention on behalf of the Protestant cause in Europe. Lady Vere (a "Calvinist bluestocking" who survived her husband by three dozen years), the Veres' daughter Mary, and Mary's husband Sir Roger all mirrored this religious concern, and

3. Smith, *County and Court*, 169–73; Townshend, *Townshend Family*, 9, 19–20, 126–28; T. Fuller, *The History of the Worthies of England*, 3 vols. (London, 1840; reprinted New York, 1965), 2:486. *DNB*, "Sir Richard Townshend," describes Sir Roger as a Presbyterian.

4. G. Owens, "Norfolk, 1620–41: Local Government and Central Authority in an East Anglian County" (Ph.D. diss., University of Wisconsin, 1970), passim, but especially 64, 303–4, 571, and chaps. 6–9.

5. J. Harris, "Raynham Hall, Norfolk," *The Archaeological Journal* 118 (1963): 180–83, and "Inigo Jones and the Prince's Lodging at Newmarket," *Architectural History* 2 (1959): 38–40; J. Spelman to Sir Roger Townshend, 19 April and 27 July 1622, Add. 63082, ff. 25, 27.

6. A. Townshend to Sir Roger, n.d. and 29 November 1619, Add. 63081, ff. 83, 89, 91.

7. C. Holmes, *The Eastern Association in the English Civil War* (Cambridge, 1974), 14, notes that 70 percent of the county gentry married endogamously.

8. The marriage date is unknown but the couple's first child, Roger, was baptized in December 1628: Stiffkey register 1, NRO, temp. loan 25.4.78; B. Schofield, ed., *The Knyvett Letters (1620–1644)*, Norfolk Record Society 20 (1949), 72; GEC, *Peerage*, "Townshend," "Vere of Tilbury," and "Westmorland"; jointure settlement, 14 May, 3 Charles I [1627], NRO, BRA 926/72, 372x9. On Vere see *DNB* and C. R. Markham, *The Fighting Veres: Lives of Sir Francis Vere . . . and Sir Horace Vere . . .*, Boston and New York, 1888.

Horatio Townshend was thus raised in a Puritan household. Little religious fervor was conveyed to him, however, and he later noted with some distaste that he "might have bine a presbiter or phanatick" himself, had he not been "forwarned by theire jesuisticall practices & insinuations."[9]

Sir Roger Townshend died on New Year's Day 1637, shortly after Horatio's sixth birthday; within eighteen months Lady Townshend married again, this time to Mildmay Earl of Westmorland.[10] After Sir Roger's sudden death, his executors maintained the six Townshend children without difficulty, but the provision of portions for the four girls would later strain Horatio Townshend's finances. Who made decisions for the fatherless children is unclear, but Lady Westmorland resided at least part of the time in Norfolk and we know she was apprised of the labor involved in raising the portion of one of her daughters.[11] She presumably helped decide where her sons would be educated when Horatio and his elder brother, now Sir Roger, matriculated together as fellow commoners at St. John's, Cambridge, in November 1644. They received their M.A.s in 1645, but there is slim indication of how they spent their time at university.[12] In December 1646, however, they received leave from parliament to travel abroad. The tug of allegiance during these troubled times cut both ways with them: their religious background was Puritan, but the family's politics and connections were mixed. In Norfolk their cousinly ties were both royalist and parliamentarian; their stepfather was a sequestered royalist. Such confused antecedents probably made the opportunity to escape from England welcome.[13]

On the continent the boys visited France and Switzerland and planned a trip to Rome, but while studying in Geneva in the spring of

9. [Draft] HT to [Lord Clarendon], n.d. [summer 1663], Folger Library, Bacon-Townshend, L.d.995. By contrast, HT's brother Roger displayed remarkable piety: Townshend, *Townshend Family*, 128/2–3. For Lady Vere, see N. Tyacke, "Puritanism, Arminianism and Counter-Revolution," in C. Russell, ed., *The Origins of the English Civil War* (New York, 1973), 137.

10. On Westmorland see GEC, *Peerage*, "Westmorland"; C. Leech, ed., *Mildmay Fane's Raguaillo D'Oceano 1640* . . . , in *Materials for the Study of the Old English Drama*, n.s., 15 (1938): 3–18.

11. Executors' a/cs 1637–47, Add. 41308; executors' a/cs 1644–52 and 1644–48, NRO, Bradfer-Lawrence, VI a ii. W. Symonds to Lady Westmorland, 13 July 1648, Folger Library, Bacon-Townshend, L.d.583, mentions the portion.

12. J. and J. A. Venn, *Alumni Cantabrigienses*, pt. 1 (1922), 4:259. The boys gave plate to the college: St. John's College Archives, Plate book, C3.1. I am grateful to M. G. Underwood for this information. The tutor at St. John's suggests that the boys pursued a normal course of study: Townshend, *Townshend Family*, 128/1–8.

13. *CJ*, 5:14. Two Vere aunts and a Townshend aunt were married to royalists; another Vere aunt had married the parliamentary general, Thomas Lord Fairfax: GEC, *Peerage*, "Clare," "Fairfax," "Poulett," "Vere," and "Westmorland."

1648, Sir Roger Townshend unexpectedly died.[14] At less than eighteen, Horatio Townshend, now third baronet, became head of one of Norfolk's most prosperous and distinguished families. He quickly returned to England and shortly thereafter married, choosing for his bride Mary Lewkenor, daughter of the late Edward Lewkenor of Denham, Suffolk, and sole heiress to a modest estate. The wedding apparently took place in October 1649, when the bride was fifteen and the groom almost nineteen, quite young by gentry standards.[15] Although he married outside Norfolk, Townshend, like his father, made a regional alliance and one that strengthened his ties among the county elite. Mary Lewkenor's aunts had each married into the Norfolk gentry, and it may have been connections here that brought the new couple together.[16]

These channels within the local elite, and others like them, undoubtedly influenced Townshend's entry into Norfolk's political world as well, if only by marking him as a man of substance whose presence in local government was desirable to a republican regime seeking legitimacy. Northwestern Norfolk was generally more royalist than the rest of the county (the port of King's Lynn overtly demonstrated its royalism in 1643), but Townshend had been too young to have engaged in wartime activities, a fact that perhaps recommended him for office. He was nominated to parliamentary commissions beginning in 1649 and was made a justice of the peace in 1652, although there is no sign he was active in these roles or that the government appointed him on the basis of overt indications of his loyalty. Perhaps in Norfolk, as in Hampshire, "the most grudging acquiescence" in the new regime was sufficient qualification for recruitment to local office during the Interregnum.[17] In Townshend's case, his family ties gave him little help in deciding his loyalties, although he socialized with local moderates, and his exposure to royalists increased during his unsettled early

14. Townshend, *Townshend Family*, 128/6–7; executors' a/cs 1644–48, NRO, Bradfer-Lawrence, VI a ii.
15. Articles of agreement, 22 October 1649, RUS, speak of the marriage shortly to take place. See three drafts of new settlement agreement, n.d. [1655], in Add. 41655, f. 118, RL drawer 112, and RUS; also indenture, 29 November 1655, RL drawer 94.
16. The ties were with the L'Estrange and Calthorpe families, the former royalist, the latter not: H. J. Lee-Warner, "The Calthorps of Cockthorp," *Norfolk Archaeology* 9 (1884): 155; R. W. Ketton-Cremer, *A Norfolk Gallery* (London, 1948), 56–94.
17. R. W. Ketton-Cremer, *Norfolk in the Civil War* (London, 1969), 156, 206–15, 275–77; A. Coleby, *Central Government and the Localities: Hampshire, 1649–1689* (Cambridge, 1987), 31; *HP 1660–90*, 3:579. C. H. Firth and R. S. Rait, *Acts and Ordinances of the Interregnum, 1642–1660*, 3 vols. (London, 1911), 1:1240, 2:304–5, 473, 670–71, 1075, 1375, give the commissions. The list of justices for summer assizes of 1653 (the sole Commonwealth survival) is damaged but appears to indicate that HT did not attend: PRO, ASSI 16/1/3.

married life.[18] Nonetheless, he negotiated the changing political streams of the 1650s in some confusion, somewhat as he would later cope with party politics in the late 1670s. Accepting appointments and even selection to parliament in the 1650s, he remained an inactive public figure, nonetheless fascinated by politics, as shown by his plea in 1651 to a cousin for news. Writing "from my lady's bedside," perhaps a sickbed, Townshend importuned Sir Edward Harley to write, "knowing how much I thinke my selfe as it were lost & out of the world if I heare not from my friends & how the world goes." Perhaps the hyperbole of a husband bound to an ill spouse and longing for worldly companionship, or perhaps the cry of a young man (not even twenty-one) lost in disordered times, the request also rings like that of an outsider looking in, the country man out of touch with the center of politics. The unsettling conviction that he was "lost & out of the world" would return to Townshend in later years.[19]

Townshend was selected for Norfolk to both Protectorate parliaments. In 1654, in a show of near-unanimity concerning his fitness for service, the electors placed him second in the poll, just behind Sir John Hobart, an ardent parliamentarian who later sat in Oliver Cromwell's "Other House." Townshend was apparently inactive when parliament met. In 1656 he was less universally endorsed by the electorate, placing fifth among seventeen candidates, and he was no more active in the House. In the second election, however, he and five others apparently formed a Norfolk group opposed to Cromwell, who had been rebuffed in the poor showing his son-in-law Charles Fleetwood, East Anglian major general, made at the poll. Such repudiation of Cromwell's regime was typical of many more counties than Norfolk, and might have placed Townshend in a position to widen his range of friends and allies. Yet even if he had little sympathy with the Protectorate in 1656, he was not seen as an enemy, and unlike five other Norfolk members, he was allowed to take his seat when parliament met.[20]

Townshend's very inactivity in parliament suggests the government's wisdom in allowing him to sit. It also signals that the honor he received from his county mattered more to him than the opportunity to pursue specific policies in parliament. His vision of parliamentary service was expressed in a speech of thanks he made when chosen in 1654. He spoke feelingly of the "honnor & truest," "incouragement &

18. He often visited Apthorpe, home of his royalist stepfather, the Earl of Westmorland. His sister Mary's father-in-law, Lord Crew, was also royalist.
19. HT to E. Harley, 2 March 1651, BL, Loan 29/84.
20. "Persons that stood for the county Anno 1654 and their polls," NRO, MS 10999, 34E1; election results for 1656 "from Robert Marsham of Stratton, Esq.," NRO, Rye MSS 9, Norris's Collections, vol. 2; R. W. Ketton-Cremer, *Forty Norfolk Essays* (Norwich, 1961) 34–36.

confidence" bestowed upon him by his "countrie," which he accordingly discharged from an obligation to pay him as an MP. Further, he promised to conduct himself "as becomes a faithfull servant to his countrie & the comonwelth," declaring that he had "always thought myself born for no other end then to serve God & my countrie."[21] On a later occasion, Townshend's acknowledgment of the honor done him mingled more clearly with a sense of obligation: he took the honor "as an assuerance & demonstration of your kind acceptance of my faithfull & former indevers for your service in the same capacity." In some measure he expected to be judged by the body of the county which gave their voices for him. Yet although he spoke of his "intier devotions for your service," it is unclear of what Townshend thought that service to consist. His rhetoric remained vague and conventional: he was willing to "laye downe my life, my estate, my all at the foote of your interest . . . there being nothing I am more ambitious of than . . . being accounted . . . as your most faithfull & humble servant."[22] The precise nature of this service was left undefined.

These sentiments, and the trust that Townshend explicitly acknowledged, seem to reveal the changed circumstances of what has been identified as a transitional era in parliamentary politics. Townshend's rhetoric (albeit pronounced after he had been selected) may reflect conditions in which the electorate had, in Mark Kishlansky's terms, begun to consent rather than assent to parliamentary choices.[23] Yet at the same time Townshend appears to be more comfortable with an older vision of parliamentary selection and of politics in general. The absence from his electoral addresses of any substantive comment about principles—whether religious or political—and his parliamentary inactivity together suggest an absence of ideological motivation.[24] The lack of clarity among contemporaries about Townshend's positions confirms the impression of one less than decisive in his commitments. This is not to suggest that Townshend had no positions, but it appears that he took them for reasons of expediency and that he viewed them as tactical postures to adopt or drop in the advancement of his personal interest.

Evidence for this chameleonlike behavior emerges in the parliament

21. HT's n.d. draft, "Gentlemen, I am very sensible," RUM/HT: mention of the "comonwelth" and absence of any reference to prior service for the county (which occurs in later addresses) suggests a date of 1654.
22. Draft and fair copy, n.d., "Gentlemen, I am so highly sensible," RUM/HT.
23. *Parliamentary Selection: Social and Political Choice in Early Modern England* (Cambridge, 1986), 6, 14–16, and especially chap. 5.
24. His outlay of £95 at the poll in 1659 is meager enough to suggest that it was intended for feasting after the selection rather than for treating beforehand: entry, 9–16 April 1659, Raynham household a/cs 1659–70, RUBV. Cf. Kishlansky, *Parliamentary Selection*, 121.

of Richard Cromwell. Although Townshend apparently helped to stir opposition to the government during this parliament, his game must have been subtle. A leading royalist, who thought him one week to be "very carefull of his Majesty's concerne," noted the next that he was "courted so highly [by the commonwealth government] that did I not know [him] well, I should feare apostacy."[25] Despite acting cautiously, Townshend finally impressed royalists with his parliamentary performance. The king encouraged him and sent a royal commission in May 1659.[26] Because the wealth and the strategic ports of Norfolk made it an important county to secure, Townshend, well-connected and able to recruit followers, was a key ally in any effort to gain the crucial port of King's Lynn for the royalists. As the Earl of Clarendon later put it, he was "a gentleman of the greatest interest and credit in . . . Norfolk," and since he "had been under age till long after the end of [the] war . . . [he was] liable to no reproach or jealousy" from others.[27] He was, in short, an uncontroversial leader. The same characteristics that made him a logical choice as parliament man, regardless of politics, made him a desirable royalist ally. Throughout much of 1659, talk of seizing King's Lynn, and of Townshend's part in achieving this goal, bulked large in royalist schemes.

Whatever his credentials and commitment, Townshend continued occasionally to be suspected of playing a double game, and royalist doubts were expressed about his loyalty when the reconstituted Rump nominated him to the Council of State in the spring of 1659.[28] Reassuringly, he sought the king's approval before sitting, and after being publicly accused of royalism by another councillor, an ostensibly outraged Townshend declined to reply to the charge and went down "in a great huff" to Norfolk, never to sit on the Council.[29] Instead, he threw

25. D. Underdown, *Royalist Conspiracy in England, 1649–1660* (New Haven, 1960), 240; J. Mordaunt to Sir E. Hyde, 8 March 1659, Bodl., MS Clarendon 60, f. 210; same to Charles II, ibid., f. 219. HT is recorded as speaking only once in this parliament, crying "no" when a member was made to kneel before the House: J. T. Rutt, ed., *Diary of Thomas Burton Esq. . . .* , 4 vols. (London, 1828; reprinted New York, 1974, ed. I. Roots), 4:4.

26. HT's contribution in parliament was judged "as forward but not so able" as other speakers, an assessment that epitomizes his limited political skill. Mr. Hayworth to Sir E. Hyde, 25 March 1659, Bodl., MS Clarendon 60, f. 249; A. Broderick to same, 10 April 1659, ibid., f. 336; Hyde to J. Mordaunt, 4 April 1659, ibid., ff. 244–45; Mordaunt to Hyde, 2 May 1659, ibid., ff. 466–67.

27. Edward Hyde, Earl of Clarendon, *The History of the Rebellion and Civil Wars in England*, ed. W. D. Macray, 6 vols. (Oxford, 1888), 6:111–12.

28. HMC, *10th report, appendix vi*, 196; Sir E. Hyde to J. Mordaunt [?May 1659], Bodl., MS Clarendon 60, f. 533; same to N. Wright, 23 May 1659, ibid., f. 544. HT was nominated perhaps because he was Lord Fairfax's nephew.

29. J. Mordaunt to Sir E. Hyde, 16 May 1659, and same to Charles II, 19 May 1659, Bodl., MS Clarendon 60, ff. 553–55, 559–60; S. S. to Lord Chancellor, n.d. [?22 May 1659], Bodl., MS Clarendon 61, f. 1; G. Davies, *The Restoration of Charles II, 1658–1660*

himself into plans for a royalist rising in Norfolk to be coordinated with similar actions elsewhere. He apparently agreed "to raise Norfolk, but ... was not widely trusted and his engagement was conditional on Lynn being secured for the landing of foreign forces."[30] His "activity" in Norfolk received favorable notice, yet when the chief conspirator, Sir George Booth, undertook his abortive royalist rebellion on 1 August, East Anglia (along with other areas) failed to rise. Three weeks later it was nonetheless falsely reported that Townshend had raised Norfolk, "which (if soe) will be of very ill consequence, for hee is a very popular man in those parts and may doe much mischief."[31] Why Townshend's plans came to naught is unclear, but the rebellion was an ill-coordinated affair, and Townshend may have waited on events. The conspiratorial nature of his activities obscures them, but his household accounts indisputably prove involvement; they also curiously reveal that, shortly after the rising miscarried, Townshend spent time in Norwich "about the militia." These almost simultaneous activities on behalf of and in opposition to current legal authority demonstrate how confused the times were—and how Townshend straddled the fence.[32]

Townshend's commitment to the monarchy was again tested in late November 1659, when a nebulous group of Commonwealth men and Presbyterians, hoping to resurrect the late Council of State, solicited his support. He was promised the "intire command of his country," but despite the tempting offer, Townshend asked the king's approval before proceeding and by delaying received nothing.[33] Instead, he went with Robert Harley to Yorkshire late in the year to persuade Townshend's uncle, Lord Fairfax, to join Gen. George Monck in his campaign for a "free" parliament. Harley's account of the journey leaves unclear the source of instructions, although it may have been the

---

(San Marino, 1955), 101; K. H. D. Haley, *The First Earl of Shaftesbury* (Oxford, 1968), 113.

30. Underdown, *Royalist Conspiracy*, 269.

31. Unk. to unk., 19 August 1659, Bodl., MS Clarendon 63, f. 263. Clarendon claims that HT was seized and imprisoned at this time, but there is no confirmation of this story: *History*, 6:118–19. See Bodl., MS Clarendon 61, ff. 141–43, 264, 284–85 for HT's activities. See Underdown, *Royalist Conspiracy*, 254–85, and R. Hutton, *The Restoration: A Political and Religious History of England and Wales, 1658–1667* (Oxford, 1985), 57–59, for the rebellion.

32. Raynham household a/cs 1659–70, RUBV. A coded entry for July 1659 bears the bailiff's later comment that 10s. was paid "for helping to secure plate & household stuff in Sir G Boothes his busines, which things weare hide att the lower house, and I write the characters for feare it should be discovered for what I paide him; in case I should go away or dye before the times weare better." Cf. January 1660 entry for expenditure on "gunn powder bought in Sir Geo Boths busines."

33. [G. Rumbold] to Charles II, 22 November 1659, Bodl., MS Clarendon 67, f. 11; Davies, *Restoration*, 260, 294–95.

The Failed Politician

king, but the pair's pleadings served the turn. Harley and Townshend then made their separate ways south, rallying support as they went, and met in London in late December.[34]

In the next five months Townshend moved back and forth between London and the country, travel characteristic of the conflicting structural demands of province and capital, which drained much of his energy, prestige, even power. He went from London to Norfolk in January 1660 to take the Rump a county address which, like similar addresses from other counties, sought the return to parliament of members secluded in 1648, and elections to fill vacant seats. Norfolk's address, however, ominously asserted that in the absence of the actions demanded, "the people of England cannot be obliged to pay any taxes." A compromise document representing both gentry opinion and that of the city of Norwich, it alarmed the House of Commons, which threatened its bearers with the Tower.[35] By mid-February Townshend returned to the country, where he mediated quarrels in King's Lynn among the townsmen and two unpaid and fractious companies of soldiers. He electioneered there on his own behalf and garnered an invitation to sit for the corporation, but he had grander plans for what he disarmingly called "that little interest I have in these parts."[36]

Despite the exaggeration of one observer's verdict that he could nominate MPs for any county constituency,[37] Townshend can be credited with a major role in Norfolk's elections to the Convention of 1660.[38] His public activity had brought him much approving attention. He stood for the county seat and won in a heavy poll at Norwich, where voters he marshaled from west Norfolk contributed greatly to

---

34. Harley's account is from c. 1671: BL, Loan 29/206, ff. 53v–54; Clarendon, *History*, 6:165; Davies, *Restoration*, 177–80; Hutton, *Restoration*, 73–84.

35. Hutton, *Restoration*, 90; Davies, *Restoration*, 271–72; J. T. Evans, *Seventeenth Century Norwich* (Oxford, 1979), 223; A. W. Morant, "Notes on a Letter and Declaration," *Norfolk Archaeology* 7 (1872): 312. The address was later presented to Monck and then published. See a draft petition from "the barronets . . . & others of the county of Norfolke," RL drawer 107, pinned to a copy of the declaration that was published. The draft, annotated by HT, mourns "the attempts of some . . . by force & fraud" to destroy a free parliament, an obvious attack on the army.

36. [Draft] HT to "My Lord" on envelope addressed to HT at Raynham, and [draft] HT to "Sir," [March/April 1660], RBF/HT misc. HT received an informal charge to command at King's Lynn from General Monck: Mr. Blinks to HT, March 1660, RUM/ HT; cf. Mr. Barwick to E. Hyde, 19 March 1660, Bodl., MS Clarendon 70, f. 196. See also R. Stewart to HT, 23 February 1660, Add. 41656, ff. 12–13, and HT's draft, c. March 1660, Add. 41140, f. 166; Gen. Fleetwood to HT, 22 March 1660 and HT's drafts to Monck and his secretary, RBF/HT misc.

37. Lady Mordaunt to Lord Hyde, 27 April 1660, Bodl., MS Clarendon 72, ff. 63b–c.

38. *HP 1660–90*, 1:323, 324, 329; R. Stewart to HT, 25 February 1660, Add. 63081, f. 100; household a/cs 1659–70, RUBV.

the victory.[39] As confirmation of his stature, Townshend received a commission from the Council of State immediately after the election as colonel of a local horse troop. A royal letter also applauded his efforts, and when he attended parliament in April 1660, Townshend helped lead opinion on the king's behalf. In consequence of his diligence and local influence, and perhaps out of deference to his ties with the renowned military leader, his uncle Thomas Lord Fairfax, the Convention chose him seventh among twelve members sent to Charles II with its reply to the royal declaration from Breda—a delegation that then accompanied the monarch back to England.[40]

All this endeavor allowed Townshend realistically to hope for advancement in the county and at the center of affairs in London. After obtaining a "favourable & charitable representation of my humble duty to his majestie," Townshend was obligingly entrusted with the care of King's Lynn, where he investigated suspicious activities among former soldiers.[41] The lord lieutenancy of Norfolk was an honor as yet out of his reach, but when the Earl of Southampton received the post, Townshend was treated as leader among the county's sixteen deputy lieutenants.[42] Receipt of a colonel's commission from Southampton brought Townshend the opportunity to exercise modest patronage in appointing junior officers, including his tenant Nicholas Rookewood, a long-suffering royalist, John Dillingham, a former steward, and Richard King, another tenant. The appointments served to reward friends and secure the service of trusted men; they display the integration of estate interests with political ambition.[43]

39. M. Barton to Sir E. Hyde, 6 April 1660, Bodl., MS Clarendon 71, ff. 156–57; Sir W. Doyly to HT, 20 March 1660, Add. 41656, f. 14; household a/cs 1659–70, RUBV. "The Sheriffes Booke delivered at an Eleccon for knights of this country," n.d., RUSL [NRO], dates from this or the 1659 election.

40. Commission, 7 April 1660, NRO, Bradfer-Lawrence, VI b 4; entries, 21 April–12 May 1660, household a/cs 1659–70, RUBV; G. Townshend to HT, 12 April [1660], NRO, Bradfer-Lawrence, Raynham misc. mss, VII b 2; draft letter endorsed "the kinge to Sir Ho. To. 4 Aprill [1660]," Bodl., MS Clarendon 71, f. 43; Clarendon, *History*, 6:229; Davies, *Restoration*, 349–50; Lord Mordaunt to Sir E. Hyde, 5–7 May 1660, Bodl., MS Clarendon 72, ff. 234*; *CJ*, 8:11, 15.

41. Militia commission NRO, NNAS 6158, 20F1; PRO, SPD 29/11, f. 174; *CSPD 1660–61*, 283; HT's notes endorsed "Lynn buisnes," n.d., RUSL [NRO]; draft [after 5 September 1660], RBF/HT misc. See also draft, probably to the Earl of Southampton, n.d., on an envelope to "My worthy and much honored friend Sir Horatio Townshend at Raynham," ibid.

42. Letters from Southampton to the Norfolk deputies were addressed specifically to HT and only generally to the others, e.g., Bodl., MS Tanner 177, ff. 36, 37v; *Calendar of Treasury Books, 1660–67*, 184. The almost identical choices of deputy lieutenants made by both men betrays HT's hand in Southampton's selections: cf. NRO, NNAS 6158, 20F1, and Add. 41656, f. 17.

43. "A General Certificate of the Commission Officers . . . 1661," RUSL [NRO]; list of militia officers, RL drawer 74; entry 2–9 February 1661, household a/cs 1659–70, RUBV. Rookewood had been arrested in July 1659: R. Woolmer to the Council of State,

Known to the king and deserving of reward for his loyal service, Townshend may have anticipated his elevation as Baron of Lynn Regis on 20 April 1661.[44] Presumably aware of the impending honor and despite the importunities of friends, he did not put himself forward at the elections to the Cavalier Parliament, but in foreswearing that intention he reiterated his hope "effectually [to] serve my countrie, it being that wee were borne for."[45] In Norfolk the promotion placed him a distinct level above his fellows. The county's only other noblemen were Lord Richardson, a Scottish peer excluded from the House of Lords, and the nonresident, lunatic fifth Duke of Norfolk (just restored to the title), whose brother Lord Henry Howard, later sixth duke, maintained the family's county interest. With his barony, Townshend in fact became Norfolk's first resident peer of note since the eclipse of the Howard dukedom in 1572.[46] This new status elevated him in his own eyes; whether the promotion, or the visible changes he made in his style of life,[47] gained him the respectful submission of those who had recently been his fellows is doubtful. Clearly he was no upstart whose rise might understandably have been taken ill, but the uncertainties of the early 1660s and the long absence of a single ascendant figure in the county almost guaranteed opposition to Townshend's ambitious effort to dominate Norfolk.

These ambitions were initially abetted by the government's needs, not so much in Westminster, where Townshend was only marginally active in the Lords,[48] but in the country, where the new regime's quest for security and loyalty were played out. The Earl of Southampton, as a distant absentee, was not the ideal royal agent in the county, and as a result Townshend was made lord lieutenant in August 1661, in what he considered the greatest single honor of his life. His effective performance in this office mattered greatly to the central authorities for several reasons. Most obviously, since Norfolk had exhibited support for the parliamentary cause, the "disaffected" elements in the

---

16 September 1659, Bodl., MS Clarendon 64, f. 90. Dillingham may be related to William Dillingham, editor of *The Commentaries of Sir Francis Vere* (Cambridge, 1657), dedicated to HT.

44. GEC, *Peerage*, "Townshend"; "Warrants for creations," RL drawer 70.
45. HT's draft, "Christmas" [1660], RBF/HT misc.
46. Ketton-Cremer, *Norfolk in the Civil War*, 26; Smith, *County and Court*, chap. 2 and 47–48.
47. Bills for 1661–62, RL drawers 70, 74; inventories of clothes, 1660–61, RL drawers 70, 80, and Add. 41306, ff. 104–22; C. Spelman's and S. Phillips's disbursements, RUEA 1663.
48. He was named to few committees early on and was absent when a dispute of some regional importance between Lowestoft and Great Yarmouth was heard: *LJ*, 11:240–435 passim. A copy of "Proposals for the Better Management of His Majesty's Customs," n.d., Add. 41656, ff. 97–104, may pertain to HT's membership on the committee for regulating the customs.

population required close watching.[49] During the 1660s, running battles with Norfolk nonconformists and the persistent analysis of partisan quarrels in light of earlier divisions demonstrated the basis for central government concern. In addition, the king and his advisors knew Norfolk's strategic significance and vulnerability from their own experience. During two Dutch wars, Townshend as lord lieutenant and vice-admiral was given the task of preparing the county against invasion. He also was expected to be the conduit of information and orders between center and locality, between Whitehall and the Norfolk countryside, to serve as royal agent perhaps, but as go-between as well.[50] In short, while he craved a role in affairs at the center of government, Whitehall's interest lay in keeping him in Norfolk. In this sense consigned to the county, Townshend tried to use his lieutenancy to build a local interest sufficient to demonstrate his merits (or power) and pry loose from the king some central government appointment. Building an interest, however, meant that Townshend inevitably politicized the lieutenancy and local government. The politicization helped to spawn an opposition, not of dangerous republicans but of men akin to Townshend's adherents, who nonetheless argued to the central government that Townshend's interest was neither unassailable nor indispensable, that he was not a figure on whom local security depended and whose demands therefore had to be met. In the absence of unquestioned local influence, Townshend could not gain an unchallenged hearing at court; without full backing from the center, he could not dominate the locality. From this dilemma, Townshend found no escape.[51]

The Lord Lieutenant in the King's Service

Because Restoration government on the whole failed to reestablish the Privy Council's control in the counties, the office of lord lieutenant

49. For antiroyalist plots and risings elsewhere, see Hutton, *Restoration*, 150–51, 164–65, 179.
50. HT's credibility and effectiveness as a link were nonetheless diminished by the fact that he was not a Privy Councillor. See Smith, *County and Court*, 127–28; T. G. Barnes, *Somerset, 1625–1640: A County's Government during the "Personal Rule"* (Cambridge, MA, 1961; reprinted Chicago, 1982), 98–101; Coleby, *Central Government and the Localities*, 97–99; A. Fletcher, *Reform in the Provinces: The Government of Stuart England* (New Haven, 1986), 335.
51. Kishlansky notes that "[n]ot the least of the qualities necessary to rise at Court was local influence": *Parliamentary Selection*, 149. See K. Sharpe, "Crown, Parliament and Locality: Government and Communication in Early Stuart England," *English Historical Review* 101 (1986): 332; A. Fletcher, "Honour, Reputation and Local Officeholding in Elizabethan and Stuart England," in A. J. Fletcher and J. Stevenson, eds., *Order and Disorder in Early Modern England* (Cambridge, 1985), 106. Fletcher, *Reform in the Provinces*,

after 1660 "came a little nearer to a viceroy" than local leader of the militia. The appointment was one of power and great reputation, which its recipients approached conscientiously.[52] It was an honor that Townshend cherished to the end of his life. Yet the mechanics of his initial appointment to replace the Earl of Southampton resulted in the kind of humiliating debacle characteristic of Townshend's career. The original commission, dated 15 August 1661, mistook Townshend's Christian name, an error sufficiently material to make him unwilling to appoint deputies or act as lord lieutenant until it was corrected. Before any amendment, however, Southampton, ignorant of the change and in obedience to Privy Council orders, instructed his deputies to view and account for the county's militia. When the deputies met in Norwich in early September to implement these orders, Townshend, though known to be the new lord lieutenant, was present as a deputy only, charged moreover to prepare his own horse troop for a militia review the next month.[53] Disconcerted by this embarrassment, Townshend turned anxiously to Lord Chancellor Clarendon, who counseled prudence, arguing that although Townshend might order his own militia muster as putative lord lieutenant, Southampton was "to[o] greate a person to disoblidge" by doing so, even if refraining implicitly disparaged Townshend's standing in Norfolk.[54] It took until mid-October to resolve the embarrassing problem.

Once firmly in place, Townshend quickly became an effective agent of central government authority, accomplishing the tasks set him without forfeiting the cooperation of his Norfolk colleagues. In the first months of his lieutenancy, militia assessments, methods of communication within the lieutenancy, and details of military musters were all arranged at meetings where he presided. The generally smooth response in Norfolk to the military threats of the second Dutch war testified to his beneficial guidance, and as lieutenant he attended on average two lieutenancy meetings per year.[55] In line with the govern-

---

335–41, briefly examines the politicization of Norfolk's lieutenancy under HT and his successor.

52. G. Aylmer, "Crisis and Regrouping in the Political Elites: England from the 1630s to the 1660s," in J. G. A. Pocock, *Three British Revolutions: 1641, 1688, 1776* (Princeton, 1980), 156.

53. *CSPD 1661–62*, 64; *CTB 1660–67*, 280–81; Add. 27447, f. 302; *NLJ 1660–76*, 24–28. [Draft] HT to "My Lord," n.d. [after 15 August 1661], RBF/HT misc., mentions the problem with the name.

54. [Lord Cornbury] to [HT], 26 September 1661, RBF/HT misc.

55. *NLJ 1660–76*, 17–18, 28–33, 37; J. Kendall to [unk.], 22 January 1662, RBF/HT misc.; R. Bendish to [unk.], 15 January 1662, Add. 41656, f. 27. A splendid, colored parchment certificate to militia officers, c. October 1661, survives in RUSL [NRO]. HT's successor, Viscount Yarmouth, came to lieutenancy meetings half as often, and Yarmouth's successor, the Duke of Norfolk, came even more rarely. My figures for

ment's campaign to secure docile corporations, Townshend helped to direct commissions which reviewed and purged the borough magistracies in Norfolk, as authorized by the Corporation Act. His interaction with the boroughs, however, illustrates the limits to his local power rather than his effective exercise of it. Considering his ambitions to move on a political plane above that of the county, his continuing, unavoidable embroilment in borough politics must have been frustrating, especially when he reaped no electoral influence or enhanced prestige in return.[56]

The corporation of Great Yarmouth posed particular problems, and Townshend enforced religious conformity and obtained military cooperation only with difficulty. He worried about the "badd consciences and wicked lives" of those who inhabited that "nest of schismaticall roages" and lamented the exclusion of churchmen and former royalists from town government.[57] His unsympathetic view of this notoriously nonconformist and republican community[58] apparently stemmed more from a concern for political order than from religious convictions, although his beliefs were overtly orthodox.[59] The extensive stockpile of arms in the unreliable hands of the town's bailiffs caused the greatest anxiety. In October 1661 Townshend ordered the bailiffs to surrender the town's ordnance and powder to a reliable designee.[60] When a committee named by the assembly obstructed the surrender, Townshend demanded obedience, warning the bailiffs, "if I have not authority so to [order], you may doe well to question mee,

---

HT's attendance, computed from the original lieutenancy journal (Add. 11601), credit him with 29 meetings; Dunn in *NLJ 1660–76*, 155, gives 22.

56. On the borough purges see J. H. Sacret, "The Restoration Government and Municipal Corporations," *English Historical Review* 45 (1930): 232–59, especially 245–52; Hutton, *Restoration*, 158–62; Evans, *Seventeenth Century Norwich*, 238, n. 1.

57. [Draft] HT [in a clerk's hand] to "My Lord," n.d. [after 15 August 1661], RBF/HT misc.

58. Miles Corbet, town recorder and regicide, was incredibly chosen (although later unseated) in a double return to the Convention in 1660: *HP 1660–90*, 1:324. The town had an "alternative" church as early as the end of the sixteenth century: P. Collinson, *The Religion of Protestants* (Oxford, 1982), 274.

59. There is no unambiguous evidence of Townshend's nonconformity; the contrary is in fact indicated, despite the claim in *HP 1660–90*, 3:579, that he was a Presbyterian. He was not on a list of Presbyterians in the Convention: see G. F. T. Jones, "The Composition and Leadership of the Presbyterian Party in the Convention," *English Historical Review* 79 (1964): 307–54. HT appointed orthodox men to livings in his gift; he also saw to the ejection of a minister who usurped the benefice at Helhoughton in the 1650s: see F. Barber to HT, n.d. [1660–61], NRO, Sotheby purchase 13.3.80, S154D. Judging by the books he intended to take to London in September 1687, HT had an unexceptional faith: "Memorandum of severall things to be taken care of now before I goe to London," 4 September 1687, RL drawer 66.

60. [Draft] HT to "My lord" [after 15 August 1661], RBF/HT misc. *NLJ 1660–76*, 30–31; "Yarmouth list," n.d., NRO, Bristow purchase 4.6.76, S187A; "For the Corporation of Yarmouth," n.d., NRO, Sotheby purchase 13.3.80, S154D.

The Failed Politician 27

... [but] if I have, it is my duty to expect your obedience to the same." This concern for his personal "authority" was characteristic: in the process of disarming dangerous persons, he saw himself perhaps as a royal agent but also as one to whom deference was due in his own right.[61]

The threat brought the bailiffs' ungracious compliance [62] but did not prevent other clashes with Townshend, especially over the borough's harboring of ministers "against the king & the liturgy." He targeted those "not comfortable unto the government of the church" (who he believed could not be "good subjects unto the king"), identifying as Presbyterians or independents two-thirds of the city's elected officials.[63] The severe purge of the borough's government under the Corporation Act was consequently no surprise,[64] but it failed to take the fight out of the town, which quarreled in 1663 with its high steward, the Earl of Clarendon.[65] Townshend's relations with the port were still troubled when the prospect of a Dutch war grew in the fall of 1664 and the men of Great Yarmouth hindered the impressment of sailors, which as vice-admiral he had ordered. The citizens, reported his agent in Yarmouth, "thinke it better to secure a trade with herrings, pretendinge [that] the concerne of the towne [is] more then his Majesties affaires, & that my actinge by your Lordshipps commands is to their prejudice." Townshend took such localist obstruction seriously and reported it to a concerned Whitehall, which stopped issuing protections.[66] Recruitment picked up, but this belated sign of loyalty did not last. When the king tried to coerce the borough's choice of bailiffs in 1665–66 (relying on power given him by the Corporation Act), the town brazenly rejected one of his nominees and chose instead a suspected nonconformist who had taken up arms "against our late

61. Sir T. Medowe to HT, 8 November 1661, and [draft] HT to bailiffs of Yarmouth, c. 11 November 1661, NRO, Sotheby purchase 23.12.76, R160B; F. Cook to HT or Lord Richardson, 4 November 1661, RBF/HT misc.
62. Bailiffs of Yarmouth to HT, 22 November 1661, RBF/HT misc.
63. HT's notes, endorsed "Yarmouth" [after May 1662], NRO, Sotheby purchase 23.12.76, R160B.
64. Evans, *Seventeenth Century Norwich*, 238. Fletcher says HT voted against this act, which he later enforced—behavior in line with his flexibility: *Reform in the Provinces*, 335.
65. E. Duncon to Lord Clarendon, 26 August 1663, and Edward Bishop of Norwich to same, 28 August 1663, Bodl., MS Clarendon 80, ff. 161, 167; HT's three drafts [to Clarendon], n.d. [late August 1663], beginning "My Lord, I must not omit," "My Lord, I doe in this affair" (both in RBF/HT misc.), and "My Lord, In obedience to your Lordps commands" (RUFP [NRO]); R. Pell to [HT], 25 August [1663], Folger Library, Bacon-Townshend, L.d.463.
66. Vice-admiral's commission, 6 August 1663, RL drawer 99; Sir T. Medowe to HT, 2 and 21 November, W. Lewin to HT, 10 November 1664, RBF/HT misc. Note of men impressed, 31 October 1664, RUSL [NRO]; bailiffs of Yarmouth to [HT or Privy Council], 21 November 1664, NRO, Bradfer-Lawrence, IV a ii, Townshend MSS; W. Lewin's pressmaster's a/c, RL drawer 70.

Southeastern England in 1680, showing London and the county of Norfolk, from *A travelling mapp of England,* by Arthur Tooker
Courtesy, Yale Center for British Art, Paul Mellon Collection

Detail of Emanuel Bowen's 1749 map of Norfolk, showing "Rainham Hall" to the east and "King's Linn" to the west

Courtesy, Yale Center for British Art, Paul Mellon Collection

king" in the Civil War.[67] Only in the 1670s did fears generated by plague and by hostilities with the Dutch temporarily reduce the town's political turbulence.[68]

Great Yarmouth was neither the only borough with which Townshend had to deal nor the only one to resist his efforts to dominate local affairs. At King's Lynn his activities in the 1650s and the fact that he lived nearby gave him influence that was reinforced by his appointment as high steward in 1664.[69] His electoral power was nonetheless scant there and elsewhere. At Thetford the Howard family held sway: Townshend and Henry Howard (later Baron Howard, Earl of Norwich, Earl Marshal of England, and finally sixth Duke of Norfolk) probably shared control of the borough's seats in 1660–61, but thereafter they became rivals.[70] The source of rivalry is not far to seek: as a leading national Catholic, Howard aspired to influence in the county, and Townshend's elevation to the peerage presented a countervailing power. Through their supporters in Thetford, Howard and Townshend recurrently quarreled by proxy in the mid-1660s, first over replacing the local postmaster, whose alleged deficiencies included speaking ill of Townshend and refusing to accept his frank. This dispute became entangled with other issues: the borough's efforts to secure a new charter, the dismissal of the town clerk by a Council order, the appointment by Townshend of a Thetford man as county mustermaster.[71] It is clear that a faction in Thetford looked upon Townshend with hostility. They resented his intrusion into local affairs, and when the corporation considered renewing its charter in 1664, this group eschewed Townshend's help, claiming that "they had

---

67. Bailiffs of Great Yarmouth to HT, 30 August 1665, RBF/HT misc. [Draft] HT to "My Lord," n.d. [September–October 1665], RUC [NRO], mentions that only the plague prevented sending to London "thos persons who have so notoriously misbehaved themselves . . . at Yarmouth." *CSPD 1667–68*, 186; C. J. Palmer, ed., *The History of Great Yarmouth by Henry Manship* . . . (Great Yarmouth, 1854), 247; Le Strange, *Lists*, 162.

68. Great Yarmouth's obstruction is in marked contrast to the welcome accorded "government involvement in . . . the defence and security" of the Hampshire borough of Southampton: Coleby, *Central Government and the Localities*, 106.

69. Le Strange, *Lists*, 199: the high steward's position had been vacant since 1646; patent, 30 January 1665, RUSL [NRO].

70. H. K. S. Causton, *The Howard Papers* (London, n.d.), 120–32, on Howard; GEC, *Peerage*, "Norfolk"; *HP 1660–90*, 1:332–33.

71. *CTB 1660–67*, 73; J. Sotherton to J. Kendall, 18 January 1664, Folger Library, Bacon-Townshend, L.d.545; "Articles agst Sotterton & Waller of Thetford," February 1664, RUSL [NRO]; Sir R. Kemp to HT, 16 March 1664, RBF/HT misc.; Sir J. Astley and Sir R. Kemp to HT, same date, Add. 63081, f. 106; M.M. to HT, 28 March, 18 April, 2 May, and 20 December 1664, RBF/HT misc.; H. Bedingfield to HT, 15 April 1664, ibid., and same to HT, n.d., Folger Library, Bacon-Townshend, L.d.884; affidavits of C. Windut, 12 December 1664, RUSL [NRO].

a friend worth forty of my Lord Townshend who would doe it for them . . . Mr. Henry Howard."[72]

This factional division lay behind a complicated municipal dispute between Thetford's mayor and the town clerk that the Privy Council appointed Townshend to investigate. His attempt at mediation in 1664 was met by obstruction and the corporation's public and insulting opposition to some of his suggestions.[73] The clash marked the low point in Townshend's relations with Thetford, the calculated insults constituting a rejection of his role as the county's leader. In 1668 the corporation pointedly bypassed him when approaching the lord keeper for a new commission of the peace, an affront compounded by the inclusion among the proposed new justices of men who had earlier reviled Townshend publicly. The Thetford quarrels underscore the significance of the commission of the peace as a patronage vehicle and political instrument. In the aftermath of the mayor–town clerk quarrel, the lord lieutenant was assured that the best way to attack (and perhaps win over) his leading opponent was by "turning [him] out of [the county] commission, and then hereafter as he carryes him self . . . [he may] be brought in agayne by your lordship's hand."[74] Yet the central government's willingness to grant the new commission at Thetford had undercut Townshend's reputation and made him fear that other corporations would try to place men in public office without his input. This development simultaneously raised questions about his ability to perform the king's service in Norfolk, highlighted the political independence of Norfolk's boroughs, and showed that the Howards' longstanding interest could outweigh that of a new nobleman whose value as patron was still uncertain.[75] Without the support of central authorities, the lord lieutenant's influence and power—his political interest—remained qualified.

In Townshend's relations with Norwich, the Howard interest appears again, not strictly opposed to the lord lieutenant, but drawing local men's attention from him, diminishing his stature in their eyes and those of the central government. Townshend generally enjoyed good relations with the borough, helping it gain a new charter and assisting in the mid-1660s when plague, threats from the Dutch, and the activities of Quakers and nonconformists disturbed the city. Yet he had no electoral influence there in the 1660s and on more than

---

72. M.M. to HT, 2 May 1664, RBF/HT misc.; J. Piddock's affidavit, 12 December 1664, RUSL [NRO].

73. HT's three draft reports to the king "of the Thetford business," Add. 41656, f. 95; Folger Library, Bacon-Townshend, L.d.398 [dated 7 November 1664]; RBF/HT misc.; E. Hunt's affidavit, 19 December 1664, RL drawer 70.

74. M.M. to HT, 20 December 1664, RBF/HT misc.

75. [Draft] HT to Lord Keeper Bridgeman, 10 January 1668, ibid.

one occasion—when a new town clerk was appointed or when some citizens tried to drive out a troupe of players[76]—he found, as in Thetford, that the corporation officers listened, deferred to, and approached others (specifically Henry Howard) in preference to him.[77] Townshend got his own back when the corporation came to him in 1670 for a favor, and he chided them for laying him aside before he had become "entirely insignificant" to them: as lord lieutenant he clearly was not that. Townshend sarcastically promised, as requested, to serve the city in resisting demands to contribute to Great Yarmouth's defenses; he simply referred the matter back to "those gentlemen whome you have [already] employed in that affaire."[78] Nevertheless, in Norwich and throughout the county's boroughs, it was evident, by 1670 if not before, that Townshend had failed to establish his interest and power throughout Norfolk. Despite his work during the Dutch war, despite his enforcement of religious legislation, despite spending much of his own money, he had not overcome local challenges, partly because he did not receive the unqualified backing of the central government.

To Townshend, his recurrent pleas for further government reward throughout the 1660s were justified by his local activity.[79] He had an especially busy time during the second Dutch war, from February 1665 to August 1667, as the foreign threat made Norfolk's dissenters bold and heightened awareness of their presence. Fear of internal subversion went hand in hand with fear of Dutch invasion, and from the first major engagement with the Dutch off the coast of neighboring Suffolk in June 1665, anxiety in Norfolk ran high. From the beginning of the crisis, Townshend attended carefully to Norfolk's military preparations.[80] He saw to it that the militia mustered and that troops patrolled the countryside and coast. Even when parliament was in session he spent much time in the county, dealing alike with militia defaulters and religious dissenters.[81] During the traumatic weeks sur-

76. *CSPD 1663–64*, 512; *CSPD 1668–69*, 627; *CSPD 1670*, 39, 71; C. Jay to J. Payne, 11 June 1664, RBF/HT misc.
77. Mayor and citizens of Norwich to HT, 1 May 1663, NRO, uncat. mss, Box M, P168C; *CSPD 1661–62*, 432, 453; *CSPD 1663–64*, 80, 188, 333, 560; *CSPD 1664–65*, 40; R. H. Hill, ed., *The Correspondence of Thomas Corie Town Clerk of Norwich, 1664–1687*, Norfolk Record Society 27 (1956): 23; Norwich citizens' petition to HT, [1667], RBF/HT misc.; and Evans, *Seventeenth Century Norwich*, 238–43, which notes the corporation's belief in 1661 that Howard "would intercede at Court on their behalf": 239.
78. [Copy] HT to Norwich corporation, 30 March 1670, RBF/HT misc.
79. See HT's undated drafts (mostly to Clarendon) in RBF/HT misc., RUM/HT, and Add. 41654, ff. 62, 68, 69–70.
80. Before the war he had urged creation of a garrison at Great Yarmouth: "Why Yarmouth should be a garrison" [c. 1664], RBF/HT misc.
81. HT to deputies, 6 April 1665, NRO, "Documents from Le Neve-Blomefield collections," Hamond deposit 21.8.75, S116C; Sir R. Paston to wife, 2 March 1665, and T. Townshend to Paston, 19 June 1665, NRO, Paston letters, vol. 1; Sir R. Kemp to

rounding the Dutch attack up the Medway in June 1667, Townshend shuttled almost nonstop around the county. In addition to his tasks as lieutenant and vice-admiral, he helped raise a regiment of soldiers, encouraged the gentry to lend money to the hard-pressed government, and secured the deputy lieutenants' compliance to a royal request asking for the return to London of surplus militia funds. To portray him at this point as an "absentee lord lieutenant" is unjust and inaccurate.[82]

For what he did during the second Dutch war, Townshend earned numerous commendations.[83] Nonetheless, his effective performance did not bring the promotion, office, or financial reward he sought as a sign of government gratitude for work well done; nor did it discourage the schemes of a rival, Sir Robert Paston, who worked to displace him. In the final analysis, Townshend made a problematic lord lieutenant. The fact that he was not involved in the conflicts of the 1640s meant that when contemporary quarrels at least partly reenacted those divisions, Townshend was not fully trusted by either side. While the Earl of Clarendon, his early patron, continued in power, supporting and assisting Townshend, the lord lieutenant's position was secure, but Clarendon eventually turned a deaf ear to cries for further reward, and with the lord chancellor's fall in 1667, Townshend had no one to whom he could turn. His modest stature in the eyes of central government and court left him unprotected against those, like Paston or Henry Howard, who were better connected than he.

While the aftermath of the Dutch war revealed that nothing Townshend did in the county would earn him the recognition he sought, it also indicated some of the limits of his political talents. Presented with uncontroversial and straightforward demands from the government, Townshend had little difficulty in performing his duties to the satisfaction of local community and central authority. When the interests of the two were in conflict, however, he experienced the countervailing tugs which made the office of lord lieutenant both trying and essential.

[HT], 20 April 1665, Add. 63081, f. 108; T. Greene, mayor of King's Lynn, to HT, 26 April 1665, ibid., f. 109; *NLJ, 1660–76*, 11–12, 75–84, 89–97. HT was absent from the House of Lords from January 1665 until September 1666: *LJ*, 11:658 et seq., 12:1.

82. *CSPD 1666–67*, 15, 114, 124; Duke of York to HT, 12 May and 16 November 1666, RUEM/HT; same to HT, 19 July 1666, RL drawer 70; W. Coventry to HT, 12 June 1666, Add. 41656, f. 50; HT's captain's commission, 13 June 1667, RU, commissions/patents; *CSPD 1665–66*, 458, 476; *CSPD 1667*, 180; *NLJ 1660–76*, 17–18, 94, 96, 113; Add. 41656, f. 41. See *NLJ 1660–76*, 105, n. 125, where the editor calls HT an absentee despite the evidence of the journal (pp. 99–101), of Hill, "Corie Correspondence," 27, and of *CSPD 1667*, 201, 210, 278.

83. *CSPD 1665–66*, 40, 458, 498; *CSPD 1667*, 227 [dated 24 June here but 24 July in Hill, "Corie Correspondence," 27], 388; bailiffs of Yarmouth to Townshend, 23 November 1667, RBF/HT misc.

During the war his deputy lieutenants placed him in an awkward spot when they twice refused to respond to government financial requests. Having already sent up £6,600 in surplus from militia assessments in Norfolk, the deputies rejected the call for more money in 1666 and for loans in 1667. Plague and trade disruptions had impoverished the county and created dangerous conditions, they argued; this, along with the need to meet a local Dutch threat, required the retention in Norfolk of all militia funds.[84] The king's ministers could do little about refusals to lend, but they tried to browbeat the lieutenancy into releasing the militia surplus, a tactic that caught Townshend awkwardly between central masters and local colleagues. He argued the deputies' case before the king but received another order for them to remit the militia money. Conveying the orders to his deputies, he then refused to help them decide how to proceed, claiming it was "no part of my buisnis to concern my selfe, any three [deputies] . . . having more power as to the concernes of [the militia] money then my selfe, & I nothing without them by the stat[ute]."[85] He employed a technicality to avoid committing his political loyalty, and in this case (which saw the lieutenancy keep its money) managed to stay on the fence between locality and center. He could not count on the permanent success of such a policy.

The issue of religion was potentially another source of tension to bedevil the lord lieutenancy. Townshend acted to neutralize it in a number of instances. Twice he appeared at King's Lynn to deal with nonconformists, and he closely followed a trial of dissenters at Norwich. In October 1667 he sternly ordered his deputy lieutenants to suppress "a conventicle at Wymondham, which, if I be rightly informed, is soe numerous that I can not but wonder that you have not allready taken notice of it."[86] Substantial concentrations of dissenters or disruptive manifestations of religious nonconformity thus elicited repressive measures from the lord lieutenant. Otherwise, nonconformists were largely safe, and in Norfolk as elsewhere there is evidence that the fear and prosecution of dissent was easing off even before the Conventicle Act of 1664 expired in 1668.[87] So much is suggested by Townshend's apparent indifference to dissent at Great Yarmouth, where conventicles abounded and many leading citizens were dissenters.[88] Perhaps it appeared prudent to ignore their reli-

84. *NLJ 1660–76*, 13, 18, 91–96, 104. See Hutton, *Restoration*, 270, for the loans.
85. [Draft] HT to Lord Arlington, [early August 1666], RL drawer 120.
86. *NLJ 1660–76*, 105; *CSPD 1665–66*, 40; *CSPD 1666–67*, 114, 124; Sir R. Kemp to [HT], 20 April 1655, Add. 63081, f. 108; depositions, Add. 41656, ff. 47, 52; depositions of 11 September 1665 and n.d., RUSL [NRO].
87. Hutton, *Restoration*, 263–66.
88. *CSPD 1666–67*, 15, 568.

gious practices so long as they helped secure the town from external threat, but by 1670 Townshend's politic indifference was transformed into political alliance with the dissenters themselves.

A Political Shift

In the late 1660s and early 1670s Townshend's forays into local electoral politics marked a significant development in his career. Hitherto a reliable servant of the crown, at by-elections in the early 1670s he pushed forth candidates whose ideological orientation signaled Townshend's personal disenchantment with the government. This disenchantment mirrors that current in the country at large, an outgrowth of the humiliations recently suffered at the hands of the Dutch.[89] Yet on Townshend's part the alienation seems more personal than principled, growing from his resentment at the mistreatment he believed the government had given him. As significant for Townshend's future as his own dissatisfactions with the government, the fall of Clarendon in late summer of 1667 removed Townshend's friend and patron.[90] Lacking a new patron during this "period of changes, ambiguities and deceptions" (as J. R. Jones describes the years from Clarendon's fall to Danby's rise in 1673),[91] Townshend used parliamentary elections to demonstrate to the crown and ministers the strength of his interest in the county by securing the choice of clients or friends.

His friends now numbered members of the nonconformist faction he had previously tussled with at Great Yarmouth. After the quarrel over the town's arms, he had continued to work against some of the powerful interests there, supporting development of Little Yarmouth as a rival port, pursuing the most hotheaded dissenters, and backing local churchmen.[92] By 1669, however, he grew lax when investigating Great Yarmouth's nonconformity at the Privy Council's behest. The town boasted unprosecuted meetings of dissenters the next year; after

89. Hutton, *Restoration*, 270–72.
90. HT was counted as a supporter of Clarendon in July 1663 and there is no evidence he ceased his support: R. Davis, "The 'Presbyterian' Opposition and the Emergence of Party in the House of Lords in the Reign of Charles II," in C. Jones, ed., *Party and Management in Parliament, 1660–1784* (New York, 1984), 33.
91. J. R. Jones, *Charles II, Royal Politician* (London, 1987), 81.
92. The implication in *HP 1660–90*, 1:325 and 2:620, is that HT showed sympathy to nonconformists in the mid-1660s, but this is not so. Even in January 1669, when HT and the Norwich sessions treated the dissenting minister, William Bridge, with what seemed to a staunch Anglican as undue respect, HT "rose up in a passion" at Bridge's unwillingness to comply voluntarily with the Five Mile Act and then ordered Bridge not to come within five miles of Yarmouth or into Norfolk: *CSPD 1668–69*, 159–60.

complaints, the Council referred the investigation to Townshend a second and then a third time, but in the end he showed his changing sympathies by "not in the least inquiring into the thing."[93]

This inattention to nonconformity (which would not have upset ministers like the Duke of Buckingham) coincided with a shocking appointment in autumn 1670, when Townshend made Richard Huntington a captain in the town's militia. To some, Huntington's service in the parliamentary army, his wife's attendance at conventicles, and his tolerance of dissent as a JP, all proved his ineligibility for the captaincy. So much was reported to London, and the impeccably Anglican Sir Thomas Medowe, a major of Yarmouth's militia, resigned in protest, yet Townshend held to the appointment and named James Johnson, an alderman ejected from office for Presbyterianism, as major in Medowe's stead.[94] Why Townshend embraced these former parliamentarians is unclear, although the government informer at Yarmouth, Richard Bower, credited the local MP, Sir William Doyly, with working his friends into the lord lieutenant's favor.[95] Despite Bower's critical reports concerning Townshend's actions, the lieutenant received no censure for them, and when the king visited Norfolk in September 1671 and took in Great Yarmouth while there, Townshend procured knighthoods for Johnson and for another former parliamentarian.[96] It was said in Yarmouth at this time that "none . . . is in favour with his lordship but what are of the old stamp of late times,"[97] although the king was unlikely to have shown Townshend his own favor on this visit (including a stay at Raynham Hall) had this literally been true. The comment reflects nonetheless both the distance Townshend had fallen away from an alliance with a self-consciously "Cavalier" group in Norfolk and the persistent casting of current quarrels in terms of the allegiances of the revolutionary years.

Townshend's identification with men whom he had previously opposed gained fuel from his growing resentment over what he deemed inadequate reward for extraordinary service. Since the fall of Clarendon in 1667, Townshend had enjoyed no patron to help him through political waters, and he apparently fell afoul of Secretary Arlington.[98] He was thus particularly vulnerable to stratagems by Sir Robert Paston

93. *HP 1660–90*, 3:211; *CSPD 1668–69*, 38, 95–96, 99–100, 159–60; *CSPD 1670*, 321, 353, 358–59, 440, 473–74, 519, 580, 585, 593. The quotation is at *CSPD 1671*, 463–64.
94. *CSPD 1670*, 473–74, 494, 512; *CSPD 1671*, 46–48.
95. *CSPD 1670*, 473–74.
96. *CSPD 1670*, 540; *CSPD 1671*, 46, 419, 463–64; *HP 1660–90*, 2:266–67.
97. *CSPD 1671*, 517.
98. *CSPD 1668–69*, 424. HT's doubts about Arlington's willingness to inquire into some seditious talk seem to have generated their quarrel.

to displace him as lord lieutenant. Paston, almost exactly Townshend's contemporary, had been knighted in 1660 and succeeded his father as baronet in 1663.[99] A Fellow of the Royal Society and devotee of alchemy, a man who "could not live without a castle in the ayre,"[100] he came directly to royal attention in November 1664 in the House of Commons, when he moved a supply of £2,500,000 for the impending Dutch war. This service combined with other factors to bring him both reward and, what Townshend never gained, a place at court. The Paston family's energetic royalism counted for something, as did his family connections and the efforts of his ambitious wife, who aggressively and on the whole successfully pressed his interests in London and especially at court.[101] Paston's mother was daughter of the first Earl of Lindsey, which linked Paston in a beneficial cousinship with Sir Thomas Osborne, future Earl of Danby, who had married the daughter of the second earl.[102] In 1667 Paston became a gentleman of the privy chamber and obtained a twenty-one-year lease on a lucrative customs farm. He angled strongly for a peerage and was elevated as Viscount Yarmouth in 1673, in recognition of his son's marriage to a bastard daughter of the king; this connection, and friendship with Lord Henry Howard, further served Paston well. Although he had once called his early ally Townshend "the best friend I have in the world,"[103] Paston found those at the center of government who could better assist him than his county's lord lieutenant,[104] and it was ultimately at the expense of this best friend that Paston attempted to rise.

Casting about for allies to aid him against Paston, Townshend found local support among men unhappy with the foreign and domestic policies emanating from Whitehall, but that he joined them for ideological motives may be questioned. As will be seen, his position on such issues was determined largely by the local contest for dominance and by the influence on him of the allies he procured in the county and in London. Having embraced the outspoken Sir John Hobart in 1673, for example, Townshend could not accommodate Hobart's fiery partisanship before the decade was out. In this regard Townshend appears a man out of touch with his times: while willing to engage in highly

99. For what follows, see *HP 1660–90*, 3:210–12; R. W. Ketton-Cremer, *Norfolk Portraits* (London, 1944), 22–57; GEC, *Peerage*, "Yarmouth"; Rosenheim, "Oligarchy," 213–51.
100. T. Henshaw to Sir R. Paston, 5 August 1671, NRO, Paston letters, vol. 1.
101. Although the surviving correspondence between Sir Robert and Lady Rebecca is one-sidedly his, her personality comes through with great force in NRO, Paston letters, vols. 1 and 2.
102. *HP 1660–90*, 3:185.
103. Ibid., 3:211.
104. Note, however, that HT intervened on Paston's behalf with the Earl of Clarendon: HT to Clarendon, 23 July [1666], Bodl., MS Clarendon 83, f. 422.

political struggles for power, employing every possible tactic for competitive advantage, Townshend felt uncomfortable with the ideological baggage that necessarily accompanied the politics of party.[105]

It is in electoral politics, in which Townshend had taken little part before the 1670s, that his new alliances mattered most, and his discomfort with the changing world of parliamentary selection became most evident. Because of Raynham Hall's proximity to King's Lynn and his services on the town's behalf, Townshend understandably attempted to sway elections there: his failures demonstrate the town's independence and the limits of his power.[106] Three by-elections in 1673 (at King's Lynn and Castle Rising, and for a county seat) testified as much to the continued strength of the Howard family interest as to the potency of Townshend's friends. Lord Howard's nominee easily won the day at Castle Rising. The forwarding of "strangers and courtiers" there, however, generated local resentment against Howard at King's Lynn, where it was feared he would attempt the same imposition, instead of leaving the voters "to a free competition without concerning himself." Howard's choice, Sir Francis North, although an outsider, nonetheless proved acceptable at King's Lynn because he had the "court interest to procure convoys and guardships" for the local fleet.[107]

At the election for knight of the shire, where Townshend as lord lieutenant could for the first time exert muscle in his official capacity, Lord Howard's influence again was felt. His son, the future seventh Duke of Norfolk, was rumored likely to contest the vacant place against the announced candidate, Sir John Hobart of Blickling.[108] Hobart, a man of intense religious convictions and long-standing ties with nonconformists, had sat for two Protectorate parliaments and been nominated to Oliver Cromwell's "Other House." Ever since his defeat by Townshend and Lord Richardson in the county election to the Convention, he had been active in local politics only, but he had been an energetic deputy lieutenant and magistrate, and his candidacy was

---

105. Kishlansky notes the frequent combination of personal, local, and familial issues in electoral contests, but attests to the pervasive presence of ideological issues as one of the novel characteristics of politics after the 1640s: *Parliamentary Selection*, 171–74. Where HT seems left behind is in his apparent inability to accept the legitimacy of ideological politics.

106. *HP 1660–90*, 1:327–28.

107. T. Povey to S. Pepys, 31 August [1672], Bodl., MS Rawlinson A174, ff. 444–45v; *CSPD 1672–73*, 485, 555; R. North, *The Lives of the Norths*, ed. A. Jessopp, 3 vols. (London, 1890; reprinted 1972), 1:110–13. North's unopposed election in January was invalidated by the House of Commons, because the writ had been improperly issued during parliament's recess; at the new poll North defeated Alderman Simon Taylor.

108. *CSPD 1672–73*, 572.

popular with the electorate.[109] As was the case at many county by-elections to the Cavalier Parliament,[110] the selection occasioned much interest, and the possibility of a contest roused the electorate, although Hobart in fact met no opposition. Encouraged strongly by Townshend, the selection of Hobart (with much dissenting support) brought Norfolk a forceful voice in the House of Commons, where it was said Hobart never once voted for the king. Townshend's endorsement of one unlikely to sit well with the government points up his own alienation from the court.[111]

The election of Hobart heralded Norfolk's division into two camps, those of Townshend and the soon-to-be-ennobled Paston, foreshadowing party rivalries of the exclusion years. The precise date of the two leaders' split cannot be determined: when Charles II visited Norfolk in September 1671, they were on friendly terms, but by year's end it was known that the bond was weak.[112] The two men maintained civilities, but by late 1674 Townshend and Paston (Viscount Yarmouth since August 1673) were seen as possessing their own opposing interests in Norfolk, this four years before the partisanship generated by the Popish Plot.[113] The rivalry between the two men—if not between their followers—is explicable primarily in personal terms. Townshend adopted toward Paston an attitude that was vaguely condescending, disarmingly self-deprecating, one of patron to client.[114] Royal rewards to Paston undid that relationship and stirred Townshend's animosity: although Townshend received earlier recognition for his service, what Paston got was more significant, both materially and politically. Townshend's resentment grew with perceived slights from his erstwhile protégé. The ultimate reward for Lord Yarmouth came with his appointment to Norfolk's lord lieutenancy in early 1676, displacing his rival, Townshend.[115]

109. For Hobart, see *HP 1660–90*, 2:552–53; J. M. Rosenheim, "An Early Appreciation of *Paradise Lost*," *Modern Philology* 75 (1978): 280–82; and his correspondence with John Hobart of Norwich, Bodl., MS Tanner 42 and 43, passim. His activity as a JP is shown in Rosenheim, "Oligarchy," appendix 4.
110. Kishlansky, *Parliamentary Selection*, 136–37.
111. *HP 1660–90*, 2:553; *CSPD 1672–73*, 572. D. R. Lacey, *Dissent and Parliamentary Politics in England, 1661–1689* (New Brunswick, N.J., 1969), 104, mistakenly claims that Hobart was a moderate Anglican.
112. Sir R. Kemp to HT, 8 December 1671, NRO, WKC 7/75, 404x4.
113. *CSPD 1673–75*, 475–76; Le Strange, *Lists*, 169. Paston visited Raynham with his wife in November 1671: Raynham household a/cs 1671–86, RUBV. See also HT to Sir R. Paston, 12 August 1672 and 10 August 1673, NRO, Paston letters, vol. 1.
114. HT to Sir R. Paston, 25 May 1667, NRO, Paston letters, vol. 1.
115. HT received the farm of customs duties on coals in 1665 but then obtained nothing until a belated viscountcy in 1682. Paston rose only after 1665, receiving the potentially lucrative wood farm; his son's marriage into the illegitimate royal family was a coup; and his viscountcy in 1673 and his earldom in 1683 were each a promotion to

Paston might not have worked Townshend's ruin, if Townshend had not undermined his own standing with the crown. Having endeavored during the 1660s to persuade the king of his merits, by the 1670s Townshend realized that his arguments were falling on deaf ears, and he gave rein to his pique. His endorsement of Sir John Hobart in 1673 had an anticourt flavor. His support for Sir Robert Kemp to succeed Thomas Lord Richardson as the other county MP was initially far less controversial, but during the year between Richardson's death in May 1674 and the election of his successor, the county atmosphere grew charged with political tension, and Townshend's identification with oppositionist forces became obvious.[116] Kemp, whose father had been a "great sufferer" for Charles I, was a malleable character "whose judgment depends soe much on others," one observed, "that raither [than] not gratify, he will debauch his reason." As a magistrate he had shown some sympathy for dissenters, but his personal religious predilections are uncertain.[117] Townshend in effect nominated Kemp, following a lord lieutenant's common practice, but he did not take public credit, in order not to compromise the "free" electorate. Still, he persuaded the reluctant Kemp to stand when the latter balked at charges of Presbyterianism brought against him (and Townshend) by the local clergy. Kemp was not ready to identify with dissent in the way that Hobart had, and Townshend reassured him that he need not do so.[118]

When Kemp formally agreed to put himself forward, Townshend craftily wrote Lord Yarmouth to solicit his support, revealing his belief that old values still applied in politics, that one's "pledge [of support] was not lightly given and could not ordinarily be withdrawn."[119] With the incumbent recently dead, the date of a new election unknown (since parliament was in recess), and no alternative candidate in view, Lord Yarmouth could not plead preengagement to another and thus had to endorse Kemp, ostensibly signaling unanimity in the county

---

a rank higher than HT's. See GEC, *Peerage*, "Townshend" and "Yarmouth"; *HP 1660–90*, 3:211–12, 579–80.

116. Ibid., 2:552–53, 671–72, and 3:330–32 on Hobart, Kemp, and Richardson, respectively. Sir W. Cooke to W. Sancroft, 12 May 1675, Bodl., MS Tanner 42, f. 148. From January 1672, HT received visits from Hobart at Raynham: household a/cs 1671–86, RUBV.

117. O. Hughes to Sir R. Southwell, 4 June 1675, Folger Library, Bacon-Townshend, V.b.305, f. 34. Cf. *HP 1660–90*, 1:320, where Kemp is labeled "a churchman," and ibid., 2:671, where the same author claims he "was known to have absorbed his mother's puritan principles." Kemp's alarm at being charged with Presbyterianism in 1675 suggests that Anglicanism overbalanced Puritanism.

118. Sir R. Kemp to HT, 30 May 1674, RBF/HT misc. Sir J. Holland to HT, 22 May 1674, RBF/HT Felton.

119. Kishlansky, *Parliamentary Selection*, 30.

but yielding a tactical victory to Townshend.[120] Despite Townshend's gambit, the well-orchestrated campaign that made Lord Yarmouth high steward of his namesake town in December 1674 underlined the latter's growing power. It exposed Townshend's shaky influence and helped to destroy "that tranquil good understanding that [had] a long time continued" within Norfolk's political community.[121] Unanimity was desirable, but it could not be long preserved.

A by-election at King's Lynn presaged the entire county's politicization. A vacancy at the end of 1674 involved Townshend in a battle over the borough seat with the Earl of Danby, who promoted his son-in-law, Robert Coke, against Townshend's choice Alderman Simon Taylor. Danby's boldness in insinuating his interest into a constituency where he had no prior influence was part of his campaign to build a reliable court party, in part by reviving the divisions of the civil wars. This effrontery evoked Townshend's vehement and perhaps rash response: he declared openly and early against Coke; he "used his interest and aut[h]ority" for Taylor (who was suspected of Presbyterianism); and he vowed to submit Danby's letter of endorsement to the committee on elections, if Coke should win.[122] Two visits to King's Lynn by Townshend nonetheless failed to counter Danby's huge expenditures there, estimated at £7,000 to £10,000, and in April 1675 the voters overcame their suspicion of an outsider and chose the well-connected Coke.[123] The loss—a clear sign of his limited influence—was humiliating for Townshend, and it is difficult to know what hurt him more, the blow to his local prestige or the public opposition he made to Danby, which determined the lord treasurer to remove him as lord lieutenant, a dismissal effected in less than a year.[124]

As much as Danby's animosity, Townshend's own behavior during the ensuing by-election for knight of the shire, which culminated in Sir Robert Kemp's victory two weeks after Coke's at King's Lynn, equally contributed to his loss of the lieutenancy. The fact that Kemp, now facing a rival candidate, had been characterized as an enemy of

120. [Draft] HT to Lord Yarmouth, n.d., and Yarmouth to HT, 2 July 1674, RBF/HT misc.

121. H. Astley to J. Hobart, 1 May 1675, Bodl., MS Tanner 285, f. 153; bailiffs of Yarmouth to Lord Yarmouth, 4 January, and R. Flynt to same, 6 January 1675, Paston letters, vol. 1; *CSPD 1673–75*, 475–76; Lord Yarmouth to Yarmouth corporation, 7 January 1675, Add. 18621, f. 29; Sir J. Hobart to HT, 19 March 1675, RBF/HT misc.

122. O. Hughes to Sir R. Southwell, 18 January and 5 February 1675, Folger Library, Bacon-Townshend, V.b.305, ff. 26, 28.

123. *CSPD 1673–75*, 468, 485, 517, 532, 560, 586; *CSPD 1675–76*, 42, 61, 73; North, *Lives*, 1:121 (where Jessopp incorrectly dates this election to 1673); *HP 1660–90*, 1:327–28; A. Browning, *Thomas Osborne, Earl of Danby and Duke of Leeds*, 3 vols. (London, 1944–51), 1:206.

124. *CSPD 1682*, 55.

the church, made him scarcely the sort of man for Townshend to promote in the face of a ministry ever more strongly identified with the Anglican interest.[125] The Norfolk clergy, angry that Kemp thought churchmen owed political loyalty to their lay patrons, led a campaign to promote Sir Neville Catelyn in opposition. Although an uneager candidate, Catelyn never explicitly discouraged his promoters, who were cheered by Coke's victory at Lynn: one successful challenge to the lord lieutenant engendered confidence in another and more significant attempt. The earlier struggle had been for a borough seat, but this was for the more prestigious place as knight of the shire. Townshend's open support for Kemp also raised the question about the nature of parliamentary selection in the county, and Catelyn gained the backing of those unhappy with "another imposition upon the people," which is how Sir John Hobart's election in 1673 was now construed.[126] More than one freeholder shared the resentment of the observer who bridled at the fact that "my Lord T[ownshend] by his greatness alone made Sir John H[obart an MP], and now Sir Robert K[emp] must be an addition to his glory, soe our parliament men are made by the peer, not the gentry and commoners."[127] Despite the fact that this observer and others like him would welcome the impact of Lord Yarmouth's electoral "greatness" in a few years' time, such comments testify to the growth of a less deferential, if not truly independent, electorate in Norfolk.

Had Lord Yarmouth been free to work on Catelyn's behalf, and had Catelyn declared himself sooner, Townshend's nominee, Kemp, might well have lost. But Lord Yarmouth was true to his word and even rallied his tenants for Kemp. £1,500 spent on Kemp's behalf played a part, too, and Townshend intervened dramatically to secure victory. He ordered deputy lieutenants, justices "& all men of power & influence . . . by all ways & meanes to make voyces for Sir R[obert] K[emp]." He persuaded the Bishop of Norwich to intervene and, predictably but potently, he condemned Catelyn's adherents as "a popish faction."[128] In May the "triumvirate" of Townshend, Hobart, and Sir John Holland, fearful of a miscarriage at the polls, came down from

125. Jones, *Charles II*, 116–17.
126. [Copy] Sir J. Holland to Mr. Barnard, 1 April 1675, NRO, Paston letters, vol. 1, and Add. 27447, f. 342; Sir J. Hobart to HT, 19 March 1675, RBF/HT misc. J. Hurton to Lord Yarmouth, 26 April 1675, NRO, Paston letters, vol. 1; *CSPD 1675–76*, 54; Sir W. Cooke to W. Sancroft, 12 May 1675, Bodl., MS Tanner 42, f. 148.
127. O. Hughes to Sir R. Southwell, 5 February 1675, Folger Library, Bacon-Townshend, V.b.305, f. 28.
128. J. Hurton to Lord Yarmouth, 26 April, and J. Gough to same, 7 May 1675, NRO, Paston letters, vol. 1; M. Bedingfield to Lady Yarmouth, 25 July 1675, Add. 36988, f. 106; Sir W. Cooke to W. Sancroft, 12 May 1675, Bodl., MS Tanner 42, f. 148.

parliament "to awe & terrifie" the voters on Kemp's behalf.[129] By all accounts, their tactics *were* awesome. Coming to Norwich before the poll, Kemp's partisans took over the inn where Catelyn's supporters intended to meet, and on election morning Townshend sat outside to discourage arriving Catelynites. He later appeared at the polling place and at day's end helped persuade the sheriff to total the votes and declare for Kemp, disregarding Catelynite complaints that many of their number had not had a chance to vote. His personal intervention indicates the importance this election had for Townshend as a gauge of his interest in the county.[130]

In the eyes of others, the affair destroyed what was left of the county's long-standing electoral harmony.[131] Although a local disturbance, it had broad implications: "We in the country," lamented one farsighted observer, "fancy the humors begin to grow & wax & threaten a paroxisme at Westminster."[132] The election in addition demonstrated "how the malitia of Norfolk governe their poore countrey men," an indictment borne out by the appearance of voters who claimed to vote not for Kemp but on behalf of the lord lieutenant or some militia officer, statements that themselves qualify the "overtly ideological" nature of the contest.[133] The substantial size of Catelyn's following, claimed to be four thousand strong, revealed the limited extent of Townshend's interest, even after fourteen years as the county's lieutenant. Despite exercising every ounce of influence and using coercive methods, he barely won the election even with a hand-picked, long-endorsed candidate for whom he appeared publicly. He ventured his personal reputation and had it smudged, bearing out the claim that patrons could no longer "assume that their [electoral] influence would go unchallenged."[134] Castigation of Kemp as the church's enemy, and open championing of Catelyn as its ally, effectively identified Townshend with sectaries, however inappropriately. Yet even before the election it was clear that he and his followers—"the Grandees," as one called them—would "extreamly lose themselves by this businesse

---

129. Sir J. Hobart to J. Hobart, 20 April 1675, Bodl., MS Tanner 42, f. 146; J. Gough to Lord Yarmouth, 7 May 1675, NRO, Paston letters, vol. 1.
130. This account is based on an unsigned, unaddressed report, hostile to Kemp, dated at Norwich, 10 May 1675, NRO, Paston letters, vol. 1. The version calendared in HMC, *6th Report*, 371–72, appears to be the basis for the accounts in *HP 1660–90*, 1:320; D. Ogg, *England in the Reign of Charles II*, 2nd ed. (Oxford, 1956), 474–76; and R. H. Mason, *The History of Norfolk* . . . (London, 1884), 356–58. See also O. Hughes to [Sir R. Southwell], 29 May 1675, Folger Library, Bacon-Townshend, V.b.305, f. 33.
131. H. Astley to J. Hobart, 1 May 1675, Bodl., MS Tanner 285, f. 153.
132. Sir W. Cooke to W. Sancroft, 12 May 1675, Bodl., MS Tanner 42, f. 148.
133. Account of 10 May 1675, NRO, Paston letters, vol. 1; Fletcher, *Reform in the Provinces*, 337.
134. Kishlansky, *Parliamentary Selection*, 191.

in the affections of the country," and not just on the religious issue.[135] In the wake of the lieutenancy's show of force, especially in the persons of the Hobart-Holland-Townshend triumvirate, one observer asked "whether the freeholders had then, or were likely hereafter to have that effect of their birth rights, free voices; or whether they were not all virtually comprehended in the will and disposure of 3 great ones, I might have said in one."[136]

Clearly, Townshend's ambition to dominate the county was not easily swallowed. "[T]he love and affection of the gentry, the duty, respects and submission of the commonalty" that he had enjoyed in the 1660s, were lost forever by his highhandedness in 1675. Norfolk men, even his enemies, might well "with joy and pleasure remember his great zeale, and adventure of his life and fortunes, immediately before the . . . restauration," but they forgot this service when he joined with dissenters and former parliamentarians, reviving memories and disputes from the 1640s.[137] Such past battles, however, counted little with the lord lieutenant: he sought personal achievement. He cared deeply that the elections of Hobart and Kemp were ascribed to his influence; it was of far less consequence that both men, when elected, would take positions in the Commons "against the court" or that some of their followers had opposed the current king's father. That the pair attracted nonconformist voters meant less to Townshend than that the gentry had turned out at his behest.[138] This preoccupation with his own interest—not that of Kemp or a "party"—explains the importance that Townshend ascribed to this election and reveals his fundamentally nonideological approach to politics. Kemp's victory demonstrated the lord lieutenant's might, and the appearance of malleable gentry seeking "to gratify and oblige my L[ord] T[ownshend]" especially did so.[139] The hope of some was that this power would next be employed in a national forum, to bring the government to new policies; Townshend, however, evidently hoped it would bring him—as a potent regional figure—the recognition (and reward) that he felt was his due.

Such optimism was not borne out by events. Where Townshend's behavior drove memories of his prior service from his countrymen's

135. J. Gough to Lord Yarmouth, 7 May 1675, NRO, Paston letters, vol. 1; J. R. Jones, "The First Whig Party in Norfolk," *Durham University Journal*, n.s., 15 (1953): 14–15.
136. O. Hughes to [Sir R. Southwell], 29 May 1675, Folger Library, Bacon–Townshend, V.b.305, f. 33.
137. Same to same, 29 May and 4 June 1675, ibid., ff. 33, 34.
138. Same to same, 5 February, 29 March, and 4 June 1675, ibid., ff. 28, 31, 34.
139. Same to same, 29 March 1675, ibid., f. 31.

minds, it might do the same with the king. In Norfolk the King's Lynn victory of Robert Coke and Catelyn's impressive showing in defeat encouraged Lord Yarmouth's ambitions: in September 1675, after recovering from a highwayman's attack, he made a triumphant processional entry into Norfolk, which evinced his rising popularity and proved that the county was ready, as had been claimed in the spring, "to receive another, who will stand by them, into their hearts."[140] The incapacitation of Yarmouth (Townshend's only logical successor, since Lord Howard was a Catholic) and perhaps the king's reluctance to dismiss Townshend, a formerly faithful servant (for whose baby son the king had recently become godparent), may have delayed the change in lord lieutenants.[141] By November 1675, however, when Charles II chose as sheriff the one man, John Pell, whom Townshend asked to be overlooked that year, the signs of impending disgrace were clear.[142] Townshend's participation in a novel and alarming scheme to help defray the expense of the sheriff's office merely hastened his downfall. An agreement, originally signed by forty gentry (Townshend's adherents almost to a man), provided guidelines to govern the expenses of any subscriber who might be chosen sheriff, minimizing the heavy burden of office. There was undoubtedly a connection between the selection of Pell as sheriff against Townshend's request and the composition of this manifesto. To some, the agreement appeared sinister, since it undercut the king's punitive power of appointing an opponent as sheriff. Moreover, if a subscriber were chosen sheriff, his fellows might then dominate local government and even the militia by their "correspondency . . . with one another."[143]

Townshend's involvement with this combination, his vote for an address to the king calling for the dissolution of parliament,[144] the enmity of Danby, the reverberations of the Kemp-Catelyn election, all contributed to his replacement as lord lieutenant by Lord Yarmouth in late February 1676. One rumor further claimed that he was turned out "for tyrannizeing in his country, caballing with Shaftsbury, Sir S[amuel] Barnardiston &c. Most believe the whole story true & con-

---

140. J. Fisher to Lady Yarmouth, and Lord Yarmouth to same, both 29 September 1675, NRO, Paston letters, vol. 1. Cf. Fletcher, *Reform in the Provinces*, 337–38, who sees this welcome as convincing Yarmouth to move against HT.

141. H. Astley to J. Hobart, 1 May 1675, Bodl., MS Tanner 285, f. 153; Sir J. Hobart to J. Hobart, 20 April 1675, MS Tanner 42, f. 146. Hutton notes that Charles II's "full vindictive anger . . . was reserved for the vulnerable and expendable," both of which HT clearly now was: *Restoration*, 204.

142. *CSPD 1675–76*, 424.

143. O. Hughes to Lady Yarmouth, 17 January 1676, NRO, Paston letters, vol. 1. On the subscription, see James M. Rosenheim, "Party Organization at the Local Level: The Norfolk Sheriff's Subscription of 1676," *Historical Journal* 29 (1986): 713–22.

144. Davis, "The 'Presbyterian' Opposition," in Jones, ed., *Party and Management*, 33.

demne him exceedingly. Some are infidells & will not believe his caballing because, as they say, hee has offered to foresweare Shaftsbury & all his worke &c."[145]

The report leaves in doubt Townshend's full identification with the Shaftesburian opposition; his parliamentary positions during 1675 reinforce the uncertainty.[146] Although he had aligned himself with opposition to the government, the assumption that he might "forsake all [Shaftesbury's] worke" suggests that the issues at hand—comprehension or toleration, an anti-French foreign policy, the government's financial accountability—mattered less to him than the personalities involved. The "caballing" in which Townshend engaged was aimed primarily at Danby (whose fall the summons of a new parliament might precipitate), rather than at maintaining a particular political position.[147] Townshend's efforts to maintain his honor and reputation explain his quarrels with Lord Yarmouth far better than any specific position either man took. Yet it was the imperious manner in which Townshend forwarded his interest that led some in the county to rejoice at his downfall "as they did when the king was restord."[148] For one as closely identified with the Restoration as Townshend, this was cruel irony.

Retreat, Not Retirement

Shaken by his removal, Townshend temporarily retreated from political affairs. He was, by later account, particularly upset at being supplanted by Viscount Yarmouth, "one he looked on as a creature of his own," one whom he had helped advance "from a mean fortune to his present share in the king's favour." Almost as if in shock, Townshend left London and remained in Norfolk until the end of 1678, acutely aware, as he said, that he had "neither interest to gaine a

---

145. R. Doughty to Lord Yarmouth, 6 March 1676, NRO, Paston letters, vol. 1.

146. He was considered by Danby to be an opponent of the nonresisting test, but in April 1675 signed neither of two protests against the government's bill "to prevent dangers which may arise from persons disaffected to the government," i.e., Puritans and parliamentarians: Browning, *Danby*, 3:125; Haley, *Shaftesbury*, 373–75. Cf. the protest of November 1675, where he joined Lord Yarmouth against the Lords' rejection of an address for the dissolution of parliament: *LJ*, 13:33.

147. A further indication of Townshend's purpose may be seen in his recruitment of Sir Robert Carr, who was related to Danby's foe, the Earl of Arlington, to work with him at the King's Lynn election against Robert Coke: *CSPD 1675–76*, 42; *HP 1660–90*, 2:21.

148. *CSPD 1675–76*, 567–68, 577; *CSPD 1682*, 55; H. Bedingfield to Lord Yarmouth, 13 March 1676, Add. 27447, ff. 503–4; Sir J. Pettus to same, 13 March [1676], Add. 36540, f. 25 ("king was restord"); *HP 1660–90*, 1:596.

hearing [at court] nor credite to be beleeved upon indifferent tearmes."[149] This retreat from the center of power was in some sense an admission of defeat by one who pinned his hopes on central favor and knew that his local stature rested heavily on perceptions of his interest at Whitehall.

On the other hand, Townshend was by no means a recluse after his fall: following his dismissal he pluckily attended assizes to encourage the sheriff's subscription and show the county that he was not broken. He may have planned a meeting at Raynham for April 1676 with the Earl of Arlington (an erstwhile foe) and the Dukes of Monmouth and Ormonde, but it never came off, if it was seriously considered. Hostility to Danby drove Townshend on: he was reported as declaring that "the king should never have [a] penny of money in parliament as long as [Danby] was lord treasurer."[150] Townshend's ties to Sir Robert Carr, Arlington's kinsman and an old enemy of Danby, suggest the same, although Sir Samuel Barnardiston, a noted country MP, was entertained at Raynham in autumn 1676.[151] That Townshend dealt with these disparate politicians—and largely on his own terms and in his own county— underscores his inability to see politics as anything but primarily personal. Moreover, he seems to have decided that the recovery of his fortunes depended on proving his continued power in Norfolk, and he stayed away from parliament until December 1678, even when explicitly solicited by Shaftesbury and Lord Holles. In minor ways he harassed the new lord lieutenant, and fanned the flames of partisanship by pursuing a suit for scandalous words against Dr. Owen Hughes, commissary of the Norwich and Norfolk archdeaconries and confidant of Lady Yarmouth.[152]

This affair had wide-reaching implications and long antecedents. Hughes, a client of Sir Robert Southwell, clerk to the Privy Council, was an ambitious man involved in local disputes ever since his controversial appointment as commissary in 1672–73.[153] Not content with the commissaryships, Hughes had himself placed on the commission of the

---

149. *CSPD 1682*, 54–55; [draft] HT to [? Henry Bedingfield], c. 9 July 1677, Add. 41654, ff. 66–67; Raynham household a/cs 1671–86, RUBV.
150. Lord Yarmouth to wife, 14 April 1676, Paston Letters, vol. 1.
151. See *HP 1660–90*, 1:595–97, 2:23–26, for Barnardiston and Carr. See household a/cs 1671–86, RUBV, for the visit.
152. Haley, *Shaftesbury*, 569–70; Lord Yarmouth to wife, 14, 19, 21 April and 5 May 1676, Paston letters, vol. 1; M. Peckover to Lord Yarmouth, 1 March 1676, Add. 27447, f. 354; [drafts] HT to Lord Holles and to Shaftesbury, 2 February 1677, Add. 41654, f. 30; *LJ*, 13:66; R. Walpole to HT, 9 May 1676, Yale University, Osborn files, "Walpole."
153. *HP 1660–90*, 3:459–60. See especially Hughes's letters to Southwell, Folger Library, Bacon-Townshend, V.b.305, ff. 2–12, 19–21.

peace and made judge of the Norfolk vice-admiralty court. Both appointments, in which the ubiquitous Henry Howard played a part, affronted Lord Townshend, who was consulted about neither. Hughes made enemies on the bench by attacking dissenters,[154] and, just as significantly, promoted the candidacy of Robert Coke at the Lynn by-election in 1675, while condemning Townshend's support for Sir Robert Kemp.[155] Through Sir Robert Southwell and others, Townshend cautioned Hughes to display "better comportment" in the future, and this Hughes attempted to do at a conciliatory interview with Townshend in July 1675 that nonetheless proved disastrous.[156]

Hughes came to Raynham, making symbolic submission, and begged Townshend's pardon, only to find that the "angry and passionate lord" could not be placated. Townshend accused him of libel for a scurrilous paper he had circulated during the election campaign, and the two quarreled over the merits of Sir Robert Kemp and the recent election. Townshend grew so angry, Hughes reported,

that it caused him to transgress the rules of civility, especially in his own house, and he called me sawcy and pragmaticall over and over again, all the while I takeing all, only alleging that I was a gentleman, and was not used to such language, nor never deserved it. . . . Whereupon [Townshend] gave a loose to his passion in words very hard, and disobliging, and commanded me to be gone out of his house, out of his doores, following me with his cane in his hand, as if he had bin a driving a brute, or designed to strike me, which I should not have taken patiently.[157]

Thus ended the effort at reconciliation.

Townshend subsequently turned Hughes's patron against him and complained in parliament of Hughes's scandalous words.[158] In early 1676 he brought legal action under the ancient statute *scandalum magnatum,* accusing Hughes of libel. An assize jury impaneled by a sheriff friendly to Townshend gave the verdict and damages of £4,000 to the peer. Many expected he would remit the award and by this magnanimity regain lost credit in the county, but Townshend had publicly disdained to yield on the matter, so Hughes carried the case on appeal to the Court of Common Pleas.[159] There, in Hilary term 1677, the

---

154. O. Hughes to Sir R. Southwell, 12 March 1673, 20 November, and 2 December 1674, ibid., ff. 15, 24, 25.
155. Same to same, 18 January, 5 February, 29 March 1675, ibid., ff. 26, 28, 31.
156. Same to same, 29 May, 4 and 21 June 1675, ibid., ff. 33–35.
157. Same to same, 12 July 1675, ibid., f. 36.
158. Same to same, 21 July, and [copy] Southwell to Hughes, 30 July 1675, ibid., ff. 37, 38; *LJ,* 13:23, 30.
159. Lord Yarmouth to wife, 30 April 1676, NRO, Paston letters, vol. 1; same to same, 17 July 1676, Add. 27447, f. 326; Sir J. Holland to HT, 28 July and 6 August 1676, RBF/HT Felton; HMC, *Townshend MSS,* 36.

justices upheld the verdict for Townshend; whether he received his damages is uncertain, but Hughes was destroyed.[160]

The immediate lesson the verdict gave mattered more than payment of the award: Townshend remained a force to reckon with in Norfolk, "a person dangerous" in his friend Sir John Holland's words. Townshend apparently hoped that the evidence of his potency would impress the court with the need to make up with him, but Holland urged him to use his power in a conciliatory fashion, to emphasize "the constancy of your loyall & faythfull affections towards his majestie . . . & that no disobligations shall or can make you depart from your duty."[161] Patient adoption of an inoffensive profile might reestablish Townshend, especially if Danby fell and Lord Yarmouth's interest collapsed as a likely result.[162] Yet the set-to with Hughes confirmed the impression of Townshend as a would-be tyrant and made him an ever greater target for partisan attack, guaranteeing that contention would win out over conciliation. Scurrilous accusations that he attended religious conventicles left him with no misapprehension about his opponents' goal: "that they who wright mee out of my commission & the king's service have a mind to worke mee out of the country too is no news to mee, who know I can never be other than an eie sore to them."[163] The attacks of his enemies combined with Townshend's temper, ambition, and self-importance to draw him back into political activity. Through much of 1677 and 1678 he was ill but not incapacitated, and at the end of 1677 Lord Yarmouth identified him as a moving force behind opposition to Yarmouth's son at a Norwich by-election. "The artifices of Rainham & Blickling [Hobart's residence]" were the focus of Lord Yarmouth's concern, but victories for Yarmouth's interest at the Norwich by-election in 1678, and at King's Lynn for the first Exclusion Parliament in 1679, revealed Townshend's weakness as a political leader.[164]

At King's Lynn, the death of Robert Coke in mid-January 1679 removed a popular incumbent and a court supporter. It created an

---

160. O. Hughes to Lord Yarmouth, 5 May 1676, NRO, Paston letters, vol. 1; A. Briggs to [?S. Philips], 29 November 1676, filed with P. Tubbing's sheepreeve's a/c, RUEA 1676. For the case, see *English Reports*, 89:994–1003. Hughes resigned his commissaryships in 1679: F. Blomefield, *An Essay towards a Topographical History of the County of Norfolk*, 11 vols. (London, 1805–11), 3:656–57.

161. Sir J. Holland to HT, 6 August 1676, RBF/HT Felton.

162. Sir J. Holland to HT, 28 July and 6 August 1676, ibid. Danby's Norfolk visit in 1676 underscored Yarmouth's reliance on the earl: Lord Yarmouth to his wife, 28 March, 3, 9, 12 April, and 17 July 1676, NRO, Paston letters, vol. 1.

163. [Draft] HT to [? Sir H. Bedingfield], c. 9 July 1677, Add. 41654, ff. 66–67.

164. *HP 1660–90*, 1:329–30; Lord Yarmouth to wife, 26 October and 21 December 1677, 14 April and 13 December 1678, and J. Doughty to Hon. W. Paston, 21 December 1677, NRO, Paston Letters, vol. 2.

unlooked-for opportunity in the borough for those still smarting over Danby's success with Coke in 1675, and Sir John Hobart therefore urged William Windham, Townshend's brother-in-law, to consider standing. That the suggestion came from Hobart shows Townshend's reduced county role and Hobart's seizure of initiative from him. Windham, an unprepossessing country gentleman, interested more in his garden than in politics,[165] was leery of the expense the contest was sure to impose. Hobart, in encouraging him, at first optimistically assessed the influence of Townshend at King's Lynn. "Your relation to & friendship from my L[ord] T[ownshend]," Hobart avowed, "will certainly secure you intirely his interest. And although perhaps the towne of Lynn have not acquitted themselves (of late) well toward him, yet I looke upon that rather as a stronger . . . argument that they will doe much better now, for as they are sensible of my Lord's resentment soe they are of their errour, & wilbe very glad of this occation to restore themselves to my lordship's good opinion."

But Hobart's confident prediction was wrong. Angry with the voters of King's Lynn because they had favored Danby's man over his in 1675, Townshend refused to appear there on Windham's behalf in 1679 unless invited by the corporation; the corporation, caring little about Townshend's "resentment," made no such plea and ignored Townshend's indirect solicitation on Windham's behalf. Windham never became a candidate at King's Lynn, which turned to a resident nominee.[166]

Townshend's unwillingness to solicit the borough reveals more than his anger over the earlier election there. On the one hand it is suggestive of the continuing breakdown in the organic and symbiotic nature of patronage relations, where patronage once "embedded in an ongoing social matrix" was now "enforced by political power."[167] It was precisely this new kind of patronage that Townshend did not fully understand, so that when he attempted to use political power, as in the election of 1675, it was in a ham-fisted, overbearing way. On the other hand, the Lynn election in early 1679 also signaled that even if he chose to play the political game by its new, more partisan rules, Townshend currently lacked the political interest to do so effectively. In the aftermath of this failure, Lord Yarmouth accurately judged that "my Lord Townshend's influence prevailes nott . . . at all" at King's Lynn. More generally, Townshend took so small a part in the

---

165. R. W. Ketton-Cremer, *Felbrigg: The Story of a House* (London, 1982; paperback ed.), chap. 4, especially 60–70.

166. Sir J. Hobart to W. Windham, 16 January 1679, Add. 37911, f. 3, which indicates Coke died on 15, not 19, January as in *HP 1660–90*, 2:102; same to same, 25 January 1679, NRO, WKC 7/6, 404x1.

167. Kishlansky, *Parliamentary Selection*, 47–48.

elections to the first Exclusion Parliament in January and February 1679, the first countywide elections in nearly twenty years, that Sir John Hobart gloomily concluded that the sickly man's interest was "not much stronger . . . than his present constitution of body."[168]

The upsetting result of the county election in January 1679 nonetheless served to invigorate Townshend, as two court supporters and adherents of Lord Yarmouth (Sir Neville Catelyn and Sir Christopher Calthorpe) were returned over Sir John Hobart for the county. That Hobart stood alone perhaps signals the county's desire for unanimity and conciliation, which therefore discouraged partisan contesting; at the same time, minimal opposition to the two successful candidates betokened Lord Yarmouth's rising power. Whatever its meaning, Hobart challenged the result as fraudulent. Even before his petition was heard in the Commons (where on 21 April the return was vacated and a new election ordered), Townshend promised personally to appear against Lord Yarmouth "at the day & place of combate," agreeing to give the Norfolk Whigs, as they may now be called, "all the little interest I may pretend too in Norfolke."[169]

Despite the promise, Townshend characteristically blew hot and cold during the ensuing Whig crisis in Norfolk. He loudly endorsed Hobart and William Windham for the special election in May and apologized to Windham (who ran last) for not serving him better.[170] Nonetheless, Townshend claimed to be "abundantly satisfyed" with a split representation and one Whig seat, especially since Windham in losing had received more votes than any previous victor. As a result, the peer refused to countenance Hobart's plan to petition on Windham's behalf, and this lack of partisan zeal deeply irritated Sir John. "Our friend in Newport Street," wrote Hobart, referring to Townshend, "is almost as dead as a herring, & talkes of goeing downe into the countrey next week: some men's tempers are like spring tydes, suffer[ing] great ebbs & flowes."[171]

This evaluation of Townshend's political persona was on the mark. In London he was a wavering exclusionist, largely absent from the House of Lords until May 1679. He served as a go-between when the

168. Lord Yarmouth to wife, 28 February 1679, NRO, Paston letters, vol. 2; Sir J. Hobart to W. Windham, 30 January and 1 March 1679, NRO, WKC 7/6, 404x1; *HP 1660–90*, 1:319–34. But see HT to Mr. Tyrell, 28 January 1679, Add. 27447, f. 398.

169. Sir J. Hobart to W. Windham, 1 and 20 March 1679, NRO, WKC 7/6, 404x1; HT to "my worthy friends and acquaintance" in Norfolk, 22 April 1679, Add. 37911, ff. 9–10; J. R. Jones, "Restoration Election Petitions," *Durham University Journal*, n.s., 22 (1961): 52–56; Sir J. Hobart to W. Windham, 27 March and 3 April 1679, NRO, WKC 7/6, 404x1.

170. HT to W. Windham, 22 March 1679, Add. 37911, ff. 7–8; 12 May 1679, NRO, WKC 7/6, 404x1.

171. Sir J. Hobart to W. Windham, 15, 17, 20, 24 May; Sir J. Holland to same, 5 May; and Windham's draft reply to Hobart, 20 May 1679, NRO, WKC 7/6, 404x1.

Duke of York made an abortive approach to the Earl of Shaftesbury, newly appointed to the Privy Council,[172] but he attended erratically during the rest of the parliamentary session and did not always join with Shaftesbury in the House's disputes.[173] In Norfolk, Townshend was somewhat more decisive, and when he learned in mid-June of the sitting parliament's dissolution and the summons of another, he immediately gathered the leading Whigs at Raynham Hall. While gentry meetings were traditional mechanisms to winnow candidates,[174] this colloquy at Raynham was not intended to obtain unified choices acceptable to the county at large. Under Townshend's aegis, Sir Peter Gleane and Hobart were chosen as Whig candidates for the August election, which they won, but having hosted the caucus, Townshend took little part in the ensuing campaign. Illness may have been one reason, but the strictures handed out against noble interference in elections restrained him (as well as Lord Yarmouth) from electioneering. It is also likely that Townshend was already losing his taste for party conflict, which only grew in the election's aftermath.[175]

The Whigs enjoyed great success at the polls, returning ten of the county's twelve MPs for the second Exclusion Parliament,[176] but this strong showing masked problems among them. The delay between the election and the meeting of parliament in October 1680, over a year later, eroded the Whigs' unanimity; they squabbled over election expenses, grew suspicious that Gleane might "turne pentioner," and disagreed about tactics that included regular meetings in Norwich, which to some appeared improperly factional.[177] Townshend's hesitant embrace of the Whig organization (and cause) is the best index of his nonparty approach to politics.

Townshend attended neither the second nor the third Exclusion Parliament and could not be counted as an avid Whig whether in Norfolk or in London.[178] He remained antagonistic to the local faction

172. Haley, *Shaftesbury*, 515.
173. *LJ*, 13:565–94; Haley, *Shaftesbury*, 522–28.
174. Kishlansky, *Parliamentary Selection*, 141–44.
175. Sir J. Hobart to J. Hobart, 14 and 16 July 1679, Bodl., MS Tanner 38, ff. 55, 58; R. Bendish to Hon. William Paston, 23 July 1679, Bodl., MS Gough, Norfolk 33, f. 29c; E. L'Estrange to Lady Yarmouth, 8 and 27 August 1679, Add. 36988, ff. 147–50. Raynham household a/cs 1671–86, RUBV, note a visit by Sir T. Browne, suggesting HT's illness.
176. *HP 1660–90*, 1:319–34.
177. E. L'Estrange to Lady Yarmouth, 27 August 1679, Add. 36988, ff. 149–50; Lord Yarmouth to same, 3 September 1679, Add. 27447, f. 431; T. Townshend to HT, 17 December 1679 and 21 June 1680, and Sir J. Holland to HT, 15 June 1680, RBF/HT Felton.
178. The rumor in Norfolk reporting him among peers presenting Charles II with an address urging that parliament meet in January 1680 was inaccurate: he had actually

headed by Lord Yarmouth—clearly the party of "Tories," although the word was not yet used in Norfolk—and thus in some basic sense he may be deemed a Whig. But Townshend disapproved of the extreme Whigs' conclaves in Norwich, which "in these jealous tymes" appeared to be a sign of "forming a party" when there was "no occasion" for it, that is, when no election was in view. Overt partisan organization gave him discomfort.[179]

By early 1680 he was talking of "accommodation" in Norfolk, hoping by his personal leadership to reconcile men whose political quarrels he only partly understood. Townshend apparently visited Newmarket when Charles II was there in April, and the following month reportedly proposed to manage parliament for the king, if he would end the series of prorogations and allow it to meet.[180] Nothing in Townshend's career prepares us for this bold move. His absence from the last parliament scarcely suggests he had a group of supporters behind his optimistic scheme, and the undertaking he supposedly offered had no realistic chance, since the king would not allow parliament the free rein Townshend wanted. Moreover, Sir Robert Reading, who retailed this account to the Duke of Ormonde, claimed rather surprisingly that Shaftesbury had also rejected Townshend's proposal, because he wanted "to keep of[f] the parliament for some time yet longer . . . [so that] the king's [financial] affaires may be more desperate."[181] This is a surprising posture for Shaftesbury to have adopted, since he had recently orchestrated a petitioning campaign aimed at forcing the king to meet parliament.[182]

Perhaps to give credibility to his extraordinary proposal to the king, Townshend seized upon a pretext (the outgrowth of quarrels over election costs) to part company with Sir John Hobart, Norfolk's leading exclusionist, and declare himself unwilling to support Sir John at a new election. Hobart saw through the charade, noting that his lordship had said for some time past that "he [had] expected a command from Co[urt?] to quitt me &c."[183] Townshend's negotiations with the king

---

been in Norfolk at the time. *LJ*, 13:476, 565, 594; Haley, *Shaftesbury*, 560–61; T. Townshend to HT, 17 December 1679, RBF/HT Felton.

179. T. Townshend to HT, 29 December 1679, 21 June 1680, and TF to HT, 27 April 1680, ibid.

180. C. Roberts, *Schemes & Undertakings: A Study of English Politics in the Seventeenth Century* (Columbus, Ohio, 1985), 98–99.

181. Sir R. Reading to the Duke of Ormonde, 11 May 1680, Bodl., MS Carte 243, ff. 473–74. Reading qualified his account with the phrase "it is said."

182. Haley, *Shaftesbury*, 559–64.

183. Sir J. Hobart to W. Windham, 26 June, and [draft] Windham to HT, 30 June 1680, NRO, WKC 7/6, 404x1. On expenses, see T. Townshend to HT, 21 June 1680, RBF/HT Felton; Hobart to HT, 25 June 1680, RBF/HT misc.; HT to Windham, 26 June 1680, Add. 37911, ff. 12–13.

indicate that Hobart's suspicions were well-founded, but when the approach to the king proved abortive, Townshend typically reversed ground and ultimately backed Hobart in the elections to the third Exclusion Parliament, further evidence of his changeability.[184]

When it came to political action, Townshend combined old attitudes and new; he was driven by social considerations and his sense of public duty, as well as by a desire to build his interest. All the same, his maneuvers during the exclusion crisis expose his old-fashioned, non-ideological conception of politics; exclusion was not a fundamental issue for Townshend, but his own future was. Although he had once, according to Hobart's later report, "twenty times declare[d], that there would be noe other security for our religion & propertyes but by the passing the bill of exclusion," he compromised on the bill's necessity (as when approaching the king) and finally abandoned it altogether.[185] Hobart's principled extremism sat ill with Townshend, in part because such an extreme ally was a liability for one scrambling to regain government favor. It is not surprising that, after endorsing Hobart, Townshend did little actively to campaign for the Whigs, who won only narrowly in Norfolk.[186]

Perhaps regretting that he had yielded to Hobart's candidacy, Townshend was disturbed by the thin margin of victory, not because of what it said about the Whig cause as such, but because the permanent ascendancy of his opponents would not afford him room to regain power. He had to be seen by the government as puissant, but not excessively partisan, if he was to recover his lieutenancy. Hobart's continued provocative candidacy might well ensure the future of Lord Yarmouth's party, so even before the third Exclusion Parliament met, Townshend planned for new elections—without Hobart. He agreed that Hobart's frequent candidacy was resented, "as if ther were noe other [but him] worthy to serve ther country," and proposed another caucus at Raynham in the summer of 1681, a gathering that would exclude Hobart and explore the possibility of sharing county representation between the two parties. Townshend clearly believed that retaining one seat was better than losing both. The suggestion to meet under his personal sponsorship, to "debate freely and honestly, how matters

184. Sir P. Gleane to T. Townshend [but with HT's endorsement], 4 September 1680, RBF/HT misc.; Sir J. Hobart to W. Windham, 20 January 1681, NRO, WKC 7/6 404x1.
185. Sir J. Hobart to W. Windham, 14 January 1682, NRO, WKC 7/6, 404x1.
186. G. Keynes, ed., *The Works of Sir Thomas Browne*, new ed., 4 vols. (Chicago, 1964), 4:182; Sir J. Hobart to W. Windham, 2 February 1681, NRO, WKC 7/6, 404x1; Sir J. Holland to HT, 19 February 1681, RBF/HT Felton. Vote totals (not given in *HP 1660–90*, 1:319) were Hobart 3,071; Gleane 2,994; Sir J. Astley 2,978; Sir R. Hare, 2,844: "Norfolk Candidates with the number of their polls," NRO, Rye MSS 9, Norris's Collections, vol. 2.

should bee carryed on, and [how] wee should dispose of our selves for the future," shows that he still aspired to a role of leadership within the county, but one of conciliator, rather than advocate of partisan causes. Unfortunately for Townshend's hopes, many voters saw Hobart as the "support of our religion and libertyes," and Sir John himself would not consider standing aside.[187]

The staunch Whig faction wanted to meet prior to the scheduled caucus at Raynham, because they feared that "the country" would not remain uncommitted while Townshend made his choice: the electorate was far too roused (and independent) to be channeled or curbed by the former lord lieutenant. Compromise with their opponents was, moreover, anathema to the true Whigs. Such an idea, Sir Robert Kemp frankly told Townshend, would, first, make the Tories

> laugh at us . . . when they are as they think like to have a victory; 2nd, they wil judg your yeilding to be a diffidence of your interest or alteration of your principles; 3rdly, how can any man that is upon one principle be an instrument to send a man of another principle to the House of Commons. . . . Were our religion, our propertyes secure, it were a time for complecency. Were you restored to your former trust and al[l] those that have stood closest to you out of disgrace, it would look like a good naterel compliance in us . . . but what will itt now be called but a truckling and at best a politick giving upp, of what you cannot hold.

To Kemp, to Hobart, even to the irresolute Sir Peter Gleane who wavered but then determined, "I will no more foresake my freinds . . . then I will my principalls," what was at stake was exactly that, a matter of principle, and for this reason they rejected the idea of compromise. For Townshend, in sharp contrast, power, prestige, personal ambition overrode the principled issues at hand.[188]

Although no new election took place in Charles II's reign, tempers continued to run high in the county, as when a King's Bench grand jury presented the address of some Norfolk Tories as libelous in May 1681.[189] Townshend, however, grew aloof from the Whig cause and was charged with encouraging the court party in Norfolk by his "soe unexpected falling off from them whom you . . . sett up & hetherto so industriously and powerfully supported." He rejected these accusa-

---

187. Sir J. Holland to HT, 19 February, 7 and 28 March, [copy] Sir J. Hobart to Holland, 8 March, [copy] HT to Holland, 10 March, and [copy] Holland to Hobart, 11 March 1681, all in RBF/HT Felton; also Hobart to W. Windham, 8 March 1681, NRO, WKC, 7/6, 404x1.

188. Sir J. Hobart to J. Hobart, 5 April 1681, Bodl., MS Tanner 36, f. 4; Sir R. Kemp to HT, 2 May, and Sir P. Gleane to HT, 16 and 30 May 1681, RBF/HT misc.

189. *CSPD 1680–81*, 285; J. R. Jones, *The First Whigs*, rev. ed. (London, 1970), 186–87.

tions self-righteously and isolated himself further. His tactics of conciliation having failed miserably, Townshend tried to make a virtue of his position outside the Norfolk Whigs' inner circle and said he was prepared to stand and fall alone. "My high and mighty crime," he complained sarcastically, "is no more than that I have without leave pretended to assume a liberty of disposeing of my selfe. The which if I might not doe now, I did not know when I might without offence be at that liberty, & you know liberty & property is what wee Englishmen are inclined tow generally."[190] By the end of 1681 he was publicizing his renunciation of Whig parliamentary candidates, and at quarter sessions early in January 1682 the county at large learned where Townshend stood.[191]

On that occasion, the moderate Whig Thomas Townshend read from a letter that his cousin the peer had written. "I desire you not to bee nyce," wrote the latter,

in saying & owning to any body that I will not concerne my self in the next eleccons, nor shall not desire or advise anybody as my freind to appeare either for Sir J Hob[art] or Sir P Gl[eane]. Pray bee playne & open in this affayre, for it is most agreeable to mee and my principles always to appeare so, it being my opinion that there are other securityes as effectual & powerfull against popery as the bill of exclusion. And therefore I cannot give my consent to the chusing of any person, who hath for 3 parl[iaments] & will in the next give his vote & insist upon that bill.

According to Thomas, this constituted a statement that left all men at liberty to pursue their consciences. If it did so in theory, however, it clearly was not meant to do so in fact; by discountenancing the Whig pair and the policy of exclusion, Townshend had abandoned the Whig party, a step he obviously thought others might follow.[192]

The Whigs who had gathered in Norwich for the sessions reacted unfavorably to this letter: they drank Townshend's health, but forty of them then "declared jollily" for Hobart and Gleane as prospective candidates. An overlapping conclave of extreme Whigs was bolstered by the general meeting and emphatically rejected a proposal to put

190. Sir J. Holland to HT, 22 and 29 August, and HT's draft reply of 25 August 1681, RBF/HT Felton; Sir P. Gleane to HT, 22 August 1681, and same to T. Townshend, 27 February 1682, RBF/HT misc. Six years later HT would "seeke none that I fiend are not ready to owne mee, being growne old & out of date": HT to T. Townshend, enclosed in mortgage of 10 September 1669, RL drawer 109.

191. HT's draft reply to Sir J. Holland's of 29 August 1681, Add. 41654, f. 64; Holland to HT, 5 September 1681, RBF/HT Felton; HT's draft to Holland on back of letter from W. Harbord to HT, 5 September 1681, RBF/HT misc.; *Prideaux letters*, 120; *CSPD 1682*, 56; letters of December 1681 between Sir J. Hobart and W. Windham, NRO, WKC 7/6 404x1.

192. T. Townshend to HT, 23 January 1682, RBF/HT Felton.

up compromise nominees; they would carry on the party battle.[193] Partisanship, not compromise, was the order of the day. "At sessions," it was reported, "they do not debate, but immediately cry, Put it to the vote, and the cause is carried as the person concerned has an interest in the bench." So long as this factionalism persisted, Townshend's hope to depoliticize discourse could not prosper. Moreover, his "standing newtral" was itself a political stance, and in early 1683 one observer plausibly argued that the county political world contained three groups, those of Hobart, Townshend, and Lord Yarmouth.[194] Despite rumors that Townshend and Lord Yarmouth had agreed between them to advance moderate men for knights of the shire,[195] their reconciliation was unlikely, and considering the animosity that now existed between Townshend and Hobart, it was no more probable that they would patch up their differences. In the end Hobart was philosophical. "If," he sighed, "I had not been well acquainted (even a great parte of my life) with the various, uncertaine & changable stepps (to say no more) of this noble person, I should have been much more surprised at the whole series & carriage of this affayre."[196]

To others, too, Townshend's switches and reversals were predictable or half-expected, although nonetheless vexing for that,[197] but in early 1682 he went further than any might have guessed. Rumor was current at the end of January that "Lord Townshend is entirely come over to the court party."[198] Here was a shift of major proportion, yet the conversion brought Townshend no immediate benefit. Having lost the Whigs as allies, having made no progress as a parliamentary undertaker, having failed as a moderator in Norfolk, he had, as Hobart said, neither new nor old "freinds on eyther side to cast a favourable mantle over him."[199] Rumors that Townshend would return as lord lieutenant, because of his influence in the county, must be dismissed as unrealistic, considering how shaky that influence was. Admittedly, one observer thought Townshend could create a strong grouping if he openly declared for the king, especially if the king promised to return his friends to the commission of the peace.[200] The reality, however, was that the

193. Same to HT, 13 January 1682, ibid. *CSPD 1682*, 55, notes that Thomas Townshend was greeted with tumultuous cries of "A Hobart, a Gleane."
194. Ibid., 54–55.
195. T. Townshend to HT, 23 January 1682, RBF/HT Felton.
196. Sir J. Hobart to W. Windham, 14 January 1682, NRO, WKC 7/6, 404x1.
197. Sir J. Holland to HT, 5 September 1681, RBF/HT Felton.
198. N. Luttrell, *A Brief Historical Relation of State Affairs . . .*, 6 vols. (Oxford, 1857), 1:161.
199. Sir J. Hobart to W. Windham, 2 February 1682, NRO, WKC 7/6, 404x1.
200. A. Sparrow to W. Sancroft, 8 February 1682, MS Tanner 36, f. 228; *CSPD 1682*, 54–56; *Prideaux letters*, 123–24.

king "had no need to buy off [the Whigs'] opposition" in Norfolk or nationally. He deprived them of a parliamentary forum, pursued their leaders, and allowed them to fall out among themselves.[201] In Norfolk, purges of the commission of the peace strengthened the Tory hand, and at assizes in March 1682, magistrates, deputy lieutenants, and grand jury drew up a strong, loyal address to the king. Aware of Townshend's attempt at rehabilitation, Lord Yarmouth increased his local activities through the spring and summer of 1682, especially in Norwich.[202]

Townshend's attempt to work his way back into the king's good graces made slow and frustrating progress; perhaps we may see Townshend as the victim of the "cold streak of cruelty and indifference" which J. R. Jones finds appearing in Charles II's personality during the 1680s.[203] In spring 1682 Townshend was "dayly alarumed . . . with the forfituer . . . of all my Norfolke old friends," since he had as yet "got no new ones." How he expected to retain old friendships is unclear, considering his frequent shifts of position, but he seems to have been genuinely puzzled by political ostracism: "I have not betraied," he lamented, "at worst only failed, when I thought I was no longer bound, to performe."[204] He could not see that inactivity might be as much a sin as excessive activity. Nor did he comprehend that, for some, politics was a matter of political principles as well as personal ones, that proper conduct toward friends and allies might count for less than support over substantive issues. Frustrated by the meager result of his politicking in the capital, he returned to Raynham Hall in May 1682 after a two-and-a-half-year absence in London.

He remained, as always, keenly sensitive of his reputation, and for one anxious to restore his status, he was quick to imagine slights and slow to mend breaches. He fell out again with Sir Peter Gleane over old election expenses, and although Lady Townshend and Lady Hobart resumed friendship, between the husbands there were differences "grounded upon such indispensable reasons as cannot in prudence & honor be ever . . . obliterated."[205] Townshend made no more headway

201. Jones, *The First Whigs*, 196–97; Jones, *Charles II*, 170–74.
202. HT's note of changes on the bench at Lent assizes 1682, Add. 41656, f. 59; copy of the address with signatures, Add. 36988, f. 180; Lord Yarmouth to Edward L'Estrange, 22 April 1682, ibid., f. 185; *CSPD 1682*, 80; [? J. Shadwell] to Lady Yarmouth, 25 April 1682, Add. 36540, f. 41. Lord Yarmouth to same, [?autumn 1682], Add. 27448, f. 127, notes that his son's visit to Lynn "will be a great eyesore to" Townshend. See also Evans, *Seventeenth Century Norwich*, 280–93.
203. Jones, *Charles II*, 10.
204. HT to W. Windham, 4 March 1682, Add. 37911, f. 18.
205. E. L'Estrange to Lord Yarmouth, 3 July 1682, Add. 27448, f. 96; J. Fountaine to HT, 26 June 1682, RBF/HT misc.; Sir J. Holland to HT, 1 May and 5 August 1682, RBF/HT Felton; Sir P. Gleane to T. Townshend, 27 February and [copy] HT to same,

The Failed Politician

with the moderates and Tories than with the Whigs, although the monarch rewarded his apostasy from the latter by elevating him to a viscountcy in December 1682.[206] Yet when he was urged, even by the king, to reconcile himself with Lord Yarmouth, Townshend refused to make the first move. When the lord lieutenancy became vacant on Yarmouth's death in March 1683, this impolitic obstinacy overbalanced Townshend's recent efforts to cultivate the king, and despite Townshend's optimism, it was apparent to the knowledgeable that the Earl of Arundel, Protestant son of Henry Howard, sixth Duke of Norfolk, would be the new lord lieutenant. The Howard nemesis struck again.[207]

News of Arundel's appointment came to Norfolk in late March 1683, accompanied by a remarkable story concerning Townshend's suits at the royal court, which Sir John Hobart retold with vengeful satisfaction. The new viscount had recently traveled to Newmarket for an interview with the king; there, according to Hobart's eyewitness, Townshend's hopes for rehabilitation beyond that symbolized by his new title were quickly dashed. Received civilly by Charles II, Townshend sought further reconciliation and approached the target of his former exclusionist allies, the Duke of York, "who sayd, My Lord— you are wellcome thus farr on your way to R[aynham] & imediatly turn'd his back. This was not well resented, but with some trouble of minde [Townshend] presently went out of towne. Upon this, an honest gentleman who was prevy to this & former passages spake freely his minde to [Townshend], which I presume would produce noe other effects then encreasing a little the mortefication." In the wake of this "mortefication" and the harsh truths he apparently was told after the snub, Townshend's only hope was that time might regain him more than a titular indication of the central government's favor.[208]

In the next several years Townshend did not retire from local affairs, but he stood back from national ones. In concert with Sir John Holland, he kept up his fruitless efforts to create a nonpartisan interest in Norfolk. His failure to do so stemmed in part from the ferocity of local political battles, which had disrupted social patterns, broken

---

11 March 1682, RBF/HT misc.; Sir J. Hobart to W. Windham, 11 January and 15 March 1683, NRO, WKC 7/6, 404x1; HT to same, 16 January 1683, Add. 37911, f. 20.
206. GEC, *Peerage*, "Townshend."
207. E. L'Estrange to Lord Yarmouth, 3 July 1682, and Yarmouth to wife, 23 August and n.d. [but autumn] 1682, Add. 27448, ff. 96, 114–15, 127; J. Houghton to Yarmouth, 25 December 1682, ibid., f. 171; Sir J. Holland to HT, 20 October 1682, RBF/HT Felton; Sir J. Hobart to W. Windham, 15 March 1683, NRO, WKC 7/6, 404x1 (suggesting that HT's hopes of reinstatement "were not altogether desperate"); *CSPD 1682*, 551; *CSPD January–June 1683*, 97.
208. Sir J. Hobart to W. Windham, 22 March 1683, NRO, WKC 7/6, 404x1.

friendships, and kept raw the sores of earlier divisions. His attempts were also undercut because all could see that his motives included a large measure of self-interest. If a middle party emerged in Norfolk, only Townshend could lead it—and gain the credit for doing so. Awareness of this fact discouraged some from joining him, and when he signed an address in August 1683, congratulating the king on his deliverance from the Rye House Plot, it rankled "disgruntled" Tory gentlemen, angry at having to associate with him.[209] The death of Sir John Hobart the same month nonetheless seemed to remove "the great obstruction to the work of accommodation" between parties. Townshend became reconciled with Sir Peter Gleane and endorsed, but did not attend, a meeting of "accommodators" held in the autumn. Still, Gleane and Sir Robert Kemp did not respond to the meeting's call to share the county seats with the Tories at any new election, and since news from London spoke of a parliament to meet in March 1684, the silence of the two Whigs was construed as boding further party battles.[210]

The next election in Norfolk actually took place after Charles II's death in early 1685. Townshend's role, while not prominent, demonstrates how fully he had abandoned his Whiggish past: having promised his service to the new sovereign, he was called on by the government to help elect well-affected MPs to James II's parliament. When the county's lord lieutenant (seventh Duke of Norfolk since his father's death in 1684) asked his deputies to find candidates who might be chosen unopposed, he had them consult Townshend in the process.[211] A large array of deputies and gentry nominated Sir Jacob Astley and Sir Thomas Hare, unsuccessful Tory candidates from 1681. In the face of this show of Tory force the disorganized Whigs, although weak in Norfolk as everywhere in the country, nonetheless put forward Sir Henry Hobart, their late champion's son, and the great compromiser himself, Sir John Holland. Between them these two gathered only 1,100 votes (Holland just 410), compared to over 3,400 for each of the Tories, a sign not only of Tory strength but of the county's satiety with party battles.[212]

209. "The Address of Norfolk 1683," Add. 41656, f. 60; Sir J. Holland to HT, 23 August 1683, RBF/HT Felton.

210. Sir J. Holland to HT, 10 September, 5 October, 16 November 1683, ibid.; same to W. Windham, 23 September 1683, with Windham's draft reply, NRO, WKC 7/6, 404x1.

211. [Draft] HT to Lord Rochester, 10 February 1685, RBF/HT misc. *CSPD February–December 1685*, 21; [copy] F. Negus to E. L'Estrange, 10 February 1685, NRO, L'Estrange P20, f. 110v; *The East Anglian*, n.s., 2 (1887–88): 28–29.

212. *NLJ 1676–1701*, 63, 65–66. Vote total from "Norfolk Candidates with the Number of Their Polls," NRO, Rye MSS 9, Norris's Collections, vol. 2, gives Astley 3,415, Hare 3,414, Hobart 692, and Holland 410–figures which differ slightly from

The Failed Politician

Townshend's quiet work on the Tories' behalf gained him some credit at court but not enough to reestablish him as a person of weight. Ill health dogged him and excused his absence from James II's coronation; he came only to the first session of the king's parliament, from May to June, where he was introduced in his new rank as viscount.[213] The death of his second wife in December 1685 left him grief-stricken and precluded further campaigns to regain lost political ground. Surviving memoranda reveal a continued interest in national politics that was never realized in concrete activities.[214] In Norfolk, however, Townshend in 1685 became embroiled in a local dispute concerning quarter sessions jurisdiction that reemphasized his abiding parochialism and extravagant sensitivity to his reputation in the county. It also helps in the final analysis to explain his failure as a politician on the national stage.

The controversy arose when JPs who met at Norwich, for one of Norfolk's three administrative divisions, passed an order in January 1685 regulating county pensions and stipulating that no money was to be paid from the county treasuries unless authorized by the justices who sat at Norwich, rather than those of the King's Lynn or Fakenham divisions.[215] The Norwich magistrates justified this power play by arguing that the county treasurers did not attend the other two divisions' meetings, but the justices outside the Norwich area thought the order illegal, since the Norwich session had no special power to bind the entire bench. The dissatisfied magistrates turned to Townshend as their champion, since he lived in one of the maligned, implicitly second-class divisions, and he rallied to defend his and their rights, privileges, and honor. He "espoused the busines & gave out that if those justices of the peace of the Norwich division did not revoke this order that hee would bring the complaint before the king & councell."[216] The threat to approach higher authorities, even if a bluff, demon-

---

those in *HP 1660–90*, 1:319. HT to the Earl of Rochester, 17 March 1685, Add. 15892, f. 194. Why Holland stood, especially in the face of the duke's call for unanimity, is mysterious: his abysmal showing may mean that he never fully countenanced his own candidacy.

213. *LJ*, 14:6–54; HT to Rochester, 17 March 1685, Add. 15892, f. 194.

214. East Raynham register 1627–1716, NRO, PD 369/1; HT to Sir J. Holland, 26 December 1685, Bodl., MS Tanner 259, f. 8v; *CSPD February–December 1685*, 169. HT's note on "The Judges 5 Reasons in dispute," n.d., in HT's memo and a/c book 1685–99, RUBV, records the arguments advanced on behalf of the crown's dispensing power in the judgment in *Godden* v. *Hales:* see J. P. Kenyon, *The Stuart Constitution*, 2nd ed. (Cambridge, 1986), 404.

215. What follows is based on Sir J. Holland's copy correspondence in Bodl., MS Tanner 259, ff. 1–10.

216. Sir J. Holland's note [damaged], prefacing the copy correspondence concerning this dispute, Bodl., MS Tanner 259, f. 1v.

strates how seriously Townshend took the affair and how far he thought he could claim to have recovered government favor. After Sir John Holland, the Norwich JPs' spokesman, spent much time soothing Townshend, a compromise was adopted a year after the matter had first been broached.

Townshend's involvement in the dispute reveals how touchy he remained about perceived slights to his reputation or interest. When Holland justified the passage of the offending order by explaining that an eminent sergeant-at-law had been present at sessions to sanction it, Townshend grew irate. Although the JPs of the other divisions were not legal experts, he railed, they worked their best to serve king and country and would not be "clerks of ease" for the Norwich magistrates, whose order he considered illegal, unprecedented, and rude. Even if the Norwich meeting attracted the largest attendance of justices, he continued, those from west Norfolk made up in substance what they lacked in numbers. For Townshend, the issues at stake involved not the efficiency and probity of the bench but rather personal and regional competitions and antagonisms within Norfolk; as a result, the quarrel's solution had to be honorable more than necessarily equitable or rational. A decision not to repeal the original order, but to pass a new one requiring pension orders to be signed by ten JPs at the sessions authorizing them, achieved this end.[217]

Townshend's intense reaction to this minor county matter exemplifies the circumscribed ambit of his political vision. Had he still been lord lieutenant, his interference in the details of county administration would be understandable. A greater man could have dominated in such circumstances; a national figure might well have ignored them. That Townshend could do neither provides some measure of the man. As a discredited political figure who nonetheless possessed title and wealth, his activity in this mundane affair seems inappropriate, yet because he always measured and defended his reputation within a provincial arena, his response is predictable and, like much in his career, rouses sympathy. His ambition, if ample, was not grossly disproportionate to his talents or status. His strategy in pursuit of new favors, office, or power was not vicious or particularly devious. If, as was once suggested, he could not be trusted,[218] it was not because he

217. For the new order, see Add. 41656, f. 64, and Bodl., MS Tanner 259, ff. 20v–21. For its acceptance by the other two divisions, see [copy] I. Motham to Sir J. Holland, 25 January 1686, ibid., ff. 19v–20. See Rosenheim, "Oligarchy," 116–25, and Rosenheim, "County Governance and Elite Withdrawal in Norfolk, 1660–1720," in A. L. Beier, et al., eds., *The First Modern Society: Essays in English History in Honour of Lawrence Stone* (Cambridge, 1989), on general changes in county administration at this time.

218. A. Sparrow to W. Sancroft, 8 February 1682, Bodl., MS Tanner 36, f. 228, notes that "his word is not to be taken & . . . he is not to be trusted."

The Failed Politician

was sly or conniving but rather because he was ingenuous in his search for means to promote himself. He could be secretive,[219] but out of uncertainty and insecurity rather than Machiavellian motives or gross distrust of the rest of the world.

His inclination was to make clear to others where he stood on issues, provided that he knew himself, but Townshend's infrequent references to the protection of English religion and liberties ring rather hollow. He had no successful legislation to his credit, no role as royal councillor and shaper of policy. His accomplishments lay in his actions as lord lieutenant, and that office, which his "tyrannizeing" apparently cost him, symbolized all that he had striven for in life.[220] The lieutenancy gave him stature above his erstwhile Norfolk peers, and he believed it was an emblem of his merit in the eyes of those who ruled above him. He had confronted the king and his ministers in the 1670s, but his labors as lieutenant provided evidence "of what I was" (as his funeral monument said), "that I had the honor to serve the king as lord lieutenant . . . by the space of seventeen years."[221] Like most seventeenth-century government servants, Townshend mixed a sense of duty with ambition: as he said in 1659, "effectually [to] serve my countrie . . . [is] that wee were borne for."[222] It was not in his conception of public service that Townshend was mired in the past, but rather in his inability to adapt to the political character of that service in an emerging world of party. Yet if cast from an older mold in the public life he led, he managed in his personal and financial life, as the next chapter shows, to adjust and innovate in ways that accorded with and were even ahead of his times.

219. Sir J. Holland to HT, 1 June 1685, Bodl., MS Tanner 259, f. 1v: "For newes, my lord, I never expect to receive much from your lordship. You have ever a pretty faculty of keeping of what you heare or know of the publick to your selfe."
220. R. Doughty to Lord Yarmouth, 6 March 1676, Paston Letters, vol. 1.
221. Will, 18 November 1678, RBF, Norfolk wills (ii). HT's arithmetic was wrong, since his lieutenancy ran from 1661 to 1676. His funeral monument did not survive when East Raynham church was rebuilt.
222. Townshend's draft, "Christmus" [1660], RBF/HT misc.; Fletcher, "Honour, Reputation and Officeholding," 114–15.

Chapter 2

Horatio Townshend
From Spendthrift to Patriarch

Land provided the base for the English aristocracy's wealth, position, and power,[1] a fact of which Horatio Townshend was well aware. Inheriting a family estate was much akin to inheriting a business, considering the work required to keep it in order, yet running an estate involved a literal and figurative trust that it was the heir's duty to preserve. Religious teaching, social expectations, economic reality, and family influences all encouraged landowners to fulfill that trust—and restricted their freedom.[2] At the same time, estate management was a personal matter as well as an economic one. The story of the Townshend estates, of the viscounts' income and expenditure, is a story that requires telling because it helps explain the concrete framework within which their political careers unfolded. But beyond this, their economic histories help to expose what manner of men these were and to lay bare the complex process whereby the early modern aristocracy was transformed.[3]

Estate management under the later Stuarts benefited from changes in accounting practices that had occurred in the preceding century, but much remained to be done before the aristocratic landowner

---

1. Beckett, *Aristocracy*, 43–49.
2. L. Stone and J. Stone, *An Open Elite? England 1540–1880* (Oxford, 1984), 266–67.
3. The Townshend estates pose the same problems for an assessment of income and expenditure as other elite landholdings. Multiple bailiffs and receivers, the absence of balance sheets, use of the charge-discharge method of accounting, gaps and inconsistencies in records, all impede analysis of financial management. Yet what we can reconstruct says much about agricultural practices and management techniques.

would accurately be able to calculate matters as fundamental as gross income or expenditure. Similarly, the often chaotic hierarchy of administrative personnel of the late medieval aristocratic household persisted well beyond the Restoration, as did many problematic agricultural practices.[4] All the same, change was in the air, and the estates of the Townshend family illustrate the slow victory of more economically rational methods over older practices. The change is as visible in the consolidation of scattered lands into a few large farms as it is in the consolidation of numerous accounts into a few men's hands.[5] Horatio Townshend's continued preoccupation with quit rents and symbolic manorial rights nonetheless should remind us that old habits died hard and were long retained, perhaps in the face of logic, precisely as new methods were often adopted by chance rather than calculation.

Although a failure as a politician, Horatio Townshend enjoyed success as a landlord and landowner. In some measure, the arc of his political career was the mirror opposite of his economic profile: as his life progressed he overcame a large burden of debt, formalized the direction of estate business, consolidated lands, and imposed new, advantageous terms of cultivation on his tenants, all this while his influence as a public figure withered away. Despite expressing the sentiment that one needed to be "master of monnies" in order to be "master . . . of himselfe," Townshend lived in a way to suggest that he disbelieved it. Throughout his active life in politics his attempts to master his "monnies" consisted of opportunistic efforts to increase income rather than of careful programs to control expenditure. When Townshend did attempt to control expenditure, it was through cracking down on what was essentially marginal leakage by scrutinizing his books and bookkeepers rather than his expenses, and even this scrutiny was abandoned when the press of political business grew.

It appears that the first Viscount Townshend could have easily profited from his inheritance. The ostensible rental value of his lands amounted to £4,200 in the 1650s, and when he died in 1687, it had grown to £5,500. In addition, Townshend enjoyed an annual income of £2,100 after 1668 from his lease (or "farm," as it was called) of part of the customs tax on coal, granted him by the king. By the time of his death, he left his twelve-year-old son Charles an enviable inheri-

---

4. L. Stone, *The Crisis of the Aristocracy, 1558–1641* (Oxford, 1965), chap. 6, especially 274–94, 313–22.
5. Timothy Felton, HT's auditor for over thirty years, served much as a latter-day professional land agent. See Beckett, *Aristocracy*, 142–49, on professional estate management.

tance. Yet the path to this eventual prosperity was uneven: early on, he bore the burden of providing portions for his sisters and was unable to enjoy the fruits of lands settled on his mother and mother-in-law as jointure; in the 1660s he incurred the expense of completing and properly furnishing Raynham Hall; and in the late 1670s and early 1680s there was great disparity between the rental and real value of his estates, because much land was held unrented in his own hands, and tenants were falling behind in their rent. From the late 1650s into the 1670s, Townshend's debt grew, but he managed not to overextend himself permanently and largely avoided selling land. Oddly enough, the death in 1673 of his childless first wife, his second marriage (with a portion of £9,500) the same year, his enforced but ultimately economical withdrawal from politics, and then the decay of his health, all combined to assist in the recovery of his fortunes. These accidents, a late but successful reform of estate administration, his interest in adroit, aggressive agricultural management and estate planning, and an avidity for detail, together created a climate of prosperity.

The focus in this chapter is, first, on the nature and extent of Townshend's income, his expenditure (ordinary and extraordinary, necessary and extravagant), and the occasions for and management of Townshend's borrowings and indebtedness. After that, an examination of the viscount's agricultural and estate policy (including an analysis of leases and his approach to cultivating and acquiring land) is succeeded by a broader analysis of the administrative and managerial practices on the estates, with special attention to Townshend's role in their creation. What emerges is a vivid picture of Townshend as an improving and progressive agriculturalist—in marked contrast to his fortunes as a politician.

Income

The tale of the Townshend fortunes after the death of Sir Roger Townshend on New Year's Day 1637—a story reenacted during the second viscount's nine-year minority fifty years later—is one of the benefit a minority could enjoy under the guidance of careful executors. By 1643 the first baronet's debt of £12,000 had been almost entirely cleared. Concurrently, £3,500 was raised to compound with the Court of Wards for the heir's eventual marriage, and £500 each year was set aside to pay for the right to farm his lands. Besides these outlays, some small purchases of land were made, a marriage portion of £3,750 was paid for Sir Roger's eldest daughter Mary, and a surplus of £4,000 was put out on loan.[6] Heavy taxes during the Civil War and a temporary scarcity of tenants did not apparently have much deleterious effect on the executor's efficient preservation of the Townshend patrimony.[7] From the war's end down to the time when Horatio Townshend succeeded his older brother in 1648, an annual average of £1,500 was spent for the children's maintenance.[8] Upon inheriting, Sir Horatio was well fixed to seek an early marriage, and in 1649, at age nineteen, he married fifteen-year-old Mary, the only child of the late Edward Lewkenor of Denham, Suffolk. Townshend settled lands worth £3,000 per annum, £1,200 of which was reserved for his wife's jointure.[9] He presumably received a cash portion, but of unknown size, and obtained an interest in the Suffolk lands his wife inherited from her father, although Mary's mother enjoyed one-third of the profit until she died in 1671.[10]

Through the 1650s Townshend held land in three different counties, Norfolk, Essex, and Suffolk. The latter two estates were accounted for separately,[11] and in Norfolk, where the vast majority of his holdings lay, there were seven bailiwicks, originally overseen by four bailiffs.[12] A general receiver, who in the 1650s and early 1660s doubled as household steward at Raynham, theoretically oversaw the bailiffs; in 1663 a separate Raynham steward was appointed. As a result, and depending upon Townshend's whereabouts, whims, and needs, the

6. See executors a/cs, 1637–47, Add. 41308; 1637–43, NRO, Bradfer-Lawrence, V x 24; 1644–48 and 1644–52, NRO, Bradfer-Lawrence, VI a ii. Sir Roger's remaining debt was cleared by 1651. HT on inheriting was nonetheless left to provide for three sisters' portions.

7. Still, Mary Townshend's marriage to Thomas Crew may have been delayed owing to problems in raising her portion: W. Symonds to Lady Westmorland, 13 July 1648, Folger Library, Bacon-Townshend, L.d.583; GEC, *Peerage*, "Crew of Stene."

8. "Mr William Symonds Account . . . to Michaelmas 1652," RUEM/HT.

9. Agreement, Add. 41655, f. 116; articles, 22 October 1649, RUS. The settlement was redrawn in 1651 and 1655: final agreement, Hilary Term 1652, RUE, deeds; jointure agreement, 29 November 1655, RL drawer 94; paper concerning resettlement, [1655], RUS; "My wifes 3000:00:00 a year," RUM [NRO]; "the parcells . . . within Sir Horace Townshends . . . new agreement," n.d., RL drawer 112. See also A. Page, *A Topographical and Genealogical History . . . of Suffolk* (Ipswich, 1847), 870–71; GEC, *Peerage*, "Townshend."

10. Settlement, 23 October 1667, RUS; indenture, 22 October 1669, RUE, deeds.

11. See Suffolk a/cs for 1653 [RL drawer 105], 1654–58 [RUEA(S)], 1659 [RBF, 17C a/cs]; Essex a/cs for 1651–52, 1654–55, RUEA. See also HT's notes on his annual a/cs, RUEA 1657.

12. The bailiwicks were Stanhoe (sold in 1680); Langham and Morston; Stibbard and Ryburgh; Stiffkey; South Creake; East and West Rudham; East Raynham and its members (Raynham cum membris). The four bailiffs cared respectively for Raynham, for Rudham, for Stiffkey, Langham, and Morston, and for the other three bailiwicks, as well as serving as sheep reeve on the foldcourses or sheepwalks, where HT had the right to graze and also fold a certain number of sheep on his tenants' land. On the foldcourse, see *AHEW*, V, 1:227–29.

four bailiffs remitted rents to either the receiver, the Raynham steward, or Townshend himself. After the mid-1660s the bailiff and sheep reeve, William Clerke, approximated a general estate steward, taking on new bailiwicks when incumbent bailiffs died, but the sheep reeve's account, on which he recorded the balances of his other annual accounts, was not a general reckoning. In 1669 his replacement became sheep reeve and bailiff of all seven Norfolk bailiwicks, in an effort at consolidation; in 1686 Thomas Warde was appointed sheep reeve, bailiff, and Raynham household steward as well, unifying all country accounts into his hands. Yet even under Warde, no single account summarized Townshend's income or expenditure, and no attempt was made to strike an annual balance.[13] The resultant accounting was nearly chaotic in the early years, which may explain the ease with which Townshend overspent—a problem that could best be counteracted by generous amounts of attention from the landlord. Of course at almost any time, as Lawrence Stone long ago pointed out, "the personal attention of the landlord was of crucial importance."[14]

Part of the problem with this system of accounts derived from the fundamentally medieval view of the land that underpinned it, for the bailiwicks represented nothing more than manorial jurisdictions that now had little significance. Only in the 1730s, under the second viscount, was the artificial unit of the bailiwick dropped for an equally artificial but more useful unit, revealingly named "the collection." In the final analysis, it is the use of a confused system of accounting that makes it impossible to calculate the first viscount's gross income and thus forces reliance on rentals to provide the measure of what must have been expected.[15]

A complete set of estate accounts exceptionally survives for 1654, when expected rent on Norfolk, Suffolk, and Essex lands came to £4,150, including quit rents and fines. This figure corresponds well

13. By contrast with the procedure in Norfolk, that for Suffolk was a model of efficiency. Distant from supervision, lands there were farmed in large parcels, and the bailiff (also a major tenant) remitted rent payments directly to HT's London agent. Nominal rents and casual profits began at £1,000 p.a. and rose to £1,450 after 1671, when Lady Townshend's mother died. From the later nominal rent, the bailiff usually sent HT £1,000 each year: RUEA[S], passim, and four rentals, 1663–73, RL drawer 96.

14. Stone, *Crisis*, 332. Cf. Beckett, *Aristocracy*, 150–51.

15. The calculation of gross income is impeded by the absence of full runs of accounts; moreover, cash returns to HT from full sets of accounts ranged wildly between £2,240 and £4,294, an index of the year-to-year uncertainty of farm income: RUEA and RUEA[S] 1650–88. HT also received substantial rent not in cash but in kind: see Raynham household a/cs, 1658–70 and 1671–86, RUBV, passim; husbandry a/c 1654, RL drawer 47; husbandry a/cs 1674–75, RL drawer 74, and 1675–76, RUEM/HT; "A note of what beife [etc.] . . . have been spent," 1683–84, RL drawer 112; "Mr Philip Lowkes accompts," 1685–86, RUEM/HT; "the accompt of what corne was remaining," 22 September 1687, RUEA 1687. Cf. Stone, *Crisis*, 298–302, 555–62, 783.

From Spendthrift to Patriarch

TABLE 2.1
Rentals, 1655–1684

Year	Norfolk	Suffolk	Total
1655 [Townshend]	£ 2,951	£ 953	£ 4,217[a]
1655 [Felton]	2,600	800	3,670[b]
1663	2,958[c]	1,004	3,962
1668	3,337[d]	1,005	4,342
1670–71	4,682[e]	970[f]	5,652
1684	4,343[g]	1,214	5,557

SOURCES: Townshend's "Memorandum 1655," with calculations by Timothy Felton, RUEM/HT; "A fearmall ... 2 February 1662[/63]," RL drawer 96; "The yearly revenue of ... Lord Townshend," 20 February 1669, ibid.; "The yearely revenue of ... Lord Townshend in Norfolke," [1670–71], ibid.; "A Farmall of all the farmes ...," 26 March 1684, ibid.; Suffolk accounts for 1669–70, 1682, 1686–87, RUEA[S].

[a] Includes Essex rents of £313.
[b] Includes Essex rents of £270.
[c] Includes land worth £133 held in hand.
[d] Includes land worth £534 held in hand.
[e] Includes land worth £533 held in hand.
[f] Includes land worth £310 held in hand.
[g] Includes land worth £325 held in hand.

with two memoranda drawn up in 1655, when Townshend thought his lands worth £4,220 and his auditor, Timothy Felton, believed they ran £550 less. Further rentals (Table 2.1) indicate the upward movement of the value of Townshend's estate and testify to the underlying strength of his economic position.

The mid 1650s were times of some financial hardship for Townshend, perhaps because of his own overspending, certainly because of the need to provide his sisters' portions. He also confronted the vexing problems common to landowners of the decade, heavy taxes and falling rents,[16] and we might further speculate that the expense of £8,300 in wardship costs by his father's executors had weakened his financial standing. Together these considerations forced him to think about selling his estate in Essex. When he enumerated the motives to sell, he began by noting the burden of taxes, which had to be paid even on mortgaged land, for which he also owed interest. That heavy interest, moreover, was more irksome for having to be paid "at strict times," even though rent on the land came in uncertainly. Finally, "considering what dangerus & uncertain troublesum times these are to have ingagements upon a man in, [it was] . . . a disadvantage . . . to be without or unprovided of monnies."[17] To this litany Townshend might have added that harvest prices were low.[18] In these circumstances, the judicious sale of land might appear to have much to commend it, and in 1657–58 he sold

16. AHEW, V, 2:119–28.
17. "1655 The Charge goeing out of my Estate," RUFP [NRO].
18. AHEW, V, 2:828; W. Cherritt to HT, 23 June 1657, Add. 41655, f. 112.

Norfolk lands for £4,500 and most of his Essex lands for £10,000 in an effort to reduce some of the charge on his estate.[19] The long-term wisdom of reducing income may nonetheless be questioned, especially as Townshend's expenditure on parliamentary politics under the Protectorate and in royalist plots in 1659 put new pressure on this reduced income. When Vere, his remaining unmarried sister among four, prepared to wed Sir Ralph Hare in August 1660, raising her portion of £4,000 required alienation of Townshend's last Essex property.[20] The anticipated accession of lands controlled by his mother and his mother-in-law as jointure perhaps made the sales in Essex more acceptable, but the alienation of capital nonetheless diminished current income. It is little wonder that after 1660, led on by his royalism, Townshend joined the hordes seeking reward from the coffers of Charles II, turning to this new source in hope of securing income to put himself "somewhat forward in the world."[21]

As a leading royalist in an important county and as one of the king's escorts to England in May 1660, Townshend justifiably anticipated a sign of favor, and he was gratified by elevation to the peerage.[22] Yet he also sought material gain, and this he did not immediately receive: presumably the king thought a barony and lord lieutenancy were ample gifts of status and authority, obviating the need for financial ones. Unfortunately for Townshend, the lord lieutenancy was an economic burden. Its expense clashed with his intention to live in a style appropriate to his new position, which determination arguably hurt his pocket as much as his official duties.

When considering the consequences of Townshend's commitment to seeking central government reward, it may be that his lack of financial alternatives committed him to a political life for which he was ultimately unsuited. As he angled for financial preferment in the 1660s, he confessed, in notes meant only for himself, that his desire was to obtain "some monnie some way or other, if it be no more then to make up my parke."[23] Aristocratic ambition in Townshend's case

19. Acquittance for Stinton manor and Heydon Hall, Norfolk, 29 May 1658, NRO, NRS 14381, 29B4; sale of Wyvenhoe, Essex, 2 November 1657, RL drawer 94; sale of Much Bentley, Essex, 4 November 1657, RUE, deeds.

20. TF to HT, 10 December 1660, RUC [NRO]; TF to C. Spelman, 10 December 1661, Add. 41655, f. 128; TF to same, 14 January 1662, RL drawer 70; "A Particular of Tilbury . . . 1660," RUE, non-Norfolk [NRO]. The sale was not completed until 1662: agreement of sale, 26 April 1662, RU [NRO].

21. "1655 The Charge goeing out of my Estate," RUFP [NRO]. See R. Hutton, *The Restoration: A Political and Religious History of England and Wales, 1658–1667* (Oxford, 1985), 137–38, on favor-seekers.

22. HMC, *10th report, appendix vi*, 203.

23. HT's draft, c. 1664, "When I was last in towne," RBF/HT misc. See Stone, *Crisis*, 551, on the impulse to build felt by "one whose patent was still fresh from the mint."

was intimately related to the figure he hoped to cut in his local community. In Norma Landau's sense, he was clearly a "patriarchal paternalist" who derived his identity from his locality.[24] Title and office alone did not accord with his vision, which was a total one that required the permanent (and expensive) symbols of status and authority that elegant park and ample hall constituted.

Accordingly, Townshend did not hesitate to ask the king for money. He explained in the mid-1660s that he had not received "one farding recompence" since becoming lord lieutenant in August 1661, and he warned that he could not keep on without "a supplie . . . to inable mee to goe throw the worke as I aught & will." He claimed to need more than £2,000 pounds a year to perform adequately as lieutenant, and by 1663 he had been promised £2,500 per annum from the duties laid on exported coal. The gift did not come for another year, however, and because, as he said, he had not "clamurusly brag[g]ed" of his service to the crown, Townshend found that others more importunate got in ahead of him. The delay drove Townshend to borrow on bond, "having morgaged [his] land as fare as it would goe" "in order to his majesties service."[25] Here perhaps were sown the seeds of resentment that later bore the fruit of Townshend's opposition to the crown.

The grant in June 1664 of four shillings per chaldron on coals exported from England and Wales was intended to provide just the "supplie" Townshend needed.[26] Optimistic projections estimated revenues of £2,500–£3,000 annually, yet he feared from the start that the grant would fall short of what he had been promised.[27] The terms on which other men held comparable customs grants convinced Townshend that his was ungenerous. Shortly after receiving the grant he proposed a revision of terms, and to one whom he acknowledged as patron, probably the Earl of Clarendon, he sent the abstract of a recent estate audit, unashamedly baring his personal affairs to prove the depth of his financial plight.[28] He charged customs officials with cheating the king and him by reserving to themselves unjustified rebates,

---

24. N. Landau, *The Justices of the Peace, 1679–1760* (Berkeley, 1984), 3.
25. HT's drafts, n.d. [early 1660s], Add. 41654, f. 63, and Add. 41656, f. 148; n.d. [1663–64], "First that his lordship sees," RUFP [NRO]; n.d. [c. 1664], "When I was last in towne," RBF/HT misc. J. R. Jones notes that the king "readily promised whatever he was asked, without any intention of fulfilling his word": *Charles II, Royal Politician* (London, 1987), 45–46.
26. *CSPD 1663–64*, 630.
27. When HT first tried to sublease the farm, he was offered £800–£1,000 a year: Add. 41656, f. 148; TF to HT, 23 November 1664, RBF/HT misc.; HT's draft, c. 1664, "When I was last in towne," RBF/HT misc.
28. Add. 41654, ff. 69–70; "The difference betweene the profitts of the farmers of the Customes & the Lord Townshend," Add. 37636, f. 4.

and he tried to bribe a highly placed official with £1,000 a year out of any new grant he received.[29]

As it turned out, his argument about the coal farm's inadequacy bore fruit.[30] First it brought him a conditional grant of marshlands in Norfolk and Lincolnshire, an arrangement that did not work out.[31] Renewed approaches to the king through the still-powerful Clarendon led in March 1667 to a regrant of the coal farm for twenty-one years or the king's life, on the annual payment of £1,000, half the original reserved rent.[32] Abandoning direct involvement in the farm as unworkable, Townshend in 1668 sublet it to a consortium of Londoners who paid the king's rent and gave Townshend £2,200 a year.[33] This arrangement worked satisfactorily for the next twenty years, although in 1676, when the king granted his reserved rent payments to Sir John Duncombe, Townshend worried that "the circumstances I am in [with] reference to my Lord Treasurer [Danby]" might endanger his farm. Here is a reminder of the way that political animosities might affect not only reputation but livelihood as well.[34]

Politics could affect recipients of royal bounty in other ways; about 1680 Townshend sought an allowance on what he owed for the king's rent, since the Dutch wars had disrupted trade and lowered customs revenue. The treasury commissioners agreed that remitting part of the rent was warranted, since Townshend had sustained great expense in Norfolk during the wars and had performed "former eminent services before your Majesty's happy restoracon." Yet the commissioners warned Charles II that the royal finances could not sustain "so considerable a dimunition of your revenue," and this argument prevailed.[35] It could not have helped that Townshend's own actions had brought him into royal disfavor, and maybe this was the lesson that he

29. HT's drafts, c. 1664, "When I was last in towne," RBF/HT misc., and 1663–64, "First that his lordship sees," RUFP [NRO]; n.d. draft, c. 1665, Add. 41654, f. 65. HT was granted allowances in case of fraud, 24 April 1665: PRO, SP38/22/127.

30. J. Earle to Sir G. Palmer, 9 March 1665, RUSL [NRO].

31. PRO, SP 44/14, ff. 53–54; J. Earle to [HT], March 1665, RBF/HT misc.; Charles II to HT, 22 March 1665, Folger Library, Bacon-Townshend L.d.217; legal opinion of E. Turnour, Add. 41655, f. 236.

32. CSPD 1666–67, 569; a/c of c. 15 June 1680, RUFP [NRO]; report of treasury commissioners, 19 June 1680, NRO, Bradfer-Lawrence, IV a ii, Townshend MSS letters 17–18C.

33. Terms of agreement, 26 October 1668, appear in new articles, 11 February 1686, RUFP [NRO]. The consortium lent HT £1,650 at 6 percent interest, reducing his annual yield by £100: G. Lulls's a/c from Ladyday to Michaelmas 1671, RUEM/HT. P. Astell's a/c for 1668, ibid., and J. Wolstenholme and J. Shaw to HT, 16 June 1666, RUC, indicate direct farming.

34. [Draft] HT to Sir J. Duncombe, 12 November 1676, RBF/HT misc.

35. Commissioners' report, 19 June 1680, NRO, Bradfer-Lawrence, IV a ii, Townshend MSS letters 17–18C.

learned. Retaining his coal farm (as he later did on Charles II's death) was perhaps worth abandoning the cause of Exclusion and the Whigs.

While politics lost Townshend this sought-for break in 1680, the coal farm nonetheless steadily brought him £1,050 every six months from the late 1660s to the end of his life.[36] It was a tangible prize that proved the advantage that could be derived from the game of politics, especially as played at the center of government. The hope of further, similar reward is surely part of what kept Townshend involved in this game beyond the time when he had much hope left of winning. Access to the avenues of power brought power and status in itself, but when it brought material reward, it enabled Townshend to mold his image and enhance his reputation with a free hand.

Townshend made the most of the grant. He used it as security to borrow from his lessees and had the annual income (never entered in his country accounts) paid to a London agent, who used it mostly for metropolitan expenses and to pay interest and principal on loans. With Townshend's nominal rent roll at around £4,500, and his effective one often substantially less, royal bounty thus supplied him with half again the income he derived from land. Given the problems encountered in collecting farm rents in the later 1670s and 1680s, and the concurrent troubles he experienced with estate managers, the grant yielded a particularly useful and steady source of income. That steadiness in itself was much prized. It was his desire for reliable income that led Townshend to farm out his customs grant, just as it informed his policy of leasing land in as large parcels as possible. Predictability was a key consideration for any landlord, and that was true not only of income but of expenditure as well, even if Townshend was not so successful in this area.

Expenditure

However flexible Townshend proved as a landlord, in expenditure he was less yielding. His outlays in the king's service even from a modern perspective seem wise ones, and over his sisters' portions he had no control, but much of his expenditure was based on personal decisions and contributed to his financial difficulties throughout the 1660s and into the 1670s. Whether his outlays can be accounted extravagance or not is a fine point. The areas in which Townshend laid out

36. On Charles II's death the grant terminated, but James II regranted it until Michaelmas 1688, when the lease would otherwise have expired: articles of agreement, 11 February 1686, RUFP [NRO]; *CSPD February–December 1685*, 169; *English Reports*, 23:619. HT's a/cs with A. Felton, 1672–87, include coal farm receipts: RUEM/HT.

TABLE 2.2

Average Annual Raynham Household Expenses

Kind of Outlay	1657–58	1659–61	1661–62	1665–66	1666–69	1671–75	1675–87
Household	£1,880	£1,862	£ 462	£ 326	£ 364	£ 494	£ 448
Servants' wages	149	275	204	144	105	—	192
Stables	—	146	192	—	35	—	33
Laborers/workmen	—	151	151	362	216	—	—
Stores expended	—	136	—	—	126	—	71
Gross sums[a]	—	350	1,138	1,657	319	256	176
Raynham Hall and Park	—	—	1,420	—	136	—	—
TOTAL	£2,029	£2,920	£3,567	£2,489	£1,301	£ 750	£ 920

SOURCES: E. Bullock's accounts, 1657–58, RUEA 1657 and RUEM/HT; Raynham household accounts 1659–70 and 1671–86, RUBV; receivers' accounts 1658–87, RUBV; P. Lowke's accounts of gross sums 1666–87, RUBV; C. Spelman's account 1665–66, RUEA 1665.

[a] Gross sums were the accountant's miscellaneous and irregular outlays.

money were precisely those on which an aristocrat was expected to spend: his residence, life in the metropolis, ostentation. Although no perfect reconstruction of disbursements can be made, Table 2.2 gives an idea of domestic outlays at Raynham for a start. On the whole, the figures support Townshend's estimate of the mid-1650s that housekeeping proper cost him nearly £1,000 a year; thirty years later he offered roughly the same figure.[37] In neither case, however, did he figure on the added expenses so evident in Table 2.2.

These cold figures only suggest the magnitude and not the direction of outlay. Close examination of the objects of Townshend's discretionary expenditure at Raynham show him not only refurbishing the hall and expanding his park in the 1660s, but also remaking his bowling green and perfecting his own graces by paying a Frenchman to teach him to fence.[38] Townshend spent substantially on hunting and racing, too, attending Newmarket to cultivate the king and court and enjoy the sport.[39] Caught by society's expectation, with these outlays Townshend self-consciously cultivated an image of himself as a fashionable, worldly figure, whether he could afford it or not. There was a steady and varied flow of guests in and out of Raynham to which this image

37. "1655 The Charge goeing out of my Estate," RUFP [NRO] and "Memo [16]55," RUEM/HT, and HT's memo and a/c book 1685–99, RUBV.

38. D. Fortree's bill, c. 15 August 1664, 1663–64 file of bills, RL drawer 79; Philips's a/c, August 1663–January 1664, RUEA 1663; Philips's payments, RUEA 1663.

39. R. King's a/c, 10 March 1661, RUEM/HT; Add. 41655, f. 123; memorandum, n.d. [1650s], RL drawer 87. For purchases of race horses, see Philips's payments, RUEA 1663; Philips's bills 1662–64, and 1663–64 file of bills, RL drawer 79; 1668–69 file of bills, NRO, uncat. mss., Box D, P168C.

was presented. Some were of great stature, including the king himself, but the most frequent guests were relatives, Norfolk Whigs, and a group of local men of slight status.[40] The presence of the Whigs suggests that Townshend used Raynham Hall as a symbolic extension of his power. When there, his entertaining was not medieval in luxury or extent, but he significantly retained old forms, keeping occasional open house as lord lieutenant and feasting tenants at Christmas and on his son Charles's birthday, the latter occasions reinforcing his paternalistic relationship with his neighborhood.[41]

However free his hand on the visible scale, Townshend prudently kept an eye on the cost of this sociability: where display and gustatory excess had once been the hallmarks of aristocratic hospitality, Townshend was more frugal. When his household steward failed to identify the "strangers" whose horses had been fed with Raynham oats, Townshend sourly remarked in the household accounts that "I allow no oatts to I know not hows [whose] horses."[42] He was equally perceptive and critical of excessive consumption in the house,[43] but when occasion warranted, expense could be damned, as when the king visited in 1671, an honor which cost Townshend over £300.[44] On important matters there was no question of scrimping. Such was Townshend's expensive and protracted project at Raynham, where he finished the hall his father left incomplete and then remade the park, in which he tried to keep five hundred deer.[45] These projects brought their own rewards. They made Townshend feel that he was living as a man of his stature should, and Raynham Hall became as elegant a seat as the county could boast during the reign of Charles II.

LONDON LIFE

While for some a sojourn in the metropolis was urged as a cheap alternative to country life, the city also had its dangers—moral, political, and financial.[46] Townshend recognized the particular cost of city

---

40. These last included militia captain Richard Godfrey; militia captain and tenant Nicholas Rookewood; and William Mitchell, the rector at Stiffkey.
41. Raynham household a/cs 1659–70 and 1671–86, RUBV.
42. Entry, 29 August–5 September 1674, Raynham household a/cs 1671–86, RUBV.
43. Entries for 24–31 October 1674, 21–28 August 1675, and 13–20 January 1677, ibid.
44. This sum was expended for household preparations: entry for 24 September–6 October 1671, ibid. Some of Philips's gross sums for 1671 [RUEM/HT] may pertain to the visit, on which see R. W. Ketton-Cremer, *Norfolk Portraits* (London, 1944), 9–21.
45. See chap. 5 for this work. On the deer, see HT to Sir E. Harley, 24 January 1678, BL, Loan 29/182, f. 259.
46. See L. Stone, "The Residential Development of the West End of London in the Seventeenth Century," in B. C. Malament, ed., *After the Reformation* (Philadelphia, 1980), 181–82.

dwelling,[47] which included rent, house maintenance, and "life-style" costs—outlays on goods and services either unique to London or demanded by the attempt to maintain state there.[48] These expenditures provide a reminder that the London world ever more eagerly embraced by the gentry and nobility of early modern England extracted a major economic cost. Townshend was brought to London by the whirlwind of parliamentary politics and by the lure of urban bustle; he was kept in Norfolk not just by lieutenancy duties and the need to maintain his insecure interest there, but also by the deterrent expense of metropolitan living.

The basic costs of rent and upkeep in London varied according to the scope of Townshend's ambition, the depth of his purse, the status of his political star. He may have tried to economize by renting rather than buying a house, but as a result he moved often, occupying eight known houses and three sets of lodgings. Townshend's movement from dwelling to dwelling provides a concrete example of the urban leasing system's encouragement of mobility, and of the aristocracy's lack of psychological attachment to town houses, which Lawrence Stone has recently pointed out.[49] Townshend's choice of dwelling seems to have depended on market, shifting conceptions of neighborhood desirability, and the family's finances. In the mid-1660s, when caught up in county affairs and remodeling at Raynham, Townshend left his lady in the country and took lodgings in London, minimizing expense as he attended parliament and hunted for a royal grant.[50] Having shifted from Bloomsbury to the western edge of Westminster in 1666, a social step down, he reversed course in 1672 and moved to Piccadilly, the center of aristocratic residence, near powerful neighbors and notable dwellings: Burlington House, Berkeley House, Clarendon House.[51] The steadily increasing level of rent Townshend paid, rising from £70 a year in 1661–62 for a dwelling in the Old Palace Yard, Westminster, to £300 for the last house he took, in Soho, reveals

47. HT's n.d. draft [1663–64], "First that your lordship sees," RUFP [NRO]; HT's n.d. draft, "My Lord, I receved your Lordship's of the 17th," RBF/HT misc.
48. Travel also incurred costs: see bills of 1667, NRO, Bradfer-Lawrence, VII b 1; bills May–June 1668, NRO, uncat. mss, Box D, P168C; "the charge of my iouernie from London," RL drawer 74.
49. Stone, "Residential Development," 195–96.
50. Payments in Philips's gross sums, RUEA 1663 and 1665. This is one of the few occasions when HT's wife did not accompany him to London.
51. London County Council, *The Survey of London*, 31:58, 32:343, 33:83–84, 34:345; rent payments in Philips's gross sums, RUEA 1667–68, 1673, and 1675, and G. Lulls's 1672 a/c, RUEM/HT. On West End neighborhoods between 1550 and 1650 see M. J. Power, "The East and West in Early-Modern London," in E. W. Ives et al., eds., *Wealth and Power in Tudor England: Essays Presented to S. T. Bindoff* (London, 1978), 167–85.

TABLE 2.3
Lord Townshend's Estimate of Annual
Expenses, 1685

"Stables & table" @ £20/week	£1,000
Servants' wages	250
"My children abroad & at home"	250
House rent	150
"My owne expences & clothes"	350
Servants' liveries and journeys	300
Garden	60
TOTAL	£2,360

SOURCE: HT's memo and a/c book 1685–99, RUBV.

both an actual increase in rents in the capital and his willingness to lay out more for a smart location and a larger dwelling.[52]

More than rent was involved in the expense of London life. When leased unfurnished, a residence had to be fitted up; furnished or not, it usually required decoration. In his Piccadilly house, Townshend even altered the structure of the building to the amount of £110.[53] He spent over £160 on interior decoration and exterior improvements there, including security arrangements that provided for a higher wall, a new porter's lodge, and gates surmounted by a deterrent "spike plate for the top."[54] But more than renovations, ordinary domestic consumption illuminates Townshend's urban expenses. Housekeeping over the years cost from £13 to £25 a week for victuals, and the butler's "extraordinaries" cost some £700–1,300 annually—figures in line with Townshend's estimate of £20 per week, made in the mid-1680s, when age and political defeat enforced on him a relatively modest style of life.[55] Far more extensive than caterers' and butlers' outlays (or those for decoration), however, were "extraordinary" household payments, which in the 1660s and 1670s involved sums far in excess of the £350 per year that Townshend allotted himself in 1685 for his "expences & clothes" (Table 2.3).

52. Bill for rent, 26 November 1661, RL drawer 70; A. Felton's a/c February–December 1684, RUEM/HT; Add. 37911, f. 14.

53. Agreement, 30 July 1672, with J. Goodchild, carpenter, and bills in Philips's gross sums, RUEA 1672.

54. Bills in Philips's gross sums, RUEA 1674; see also bill, 12 February 1687, RL drawer 70.

55. R. King's a/c, March 1661, RUEM/HT; accounts for June–July 1661, March 1662, RL drawer 70; "bills of household expences London ... per anno 1670," RUEM/HT; household a/cs 1669–74 in London/Raynham household a/cs 1669–87, RUBV; London caterer's bills 1674–76, RLBV; paper headed "Your Lordship came to towne on ... 29 October 1686," RUM/HT [NRO]; London household a/cs 1685–88, RUBV.

Thomas Bullock, for example, spent £425 for Townshend in just four weeks in late 1657, including £100 to a tailor, expenditure probably connected with Townshend's attendance at the second session of the second Protectorate Parliament.[56] Perhaps this outlay was exceptional, but more typical are those from 1660–61, when housekeeping, tradesmen's bills, and servants' wages amounted to around £40 per week.[57] In fact, none of the extant London accounts stays nearly within the bounds Townshend later set for himself. After 1663 the London-based receiver Samuel Philips's "gross sums"—that is, unusual, irregular, and miscellaneous payments—survive in detail for eight years, although they are incomplete and provide few annual totals.[58] All the same, they yield a detailed picture of nonhousehold outlays made for Townshend when in London and show average expenditures running between £35 and £55 per week, exclusive of housekeeping.

Luxuries were a major component of this expenditure. Tailored goods costing over £1,000 were bought in the weeks before Townshend's elevation to the peerage,[59] and while his wardrobe was reshaped, so too was his art work, with payments to "Mr Lilly" for "picturs," among them perhaps the surviving portrait of Townshend in his baron's robes[60] (see Frontispiece). He paid "Mr. Dugdale for searching the Herauld's office" about his pedigree and bought a stamp with the family coat of arms to emboss his wine bottles. He acquired plate in 1662 worth £200 and engraved it with his arms and "supporter coronet."[61] Concern with modishness is also evident, especially in the addition of foreign-made or foreign-designed items, whether a dozen spoons "of the Italian fashion," a pair of "screwd turne . . . Damaske pistolls," or French hats, Portugal water, and Spanish tables.[62] Other items were distinguished by novelty or high quality rather than exotic origin, including Townshend's four "best" close stools, his "new-fashioned gold & silver hatband," and his new carriage, painted, gilded,

---

56. Bills, 12 November–9 December 1657, RUEA 1657.
57. "March the 10 1660 Mr. Kings account," RUEM/HT.
58. Philips's disbursements, RUEA 1663, and 1662–64 file of bills, RL drawer 79; Philips's gross sums, RUEA 1665; Philips's gross sums for 1667, 1668, 1670–71, RUEM. These London payments are mixed with country expenditures, showing that urban and rural accounts were not kept separately.
59. Bill, 30 February–20 June 1661, RL drawer 74; inventory, 5 November 1660, RL drawer 70; four inventories, Add. 41306, ff. 115–16, 117–18, 119–20, 121–22. Cf. Stone, *Crisis*, 562–66.
60. T. Bullock's payments, November–December 1657, RUEA 1657; Philips's payments, RUEA 1663; A. Felton's acquittances, May 1679–January 1680, RUEM/HT.
61. C. Spelman's 1663 gross sums and Philips's gross sums, February 1665, RUEA 1663, 1665; bills, April 1662, RL drawer 70.
62. Bill for Sir Frederick [sic] Townshend, 25 June 1656, Add. 41656, f. 132; bill, 15 July 1661, RL drawer 70; bill, 15 March 1670, NRO, MS 20446, 127x1; Philips's gross sums, RUEA 1663, 1668, and 1671.

and lacquered, equipped with a new harness and a lockable trunk, upholstered in Russian leather.[63]

If Townshend spent £20 per week on housekeeping and even £35 on these other outlays, then, omitting rent (which he calculated at £150 a year) and wages (which he set at £250, not distinguishing between London and country), he would have been spending more than £1,400 over six months in the city, a sum approaching one-fourth his nominal annual income.[64] This was no economy. There is no question that the level of his expenditure rose because of the intrinsic costs of the city and its temptations and opportunities to spend. Yet economy was not the point, as there was a social and even political direction to Townshend's consumption. His ambition to rise, on the national stage or the local one, naturally led him to the metropolis. Even so, the significance of his choice not to buy a permanent residence there merits consideration. The decision may have been made for him, because of his uneven health and lack of ready cash. And yet his commitment to metropolitan life was not complete, and his hall at Raynham and the soil of Norfolk often called him back from the city. Neither the "season" nor even parliamentary sessions regularly brought Townshend to London; the yearly political rhythm his son felt was not manifest in the first viscount's life.

LAND PURCHASES

Lord Townshend's concern for living in a style that exhibited his real and desired stature largely precluded the acquisition of further acreage for himself and his posterity. Struggling with intermittent financial problems, he was not well placed to pursue a long-term strategy of purchase nor did he engage in land exchanges with tenants on a scale suggesting any farsighted planning, by contrast with his son, who frequently exchanged land in an effort to make his holdings more compact. Horatio lacked means and possibly foresight to undertake thorough estate consolidation, and his only major attempt at land exchange had nothing to do with economic advantage but instead facilitated the creation of his extensive park.

It was perhaps with this end in mind that Townshend, after inheriting his land, continued the haphazard acquisition of small pieces in his home parish of East Raynham begun by his father's executors. The

---

63. Philips's gross sums, RUEA 1671; A. Felton's a/c July 1678–April 1679, RU estate/household [NRO]; bill, 18 December 1686, RUM [NRO]; bill, April 1684, filed with A. Felton's 1684 file of acquittances, RUEM/HT.

64. For a comparison with two gentry families' expenditures, see M. G. Davies, "Country Gentry and Payments to London, 1650–1714," *Economic History Review*, 2nd ser., 24 (1971): 20–22.

executors had spent at least £1,200 before 1649, and with Townshend's additions the "new purchased lands" brought in nearly £150 a year in 1660.[65] Other than this, Townshend made only two purchases of any substance before the mid-1670s; together they cost £2,000[66] After his second marriage brought him an heir, however, Townshend bought property in Toftrees for £1,060 in 1676,[67] and four years later he consolidated his holdings there, acquiring the remainder of the previous seller's estate for over £6,000, money obtained from the concurrent sale of his own land in Stanhoe. This last, double transaction is worth examination, because it indicates the role that purchase played in estate improvement, while also demonstrating how complicated the acquisition of land could be.

Henry Clifton, original owner at Toftrees, died before early 1670,[68] and ten years later Townshend approached Clifton's son-in-law, William Ruding, with an offer to buy.[69] The two reached agreement for sale at £6,400; the lands were reliably said to be worth £330 per annum, so the price represented about nineteen-and-a-half years' purchase, rather above the going rate of sixteen to eighteen years.[70] The property's description shows why Townshend was willing to pay an inflated price, since the lands lay in six parishes where he had substantial holdings and where Clifton's property had been interspersed with his. Significantly, Ruding signed a nine-year lease immediately after the sale to stay on as tenant, and £400 of Townshend's purchase price was discounted from Ruding's rent, a powerful inducement for the new tenant.[71] Despite a devastating fire in May 1681, probably caused by his negligence, Ruding proved reliable, and his later absence from the ranks of tenants who fell behind with their rent testifies to the value to Townshend of the purchase.[72]

65. At eighteen to twenty years' purchase (the prevailing rate in the 1650s), this rental value suggests that HT spent about £1,800 on land. See executor's a/cs 1637–47, Add. 41308, and 1644–48, NRO, Bradfer-Lawrence, VI a ii; deeds of transfer, 31 January– 12 February 1653, RL drawer 63; fragment of 1649 a/c, RL drawer 100; a/cs of new purchased land, RUEA 1650–52, 1656–58, 1660, 1662.

66. Before 1659, HT bought lands in Stanhoe valued at £62 p.a. for £1,300: note of payment [before 24 November 1658], RL drawer 74; Stanhoe a/c, RUEA 1658. Five years later, he acquired acreage around East Raynham for £700: indenture, 13 May 1663, RL drawer 63.

67. Indenture, 26 February 1676, RL drawer 103.

68. Will, proved c. 13 May 1670, NRO, N.C.C. Alden 35 and 1670 Original Will 35.

69. W. Ruding to HT, 22 April 1680, RBF/HT misc.

70. *AHEW*, V, 2:173.

71. TF to HT, 27 April 1680, RBF/HT misc. "This concerns Mr Rudings of Tofts," 25 November 1680, RUE deeds [NRO]; agreement, 3 December 1680, NRO, BRA 926/89, 373x1; conveyance, 17 December 1680, RL drawer 112; lease, 18 December 1680, RL drawer 99. Transactions with Clifton dated to 1647: NRO, MS 1482, 1F.

72. [Copy] J. Stewart to W. Ruding, 28 June 1681, RBF/HT misc.; TF to HT, 31 March, 12 July, 16 August, and 27 December 1681, RBF/HT Felton.

William Ruding was the kind of desirable tenant whose absence at Stanhoe encouraged Townshend to sell that estate, valued at £390 a year. Its distance from Raynham Hall (more than thirteen miles) made it difficult to manage. Although rents were hard to collect on all holdings in the late 1670s and early 1680s, Stanhoe was the worst example. Lease conditions could not be enforced, and tenants were retained only with difficulty. In fact, the concessionary terms of several farmers' tenancies were among the details that Townshend and his agents hammered out with the purchaser, Richard Sherwin, before the sale went through in late 1680 for £6,500.[73] Sherwin's negotiations with Townshend's former tenants were complicated by their reluctance to bind themselves to high rents at a time of low grain prices,[74] and by the difference between their new leases and those they had signed with Townshend. He had compounded with tenants for back rent when they renewed leases; he had imposed low interest rates for the sheep provided to those farming his foldcourses; he had even allowed one tenant meadow rights on an adjoining Townshend property, which a new landlord could scarcely do. Townshend had played the part, in other words, of a benevolent, almost paternalist landlord, so much so that Sherwin thought he had been misled in his purchase and demanded the execution of a clarifying indenture.[75] Such details complicated the transfer of property, but the purchase of Toftrees and sale of Stanhoe were consistent with a flexible estate strategy on Townshend's part, and in the end, selling distant and buying nearby land better enabled his bailiff to oversee tenants and attend to the minutiae of estate management, so essential when agricultural markets were depressed. Both transactions further show how important the provision of a good tenant was to any transaction: new lands without farmers were of little practical worth.

DEBT

Despite his pretensions to the contrary and his later disenchantment with the government he thought had treated him ill, there is no evidence to support Horatio Townshend's claim that he incurred a debt "of above twenty thousand pounds" serving the king.[76] His accounts

---

73. TF to HT, 19 March 1680 and 31 March 1681, RBF/HT Felton; Stanhoe a/cs, RUEA 1674–77. Problems arose over the purchase: "The defalcations demanded," n.d., RL drawer 74; list of Sherwin's queries, n.d., RBF/HT Felton.
74. TF to HT, 19 March 1680, 12 July 1681, 24 March 1682, RBF/HT Felton.
75. TF to HT, 31 March, 3 and 16 August, 27 September 1681, ibid.; indenture 11 March 1682, RL drawer 111. The meadow rights affected a farm of over one-third of Stanhoe's annual value: TF to HT, [25 July or 1 August 1681], Add. 41655, ff. 163–64.
76. Note concerning exported coals 1660–63, n.d., Add. 41656, f. 148; *CSPD 1682*, 55. Lord Mordaunt supposedly reported in January 1660 that HT had given General

record no such large expenditure, nor is there any indication that what he spent was laid out "in his majesties service" rather than "for [Townshend's] present support in the same."[77] The fact that at least £8,000 realized from land sales before 1660 paid for his sister's portions suggests that personal more than public expenditure strained his resources. He did amass some £9,000 in obligations during the one year 1660, but nearly half came from a bond entered to pay his sister Vere's marriage portion of £4,000. Debt scarcely began to grow until 1660, although it nearly tripled between then and the mid-1670s.[78]

In the 1650s Townshend's debts remained manageable, and if he showed a youthful tendency to overspend, in this he was not alone.[79] When he considered selling land around 1655, however, it was the pressure of providing portions for his sisters and the problems unique to the Interregnum that were foremost in his mind. Only after the Restoration did he begin to follow a common pattern among the aristocracy[80] and avail himself of mortgages as instruments of credit. In February 1669, Timothy Felton drew up a list of Townshend's debts amounting to £29,000, half derived from outstanding mortgages, the average value of which, at £1,500, was over two and a half times that of the average unsecured debt.[81] The chronology of Figure 2.1 suggests that something other than royalist zeal was responsible for Townshend's plight: the ability to borrow, his office as lord lieutenant, and his personal expenditure are more to blame. Townshend himself noted the "continual charge as well as disorder it must be to mee to be in towne," because of his need to come up "some times to lett [my enemies] see they can nor shall get no ground upon mee."[82]

The constraining force of debt is readily apparent. In December 1661, for example, after two days of poring over Townshend's deeds, neither his auditor Timothy Felton nor two legal experts "could . . . find that my Lord had any lands free, but all were mortgaged." Worse,

---

Lambert £5,000, but the story is hard to credit: M. Coate, ed. *The Letterbook of John Viscount Mordaunt, 1658–1660*, Camden Society, 3rd ser., 69 (1945): 164. HT is here identified by the editor as the cipher "174," having been assigned this number the previous June, but the context makes the identification dubious.

77. HT's draft, n.d. [1663–64], "First that his lordship sees," RUFP [NRO].

78. This conclusion assumes that surviving evidence fairly represents HT's debts. On this score, it should be noted that a list of debts of February 1669 (RUEA [1988] 1664–77) records only 3 of 31 debts, amounting to £1,600 out of £29,000 owed, for which confirming evidence does not exist.

79. C. Clay, "Property Settlements, Financial Provisions for the Family, and Sale of Land by the Greater Landowners, 1660–1790," *Journal of British Studies*, 21 (1981): 19–20.

80. Beckett, *Aristocracy*, 295–301.

81. "My Lord Townshend's debts the 16 of February 1669," RUEA [1988] 1664–77.

82. HT's draft, n.d. [1663–64], "First that his lordship sees," RUFP [NRO].

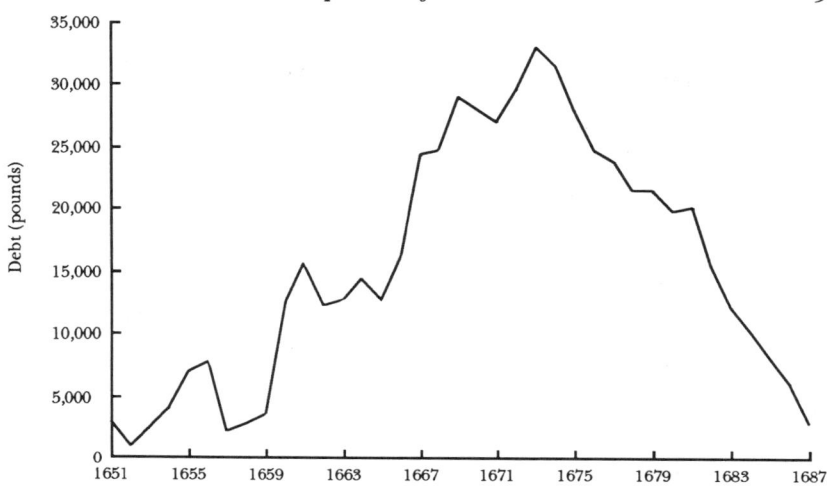

Figure 2.1
Horatio Townshend's Known Debt,
1651–1687

few would lend on bond "since my Lord was made a barron,"[83] because as a peer Townshend was immune from arrest for debt. Tight money grew tighter still. In his soliciting letters of the mid-1660s, Townshend noted that he had "spent his ammunition," that he could "no longer procuer monnies to paye intrest & live," that he had "not the wherewithal to raise £1000, my estate being all out in joynture, & setled upon marriage."[84] Admittedly, Townshend painted this gloomy picture as part of his search for a place at the public table: a posture of poverty was always congruent with a pursuit of ambition. Yet the actual costs of his ambitions were substantial, and the work at Raynham Hall particularly required ready capital and probably forced him to borrow. That he had no difficulty in finding creditors, despite Felton's plaint, corresponds with J. V. Beckett's depiction of a Restoration aristocracy taking on a growing weight of debt for longer periods of time.[85]

In a sense, debt fed upon itself; although he paid only the prevailing rate, in some years Townshend was hard-pressed to keep up with the interest payments alone.[86] In the decade from 1667 to 1676 his debt

83. TF to C. Spelman, 10 December [1661], Add. 41655, f. 128.
84. Draft, c. 1663, "My Lord, I must not omit" [probably to Clarendon], RUM/HT; draft, c. November 1664, RUFP [NRO]; draft, c. 1665, Add. 41654, ff. 69–70; draft, c. 1665, ibid., f. 65.
85. Beckett, *Aristocracy*, 300.
86. "The Acco made upp to May 1669," RUEM/HT contains HT's comment, "Nota, noe interest uppon interest demanded."

never dropped below £24,000 and ran as high as £33,000, entailing annual interest payments of £1,400–£2,000. With a realizable income of less than £5,500,[87] the drain of interest costs was severe, and it hit most at those times when Townshend was deeply involved in national and local politics.[88] This burden provides part of the explanation for Townshend's political gamble in opposing Danby in 1673 and his effort to make up with the court in 1682. Nevertheless for many years, while the first viscount sought ways to enhance his income, including steps to make himself appear so politically potent as to be worth buying off, he made no move to reduce the encumbrance of debt. His childless state may have discouraged him from long-term planning; it was his second marriage, which brought a portion of £9,500, that set him on the road to solvency. More important than the dowry, the marriage provided him with the one spur to thrift hitherto lacking, a son to inherit his estate.[89]

Townshend's first wife's death in May 1673 hit home harder than his rapid remarriage suggests. She had perhaps been ill some time, since in 1671 they had gone together to Bath and then to the hot wells at Bristol, where she found no relief.[90] Two months after she died, he wrote feelingly of the continuing "passione of grife which so justly hath taken place in my heart & thoughts."[91] Nonetheless, by late November 1673 he had married twenty-year-old Mary Ashe, daughter of Sir Joseph Ashe of Twickenham, Middlesex, a wealthy merchant.[92] Despite a gap of twenty-two years in their ages, the marriage between Townshend and Mary Ashe was loving,[93] and within a year Lady Townshend had become pregnant, a circumstance that wrought "a

87. In 1672, for example, the rent nominally owing on HT's bailiwick a/cs was £4,350 (this includes £300 on Stanhoe, for which no a/c survives); his coal farm brought him £2,100, for a total of about £6,500. Yet estate deductions on the extant bailiwick accounts lower the rent actually due by £1,100. Had a household or reeve's a/c survived, further deductions from rent would probably be revealed.

88. While HT was spending up to 30 percent of gross income on interest, this amount pales before the 50 percent paid by the sixth Earl of Salisbury in the middle of the next century: L. Stone, *Family and Fortune: Studies in Aristocratic Finance in the Sixteenth and Seventeenth Centuries* (Oxford, 1973), 159.

89. *CSPD 1673*, 599. Similarly, note that Jones, *Charles II*, 188–89, ascribes the king's disinclination to look to the future to his lack of legitimate descendants.

90. HT to Sir E. Harley, 12 June 1671, BL, Loan 29/181, f. 262.

91. HT to same, 21 July 1673, BL, Loan 29/182, f. 73. See also D. Mitchell to [same], 21 May and 12 June 1673, BL, Loan 29/80.

92. GEC, *Peerage*, "Townshend." For Ashe, see *HP 1660–90*, 1:556–57. Another of Ashe's daughters, Katherine, had married Townshend's brother-in-law, William Windham, in 1669: R. W. Ketton-Cremer, *Felbrigg: The Story of a House* (London, 1982; paperback ed.), 39–40, 45.

93. Shortly after the wedding they appeared "very happy in on[e] another, my lord very fond & my lady very affectionatly caerful to plese him": D. Mitchell to Sir E. Harley, 1 December 1673, BL, Loan 29/183, ff. 98–99.

great change upon [Lord Townshend] for the better." He made "a very joyfull father" after his son Charles was born on 18 April 1675, and the pleasures of fatherhood consoled him in the months after the loss of his lieutenancy. "God's owning his famelly now at last has taken a great impresion on him," one observed: "he growes very pious & serious."[94]

The seriousness was immediately apparent. More than his political failures, which he strove to reverse, fatherhood changed Townshend's economic behavior. Practical as well as proud, Townshend the family man abandoned extravagance for thrift. He had already applied his marriage portion to the payment of debt, and from 1673 to 1681 paid off £13,000. More strikingly, from 1682 until his death in December 1687, he liquidated another £19,000 in obligations, an average of £3,000 each year, an enormous proportion of his income. He brought off the reductions through the application of his coal farm money, through careful estate management, and through economy, even drawing up a personal budget "not to exce[e]d upon no account what ever."[95] Successive versions of his will show the accomplishment: in 1678 he planned to leave Roger, the second of his sons, a legacy of £2,000 and lands valued at nearly £4,000. Two years later he increased Roger's inheritance to £10,000; revising his will in 1683 (after the birth of a third son, Horatio), he hoped to provide £7,000 for each younger son. His final will gave each boy £8,000, sums he explicitly acknowledged he could afford because of reducing mortgage debt.[96] In less than ten years the viscount thus changed his estimate of the weight of portions and legacies his estate could bear from as little as £6,000 to £16,000. Here is the clearest possible evidence of his success in reducing indebtedness.

Analysis of Townshend's handling of debt provides some sign of his changing personal priorities. Examination of creditors illuminates the world of finance in which he operated and the changing markets open to him, especially as Townshend's early borrowing differed from the

---

94. Same to same, 8 December 1674 and 24 April 1675, ibid., ff. 166, 197. W. Mitchell said that HT took "great pleasure in [Charles], & never was better contented then since my Lord Paston's being made lord leiuetenant": W. Mitchell to same, 26 December 1676, BL Loan 29/80. Feasts at Raynham to celebrate Charles's birthdays reflect HT's pride: entries for 15–22 April 1676, 14–21 April 1677, and 13–20 April 1678, household a/cs 1671–86, RUBV.

95. Calculations of annual expenses, HT's memo and a/c book 1685–99, RUBV. Around 1680 HT "prudently assigned over the profitts ... from [his coal farm] lease for the payment of debts in course": Sir J. Holland to HT, 19 November [?1683], RBF/HT Felton.

96. Draft will, 18 November 1678, with codicil of 3 December 1680 and changes of 1683: RBF/Wills (ii); PRO, PROB 11/389, f. 196 et seq.

later, when the sums involved grew larger and the range of lenders wider but the number of them fewer. In 1661–62 he had nearly £15,000 outstanding to twenty-five different creditors, representing an average loan of under £600. The small amounts involved in many of these loans give a haphazard look to the borrowing. Lenders like the attorney general, Sir Geoffrey Palmer, or Sir Peter Killigrew, a Cornish baronet, were outnumbered by local creditors, many lending small sums on bond.[97] Local figures, like the Norfolk-born barrister John Earle, helped to procure money or pay Townshend's interest for him on occasion in the 1660s, but the employment of Earle was neither so formal nor so effective as the later use of London agents. Similarly, in the early 1660s the payment of interest was poorly coordinated, and particular payments were often made the responsibility of specific estate bailiffs, a confusing procedure that needed careful attention to ensure that obligations were met. When money was in short supply, as in August 1661, the very interest due on some mortgages had to be borrowed.

After Townshend received the coal farm grant in the mid-1660s, this convoluted situation began to improve, although Timothy Felton's list of debts, drawn in February 1669, still records thirty-one creditors.[98] All the same, Townshend's receiver had taken charge of interest payments on his "gross sums" account at this time. By 1671, most payments were consolidated with an agent in London, who received a portion of Townshend's Suffolk rents, any newly borrowed money, and the money due from his coal farm lessees. These sums were earmarked first to meet interest obligations and then to pay London expenses, as well as any principal repayments.[99] Even more formally, in the 1670s some mortgage debts were managed by professional bankers, Sir Robert Clayton and John Morris. For advancing interest when due, they received a commission of 0.5 percent of the face value of the debts they serviced, and they assisted with the renegotiation of mortgages when necessary.[100]

97. List of debts 1661–62, Add. 41656, ff. 140–41.
98. "My Lord Townshend's debts the 16 of February 1669," RUEA [1988] 1664–77. Despite the increase in creditors, the average loan in 1669 had grown to £940.
99. G. Lulls's a/cs 1671–72 and 1672–74, RUEM/HT and RUEA [1988] 1664–77; Sir J. Ashe's a/cs, 1678–82, RUEA [1988] 1678–88; A. Felton's a/cs 1678–87, ibid.
100. S. Philips's bills of interest, June 1673–February 1674, RUEM/HT; HT's a/c with Clayton and Morris, January 1676, Add. 41140, f. 224. The last payments to the two occur in A. Felton's a/c, 7 June 1679, RL drawer 87. For Clayton and Morris, see *HP 1660–90*, 2:84–87, 3:108–9, and D. C. Coleman, "London Scriveners and the Estate Market in the Later Seventeenth Century," *Economic History Review*, 2nd ser., 4 (1951–52): 221–30, where Coleman notes that arranging mortgages was probably the "most important branch" of their business (225).

Perhaps the expense of their services or Clayton's notoriety as an exclusionist Whig led Townshend to sever ties, but his debt management had permanently lost its amateur cast and remained in the hands of London men of business, even if not professional bankers. The "entertainment" at Raynham that marked the repayment of £1,000 to a creditor in 1660 was a vestige of an approach to fiscal matters uncharacteristic of the late seventeenth century.[101] Matters were handled with acuity, as shown by the reassessment of interest rates that occurred around 1680. Three debts, which totaled £3,500 and bore 6 percent interest, were paid off in December 1678 and the mortgages reassigned to a creditor who took them on at 5 percent. Rates pegged at 6 percent on outstanding mortgages worth another £8,500 were lowered to five, as Table 2.4 shows. The burgeoning national credit market, centered in London, made all these arrangements possible and indeed relatively easy to effect.

Some mortgages were unaffected by changing interest rates, and in these instances the mixture of economic with older, sometimes stronger considerations can be discerned. Townshend's £2,000 loan from Sir John Holland, for example, continued to cost 6 percent. Holland argued in 1681 that Townshend should defer the reduction for friendship's sake, since Sir John had allowed Townshend to keep the money for over twenty years and had often awaited interest payments until it suited Townshend's "owne conveniency."[102] Townshend contrarily thought his demand was just at a time "when money is at five [percent] and under," but he agreed to leave matters as they were, citing friendship in turn.[103] Two years after this arrangement was made, Townshend further accommodated Holland by delaying repayment of principal, because Holland was afraid he could not find another outlet for the capital; Holland gratefully then accepted a 5 percent rate of interest. In late 1686, however, Townshend set aside personal feeling far enough to force £1,000 in partial repayment on Holland.[104]

Similar considerations of friendship and business (and family) affected Townshend's dealings with his cousin Thomas in 1687. As with Holland, Thomas Townshend was reluctant to take full repayment of a £2,000 mortgage outstanding since 1673. He accepted £1,000 in August 1687, but his hesitation in doing so led Lord Townshend to

101. Entry for 22–29 December 1660, household a/cs 1659–70, RUBV.
102. Sir J. Holland to HT, 7 March 1681, RBF/HT Felton.
103. [Copy] HT to Sir John Holland, 10 March 1681, ibid.
104. Sir J. Holland to HT, 19 November [1683], ibid.; A. Felton's a/cs, October 1683–October 1685, RUEM/HT. Holland received the other £1,000 after HT's death: see endorsement on mortgage, 10 February 1661, RL drawer 109.

TABLE 2.4
Mortgages of the First Viscount Townshend

Date	Mortgage	Amount/rate	Disposition
3/1651	H. Ballow of London, merchant	£1,000 @ 6%	Paid 6/62
6/53	trustees for Mary, daughter of O. St. John	1,500 6%	Unknown
4/54	N. Johnson of London, vintner	1,500 6%	Paid ?6/57
4/54	Dame Margaret, widow of Sir W. Boswell of Sevenoaks, Kent	1,000 6%	Paid 12/57
3/55	S. Balmford of Aldermanbury, clerk, and J. Paynes of Christ Church, London	500 6%	Paid 12/57
6/59	N. Knyvett of Intwood, Norfolk, Esq.	500 6%	Paid by 1663
11/60(h)	R. Freeman of Aspeden, Hertfordshire, Esq.	1,500 6%	Assigned 12/78
11/60	nominees of Sir T. Bedingfield of Darsham, Suffolk (increased by 5/71 to £2,000)	1,000 6%	Paid by 12/73
1/61	Sir J. Holland of Quidenham, Norfolk (interest reduced to 5% by 4/85)	2,000 6%	Paid by 10/87
5/63	J. Hervey of Ickworth, Suffolk, Esq. (interest reduced to 5% by 6/83)	1,000 6%	Paid by 2/87
5/63 (c)	Sir R. Berney of Reedham, Norfolk	500 6%	Assigned 4/72
5/64 (a)	executors of R. Wilton of Wilby, Norfolk, Esq.	1,000 ?7%	Assigned 10/70
12/66	Sir W. Glascock of Wormley, Hertfordshire, and trustees of his wife, Mary	2,500 6%	Paid 6/77
12/67 (b)	George, Duke of Albemarle	5,000 6%	Assigned 8/71
5/69 (d)	Sir P. Killigrew of Arwanack, Cornwall	1,000 6%	Assigned 4/73
9/69	T. Townshend of Norwich, Esq. (increased 12/73 to £2,000)	1,500 6%	Paid by 6/88
1/70	J. Payne of Inner Temple, London, Esq.	2,300 6%	Paid 7/80
1/70 (i)	G. Farewell of St. Margaret's, Westminster	1,000 6%	Assigned 12/78
10/70 (f)	assignment of (a) to N. Wilton of Wilby, Norfolk, Esq.	1,000 6%	Assigned 1/76
8/71 (e)	assignment of (b) to Sir W. Ellys	5,000 6%	Assigned 11/73
4/72 (k)	assignment of (c) to Sir P. Wodehouse of Kimberley, Norfolk	500 6%	Assigned 10/79
4/73 (j)	assignment of (d) to H. Jewkes of St. Martin's in the Fields, London	1,000 6%	Assigned 12/78
11/73	assignment of (e) to J. Hervey of Ickworth, Suffolk (interest reduced to 5% by 6/83)	6,450 6%	Paid by 2/87
1/76 (g)	assignment of (f) to Viscount Halifax	1,000 6%	Assigned 11/76
11/76	assignment of (g) to Sir F. Hyde, sergeant-at-law (interest reduced to 5% by 2/82)	1,000 6%	Paid 6/84
12/78	assignment of h, i, and j to J. Gofton of Richmond, Surrey, Esq.	3,500 5%	Paid by 12/83
10/79	assignment of (k) to T. Bacon of Norwich, Esq., in trust for D. Porland	500 6%	Paid 11/80
2/85	A. Walpole of Houghton, Norfolk, spinster	1,900 5%	Paid 2/88

justify his desire to pay the other half of the money in the near future. Reflecting on the decline of his health and on his family's future, on the fact that he had "growne old & out of date," Townshend expressed the intention to pay the outstanding money in the next six months. "Longer," Lord Townshend claimed, "my affaires will not permitt mee to keep itt lyeing dead by mee, & paying interest for itt, which I am willing to doe to you, tho' to nobody els." Even in dealings with family, sound financial practice had to be considered. Yet neither of these instances necessarily exemplifies the triumph of cold fiscal prudence over social obligation to friends and relatives. The driving force behind Townshend's eagerness to make repayment was clearly his intention to assist his children by clearing away debt before his impending death.[105]

Townshend's singlemindedness at the end of his life is one of four factors that enabled him to leave his sons a solvent, thriving estate, an estate on which, it should be added, there were no pending expenses of wardship.[106] His retreat from politics, and the release (however unwelcome) from the expenditures required of a lord lieutenant, removed major drains on income. Conscious economies further helped; they are witnessed both by reformation of estate management and by vows of thrift in the mid-1680s.[107] Finally his assignment of part of his income, and in particular his coal farm income, specifically to amortize debt, helped him to reduce his obligations. The economic well-being of the estate after Townshend's death in 1687 was the measure of the strategies' success.

Agricultural and Estate Policy

In the later seventeenth century the ground was laid for the rapid agricultural change of the eighteenth century, when the role of landowners and agricultural professionals as effective propagandists for new techniques was crucial to the spread of novel practices.[108] It has recently been argued that "English agriculture developed in a landlord-conceived framework" after 1660 (and presumably before), and

105. Mortgage, 10 September 1669, for £1,500, RL drawer 109; £500 added, 11 December 1673, RL drawer 72; HT to T. Townshend, 11 October 1687, folded in a mortgage of 10 September 1669, where HT also acknowledged that his "health being departed from mee, I am not to flatter my selfe with any hope of recovering."
106. The abolition of the Court of Wards in 1660 freed families from the threat of external control over minor heirs and from the cost of retaining control of the ward by the family.
107. HT's memo and a/c book, 1685–99, RUBV, where he aimed to limit his expenses to £2,360 p.a.
108. P. Horn, "The Contribution of the Propagandist to Eighteenth-Century Agricultural Improvement," *Historical Journal* 25 (1982): 313–29.

that as a result much credit for advance in the agrarian world lies with the aristocracy.[109] Although their responses to the challenges of landownership fluctuated widely, even within an individual's lifetime, aristocrats made decisions and investments that lay at the heart of agricultural improvement. Horatio Townshend retained elements of an old-fashioned view of the nature of landlordship (congruent with his somewhat outmoded view of politics), emphasizing for example his manorial rights to negligible quit rents. Nonetheless, he embraced progressive methods on his lands and insisted that his tenants do the same. By making familiar the field preparations, crops, and cultivation practices associated with agricultural improvement, he played a less conspicuous role than his son in effecting agrarian change, but one that was in its way equally valuable.

The principles, ideas, and hopes that guided Townshend in estate management and cultivation of land are shown as much in his actions as in his words, especially in the absence of overarching statements of policy. Townshend's correspondence (where it patchily survives) reveals scrupulous attention to detail, flexibility in dealing with tenants, and a desire to maintain the estate's integrity. These characteristics are evident alike in the handling of leases, the taking of accounts, the management of periodic crises, and the guidelines occasionally drawn up for employees. In what follows, an assessment of landlord-tenant relations and of the leasing of lands addresses the economic essence of Townshend's agrarian regime. Then an evaluation of the farming methods used, and Townshend's role in shaping them, explores the relationship between employer and his estate servants, while a discussion of accounts finally shows the interaction among all three parties: tenants, employees, and landlord.

TENANTS AND LEASES

Profitable management of the Townshend estates rested upon reliable employees, dependable tenants, and productive lease conditions. Direct farming of demesne lands had been effectively abandoned by landowners before the sixteenth century, and the Townshends were no exception.[110] Direct farming was generally avoided, surprisingly often even on the home farm. The desire to keep a farm from falling in hand—that is, from coming under the landlord's direct management for lack of a tenant—was sufficient motive to make concessions when negotiating leases, and it sometimes prompted capital improvement to make an otherwise unleasable farm attractive to a prospective

---

109. Beckett, *Aristocracy*, 156–57.
110. Stone, *Crisis of the Aristocracy*, 295–303.

tenant. Considering the disparity between the rent tenants would have paid and the slim profit derived from direct-farming lands held in hand during 1685–87, the motive to avoid direct management was clear. Such management entailed high overheads for farm implements and seed, and wages for those who worked the farm, and in the short term it was difficult to implement productive rotations of crops. Renting out lands was the key to prosperity.[111]

The prevailing conditions of leasing on Townshend's estate embody many features associated with progressive agriculture in the mid- and late-seventeenth century.[112] An early memorandum Townshend himself wrote, which specified covenants to be included in tenants' leases, shows he valued highly the practice of making written leases, even in the 1650s. These instructions among other things called unrealistically for the voiding of leases if rents were not paid half-yearly and without deductions. Tenants' houses, once repaired by the landlord, were to be maintained by the tenant, and no subletting was allowed without permission.[113] For all its detail, however, this memorandum did not address cultivation practices, but leases themselves did. Those for large farms contained the most—and most detailed—covenants, regularly including provisions to prevent soil exhaustion, guarantee fertilization of fields, preserve fallow lands, and rotate crops.[114] Townshend's directions to his new bailiff in 1686 enjoined him to see that tenants kept their farms according to their leases. They were to plow "in course," distribute muck and compost on the land that gave rise to it, refrain from plowing unplowed land, and perform requisite "days workes" on repairs.[115]

Although Townshend nowhere enunciated a policy concerning the length of leases, the long terms thought appropriate in the next century to induce tenants to make capital improvements were also granted in Townshend's day.[116] Forty percent of known lease terms ran ten years or more; by the same token, half were for seven years or less. In

---

111. TF to HT, 16 August and 27 September 1681, 17 March and 3 November 1682, RBF/HT Felton; S. Smith's a/c of farms in hand, 1685–87, RL drawer 69; receipts on Rudham farms in hand 1686–87, RUEM/HT. Admittedly, lands in hand during the second viscount's minority were fairly profitable, but the practice of direct farming was abandoned as soon as practicable: see chap. 3.

112. *AHEW*, V, 2:214–24. HT's first extant lease dates from 1654: RL drawer 99. The majority of leases survive in RUEM/HT and in RL drawers 65, 77, 79, 99, 109.

113. HT's memorandum, "First I must have all my hounds at nurce," c. 1655, RUEM/HT.

114. Particularly full terms are found in a lease with C. Pirkins, 2 October 1663, RL drawer 99.

115. "Direccons for Ward . . . 3rd of June 1686," RL drawer 66.

116. S. Trowell, *A New Treatise of Husbandry, Gardening, and Other Matters relating to Rural Affairs* . . . (London, 1739), 151. See also later sources cited by Beckett, *Aristocracy*, 187, n. 99.

general, where the terms of years are known, longer ones were reserved for larger farms, a phenomenon much in evidence in the next century. Relatively frequent turnover among the smaller tenants, fewer of whose lease articles survive, also suggests that large farmers had the longest leases.

Together, Townshend's personal involvement and his belief that leases were essential for effective estate management helped set him at the leading edge of agricultural practice.[117] His employees took for granted his direct role, not just his desire to be informed, and evidence abounds of his familiarity with tenants and even subtenants and with the rotation of lands on his farms. When considering in the late 1670s whether to keep in hand the meadows of a farm in Stiffkey "& . . . bring all my haye from thence," Townshend knew the amount of hay he could expect per acre.[118] In 1678 he led a campaign to renew all leases in East Raynham; in 1680 he decided to abandon direct animal husbandry at Raynham, altering the nature of lease concessions there; and his careful instructions guided his auditor Felton in other lease negotiations. These are the actions of one fully cognizant of the disposition of his lands, not of a casual observer who let others run affairs for him.[119]

Not only was Townshend knowledgeable, he was a severe manager when necessary, although never one quick to deal harshly with tenants, if patience and cordiality might make them tractable—and able to pay rent. For example, a tenant already in default on a bond was nonetheless given time to pay part of his rent arrears; when the tenant Rowland came "with tears in his eyes" to explain his financial distress, he was coddled and encouraged to carry on farming.[120] Yet when a tenant obstructed Townshend's plans by citing the letter of his lease, he was in turn pursued for not adhering to the lease obligations. Another, who spoke of abandoning an agreement to stay on his farm eight more years, was threatened with a demand for repayment of £120 he owed Townshend. Small tenants behind in rent might, as Townshend instructed bailiff Philip Tubbing, "bee turned out imedi-

117. *AHEW*, V, 2:228–30.
118. Articles, 9 December 1676, Add. 41655, ff. 153–58; note of "leases . . . made in Sept and October 1672," RUEM/HT; "Lands to be let at Morston," RUM; memorandum, c. 1677–79, RUEM/HT.
119. Draft lease with J. Parke, March 1678, with HT's endorsement, RU leases [NRO]; TF to HT, 19 March 1680, RBF/HT Felton; TF to HT, 27 April 1680, RBF/HT misc.; TW to HT, 24 December 1686; Add. 41655, ff. 173–74. Cf. Beckett, *Aristocracy*, chap. 4, on landlords and estate management, where he shows that even as absentees "aristocrats were vitally involved in the running of their estates" (156).
120. TF to HT, 19 March 1680, RBF/HT Felton; TW to HT, 21 February 1687, RBF/HT misc. See also TW to HT, 3 April 1687, RL drawer 69.

atly by you by my express command."[121] Townshend and his agents proceeded reluctantly against delinquent tenants, but with determination when they did: if legal distraint of goods presented the only recourse to recover rent, then they were distrained.[122] Although Townshend was as sensitive as any man to the reputation he enjoyed in the countryside around him, he was not willing to obtain that reputation by sacrificing the welfare of his estate.[123]

Extreme measures were happily unnecessary with good tenants, those characterized by performance of lease covenants, a "husbandly" approach to the land, and prompt payment of rents. Such tenants were never easy to find, and when located, their relationship with a landlord, albeit based on mutual interests, was often adversarial. Depending on the agricultural market, one party often held an edge over the other, but only rarely did either have sufficient security to disregard the other's position: negotiation, rather than ultimatum, thus predominated in the relationship. Even so, the patience exhibited by Townshend as a landlord, his willingness to concede allowances to tenants or hold off from eviction, is sometimes surprising. To some extent, this leniency suggests a paternalist attitude toward landownership, further evinced by Townshend's Yuletide feasting of tenants and his use of the imposing Raynham Hall to enhance his dominance over the neighborhood.[124] In addition, although his position and wealth gave him social, political, and economic power over his neighbors (whether tenants or not), Townshend's estate management was constrained by the need to find others to farm his land for him—and take some of his economic risks. Tenants were not day laborers, easily found and easily replaced. They could not be turned out if they abided by their leases, regardless of how troublesome they proved, and they could not be recruited in the first place without sufficient inducement.

Townshend's tenants were perceptive and adept. With the depression of grain prices and rents from the 1670s, they grew wary of taking on new leases or renewing old ones on outdated terms.[125] Solvent

---

121. P. Tubbing to HT, 10 October 1681, RBF/HT misc.; TF to HT, 16 August 1681, RBF/HT Felton; "This is [a] coppy of what I sent to Tubbing," November 1681, RUEM/HT. See also HT to W. Ray, 16 July 1681, filed with RUEA[S] 1693.

122. "Mitchells note of ... cattle," 21 June 1684, RU; inventory of goods seized, Add. 41656, f. 158; "stocks seized and disposed of," 29 September 1684, RUEM/HT.

123. Cf. *AHEW*, V, 2:242–43, which suggests that some landlords' "easy going approach ... was ... a symptom of neglect"; this was not so with HT.

124. As late as 1683 tenants dined at Raynham during Christmas week, when money was spent on fiddlers, the King's Lynn waits, and much "tobakey and peyps": household a/cs 1671–86, RUBV.

125. While agricultural prices were generally depressed from the mid-1660s to 1690, there were ways, as P. J. Bowden points out, for landlord and tenant to overcome this problem, so that rents need not be equally depressed: *AHEW*, V, 2:62–85.

tenants were difficult to find throughout the 1680s, and when found, they drove hard bargains.[126] Arrangements had to be flexible, which often meant that tenants got their way, a story the estate accounts tell when leases and letters do not: what leased in East Raynham for £100 in 1675 was broken between two tenants paying £9 less two years later; a farm in Stiffkey of £375 in 1676 brought £8 less in 1683.[127] Where tenants were discovered or retained, there was work involved in doing so. When Townshend tried to lease one farm in 1680, no one would rent without the use of a meadow, storage room for grain, and "what muck is made in your lordship's stables & yeard."[128] From Rudham, the tenants came en masse to Raynham in 1682 to threaten that, unless they received rent abatements, they would sow rubbish crops like oats on their fields or leave the land. When Felton the auditor took sixpence per acre off their rent, he did so because otherwise, without tenants, the fields could be used only as less valuable grasslands: the abatement minimized loss. The same year, in Raynham no tenants would take vacant farms without abatement; at Langham and Morston, where "even the ablest" farmers had broken, it was "difficult to meet with responsible [new] tennants," while those remaining would "not heare of any increase of rent."[129] At Stiffkey, finally, a large farm had to be farmed "by halves": the new tenant paid one-third of the former rent and then gave the landlord half his crop. At a time of low prices, this practice protected the tenant when he had trouble selling the crop that normally paid his rent, but the arrangement was hard for Townshend. When the new tenant left in 1684, however, the bargain grew worse, since the land had to be farmed directly. The slow sale of the crops raised there by his employees in 1686–87 attests to Townshend's dilemma.[130]

Finding reliable tenants was all the more important because of Townshend's inclination to seek out large farmers wherever possible. Nowhere did he specifically enunciate a policy of leasing in large parcels, but it had been the practice of his father's executors, who had seen the wisdom of consolidating small holdings into larger farms, and it evidently became his own.[131] Consolidation had several managerial

126. TF to HT [30 March 1682], RBF/HT Felton.
127. RUEA 1675–83.
128. TF to HT, 27 April 1680, RBF/HT misc.
129. TF to HT, 17, 24, c. 28 and 30 March 1682, RBF/HT Felton.
130. Lease, 20 June 1677, RUE [NRO]; TW to HT, 21 February 1687, RBF/HT misc., and TW to HT, 27 February, 3 and 29 April 1687, RL drawer 69; TW's a/c of Stiffkey Hall farm, RUEA 1687.
131. "Considerations . . . for the converting of lands . . . into severall distincte farmes," [1640s], RUM [NRO]. These reflections probably pertained to Lady Westmorland's jointure lands, where the advice was apparently followed: see Stiffkey a/c, 2 February

advantages. Admittedly, the occasional collapse of substantial farmers could cause severe dislocation,[132] but only substantial tenants possessed sufficient capital to make a go of large farms. Thomas Warde urged acceptance of a new tenant on the large South Creake farm in 1687 partly because he was "thought to be a ritch fellow" who could bear the expense of farming there.[133] With large farms, the bailiff had only to deal with a few rather than many tenants, and large tenants were more likely to possess substantial assets to distrain in the event of bankruptcy. They also could unofficially oversee smaller farmers renting from Townshend in a given area.[134]

Unfortunately, in an age when good tenants were hard to find, reliable large-scale farmers were rarer, but estate records show a trend in this direction on virtually all of Townshend's holdings, and not only after the hardships of the late 1670s and 1680s, when low prices squeezed marginal producers. The estate at South Creake, for example, broken into numerous components in the 1650s, was dominated from then on by a single tenant who leased acreage valued at 90 percent of the total. The Stiffkey lands were leased mostly as one large farm from the early 1650s. At East and West Rudham, a rental that featured four major tenants in the 1650s and 1660s was split among many more in the next decade, but by the early 1680s four tenants had regained predominance.[135] The transition to large farms can be documented in another fashion, in the decline of small holdings leased at insubstantial rents. At Raynham, 52 tenants paid under £20 in annual rent in 1651, and 47 in 1665. In 1675 and 1687 there were only 36, a reduction of 30 percent since the 1650s.[136] The Rudham accounts include 34 tenants under £20 per annum in 1667; the total was down to 24 in 1677 and to 13 nine years later. Langham and Morston had over 40 small tenants in 1667, but by 1687 only eighteen.[137] The benefits of large tenants were undeniable, but emphasis

---

1654, NRO, Emmet & Tacon deposit, 29.7.74, T190A; Stiffkey a/c April–September 1656, RUEA 1656; and "note of the profitts of Stiffkey farmes," RUEA 1657.

132. TW to HT, 27 February 1687, RBF/HT misc.

133. TW to HT, 11 February 1687, RL drawer 69. Cf. TF to HT, 30 March 1682, RBF/HT Felton.

134. On a Langham tenant's death, HT sought "some trusty person" for a farmer, to see that other tenants observed their lease covenants: TF to HT, 27 March 1679, ibid.

135. RUEA passim. Large farmers also dominated at Langham and Morston and at Stanhoe; the pattern held at Stibbard and Ryburgh until about 1680. On large farms, see Beckett, *Aristocracy*, 185–87.

136. When Townshend was extending the park at Raynham, he temporarily had 66 small tenants, but the emparking ended their tenancies.

137. RUEA, passim. These figures almost certainly reflect an absolute decline of small tenants, since large farmers seem not to have sublet to others any land they rented from HT, who in any event dealt with a diminishing number of tenants himself.

on a few major farmers required close attention by estate employees (something not all of them could provide), since slackness on the part of one such tenant, paying as much as £500 a year in rent, had major consequences for the estate as a whole. As the number of substantial tenants grew, Townshend's management procedures and methods became increasingly important, and it is to them that attention must now turn.

METHODS AND PROCEDURES

Townshend's involvement with his estate was continuous and often methodical. He had precise, if not always the most efficient, accounting procedures for his employees to follow; he examined accounts and most other estate records with exemplary care, noting each misplaced sixpence; and he tried, when need arose, to enunciate the principles and considerations by which he wanted his estate managed. As he grew older and ill, Townshend's physical capacity to oversee his employees diminished, but his intellectual capacity and energy never did. His attention to detail is impressive, almost compulsive, and sometimes petulantly recorded: in the mid-1650s he carefully calculated the amount due him for two half-a-crown quit rents, unpaid for nine years. In 1681 he severely blamed his bailiff Philip Tubbing for 12s. 6d. in quit rents omitted from a balance of £1,058 and demanded to see the court rolls to be sure nothing else was left out. Spying an excessive quit rent his bailiff had paid another landlord as due from a Townshend smallholding in Stiffkey, Townshend consulted a thirty-year-old account to determine that only 1s. 8d. should have been paid, not 3s. 4d.[138]

This kind of zealous scrutiny on the surface seems miserly and even an ill-advised expenditure of energy and time. But it made a measurable economic difference early in Townshend's life, when he was no more than a wealthy country baronet, marginally active in politics, mistily involved in royalist cabals. Later in life, having withdrawn from national politics, he had plenty of time to devote to his estate, and the obsessive quality of his oversight may be explained in this light. Moreover, he cherished his role as landowner precisely in the marginal details of preeminence it gave him; it provided him with identify and fulfillment, the depth of which is best gauged by his fury when matters went awry. And finally, in the absence of sustaining external sources of income or diverse investment outlets, Townshend had to rely on his own energies and ideas—and attention to detail.

138. Memorandum, n.d. [1650s], RL drawer 87; account of farm at Stiffkey, 25 June 1681, RUEM/HT; "Mr Phill Tubbings severall debenters," Michaelmas 1681, ibid.; Stiffkey a/c, RUEA 1683.

The fact that his son's guardians and then the son himself adopted almost wholesale the methods evolved during the first viscount's life strongly suggests their value. The household and estate did not always run flawlessly, but not because Townshend was indifferent to its running, or unwilling to learn from experience.

In 1656, having the previous year considered how best to "set mee somewhat forward in the world,"[139] Townshend took the occasion of a run-in with his auditor to reflect that "estate . . . buisnes requiers one mans continnuell labor and pains," a resident agent "who miends nothing els."[140] Yet Townshend further knew his own effort was required along with that of his employees, and throughout his life he either initiated or approved virtually every expenditure and agreement that substantially affected his estate. More than that, from the 1650s until shortly after his elevation to the peerage in 1661, most major decisions actually awaited his presence in Norfolk. His attendance at the annual audit was more common than not.[141] Then, and again in the 1680s, one way to deal with troublesome tenants was to put off resolution of problems "until your lordship be in the countrey": tenants could be cowed in face-to-face negotiations with the landlord.[142]

Townshend's involvement in national and county affairs from about 1661 until the mid-1670s forced his reliance on employees like Timothy Felton (auditor almost continuously, 1644–82) and Philip Lowke (household steward at Raynham, 1667–87). Their reliability allowed Townshend the measure of release from estate concerns that he enjoyed for over a dozen years. During this period he spent his energy on the lieutenancy and central government business, and spent his money with little regard to his income. Many factors triggered his renewed engagement with the estate: the birth of a son in April 1675; a dissatisfaction with the two auditors who replaced Felton from 1669 to 1674; a shortfall in income and a rise in rent arrears that seemed likely to respond to more direction from him. Townshend's disgrace upon his dismissal as lord lieutenant in February 1676 further encouraged a readjustment of interests. It is no coincidence that the first set of estate accounts since the early 1660s on which Townshend left his

139. "1655 The Charges goeing out of my Estate," RUFP [NRO].
140. HT's draft, n.d., on letter to "My honored couzen," 25 December 1655, RL drawer 66.
141. Household a/cs 1659–70, RUBV; TF to C. Spelman, 14 January 1662, RL drawer 70. HT's X appears on receipts to bailiff's a/cs 1653–62, but then not again until the a/cs for 1675: RUEA passim. See also HT's presence in Suffolk to take a/cs, e.g., N. Cherritt's 1659 a/c, RBF/HT 17C a/cs.
142. TF to HT, 17 March 1682, RBF/HT Felton, and TW to HT, 21 February 1687, RBF/HT misc.

mark is that for 1675, which he examined in the autumn of 1676.[143] After this point, his imprimatur ("Perused—Townshend") and his distinctive, large X were once more scrawled on bailiwick, household, sheep, and general accounts alike—and often on scores of accompanying acquittances. He resumed writing comments in the margins of accounts, draft leases, and farm particulars. His lengthy indictments of mismanagement by several bailiffs were—as will be seen—a new departure in managerial intervention.

Amounts of unpaid rent increased sharply during the 1670s, as a result of a period of generally low agricultural prices that began in the mid-1660s, and Townshend understandably grew concerned.[144] On several occasions he received lists of delinquent tenants well before the annual accounts were due,[145] while in the autumn of 1679 bailiff Philip Tubbing indicated that between £3,840 and £4,040 in rent was due from current tenants, sums approximating a year's income on the Norfolk estates.[146] Townshend's angry response to this news may be imagined, and he wrote harshly to defaulting tenants. His direct intervention elicited thirty replies and reduced the outstanding arrears by one-fifth by spring 1680,[147] but the statement Townshend then received of the 1679 accounts was still dreary, as shown in Table 2.5.

Beyond assailing his tenants with calls for the money owed him, Townshend blamed the arrears on Philip Tubbing's slovenly accounting. The tenants' obligations had to be recorded systematically, Townshend instructed Tubbing, to avoid "the disorder of the notes of respitts and rentalls ... which you now gave mee ... by keeping this certaine and regular method."[148] To develop orderly procedures nonetheless took time, and the coherent directions presented to a new

143. HT took the Raynham a/c 30 October and examined the others 21–23 November 1676: RUEA 1675.

144. *AHEW*, V, 2:75–76, 847–48. Arrears reached sizable proportions on the Langham and Morston account for 1673, spreading through the other bailiwicks by 1676. Their weight is difficult to assess, because current and past respites were both carried in the accounts as part of the "charge" or debit which bailiffs had to clear. In the "discharge" or credit, a bailiff received allowance for arrears that remained unpaid, whether old or new. The total of respites in a given account thus does not measure that year's arrears. On the other hand, past arrears (some of them forty years old) did not increase from year to year, nor did they decrease unless accounts were cleared at the landlord's order or with the employment of a new bailiff. Thus change in the level of respites from year to year can indicate current rent unpaid, if one controls for decreases due to the discharge of long-outstanding arrears.

145. TF to HT, 27 March 1679 and 31 March 1681, RBF/HT Felton.

146. Papers endorsed by HT: "The respicts given mee in the 28 of Octo[ber] 79," "A note of respicts deliverd to mee this 21 of No[vember] 79," and "This paper shows the difference between the respitts," RUEM/HT.

147. HT's "Note of the severall tennants answers I sent tow," 28 November 1679, RUEM/HT.

148. "This paper shows the difference," n.d., RUEM/HT.

From Spendthrift to Patriarch

TABLE 2.5
Rents and Arrears, 1679

Bailiwick	Farm rent	Current arrears	Old respites[a]
Raynham	£1,356	£1,310	£128
East and West Rudham	812	493	130
Langham/Morston	458	528	70
South Creake	308	125	101
Stiffkey	241	120	10
Stibbard/Ryburgh	109	150	—
Stanhoe	383	353	5
TOTAL	£3,667	£3,079	£444

SOURCE: "A Note of all the farme rents and respits" [endorsed by Townshend, "As they were sent mee by Mr. Felton from my audite for 1679"], RUEM/HT.

[a] These are rents "formerly respited & unpaid."

bailiff seven years later in 1686 were distilled from various injunctions Townshend issued in response to immediate problems.[149] To give Tubbing his due, Townshend must have been a trying employer, with his keen eye for the misplaced halfpenny, unauthorized consumption of ale, or two-shilling quit rent unpaid. On the other hand, Tubbing had given signs of incompetence for years.[150]

Tubbing evidently could not manage the disparate parts of a large estate, as his disorderly records show.[151] His "double charging of persons, and leavings out and put[t]ings in" hints at dishonesty, but his inclination to collect rents only on nearby property speaks more of laziness. When Tubbing sought a harmonious relationship with tenants and accepted bills even from those who had defaulted in their rent, he received the sharp edge of Townshend's tongue. A reference to a tenant's "promise" to pay back rent provoked the viscount's rejoinder: "I will not have my accompts incumbred with a discourse of what any body sayes, nor with noe mans promises. I expect nothing of promises from you in my accompts, your duty is to receive the money for mee, and not to concerne mee in promises." Tubbing was paid to collect Townshend's due, and for the future Townshend imposed a "standing rule" on bills for repairs (which, with tax bills, made up the bulk of allowances sought by tenants): no work would be allowed that had not been authorized specifically, and no bills would be accepted except in the year the work was done. Townshend, like Tubbing,

---

149. See for example HT's seven-page indictment of Tubbing, "This is [a] coppy of what I sent to Tubbing about the 1 No[vember] 81," RUEM/HT.
150. See RUEA 1679–81 and TF to HT, 27 March 1679, RBF/HT Felton.
151. "I am at a loss in takeing of Mr Tubbin's accompts," wrote TF to HT, 24 March 1681, RBF/HT Felton.

recognized the need for peaceful relations with tenants, but he sought to ensure harmony by applying guidelines rather than by making concessions.[152]

The landlord's most revealing complaint against Tubbing had to do with the neglect of the tiny quit rents that various tenants owed. Despite the small sums involved, Townshend was furious at the omission, especially because Tubbing had been negligent for the last dozen years.[153] Such neglect was important not because it deprived the landlord of income, but because it could lead to the extinction of his manorial rights. Failing to collect quit rents encouraged tenants to claim copyhold land as free and led them to believe that they could ignore their customary obligations to the manorial lord. Little money was involved, but the principle was large: property was property, no matter how small. The rents were symbolic of Townshend's overlordship, and losing them tarnished its quality and compromised his stature as a landowner.[154]

Townshend's animadversions made Tubbing somewhat more systematic in his accounts of Michaelmas 1681, but arrears still amounted to £2,900 and the bailiff could not change a decade's practice in one year. Townshend remained petulant: "What with his neglect in gathering my rents," he wrote of Tubbing, "and the letting my tennants bring in what reparing bills they please ... I must be undone, let me take what care I can."[155] In disgust, Townshend tried to replace Tubbing, but efforts to recruit a successor were almost bound to be frustrating in a day when professional managers did not yet exist.[156] The search nearly foundered when the first candidate proved unacquainted "with our way of accompting," as Timothy Felton reported, while adducing three further reasons for his inadequacy: "he was used to inclosed grounds & your lordship's estate lyeth most in small parcells ... and then the carr[y]ing on old respitts makes it the more troublesome; and I doubt he is lasy, which he must not be who doth undertake

152. "This is [a] coppy of what I sent to Tubbing about the 1 No[vember] 81," RUEM/HT.

153. Ibid.

154. HT quarreled for several years with James Calthorpe (friend, cousin, and future executor) about minuscule quit rents each claimed of the other: TF to HT, 27 March 1679, RBF/HT Felton; "A note of the agreement betweene ... Lord Townshend and James Calthorpe, Esq.," 21 April 1680, RUEM/HT. See also TF to HT, n.d. [before 17 March] and 30 March 1682, RBF/HT Felton; TW to HT, 25 November 1686, RBF/HT misc., and 24 December 1686, Add. 41655, ff. 173–74.

155. "The monyes respited in the accompts for the years ended at Michaelmas 1681," RUEM/HT.

156. E. Hughes, "The Eighteenth-Century Estate Agent," in H. A. Cronne et al., eds., *Essays in British and Irish History in Honour of James Eadie Todd* (London, 1949), 186–90.

From Spendthrift to Patriarch

such an imployment."[157] The first two disabilities could be overcome only by someone unburdened by the last.

Townshend was thus thwarted in his search for a new bailiff and soon lacked even the help of Felton, whose thirty-five years of experience made up for others' shortcomings, but who died toward the end of 1682. Unable to replace the auditor quickly, Townshend audited the accounts for 1682 himself, which surely explains why that year was Tubbing's last as bailiff. His replacement, Bartholomew Snelling, enjoyed only a brief tenure, his service as bailiff proving a mixture of ineptitude and corruption.[158] Townshend had one query after another about Snelling's work for 1683, and recalculation of the accounts showed that Townshend was due £420 more on the year's accounts than Snelling had indicated, nearly 10 percent of nominal Norfolk rents.[159] "I had better have given £500 than imployed Mr. Snelling," Townshend complained, "who was so far from making my affairs his business, as that it appears he could not make up his owne account." Snelling had patently done little to earn his salary of £50 a year, and so he was fired.

Considering the intricacies of late Stuart estate bookkeeping, Snelling's incompetence reverberated after his tenure. Sums improperly allowed had to be disallowed; respites dropped had to be reinstated; rents Snelling received after submitting his 1683 account had to be accounted for;[160] and his balance due to Townshend had to be collected. Above all, another such debacle had to be avoided. We can imagine Townshend's anger and worry, as he, an aging, unwell man trying to settle the inheritance of his three young boys, was confronted with a management crisis that threatened his plans. The bitterness of his comments on Snelling's accounts provides a measure of his state of mind; his proceedings with Snelling's successors yields another.

Samuel Smyth, apparently a Norfolk man, followed Snelling and began hopefully: in particular, he kept much fuller accounts than his predecessor. Yet despite all Townshend's careful directives, Smyth also proved unsatisfactory.[161] Like Snelling, he left out entries that should have gone into his reckoning, but more to the point, he proved

---

157. TF to HT, c. 17, 17, and 24 March 1682, RBF/HT Felton; quotation from letter of 17 March.

158. Snelling was perhaps the former clerk of a local attorney: TF to HT, n.d. [before 17 March 1681], ibid. This paragraph is based on RUEA 1683 and numerous papers concerning Snelling, filed together in RUEM/HT.

159. Add. 41655, f. 170. See also ff. 166, 167, 169.

160. See "The severall respitts of Mr Snellings Accompt taken on to Smyths Accompt for the year 1684," RUEM/HT.

161. The paper headed "85 These papers are to make good my charge upon Mr. Snelling ... 16 April 1685," RUEM/HT, includes instructions for Smyth.

incapable of adhering to the instructions Townshend gave him.[162] A list of seven of these, meant for Townshend's auditor but also given to Smyth before an audit in March 1686, spells out what the landlord expected of his head bailiff; four sheets of Townshend's queries and notes enumerate the problems he nonetheless encountered with Smyth.[163]

The instructions to the auditor show how strongly Townshend had been affected by the difficulties he encountered with Philip Tubbing and Bartholomew Snelling. No bills of repairs would be allowed except for work ordered by Smyth for that particular year; only when these bills and other deductions granted in the tenants' leases had been specifically accepted by Townshend could they be deducted from rent. Otherwise, they would be carried as respites on the account. Because the troubles with Snelling had mostly involved repairs never done or overcharged, Townshend hoped that a system requiring his personal approval for extraordinary expenditures and allowances would prevent any recurrence.

This command to be careful with repair bills was the most important of the seven instructions given to Smyth. Three others merely specified the lands currently in hand and ordered separate accounts to be drawn for each. The remaining points, reflecting Snelling's malpractice, limited tenant allowances for carrying roof thatch; forbade allowances for carrying other repair materials; and required the entry of past arrears "in the severall accompts, mentioning the number of years due, and the yearly value exactly." These provisos were meant to check any problems before they occurred.[164]

Unfortunately, Townshend was unduly optimistic about forestalling further management problems with a detailed directive. An examination of the accounts for 1685 and part of 1686 discovered all sorts of difficulties, including a set of bills turned in by Smyth, but unsigned by the workmen or businessmen who rendered them, which amounted to £275.[165] Townshend's queries on Smyth's account once more demonstrate his intimate knowledge of estate and farm business—and his unwillingness to be cheated. He complained of grain "sold at very lowe rates" off a farm held in hand; allowances had been improperly made to tenants; reasonable expenditures had been computed at inflated

162. "Left out in Mr Snellings and Mr Smyths Acco," RUEM/HT.
163. "Instructions for . . . Lord Townshend to his Auditor, November the 1st 1685," RUEM/HT [a copy in RL drawer 112 is addressed to auditor and bailiff]; HT's notes, n.d. [after Ladyday 1686], RL drawer 100.
164. "Instructions for . . . Lord Townshend to his Auditor, November the 1st 1685," RUEM/HT.
165. "An Account of the Bills," 7 May 1686, RL drawer 74.

prices; one sheep foldcourse account was entirely incomprehensible. Considering this chicanery, it is no surprise to find the entry in Townshend's memorandum book, "I turned Smyth away for a knave, 7 May 86."[166]

Within three weeks, Townshend took on Thomas Warde as his new bailiff, and here he finally found a competent employee, as Warde proved a quick and thorough learner, partly because the landlord determined to be an excruciatingly careful teacher. Within ten days of engaging Warde, Townshend sent him extensive instructions "how to looke after my estate in Norfolk."[167] These began much like the directions to Samuel Smyth: Warde had to account for each bailiwick (there were now six) as well as each foldcourse and farm in hand by a separate account, making sure "never to mix the accounts of the farm rents with the others."[168] In a new step, Townshend required that once a month Warde bring him (or send him, if in London) an account of all money he had received, of whom and for what, whether rent, sales of grain, or the like. This way, said Townshend, "I may know what is in cash allwayes and how to call for it." This interest in cash flow was novel, and the rendering of monthly accounts from Raynham continued at least into the 1720s.[169]

As for the farm lands, Warde was ordered to enforce leases diligently, and he received guidelines, more explicit than ever, for coping with tenant repairs, an obvious consequence of Townshend's earlier problems. Warde's first obligation was to see "that no more bee done than needes." Where requisite, however, repairs were to be undertaken expeditiously, but Townshend was to be informed so as to approve *before* work was begun. He would not delegate authority in this matter and hammered home to Warde the bailiff's responsibility. "You are not," he cautioned, "to suffer the tenants to bring you any bills for repaires but such as are within your tyme and as you have ordered to bee done & will answeare for yourself." Under other conditions Townshend would not accept the allowances, and Warde would

---

166. HT's notes, n.d. [after Ladyday 1686], RL drawer 100; HT's memo and a/c book 1685–99, RUBV.

167. "Direccons for Warde," RL drawer 66; HT's memo and a/c book 1685–99, RUBV records the hiring of TW.

168. This injunction promoted a system, retained into the next century, of accounting for bailiwicks on a year ending at Michaelmas, while accounting for foldcourses and in-hand farms on a June-to-June year.

169. "Direccons for Warde," RL drawer 66. For the 1720s, see the a/cs sent monthly by William Fenn to Lady Townshend, April 1723–March 1725, RUEM/CT. In 1686 Sir Stephen Fox thought that receiving abbreviated monthly estate accounts would "tempt [his son-in-law, the Earl of Northampton] to looke over yr acctts often without much pains": C. Clay, *Public Finance and Private Wealth: The Career of Sir Stephen Fox, 1627–1716* (Oxford, 1978), 298.

be liable. Finally, Townshend demanded that every acquittance brought him for money Warde had disbursed was to have the sum written out in words, not just in figures, so as to prevent any dishonest alterations.[170]

The survival among the Raynham manuscripts of acquittances following exactly this specification is just one indication that these rules took firmer hold than their precursors. It had taken nearly ten years of trial and error, but an effective and precise method of regulating the bailiff's accounts seems to have been found.[171] Warde, far more conscientious than his predecessors, deserves much credit. In the first year of his job, he turned away tenants who claimed allowance for repairs he had not authorized and would not allow, he being "no waye conserned therein." Similarly, even in the absence of news to report, he faithfully sent off letters to his master which included the monthly account, "according to your lordship's derection to me."[172]

Yet whatever Warde's contribution, Lord Townshend's part in arriving at these exemplary arrangements must be emphasized. Directions of this amplitude and specificity presuppose a devotion to estate management lacking in many men of his stature. No matter what is said about the significant impact of aristocratic landowners as propagandists and experimenters,[173] their activities as landlords, unglamorous though they might appear, had immediate consequence. By insisting on the bailiff's responsibility, the landlord indirectly urged his tenants to a more careful consideration of how they applied their capital and labor on improvements and repairs. By employing written leases, the landlord at least theoretically determined the course of husbandry on tenants' lands. If nothing else, the use of fixed-term, rack-rent leases emphasized the need for tenant productivity. The guidelines laid down by Horatio Townshend may have directly inspired no one further afield than the northern coast of Norfolk, but they kept domestic affairs running smoothly after his death, during his son's minority and early adulthood, and in their way helped to shape England's new agrarian regime.

170. "Direccons for Warde," RL drawer 66.
171. HT also enunciated explicit guidelines for household management: paper endorsed "Cos E[dward] L['Estrange]'s his note concerning My Lord Townshends Expences in his house," c. 1688, RL drawer 66.
172. TW to HT, 30 January, 11 and 27 February 1687, RL drawer 69.
173. *AHEW*, V, 2:562–66; Beckett, *Aristocracy*, chap. 5.

Chapter 3

A Time of Transition
1687-1709

The twenty years between the death of Horatio Townshend, the first viscount, and the appointment of his son Charles as ambassador to The Hague in 1709 were turbulent and momentous years for England. Because the first Viscount Townshend was nearly forty-five when his son Charles was born, it is almost as if two generations separate the men, and this gap helps bring out in sharp relief the contrasts between the Restoration world of the one and the eighteenth-century world of the other. Many of the differences between Charles Townshend's era and that of his father were the product of the two decades when the son was first a minor and then was making his way to become a national political figure. Before the second viscount came into his own, England participated in a massive European war; religious toleration was accepted; the national debt was funded and the Bank of England created; annual sessions of parliament (and, through 1715, triennial elections) became a permanent feature of political life; political parties flowered as they had not done in the 1670s; and party competition became a "prime feature of parliamentary politics."[1] In Norfolk an older generation of elite leaders was passing from the scene, their leaving perhaps best symbolized by the death at ninety-eight, in 1701, of Horatio Townshend's friend and colleague, Sir John Holland. Although the revolutionary quality of these developments has been questioned,[2] the trajectory of Charles Townshend's life, set as it is here in contrast with his father's, is one measure of the new horizons and

---

1. H. Horwitz, "The Structure of Parliamentary Politics," in G. Holmes, ed., *Britain after the Glorious Revolution, 1689–1714* (London, 1969), 103.
2. Most notably by J. C. D. Clark, *Revolution and Rebellion: State and Society in England in the Seventeenth and Eighteenth Centuries* (Cambridge, 1986).

expectations, the new structures and mental outlooks that separated an aristocratic generation born under the second Stuart from one who died under the second Hanoverian.[3]

The score of years following Horatio Townshend's death also mark a discrete era in the management of the Raynham estate and in the fortunes of the Townshend family. For ten years after 1687, the inheritance and the care of three young boys fell to a set of executors who maintained and improved the economic well-being of the estate and who saw the heir grow into a responsible young man. Near the end of the century the second viscount returned from a protracted tour abroad, took control of his patrimony, married a well-connected heiress, and began a political career. In the ensuing ten years he balanced the competing demands of city and country life, but despite an abiding involvement in estate management, the extent of his engagement diminished during the course of this decade. Unlike his father, however, the second viscount's attachment to urban life did not jeopardize his social and political standing in the country; nor were his financial circumstances ever straitened as were the first viscount's for so long.

In agriculture Charles Townshend's energy was expended on experiment and improvement, whereas his father had devoted his time to accounting (and accountability) above all. In his experimentation the son benefited from the legacy of tested financial methods left by his father and from trustworthy estate employees. Moreover, the accumulation of capital during his minority, the promise of nearly £30,000 upon his first marriage in July 1698, and eventually the profits of public employment, all put Charles Townshend in a far more maneuverable position than his father. The son's dependence upon rents was never insignificant, but that source of income did not bear the weight for him that it did for the first viscount. Where the son was as capable as his father of spending money to maintain an appropriate style of life, he was not prodigal and never had the heavy debts that made so much personal expenditure appear extravagant in his father's day. The era of family transition, marked by ten years of executorship and ten years of the second viscount's apprenticeship on his estate and in politics, came to an end with his departure for Holland in 1709. Although the economic and agricultural priorities established before 1709 continued in effect thereafter, Townshend's prolonged absence, followed only a few years later by his elevation to a position of substan-

3. For this contrast, see L. Stone, "The Results of the English Revolutions of the Seventeenth Century," in J. G. A. Pocock, ed., *Three British Revolutions: 1641, 1688, 1776* (Princeton, 1980), 63–100.

tial political power at George I's accession, heralded for him a different sort of life altogether.

Minority and Youth, 1687–1698

The development of the Townshend estates and the young second viscount's future were partly determined by the stipulations of his father's marriage settlement and will. Despite minor quarrels between the first viscount's executors and other advocates for the interests of his younger sons, the family estates were kept intact, as the first viscount had sought. An examination of the estate strategy of his last years shows that once Horatio Townshend could secure his younger sons' financial future without settling lands on them, he took steps to avoid breaking up the estate he had nurtured during his life. In 1684, a year after the birth of Horatio, his third son, the first viscount adjusted the settlement of lands he had previously made. These alterations resettled on his heir, Charles, lands previously meant to provide for the younger boys, Roger and Horatio. No further changes were made after the death of the boys' mother (the viscount's second wife) the following year, but her demise meant that, unless the father remarried, lands intended for a widow's jointure became available to provide for sons. By settling some of these jointure lands in trust for portions to his two younger boys, Horatio the elder protected intact virtually his entire estate.[4]

The tenor of his will further reveals the first viscount's desire to pass on a unified inheritance that might help launch his heir to greatness. Instruction for a funeral monument costing up to £600 (double the price specified in earlier drafts of his will) speaks of family pride, as does the first viscount's proviso to preserve all "jewells, plate, householdstuffs . . . armes and other my goods . . . as heyre loomes" not to be sold or severed from Raynham Hall "upon any occasion or pretence whatsoever." He wanted the literal components of his heritage preserved.[5] To his younger sons he left £8,000 apiece when they reached twenty-one, money secured by Norfolk lands worth £250 per annum

---

4. See the provisions of a lease, 3 March 1684, settling in trust HT's Suffolk estate and certain Norfolk lands, which appear in HT's will and in an indenture of release on CT's marriage, 15 June 1698, RUS. See HT's settlements of 25 November 1673 and 15 November 1678, ibid., and Sir R. Baldock to HT, 9 November 1678, NRO, Le Strange P20, f. 99.

5. Will, 16 March, with codicils of 25 and 26 November, proved 7 December 1687, PRO, PROB 11/389, f. 196 et seq. Draft will, 15 November 1678 (with codicil of 1680 and alterations for a new will, 1683), RBF, Norfolk wills (ii). Extensive inventories were drawn up in 1686: "An inventory of my Lord's plate," 14 April 1686, RUFP [NRO]; "A note of linnen &c," 4 May 1686, RU, household/estate [NRO].

and by his Suffolk estate, valued now at £1,200 per annum and yielding £800–£1,000 clear.[6] The executors gave ample allowances to the younger boys, who also benefited from their father's sympathy with the plight of a junior brother. The first viscount specified that Roger and Horatio's upbringing was to be guided by a regard for "theire capacityes, abilityes and inclinacons," whether to study law or divinity or to be put to "merchandize." In the case of Roger, a false start in law was followed by a career in politics and the army, furthered by his elder brother and cut short by his own early death; Horatio, after a boisterous youth, was apprenticed in "merchandize" and made a successful career for himself, including service as a South Sea Company director, Bank of England director and governor, and Commissioner of the Excise.[7]

The first viscount's will nominated four men as executors, two of standing in the county, Sir Jacob Astley and Robert Walpole (father of the future prime minister), and two men of business and legal acumen, James Calthorpe (a Norfolk-born cousin of Townshend's) and William Thurisby. Perhaps anticipating that Astley would refuse his part in the administration and that Walpole would have little time, Townshend added a codicil to his will identifying Calthorpe as the executor in whom he reposed particular trust to manage the estate. That faith Townshend witnessed with a £100 annuity beyond the £50 legacy all four executors received; Thurisby, who proved a workhorse like Calthorpe, received an additional £40. These inducements encouraged the two lawyers in combined execution of the will in a manner beneficial to the heir and the family as a whole.[8]

When the first viscount died in London on 3 December 1687, the youngest boy, Horatio, was in the care of an aunt, and the heir Charles and his brother Roger were at Eton, where they had been sent the year before.[9] The elder sons' care in ensuing months posed something of a problem, because the Tory executors Calthorpe and Thurisby clashed with the second viscount's Whig uncle William Windham for control of Charles.[10] Young Townshend was a pawn as the ensuing

6. RUEA[S], 1675–90. The Suffolk land's nominal value in 1699 was £1,162: "An Accot of the Estate of . . . Lord Viscount Townshend . . . in . . . 1701 and 1730," RUEM/CT.

7. Le Strange, *Lists*, 52; *HP 1715–54*, 2:473. See chap. 6 for Roger's political career.

8. Thurisby was already working for HT, facilitating his London business: A. Felton's 1686 a/c, RUEM/HT.

9. HT's memo and a/c book 1685–99, RUBV; R. Hascard's bills for young Horatio are in A. Felton's 1686 a/c, RUEM/HT.

10. Windham's brother John married HT's sister Jane, and Windham himself married Katherine while HT married Mary, daughters of Sir Joseph Ashe of Twickenham: J. Burke, *A Genealogical and Heraldic History of the Commoners of Great Britain . . .*, 4 vols. (London, 1834–38; reprinted Baltimore, 1977), 2:578–79.

microcosmic struggle of Tory and Whig impinged on family affairs. In 1688 he and his brother were taken out of school and brought to the home of his grandmother, and Windham's mother-in-law, Lady Mary Ashe. There, she and Windham attempted (according to William Thurisby) "to get a prevayling interest" in the youngsters. As the boys' uncle, Windham had a legitimate family interest to assert, but he strained its limits, apparently trying, for example, to sway the young viscount to abandon the claim to a church living at Felbrigg, which was in Windham's gift but had been promised to the first viscount's former chaplain. An anxious Thurisby tried to assess "how the ill councell . . . had taken impression upon [Townshend]," and he sent the boy to another uncle, Thomas Lord Crew, who obligingly instructed Charles to heed his "sober & carefull guardians" and ignore the advice of his "evill relacons."[11]

Even so, Townshend stayed on with Lady Ashe, and despite Thurisby's effort to have him return to school, his bored charge went to London in the hot, "sickly time" of summer 1688 to visit an aunt and see a play. This venture brought a confrontation between Windham and Thurisby, who tracked the boy down in London. In front of Townshend, who "lay in bedd & sayd noething," Windham urged the viscount to ignore his guardians' advice and come to him at Felbrigg in Norfolk anytime, which left Thurisby to bemoan the "great stepp into the government of the young man" that Windham had gained.[12] Yet the guardians ultimately had their way. By the end of July 1688 the boy was back at Eton; his French valet, blamed for allowing Windham to spirit him away, had been chastised; and the masters at Eton had received orders not to let Townshend leave without his guardians' permission. The viscount himself, visited by James Calthorpe, averred "that tho' he has been much pressed to doe as the world reports, yet he will never forsake [his guardian], if it were in his power."[13] That qualifying "if" perhaps bespoke some ambivalence on the boy's part toward the parties involved. Still, legal efforts (perhaps instigated by Windham) failed to wrest control of the estate from the executors: charges that they kept poor records and failed to invest estate profits or to manage the lands competently were all rejected. The death of

11. See W. Thurisby to J. Calthorpe, 31 May 1688, NRO, L'Estrange P20, f. 120 (which letter Thurisby cautioned Calthorpe to burn), and R. W. Ketton-Cremer, *Felbrigg: The Story of a House* (London, 1982; paperback ed.), 72–74, concerning the church living. Two of Windham's sons were at Eton with the Townshend boys: ibid., 71, 81.

12. W. Thurisby to J. Calthorpe, 5 June and n.d. 1688, NRO, L'Estrange P20, ff. 121, 252. Windham said Lady Ashe or her nominee (i.e., himself) ought to help manage the part of the family inheritance that had been settled upon HT's marriage to her daughter Mary Ashe.

13. [J. Calthorpe] to R. Walpole, 21 July 1688, CUL, C(H) Corr. #14.

William Windham in June 1689 removed the guiding force behind this quarrel and brought it to an end.[14]

What Townshend made of the wrangles can only be inferred, but he weathered the storms with maturity. During several of the arguments between guardians and relatives he said nothing, an admirably politic approach, and to his uncle Crew he denied listening to ill advice. He did not in any event reject the executors: Calthorpe remained a close advisor until his death, while Robert Walpole the elder was asked for counsel in ensuing years, and his son became Townshend's friend and political ally. The boy also continued to visit Twickenham and see his Ashe and Windham cousins,[15] and the remaining years he spent at Eton left no trace of further intrafamilial difficulties. In Easter 1691 Charles matriculated at King's, Cambridge, and he went up to reside at university that July. During the next three years he attended sporadically, taking no degree and generally marking time.[16] His valets' letters to agents in London unsurprisingly spoke of clothes and other purchases, but there are no greater signs of Townshend's studiousness from other sources. He once stayed in residence at Cambridge for seven consecutive months, but more generally punctuated his time with weeks at Raynham and longer periods in London.[17] Nonetheless, it seems likely that Townshend's time at university, however brief, served the purposes of aristocratic education identified by John Cannon: to fit a nobleman for leadership, to encourage a common sense of purpose among the elite, and to create a network of acquaintance.[18] The Cambridge sojourn clearly did this last, by further cementing Townshend's friendship with his fellow collegian Robert Walpole, who had been his Eton schoolmate as well. And, as one Norfolk observer noted, it afforded him the base from which to make "his first start in London."[19]

The very fact that in late 1693 a young man not yet nineteen should

14. Legal brief, n.d., *Townshend* v. *Townshend*, RU, legal [NRO]; legal bills 1689–91, with Titley's a/c, RUEA 1691; Ketton-Cremer, *Felbrigg*, 80. Resolution did not come before Lady Ashe had peevishly sold stock she held for young Roger Townshend's use: M. Ashe to W. Thurisby, 11 April [1689?], RBF/HT misc.

15. CT was also witness to an agreement between Lady Ashe and her son, Sir James, concerning the disposal of the Ashe estate on Sir James's marriage: "Articles agreed upon between the Lady Ashe and Sir James Ashe," 1 January 1698, RUS.

16. Titley's a/c, RUEA 1691. J. and J. A. Venn, *Alumni Cantabrigienses*, pt. 1, vol. 4 (Cambridge, 1927), 258; Raynham household a/c, RUEA 1692.

17. Mons. Moret, Delaleu, and J. Stuart served as valets; see their letters and those of J. Calthorpe and C. Titley in RBF/CT 1692–1704 for residence and movements.

18. J. Cannon, *Aristocratic Century: The Peerage of Eighteenth-Century England* (Cambridge, 1984), 35–36. Cannon adds a fourth end, to give validity to the rule of the elite through its virtual monopoly of higher education.

19. *Prideaux letters*, 165–66.

make his start in London rather than in his home county points to the insinuation of metropolitan imperatives into aristocratic life.[20] The lures of the city did not, however, immediately snare the young viscount, whose "first start" proved something of a false one, since within eight months he began an extended European tour. The London "start" also postdated by several years the beginning he made as a landowner with local responsibilities. As early as 1690, when only fifteen, Townshend had inspected and signed the accounts for expenses incurred during a visit to Raynham—a practice he actually discontinued as an adult. By 1692, payments hitherto authorized by "the late Lord Townshend's executors" were now made specifically at the young heir's behest.[21] The sums in his personal control also grew, since his father's will stipulated that his allowance of £100 a year should triple when he was fourteen and rise to £500 on his seventeenth birthday. Yet daily management of the family estates and the care of his brothers did not come into Townshend's hands until he returned from abroad in 1697, and his guardians apparently saw no need to apprise him even of substantial estate matters, whether the leasing of farms or the lending of money. Social obligations were another matter, and he took to these avidly, exhausting his guardian James Calthorpe when the two were together in the country. Townshend was rivaled in Norfolk by only one other resident peer, the strongly Tory (and nearly insolvent) second Earl of Yarmouth, and was reckoned to have the county's second largest fortune,[22] so his county interest was there for the taking: unlike his father, he did not have to earn his title or the lord lieutenant's commission awarded him in 1701. If one can usefully talk of the countryside's natural leaders, the second Viscount Townshend was one.

Credit must go to his father's executors and former employees for much of the ease with which Charles Townshend assumed his position of wealth and authority. Unlike the men who oversaw Horatio Townshend's minority, they had growing financial opportunities to seize,[23] no prolonged civil disorder to negotiate, and no Court of Wards to confront.[24] On the first viscount's death they also found the estate little

20. Beckett identifies the reasons why, after 1689, life in London changed from "a pleasurable diversion . . . into a social necessity": *Aristocracy*, 364–65.
21. See CT's note "I do allow of this bill of £19.12.2, Townshend" in TW's household a/c, RUEA 1690. Cf. TW's general a/c to March 1691 [RUEA 1690] with his general a/cs to March 1692 and 1693 [RUEA 1691, 1692].
22. *Prideaux letters*, 165–66.
23. This said, it should be noted that the executors invested only in mortgages.
24. P. Roebuck, "Post-Restoration Landownership: The Impact of the Abolition of Wardship," *Journal of British Studies* 18, no. 1 (1978): 67–85. The abolition of wardship brought new legal safeguards for minors' interests, and under effective guardians

encumbered with obligations. Those imposed by the deceased's will were substantial, with £8,000 assigned to each younger son and £150 in annuities to others, but Roger Townshend was not quite eleven and little Horatio was only about to turn five, so there was time to accumulate estate profits and invest them to raise the portions. Similarly, before the time came for payment, there was the possibility that Lord Townshend would marry and receive a dowry to help provide for his brothers. From the beginning, however, the executors took steps to preserve the family inheritance by retaining employees and methods that had served the first viscount well. Edward L'Estrange remained as auditor until he died in 1717, and Thomas Warde was kept as bailiff until his death in 1710.[25] James Calthorpe, when he ceased to be guardian and executor, remained a trusted advisor to his former charge.

Continuity of personnel minimized disturbance to the estate after the first viscount's death; so did the fact that there was money to spare. In the seven years after 1687, an average of £1,800 per annum was returned from the Norfolk and Suffolk estates to London receivers, and from this profit the orphaned boys were maintained and many of the investments made. As much as £8,500 was out at loan at one time before 1694, sums invested on behalf of Roger Townshend, who received the principal and interest when he came of age in 1698. Expenses were not great: no permanent household was kept either at Raynham or in London; the younger boys' maintenance was minimal, under £200 in 1691–93 and only £250 a year for both by the middle of 1694. Charles's allowance was ampler, but his disbursements came to less than £900 in the two years to 1693, although they rose steadily during his time at Cambridge and ballooned when he went abroad in 1694. This extended stay cost about £1,000 a year over three years, a far greater rate of expenditure than before. On his return, now of age, Townshend launched into something of a spending spree, but even then the executors experienced no difficulty in meeting the demands placed on them. They had to provide for only two children beyond the heir, brothers at that, and estate income was unaffected by jointure payments, since Horatio Townshend had outlived his mother and both his wives. In short, money was available for the needs of the heir and his brothers throughout the second viscount's minority, whether for the latter's travels abroad, diamond earrings for his bride-to-be, or his brother Roger's barely occupied legal chambers in the Temple.[26]

"enabled a maximum of income to remain available for investment and improvement" (85).

25. Between 1698 and 1700, TW was replaced by William Manning.

26. HT's memo and a/c book 1685–99, RUBV; Titley's a/cs, RUEA 1691–93; receivers' a/cs 1693–1706, RUBV; bills of 1693–94, RL drawer 112.

In fact, a greater problem than supplying Townshend and his brothers was obtaining secure outlets for cash on hand; the discovery of a solid investment brought urgent calls from London to the country bailiffs for the most rapid possible return of money.[27] The desire to seize safe investment opportunities led the executors twice in the 1690s to lend money at less than prevailing rates of interest, and it caused dismay when one of these loans (£1,000 at 4.5 percent) was repaid with unwelcome promptness. For money to "lye dead at the goldsmyths" was a cardinal sin, although good security had to be safe security.[28] When the goldsmith Sir Thomas Fowles fell ill, James Calthorpe had qualms about sending any money from Norfolk to be lodged with him, and would approve only because the £300 involved was "soe small a summ" as to cause no major concern if lost, a comment that shows the prosperous state of the Townshend finances.[29]

That the estate thrived was partly the result of the energy the executors devoted to their charge. Robert Walpole the elder was busy with county and national politics, so the London lawyer William Thurisby and James Calthorpe, fundamentally a country gentleman, played the active parts.[30] Calthorpe, in particular, as an unmarried man had time to take on surrogate sons; himself a younger son, he showed sympathetic solicitude for the two junior Townshends, whose place in the world was not secure. Since he was a man of insubstantial means, his legacy of £100 a year was a significant addition to his income.[31] Yet these material considerations do not negate the affection evident in Calthorpe's deep involvement with the family, nor his sense of obligation to the dead father, both of which spurred him to conscientious performance of his trust. He neglected few details, making sure the young boys had pocket money at school and that Horatio's sweet tooth was assuaged with chocolate almonds.[32] Overseen by their guard-

27. E. Mann to TW, 20 February 1694, with TW's 1693 general a/c, RBF/CT Warde 1692–93.
28. W. Thurisby to J. Calthorpe, 29 October 1691, NRO, L'Estrange P20, f. 140; Calthorpe to C. Titley, 24 July 1692, RBF/CT 1692–1704. See same to same, 5 December 1692, ibid., for £100 lent at 4 percent.
29. J. Calthorpe to C. Titley, 15 April and 21 November 1692, RBF/CT 1692–1704. See also TW to C. Titley, 8 January 1693, ibid., and Titley to TW, 17 January 1693, with TW's general a/c, RUEA 1692.
30. W. Thurisby to CT, 10 March 1697, reports Walpole "over head & eares in disputes in Parlt country": Add. 41654, f. 42. See also Plumb, *Walpole*, 1:81–92, for a sketch of Walpole, who still took a significant part as an executor: see letters to him in RUEA[S] 1693; CUL, C(H) Corr. #38, 49, 58; and Add. 63101, f. 38. For hints of peculation by Walpole, see E. L'Estrange to J. Calthorpe, 16 May 1694, RL drawer 66.
31. H. J. Lee-Warner, "The Calthorps of Cockthorp," *Norfolk Archaeology* 9 (1884): 155. See RBF/CT 1692–1704 passim for Calthorpe's mien and means.
32. See Calthorpe's touching letter to CT on his twenty-first birthday, 18 April 1696, RBF/CT 1696–1735, as well as Calthorpe to C. Titley, 5 May, 23 October, 14 November,

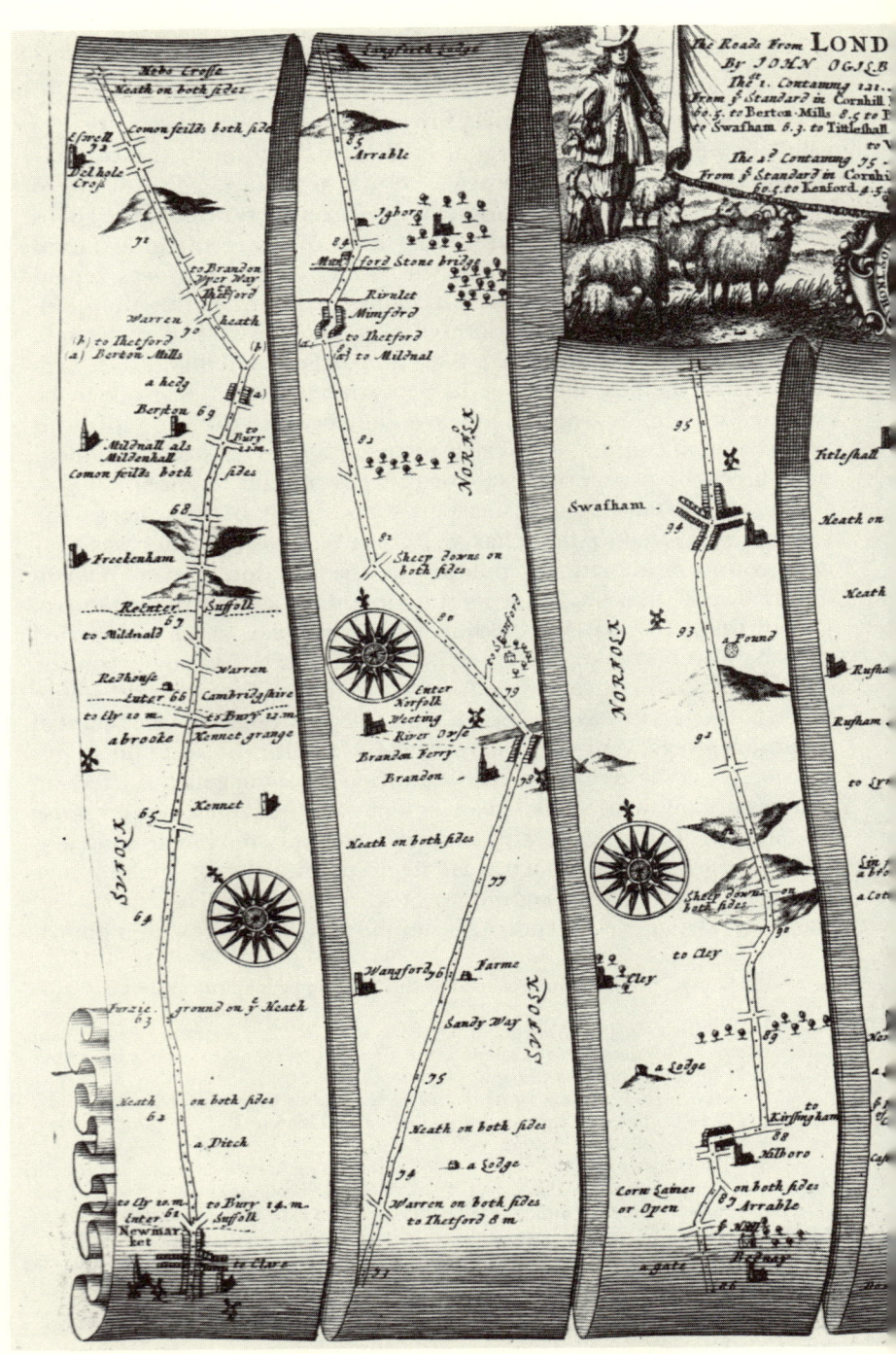

"The Roads from London to Wells in Norfolk and St. Edmonsbury in Suffolk," an engraved strip road map from John Ogilby's *Britannia*, published in 1675; Raynham Hall is depicted on the third strip from the right
Courtesy, Yale Center for British Art, Paul Mellon Collection

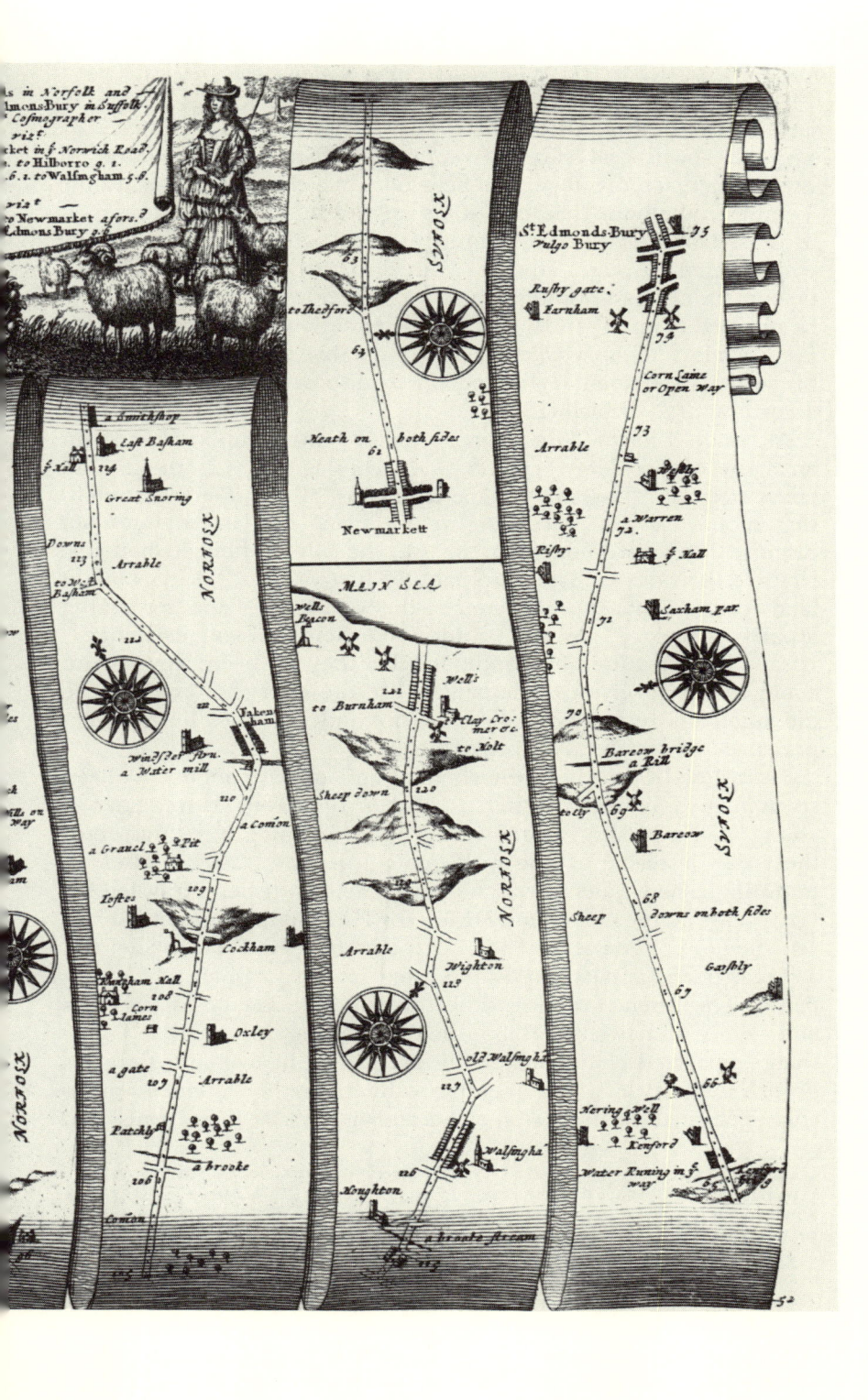

(Strip map, John Ogilby style road map of Norfolk/Suffolk)

Partial text visible on map panels:

Top left cartouche (partially cut off):
...in Norfolk and
...lmons Bury in Suffolk
...Cosmographer
...viz:
...ket in ye Norwich Road
...to Hilborro 9.1.
...6.1. to Walsingham 5.8.
...viz:
...to Newmarket afores'd
...dmons Bury

Left strip (Norfolk):
- a Smiths shop
- East Basham
- Great Snoring
- Downs 113
- Arrable
- to Mr Basham
- 112
- Windsel Stru, a Water mill — Yaxenham 111
- 110
- a Comon
- a Gravel Pit
- Iostes 109
- Cockham
- Thorngham Hall 208 Corn Iames
- Oxley
- a gate 109 Arrable
- Patchly
- a brooke 106
- Comon

Second strip (Norfolk / Main Sea):
- to Thedford
- 63
- 64
- Heath on both sides
- 61
- Newmarkett
- MAIN SEA
- Wells Beacon
- to Burnham 121
- Wells
- to Clay, Cromer &c, to Holt
- Sheep down 120
- 118
- Arrable
- Wighton 119
- old Walsingh...
- Walsingha
- 116 Houghton
- a brooke & stream 117

Third strip (Suffolk/Norfolk):
- St Edmonds-Bury / Fulgo Bury 75
- Rushy gate, Farnham 74
- Corn Laine or Open Way 73
- Arrable
- a Warren 72
- Rushy
- Saxham par.
- 70
- Bareow bridge, a Rill
- to Ely
- Bareow 69
- Sheep Downs on both sides 68
- Gasbly 67
- Hering Well 66
- Kenford
- Water Runing in ye way

ians, all three boys thrived along with their family's inheritance. By 1697, as Townshend learned from his guardians while he wound up his continental tour, Roger had been bought a chamber in the Middle Temple in the hope that legal study might lead to a stable career, "if it please God he take to it." Young Horatio, who recognized that he was no scholar, sought any other outlet for his talents: "I had better do something than nothing," he wrote his eldest brother, hoping to be released from the torture of school. He was a belligerent boy, and for a while a military career seemed suitable for him, in line with his father's testamentary injunction to dispose the boys in careers according to their inclinations.[33]

Although William Thurisby reported to Townshend in 1697 about an array of problems—trouble with a goldsmith, ubiquitous and heavy taxation, "losses by sheepe & tenants," the difficulty in remitting money to the journeying young man—his lament does not disguise his satisfaction with the way he and Calthorpe had discharged their duties. They had paid the first viscount's debts, bought land costing £900, started Roger in the world, and kept "something alwaies in bancke" for the venturesome heir's bills of exchange.[34] Affairs were in admirable condition. Had they not been, Townshend could not have given cosmopolitan life the energetic embrace he did upon his return from Europe, nor indeed could he have experienced so apparently carefree a tour.

Townshend's years between schooling and majority might have been spent in any number of ways, most of them disastrous. More than one young man wasted a fortune before ever obtaining it, by misuse of the credit available to one with good prospects. Instead, after an undistinguished, quiet stay at the university, Townshend traveled for three years on the Continent. He left for Holland in August 1694 and returned to London at the end of October 1697. Dr. William Sherard, an Oxford scholar particularly interested in botany, apparently accompanied Townshend the entire time, traveling through the Netherlands and France and as far as Italy. It may be during this trip that Townshend perfected command of the French he had obtained via his French menservants, and one may wonder whether Sherard's influence generated the interest in plants and agriculture that Townshend

---

5, 14, and 19 December 1692, RBF/CT 1692–1704; same to same, 25 April 1692, Add. 41654, f. 38; W. Thurisby to Calthorpe, 29 October 1691, NRO, L'Estrange P20, f. 140. Entries for 2 July 1694, 13 September 1695, and 10 February 1696, receivers' a/cs 1693–1706, RUBV.

33. W. Thurisby to CT, 10 March 1697, Add. 41654, f. 42; H. Townshend to CT, n.d. [1697–98], RBF/CT 1696–1735.

34. W. Thurisby to CT, 10 March 1697, Add. 41654, f. 42.

later exhibited.[35] Townshend's foreign sojourn was not cheap, but unlike young peers of a generation or two later, he neither made expensive purchases of art nor returned with grandiose plans for building, as did, for example, Thomas Coke, the builder of Holkham Hall in Norfolk.[36]

On his return, Townshend took his seat in the House of Lords, assumed legal responsibility for the trusts hitherto in the hands of his father's executors, and quickly married.[37] On the matrimonial front Townshend's cousin, Sir Nicholas L'Estrange, had earlier suggested marriage to the daughter of the viscount's uncle, Thomas Lord Crew, but Crew had rejected the proposal, especially since Townshend was "under age and nott in England." Even the assurance that the prospective groom's estate would amount to more than £5,000 a year could not change his mind.[38] The awkwardness inherent in having another seek out a partner on his behalf was overcome when Townshend paid court to Elizabeth Pelham on his return from Europe. By the end of June 1698, property settlements and marriage preparations had been made, and the pair were married at the girl's father's house in Chelsea. The eighteen-year-old bride, daughter of Thomas Pelham, future fourth baronet and first Baron Pelham of Laughton, Sussex, and granddaughter and heiress of Sir William Jones, former solicitor general and attorney general to Charles II, brought with her a substantial portion.[39] Under the provisions of his father's will, Townshend could

---

35. For dates and locations of travel see *CSPD 1694–95*, 234; E. Mann to H. Sorrell, 16 August 1694, Sorrell's a/c, RUEA[S] 1694; receivers' a/cs 1693–1706, RUBV; and Sherard's correspondence with Dr. Charlett at Oxford, Bodl., MS Ballard 27. There is no sign of later contact between CT and Sherard, beyond a gift to the doctor of £125 at the end of 1697. On Sherard, see *DNB* and J. Nichols, *Literary Anecdotes of the Eighteenth Century*..., 9 vols. (London, 1812–15), 3 (1812): 652, as well as the entry of 14 December 1697, receivers' a/cs 1693–1706, RUBV. It is unclear whether Sherard returned to England with Townshend; in August 1698 he was in Rome: Sherard to [H. Sloane], 23 August 1698, BL, Sloane MSS 4037, f. 113. On Townshend's tour, see also A. W. Moore, *Norfolk & the Grand Tour: Eighteenth-Century Travellers Abroad and Their Souvenirs* (Fakenham, 1985), 85.

36. Ibid., 33–39.

37. *LJ*, 16:174; indenture, 15 June 1698, RUS: CT agreed to pay his youngest brother's portion and to erect his father's funeral monument.

38. [Drafts] Sir N. L'Estrange to Lord Crew, 16 November, 2 and 16 December 1694, 21 January 1695, and Crew to L'Estrange, 14 December 1694 and 1 January 1695, NRO, L'Estrange P20, ff. 170–72. Lord Crew married Mary Townshend in 1650; she died in 1668, and he remarried. The daughter, from the second marriage, was no blood relation to CT: GEC, *Peerage*, "Crew." If the daughter in question was Jemima, eldest by Crew's second wife, she brought Henry Grey, Earl of Kent, £20,000 on their marriage in March 1695, a date suggesting that CT was rejected because a better offer was available: GEC, *Peerage*, "Kent."

39. GEC, *Peerage*, "Pelham"; *DNB*, "Sir William Jones," "Thomas Pelham"; *HP 1660–90*, 2:666–68, 3:220–21; notes at the end of receivers' a/cs 1693–1706, RUBV.

settle lands worth £1,200 per annum on his wife, but considering that she brought £19,000 in immediate expectation and another £10,000 on her father's death, Townshend added jointure lands to provide her with £2,000 a year in all. The portion-jointure ratio of nearly fifteen to one is nonetheless half again as high as the average for the period. She received £400 in pin money each year, a provision for maintenance never formally made in the first viscount's marriage settlements.[40]

With no substantial debts to pay off, Charles Townshend, unlike his father, invested the money he received on his marriage. In his personal account book he entered "the money I have out at interest of my wife's fortune," some £12,000 he had received immediately.[41] The infusion of capital from his bride made it easy to pay £1,000 for brother Horatio's apprenticeship in 1700, and investment income, something from which his father had never benefited, helped Townshend afford the new style of life brought by marriage. Marriage was, after all, an important step, and he commemorated it splendidly, buying his bride diamond earrings worth £1,600 and expending £1,700 on preparations for the wedding itself. The London receiver, who had recently been disbursing £1,600 a year for the bachelor Townshend, spent £5,300 in ten months surrounding the wedding date, four times the previous rate of expenditure.[42] Outlays slowed thereafter, but marriage forever altered the financial demands on Townshend's estate and household. Simple lodgings in London no longer sufficed, so he left his rooms, first for a house in York Buildings, Buckingham Street, Westminster, then for one in Soho Square and later for Bond Street. New domestic arrangements required an expanded household; on the couple's return to London from a honeymoon at Raynham, their entourage numbered at least eleven.[43] Nurses were soon required for the children who rapidly appeared, and over the coming years Lady Townshend's "great belly" often obliged

40. Abstract of settlement, 28 June 1698, RUS; marriage faculty, 29 June 1698, RUS; Add. 41656, f. 175; L. Stone, *The Crisis of the Aristocracy 1558–1641* (Oxford, 1965), 645. N. Luttrell, *A Brief Historical Relation of State Affairs* . . ., 6 vols. (Oxford, 1857), 4:398, reported that CT got £30,000 with his bride.

41. Another £10,000 was to come when Pelham died (he lived until 1712), and £7,000 from Sir William Jones's estate when Lady Townshend turned twenty-one. Of the £12,000, £5,000 was secured by a mortgage on an estate in Norfolk, and £7,000 was put into Exchequer tallies, later converted into Old East India bonds, then New East India Stock and land tax tallies: CT's personal a/c book 1697–1702, RL drawer 99; T. Wentworth to CT, 30 August 1698, Add. 63079, f. 1.

42. Entries for May 1698–March 1699, receivers' a/cs 1693–1706, RUBV. CT's personal a/c book 1697–1702, RL drawer 99, records the apprenticeship agreement, 23 May 1700. See indenture, 17 June 1700, RL drawer 111.

43. Rent payments in receivers' a/cs 1693–1706, RUBV; entry for 20 December 1698 for servants' wages; London County Council, *Survey of London*, 33 (1966): 59.

a shift from Raynham to London, where she preferred her children to be born. The first arrived in mid-August 1699, a son, Horatio; he was followed by two sisters and six brothers, the last birth killing the mother, who had produced nine living children in thirteen years of married life.[44]

Marriage did more than raise financial demands for Lord Townshend, and the significance of family cannot be overlooked in assessing his life and character. He was called "a kind husband," and his bonds with both his wives were apparently close.[45] Almost no marital correspondence survives, but when Elizabeth Townshend was at Bath in 1707, she wrote Townshend frequently, and he apparently responded in kind. She did not enjoy her stay in "this hatefull place," hoping "never [to] be so unfortunate [as] to be from you again" and finding that "every week that I get over pleases me as much as if I had gained the Indies."[46] Perhaps because of illness or because of the retiring, even submissive personality that her few letters reveal, Elizabeth Townshend's roles in the family and its business, and in Townshend's political career, are difficult to make out. She had the responsibility of communicating with Townshend's steward at Raynham when the viscount first went to Holland as ambassador in 1709, and she wrote a perceptive if brief account of the Norfolk election to her father in 1705.[47] Nonetheless, it was left not to Elizabeth but to Dorothy Townshend, whom the viscount married in 1713, two years after his first wife died, to play the more visible part in holding domestic affairs together, especially in the 1720s.

As for the twenty children Townshend eventually fathered by his two wives, his affection ran deep from the start. He proudly named his first child Horatio in his father's honor and had his next child (and ultimate heir) christened with his own name. His many offspring were well looked after when young, and as they matured they received more-than-adequate provision from their father in the form of education, appropriate marriage partners, and assistance in their careers. Sir Horace Mann much later accused Townshend of neglecting the education of his children, but domestic account books show substantial outlays on their behalf, and any deficiency in the schooling they received may better be attributed to their tutors' or their own shortcom-

44. The phrase "great belly" occurs in J. Calthorpe to E. Mann, 23 April and 19 May 1699, RUC [NRO]. For the children's births, see East Raynham parish register 1627–1716, NRO, PD 369/1.
45. BL, Stowe 308, f. 14.
46. Lady Townshend to CT, c. 23, 26, 30 April and 5 May [1707], RBF/CT 1696–1735 and 7 May [1707], RUM [1988] misc. box 1.
47. E. Townshend to Sir T. Pelham, 1 June [1705], Add. 33084, f. 177.

ings.[48] On the score of material aid, however, the Earl of Chesterfield believed that at his death Townshend "left his younger children very moderately provided for, though he had been in considerable and lucrative employments near thirty years."[49] This unqualified judgment fails to consider that providing in any fashion whatsoever for the eleven of his children who attained adulthood was in itself an accomplishment; it will be seen that Townshend's provisions, while not extravagant, were ample.[50]

Townshend the Landlord

Return to England from his tour abroad, entry into the House of Lords, marriage and the appearance of a family—these developments signaled Townshend's true coming of age, more than attainment of his twenty-first year in 1696. Increased devotion to his estate and its management further characterized his maturity. Nevertheless, none of these developments marked the transition from one family era to another as well as did Townshend's departure for Holland in May 1709 to serve as plenipotentiary to treaty negotiations with the Dutch. From his marriage in 1698 until then, Townshend spent as much time on the conduct of personal as public business. Politics and national affairs began to grip him with his appointment as lord lieutenant of Norfolk in 1701, but estate decisions still bore his stamp, and relatively minor details were referred for his approval. Into the first years of Anne's reign, Townshend experimented to find an even balance between country and cosmopolitan pursuits, political or otherwise. Only the problems created by his distance from Norfolk when abroad finally forced him away from close touch with his land; then the press of national affairs after he returned in 1711 never allowed him to bestow full attention again until he retired. Townshend's life does not describe a clean trajectory of growing or lessening engagement, whether in agrarian or governmental pursuits.

Unlike his father's, Charles Townshend's country activities were far less political than personal: if he was not already the greatest man in Norfolk at the very end of the seventeenth century, he showed little ambition to make himself so. He addressed his attention closer to home

---

48. Sir H. Mann to H. Walpole, 7 December 1745 (NS) in W. S. Lewis, ed., *The Yale Edition of Horace Walpole's Correspondence*, 19 (New Haven, 1954): 169. It is possible that Mann's reference in this letter to an ill-educated Mr. Townshend is to one of the *third* viscount's sons. Horace Walpole himself was tutored with CT's four youngest sons: ibid., 13 (New Haven, 1948): 3.
49. BL, Stowe 308, f. 14, where CT is also described as "a most indulgent father."
50. See chap. 6.

than the castle at Norwich, where county business was transacted. In 1698, the bailiff Thomas Warde happily approved that Townshend "would not conserne" himself in parliamentary elections. Despite this political inactivity (which in any case he abandoned in 1701, when helping his brother Roger to a county seat), Townshend remained socially secure in the county. His reappointment as lord lieutenant by Queen Anne in 1702 guaranteed continued local political influence.[51] But in the uncertain climate of party strife in the years immediately surrounding the turn of the century, it is not surprising that the young man (only twenty-five in 1700) felt his way cautiously in public affairs and devoted much time to private ones.[52]

The condition of Raynham Hall, however, caught the second viscount's eye as much as his father's. The renovations Townshend undertook presupposed a commitment to residence in the country, which in the early 1700s was largely undiminished by his political activity and ambitions, and which his sharply focused attention to the work itself demonstrates. Like his father, he was not indifferent to the symbolic importance of a country house, although the security of his reputation in Norfolk meant that the hall never became the focal point of politically significant socializing. Like his father, he also came to recognize, during this time of transition, the importance of direct involvement in estate affairs. This involvement, to be sure, tapered off with his appointment as a commissioner for the union with Scotland in 1706 and more dramatically when he became ambassador to the Dutch treaty negotiations in 1709; but in the early 1700s it is evident in many ways.

Shortly after his marriage, Townshend increased his application to country business, in contrast with his youthful enthusiasm for hunting and socializing on visits to Raynham. The most significant evidence of this change lay in decisions taken to abandon farming in hand and to clear the estate accounts of their respites. Between 1698 and 1701 ten of the eleven foldcourses or sheepwalks, formerly managed directly by Horatio Townshend's trustees—to no great profit—were taken out of the bailiff's hands and leased to tenants.[53] The result simplified management and lowered its cost, while making more predictable the return on these lands. In a further effort to rationalize procedures and symboli-

51. TW to CT, 10 June 1698, RBF/CT 1692–1704; Rosenheim, "Oligarchy," 412–14; patent as lord lieutenant, 21 July, 1 Anne [1702], RU, commissions. Between April and August 1701, CT was made high steward of Lynn and high steward of Norwich cathedral, and received the freedom of Norwich: ibid.
52. See chap. 6 for a full discussion.
53. See a/cs to June 1698, RUEA 1698; foldcourse a/cs, RBF/CT Manning 1699; general a/c to June 1700, RUE fragile; general a/c to June 1701, RUEA 1701. There were in hand 6 foldcourses and 3 farms in 1699, 2 foldcourses and 1 farm in 1700, 1 foldcourse and no farms in 1701.

cally make a new start with his accounts, Townshend in 1701 discharged his bailiff from £1,700 in arrears that had accumulated on the six bailiwick accounts.[54] Some of the respites now written off dated from Philip Tubbing's tenure twenty years before, but whatever their origin, by discharging them Townshend acknowledged the futility of recording unrecoverable rent charges that only cluttered bookkeeping. Where the first viscount never abandoned such claims, no matter how unlikely of enforcement, his son's approach was more practically based on financial and administrative considerations, not on a concern to maintain the traditional (and outmoded) perquisites of landownership.

Estate particulars and instructions for employees from around 1701 preserve Townshend's efforts to gain mastery of his affairs during these years, but in a different fashion from that of his father.[55] Possessed with an attention to detail his son lacked, the first viscount queried the smallest items of expenditure on his accounts, spent time haggling about unpaid quit rents, watched over his flocks and foldcourses like a worried sheepdog, and struggled with intricacies of leases no matter how little land was involved. For him, these minutiae constituted the fabric of overlordship; mastering them both characterized and justified his mastery of those over whom he enjoyed dominion and exercised authority as employer, landlord, and magnate. He had larger visions for his country estate, and the enlargement of the park at Raynham showed his capacity to follow through on them. Yet the small points fascinated and even obsessed him. It was as well they did: attention to detail is part of what kept him solvent.

Charles Townshend's interests, concerns, and social needs were different. No sign of his personal attention to bookkeeping survives in the household or bailiff's accounts of the late 1690s and early 1700s. Where his father at the same age checked over and scrawled upon dozens of vouchers accompanying each bailiwick account, verifying taxes, repairs, and allowances, the second viscount did not sign or apparently even personally approve the general, comprehensive accounts he received, much less the smaller, more particular ones. Relying on his auditor instead, he only placed his approving signature on the accounts he kept with Joseph Wilson, his broker in London, and these he passed less than once a year.[56] He manifested little interest

54. RUEA 1701.
55. "The Rents of the Farms of . . . Viscount Townshend . . . 1701," RBF/CT 1700–40s; "A rental of Lord Townshend's estate in Suffolk," 22 June 1700, RU, non-Norfolk [NRO]; "Mr. Manning's baylwick accompts explained," 14 March 1703, RBF/CT 1700–40s.
56. "Mr. Wilsons Account," 1709–20, RUBV, signed by CT seven times in eleven years.

in scrutinizing sheep and wool sales, and when it came to tenant repairs, he relied heavily on his bailiff's judgment to authorize them.[57] Nor did seigneurial rights much concern him, except in rare discussions of the profits that a manorial court had yielded. Even the leases that merited the second viscount's attention were usually those with his most substantial tenants, Tubbing and Dunn at South Creake, Ruding of Toftrees, the troublesome Stagg at Shipdham. The conclusion is clear: with the employment of more efficient accounting procedures, Townshend did not have to be as attentive to detail as his father had been.

Yet despite this indifference to the fine points of accounting and management, details that fascinated his father, the second viscount exhibited his own sort of interest. Until his departure for Holland as ambassador, he clearly ran the estate, although over the decade to 1709 the nature of his supervision changed. As this time passed, he focused more on major problems and on decisions relating to the most significant income-producing elements of his lands. He always set the date for the annual audit of accounts, controlled the disposition of timber, and followed closely the return of rent money to his bankers in London. Nor was he indifferent to peculation and the rare instances of venality he found among his employees.[58] In addition, he devoted time to the cultivation of his home farm, partly for economic reasons (it supplied many needs in city and country—oats for horses, barley for malt, meat for the table), and partly because of his interest in agricultural experiment and improvement, an interest apparently absent in his father's case.[59]

While Townshend's attention was thus fundamentally selective, he still had more than a haphazard sense of his estate. Thomas Warde, the bailiff, provided full information about country life when his master was in the city; the sheer detail of Warde's early letters assumes Townshend's continuing interest in and close familiarity with his land, its tenants, and previous decisions about cultivation and management. Into the early 1700s, Townshend knew his tenants and their personalities well enough to confront the obstinacy of one or the unreliability of another. Not surprisingly, he had more command over details about

57. Admittedly, sheep husbandry was deemphasized because CT leased most of the foldcourses, whereas HT kept them in hand. For a rare comment, see TW to CT, 10 December 1703, RBF/CT 1692–1704. On repairs, see CT to TW, 16 May 1704, RBF/CT 1692–1704, but also H. Sorrell to R. Walpole, 2 March 1699, CUL, C(H) corr. #58.

58. See CT to TW, 12 July 1704, and W. Watts to TW, 8 June 1704, RBF/CT 1692–1704, and same to TW, 29 November, 9 and 16 December 1707, RUC [NRO], and 13 January 1708, RBF/CT 1705–20s.

59. See Beckett, *Aristocracy*, 158–64, who suggests that relatively few home farms served for experimentation, or were useful models when they did.

the farms near Raynham than those elsewhere, just as he knew more about his major tenants than the small ones.[60] He was apprehensive about the "very indifferent circumstances" of John Stagg, farmer of the Shipdham estate purchased in 1704, a prescient concern, considering that Stagg, always promising immediate payment, let his rent fall deeply in arrears.[61] Peter Tubbing (with Stagg, one of "the 2 great ones" among the tenants) was the source of similar misgivings.[62] These difficulties only confirmed Townshend's tendency to address himself primarily to his largest tenants. The same was true with lease negotiations, where Townshend usually intervened directly only when Warde requested his help with the largest tenants, mostly over concessions they demanded.

The landlord's involvement helped resolve controversy no matter who was involved, and his presence in Norfolk—as was the case with his father—had a galvanizing effect on tenants large and small. Directly invoking his name helped solve all manner of problems, and not just those connected with leases. The mere rumor of Townshend's forthcoming appearance at Raynham spurred otherwise recalcitrant workmen at the hall and promoted rent payments from laggard tenants, just as his absence encouraged laxness in these matters.[63] But Thomas Warde rarely sought to engage Townshend on lesser issues, and then only in the early 1700s, when, for example, he bothered him with a minor tenant's request for his married daughter to have use of a farm renting for the inconsequential sum of £4 a year. Instances like this understandably reinforced Townshend's conviction that, because Warde referred such details to him, no large matter was being neglected. Along with demonstrations that Warde's advice was reliable, that belief in turn led Townshend increasingly to defer to his bailiff on all sorts of matters.[64] What immediately concerned the viscount were substantial affairs: what new terms could be got for the Langham farm falling vacant; the arrangement to keep one man on his land at £140 a year; the terms asked for the timber-bearing Scarndale Closes, tenantless in 1709. He played a central part in the on-again, off-again

60. CT to TW, 2 and 24 May 1704, RBF/CT 1692–1704.
61. CT to TW, 6 February 1705, and TW to CT, 23 March 1709, RBF/CT 1705–20s. In November 1706, TW (at CT's order) took a bill of sale for Stagg's goods as security for £474 in back rent: TW to CT, 20 November 1706, Add. 41655, ff. 182–83.
62. TW to CT, 15 March 1706, RBF/CT 1705–20s.
63. TW to CT, 16 February and 22 March 1704, RBF/CT 1692–1704; TW to CT, 24 April, CT to TW, 25 April and 2 May 1704, and 22 April 1706, RBF/CT 1705–20s; [copy] TW to J. Howes, 31 January, and Howes to TW, 10 February 1705, ibid.
64. TW to CT, 31 December 1703, RBF/CT 1692–1704. For example, CT accepted TW's advice on whether to put his servants on board wages in 1704: CT to TW, 25 April 1704, ibid.

negotiations with Peter Tubbing, who threatened in 1709 to leave his farm of £300 per annum when his lease expired a year later.[65] Even from the Netherlands in 1710, Townshend followed negotiations concerning the large farms at South Creake and Toftrees, each of which bulked so large in the estate economy as to warrant attention from overseas.[66] As he grew more aware that he had limited time to bestow upon estate affairs, Townshend ignored the marginal matters that had given texture to his father's landlordship, because his own proprietorship possessed a different, more economically hard-edged quality.

Townshend the Agriculturalist

Concern about his tenants and interest in a constant supply of money are to be expected of any landlord, whether an active innovator or one entirely indifferent to agriculture. Where Townshend parted company with other landowners was in his abiding attention to the estate's broad agrarian regime. Like them, however, he paid close attention to those elements of this regime that brought unique economic benefit, aesthetic satisfactions, or both. As for so many landlords, the trees on the estate, although requiring careful nurture, provided substantial income. This resource could especially be used at times of capital need, and Townshend's closest scrutiny of timber bargains coincided with his early remodeling at the hall, where he also used lumber his property supplied.[67] Both economic and aesthetic considerations influenced decisions with respect to Raynham's gardens. On the one hand, the kitchen garden supplied domestic consumption, and when supply was not required, provided income through the sale of produce.[68] On the other hand, aesthetics figured into management of the decorative features around the hall, including

65. TW to CT, 24 April 1704, 7 and 21 January, 21 June, 9 September, and 17 October 1709; TW to J. Calthorpe, 24 December 1707; CT to TW, 14 February 1709: RBF/CT 1705–20s. W. Watts to TW, 6 January 1708, RUC [NRO].

66. TW to CT, 17 October, 29 December 1709, 23 January, 13 February, 23 March 1710, and TW to S. Poyntz, 31 March 1710, RBF/CT 1705–20s; S. Poyntz to TW, 28 February and 1 April 1710 (NS), NRO, Bradfer-Lawrence, I, c, Townshend State Papers 2; 11 November 1710 (NS), RBF/CT 1705–20s; and 14 November 1710 (NS), RUC [NRO].

67. *AHEW*, 4:677–79; Beckett, *Aristocracy*, 230–31; Stone, *Crisis of the Aristocracy*, 295. TW to CT, 29 November and 10 December 1703, 21 January, 16 February, 3 March, [7–24] April, and 19 May 1704, 9 January and 22 February 1706; TW to [?J. Calthorpe], 15 February 1706; CT to TW, n.d. [postmarked 25 December (1703)], 25 April, 16 and 24 May 1704; W. Watts to TW, 7 December 1703, RBF/CT 1692–1704. General a/cs for 1703–04, RBF/CT Warde 1704; for 1705–09, RUEA 1705–09.

68. W. Watts to TW, 8 June, and TW to CT, 14 June 1704, RBF/CT 1692–1704; Lady Townshend to TW, 3 May 1709, RBF/CT 1705–20s.

orchards and at least nine acres of walk and "wilderness."[69] The salary of £130 a year paid to the gardener indicates his prestigious role in the domestic hierarchy, even if the salary was meant to defray charges (especially labor) his employer would otherwise have borne. The investment in extraordinary garden projects, which cost £350 in 1699 and 1700, testifies to their importance,[70] as does the attention that the setting of lime trees, graveling of walks, and repair of garden walls received in estate correspondence.[71]

Beyond his gardens and woods, Townshend carefully looked over his fields. Despite his nickname, turnips did not bulk large in early estate correspondence.[72] In later years provisos for turnip cultivation became standard lease clauses, but Townshend's personal interest in the early 1700s revolved less around this specific crop than around enclosure, preparation, and rotation of land itself. More earthy still was his preoccupation with ditching and hedging, muck and marl—themselves characteristic features of improvement. These are the matters to which Townshend gave much time at a period when he could do so without restricting his political activities in London. Ditching and hedging signified enclosure and the reorganization of farm land, vital elements in the effort to make production more efficient, extend full cultivation to marginally used land, and increase output per acre. Progress on ditching and hedging work, of which he was kept well informed, understandably pleased Townshend, since it was the precondition to profitable enclosure. Protecting the integrity of enclosures, and deciding where to take in new ones, were chief concerns for Townshend;[73] his greatest anxiety in the severe cold of early 1709 involved (besides the welfare of his deer) the hedges broken by the weight of snow.[74] He alone author-

69. CT was concerned in 1704 about frost damage to the park's lime trees, the "wilderness," and the garden: TW to CT, 31 May 1704, RBF/CT 1692–1704. See also J. Calthorpe to E. Mann, 23 April 1699, RUC [NRO], and entry, 30 May 1701, receivers a/cs 1693–1706, RUBV.

70. Manning's disbursements, RUEA 1703; TW's household a/cs, RUEA 1704–09; Manning's household a/cs, RBF/CT, Manning 1699 and RUEA fragile. Henry Wise from London did the special work; he may have been related to Henry Wise, gardener to Queen Anne.

71. TW to CT, 10 and 19 November 1707, 4 March, 29 April, and 17 October 1709; CT to TW, 5 March 1709; Lady Townshend to TW, 3 May 1709; TW to Lady Townshend, 3 June 1709: RBF/CT 1705–20s.

72. They were, however, grown regularly and used, as elsewhere in the region, to fodder livestock during the winter: E. Kerridge, *The Agricultural Revolution* (London, 1967), 273–74. See TW to CT, 28 May and 12 July 1706, 3 March 1707, 4 and 23 March 1709, RBF/CT 1705–20s; W. Watts to TW, 30 December 1707, RUC [NRO].

73. TW to CT, 22 February 1706 and 8 January 1707, RBF/CT 1705–20s; general a/cs to June 1706 and June 1707, RUEA 1706–07.

74. TW to CT, 2 February and 21 June 1709; CT to TW, 5 and 15 March 1709, RBF/CT 1705–20s.

ized new ditching, usually after making personal observations in Norfolk, after which he had plans of work sent to London so he could follow its course.[75]

Long-term agricultural productivity was affected not only by enclosure but by the soil's fertility, sustained through application of a fertilizing agent and through manipulation of crops.[76] In the former case, dung and marl were the scarce commodities employed, and because of their value Townshend was kept abreast of their use. Warde routinely notified him when marl-digging began each year and gave him details of progress made.[77] Like ditch and hedgework, marling took special time and labor to accomplish, so it was accounted for separately as an extraordinary expenditure in Warde's household accounts, an acknowledgment of its status as capital improvement.[78] Although late-eighteenth-century practice, according to Naomi Riches, was for tenants to undertake marling, that was not exclusively the case earlier: at Raynham the landlord's improving initiative set the pace.[79] With respect to animal fertilizer, beyond what the landlord's sheep and the tenants' stock left on the fields, the manure from the stables and the dung from the pigeon house were additional sources to be applied with discretion. Cleaning the pigeon house, as odd as it sounds, constituted a significant event in the agricultural routine,[80] and where to lay the stable muck was an important decision. Townshend himself determined the application and often had both scarce resources put on the most valuable farm crops, such as winter corn or barley. In 1704 Warde stored the precious pigeon dung, to be spread later "as is needfull where your lordship have ordered"; two years later, Townshend gave special direction *"for an experiment . . .* [to] spread some of the dung upon . . . part of the meadows in the park." These would seem to be the actions of a man engrossed by scientific elements of farming.[81]

75. CT to TW, 12 March 1706, 18 January 1707, 17 February 1708, and 16 February 1709; TW to CT, 6 March 1706, ibid.
76. On fertilizers, see N. Riches, *The Agricultural Revolution in Norfolk,* 2nd ed. (New York, 1967), 77–81; Kerridge, *Agricultural Revolution,* 240–50.
77. TW to CT, 6 March 1704, RBF/CT 1692–1704; CT to TW, 8 March 1706, TW to CT, 15 March, 22 April, 28 May, 12 July 1706, 21 June 1709, and TW to Lady Townshend, 3 June 1709, RBF/CT 1705–20s.
78. TW's general a/cs to June 1706 and June 1707, RUEA 1706–07; TW to CT, 12 July 1706, RBF/CT 1705–20s.
79. Riches, *Agricultural Revolution,* 78 and 171–83 on improvements generally.
80. Keeping pigeons regained popularity after 1660, both as an edible delicacy and for the dung, which was often reserved "for bringing on special crops": *AHEW,* V, 2:575–76.
81. TW to CT and CT to TW, 12 and 16 July 1706, RBF/CT 1705–20s; TW to CT, 16 February 1707, Add. 41655, f. 184, and 24 February 1707, RBF/CT 1705–20s; TW

This engrossment extended into the realm of animal husbandry, even though large-scale cattle breeding for the market (later a lucrative element of Norfolk farming) is not in evidence. The cattle bred and sustained through the first decade of the eighteenth century supplied the needs of the Raynham household and little more: the length of Townshend's stay in the country determined the amount of stock kept in the park.[82] Townshend was nonetheless involved in deciding how and whether to breed his cattle each year, and the presence of "Suffolk cowes" and Scots heifers suggests that livestock husbandry was forward-looking in its principles.[83] Similarly, while the viscount largely left the family's racing and hunting to his brothers, he decided on the purchase, sale, and breeding of horses himself.[84] Unlike his son and grandson, he had no evident interest in bloodlines or "scientific" horse-breeding,[85] but in 1707 he began a breeding project with fowl he obtained from London which were specially fed and segregated from his other birds.[86]

Improvement for both the long and short run lay at the heart of Townshend's estate strategy, as illustrated finally by the disposition he and Thomas Warde made of fields near Raynham in 1707, some of them on Uphill farm, which was then in hand. By early March, Warde had two plow teams working on a daunting schedule, employing Townshend's coach horses along with farm animals. Thus busy, Warde balked when the viscount sought the return of the former to London, arguing that it would delay the farm's improvement, which was intended to make it attractive to a prospective tenant. In these circumstances, Townshend reconsidered his social demands and left the coach horses in the fields of Norfolk.[87]

Sensitive byplay of landlord and bailiff lay at the heart of the successful partnership between Warde and Townshend, demonstrating the

---

to CT, 6 March 1704, RBF/CT 1692–1704; CT to TW, c. 28 February 1706, RBF/CT 1705/20s [emphasis added].

82. When he departed for Holland, for example, CT ordered TW to sell the stock and rent the dairy at Raynham.

83. CT [in W. Watts's hand] to TW, 25 March 1704, RBF/CT 1692–1704; TW to CT, 6 December 1706 and 18 March 1709, RBF/CT 1705–20s.

84. TW to CT, 31 May, and CT to TW, 5 June 1704, RBF/CT 1692–1704; TW to CT, 12 March and 22 April 1706, 3 and 9 March 1707, W. Watts to TW, 6 March 1707, and CT to TW, 15 March and 30 April 1706, 11 March 1707, RBF/CT 1705–20s; W. Watts to TW, 6 April 1706, RUC [NRO].

85. See RBF, "Horses." On the development of scientific breeding, see N. Russell, *Like Engend'ring Like: Heredity and Animal Breeding in Early Modern England* (Cambridge, 1986).

86. W. Watts to TW, 8 February 1707, RUC [NRO].

87. TW to CT, 9 and 21 March 1707, and CT to TW [11 March 1707], ibid. Uphill farm at West Raynham was in hand from 1701: "The rents of the farms . . . in . . . 1701," RBF/CT 1700–40s; a/c of Uphill farm, 20 June 1703, RUEA 1703.

A Time of Transition

importance of mutual trust between master and servant.[88] Yet these detailed interchanges between employer and employee decreased in number and changed their character as the first decade of the century came to an end. Now writing most often about money remitted to London, leases drawn, or wine left after Townshend's departure from Raynham, Warde himself began to distinguish significantly between this domestic business and "the farmeing parte," "our parte of farming," "our outward affayres."[89] This language spoke to an unmistakable shift in estate priorities. When Townshend learned in spring 1709 that he would be sent to Holland as ambassador plenipotentiary, it marked the culmination of the era of transition. The viscount's first instructions to Warde after the appointment understandably dwelt on the need "to return all the money you can" for his coming needs. Seeking cash, he ordered Warde to sell wheat, cheese, and meat left at Raynham, to lease out the dairy, and to dispose of livestock as soon as they were fat enough to sell.[90]

Adequate finance was Townshend's overriding domestic concern while abroad, and when Warde sat down to write of country affairs in late spring 1709, he began by informing Townshend of tenant leases (which related directly to expected income) rather than of crops or ditching or marling.[91] In the months until Townshend returned to England in 1711, this pattern was repeated. Warde spoke of a long lease negotiation, of problems collecting rent and returning money to London for Townshend's use, but detailed discussion of sowing crops, of patterns of cultivation, or of farm improvements was almost entirely lacking.[92] The shift in the content of Townshend's correspondence with his bailiff derived directly from the alteration in his own circumstances, for in Holland the press of official business could not be ignored or avoided, and the ambassador admitted he had "little time to think of my country affairs."[93] Nearly a year into the diplomatic mission, Stephen Poyntz, the ambassador's secretary in The Hague, apologized, saying that "affairs of the greatest moment" had interrupted consideration of the division of a very large farm, which Town-

---

88. J. V. Beckett, *Coal and Tobacco: The Lowthers and the Economic Development of West Cumberland, 1660–1760* (Cambridge, 1981), 27–30, emphasizes such trust.

89. TW to CT, 27 April and 21 June, and TW to Lady Townshend, 16 May 1709, RBF/CT 1705–20s.

90. CT to TW, 26 April, and TW's reply, 29 April 1709, ibid. The latter is unusual for the absence of any discussion of strictly farming-related matters.

91. TW to CT, 21 June 1709, ibid.

92. TW to CT, 22 July, c. 9 September, 17 October, and 29 December 1709, 23 January and 23 March 1710, ibid. TW to CT, 13 February 1710, ibid., exceptionally discusses improvements at South Creake, but in the context of a lease renewal.

93. CT to TW, n.d. [after mid-July 1709 and in reply to TW's of 21 June], ibid.

shend had "forgot to give orders about . . . till very lately."[94] One wonders how many other landlords, similarly confronted by the demands of public life, but not so well served by men like Thomas Warde, found themselves in financial difficulties because they could no longer attend carefully to the detail of estate management.[95]

All the same, Townshend had been distracted from country matters before, although never so much as now. At Christmas 1703 he apologized to Warde that he had "been so busie in Parliament that I have had no time to answer yours"; three months later he dictated a reply to some questions from Warde, leaving his secretary to explain that while Townshend had more to say, his lordship "has not time to answer them now." A similar claim made from Norfolk, where he had been electioneering, excused dilatoriness in writing his London agent during 1705.[96] Another kind of distraction, beyond the press of business, emanated from Townshend himself, suggesting that personality (especially his youth) affected estate management in his case as in his father's. As early as 1699, with Townshend in his midtwenties, some inattention on his part was excused by reference to his "not loving writing letters."[97] The brevity of much of the viscount's surviving correspondence hints that the disinclination remained with him for life. More to the point, in a man who had others to write letters for him, are recurrent signs of inattention and procrastination. More than once he forgot decisions made or choices considered.[98] Writing from Norfolk, his secretary instructed the London man of business that "when you have anything that requires an answer, don't incert it in my Lord's newes cover, but either in [a letter] to Mr. Calthorp or me, for when my Lord . . . getts the cover into his pockett, it may be 2 months . . . ere any answer can be made to it, if at all."[99]

Thomas Warde, who conscientiously sought his master's approval on significant decisions, was often frustrated by Townshend's laxity.[100]

94. Poyntz to TW, 1 April 1710 (NS), NRO, Bradfer-Lawrence, I c, Townshend State Papers 2.
95. Beckett, *Aristocracy*, 150–52, notes that landowners who failed to visit their estates invited mismanagement.
96. CT to TW, c. 25 December 1703, CT [in hand of W. Watts] to TW, and W. Watts to TW, both 25 March 1704: RBF/CT 1692–1704; CT to R. Leman, 13 June 1705, Add. 63079, f. 16.
97. J. Calthorpe to E. Mann, 8 May 1699, RUC [NRO].
98. CT to TW, 5 April 1704, RBF/CT 1692–1704; CT to TW, c. 28 February 1706, RBF/CT 1705–20s; W. Watts to TW, 17 February 1708, ibid.
99. W. Watts to R. Leman, 19 July [1703], RBF/CT 1692–1704. CT once "lost" an apothecary's bill in his pocket: W. Watts to TW, 29 November and 9 December 1707, RUC [NRO], and TW to Watts, 3 December 1707, RBF/CT 1705–20s.
100. TW to CT, 21 January, 16 February 1704, and CT to TW, c.26 January and 25 March 1704; W. Watts to TW, 25 March 1704, RBF/CT 1692–1704.

Townshend recognized his own slowness, as when he tardily returned to Warde the lease of a highly sought tenant, admitting he had been "very idle in not returning sooner the enclosed articles." Warde continually reminded Townshend of unanswered questions and urged other employees to try to elicit some response for him. "Please," he wrote Stephen Poyntz at The Hague, "reminde . . . his Excellency [Townshend] that he would thinke of what I writt . . . about, which I thinke long for."[101] And while Townshend's commitment to estate business should not be measured by his distraction during his time in Holland, the limits to that commitment are nonetheless clear. His character and ambitions diluted single-minded application to country pursuits, and his preoccupation with grand politics (what Chesterfield called his "unwearied application"[102]) eventually forced him to curtail the time given to estate affairs.

Simultaneously, this preoccupation led him to grant his servants more responsibility and trust than ever before. Curiously, perhaps, a period of transition for the Townshend family that began with the ascendancy of the family's trustees ended in a similar fashion. The era of Townshend's maturation in coping with his estate coincided with his retreat from intense involvement with it. The period is neatly marked symbolically by a letter from The Hague to Thomas Warde in mid-summer 1709. In one hundred and fifty words Townshend laid out for Warde the strategy for negotiations over a farm at South Creake; the terms were particularly important because the farm in question was large, with a sixteen-year lease at stake. But Townshend's explanation was necessarily brief. "I am persuaded," he wrote Warde, that "you will easily believe that I have little time here to think of my country affairs," and he concluded, "I have told you how far I am engaged in this matter & must leave the management of this, as well as all my other concerns, entirely to you." While this apparently complete delegation of responsibility should not be taken literally, Townshend now left far more to his employees' discretion than had been the case at any time since he had become an adult.[103] How well Warde and his successors made good on the trust reposed in them is discussed in the next chapter.

101. CT to TW, 14 February 1709; TW to S. Poyntz, 9 November 1709; TW to same, 24 October 1709; TW to CT, 23 January, 13 February 1710, RBF/CT 1705–20s.
102. BL, Stowe 308, f. 14.
103. CT to TW, n.d. [mid-July 1709, in reply to TW's of 21 June], RBF/CT 1705–20s. See S. Poyntz to TW, 1 April 1710 (NS), NRO, Bradfer-Lawrence, I c, Townshend State Papers 2.

※ *Chapter 4* ※

Getting and Spending
The Second Viscount as Landlord

Lord Townshend's appointment as ambassador to The Hague culminated a rapid rise to prominence by the young aristocrat that inevitably altered the nature of his ties to his estate. In the ensuing quarter century of his active political career, Townshend retained control of his estate business, but often he could do so only from long distance or even by proxy. He employed his second wife and then later his eldest unmarried daughter, partly as accountants, partly as conveyors of instructions. The former disbursed money to the household steward at Raynham and in London and took his accounts; there is no indication that her husband ever double-checked her work. Young Dolly Townshend kept the household accounts at Raynham after her father retired, receiving tenants' rent from his hands and paying bills as a household steward might have done.[1] All the same, the Townshend women's involvement in business management apparently did not extend beyond the household into those estate affairs that related strictly to tenants and agricultural policy.[2] In these areas, Townshend's attenuated connection with his estate led him and a succession of stewards and bailiffs to streamline and improve managerial structure

---

1. For Lady Townshend, see a/c of "money received and disbursed" 1723–32, RUBV; household a/cs 1717, 1719–23, RUBV; and W. Fenn's a/cs 1723–25, RUEM/CT. For young Dorothy, see household a/cs 1730–37, RUBV, and "Copy of my sister Dorothy Townshend's account settled at the death of my father," RUBV.

2. W. Fenn's a/cs with Lady Townshend 1723–25, for example, often had no accompanying text at all. When they did, he wrote of the children and of work on the park grounds and the hall: RUEM/CT. He only once wrote about farming business, reporting on the distraint of a tenant's farm and asking leave to plow up a pasture for his own use: 11 November 1724, ibid.

as the years went by. Direct farming was eschewed wherever possible. An inclination to rent to large farmers was facilitated by consolidation of holdings, which created more compact farms, and by granting long-term leases. These developments provided fewer tenants to manage and fewer cracks through which rent could fall before reaching the landlord's pocket. The estate accounts (which yield so much of the evidence on management techniques) took on a leaner and less informative cast over the years, as if Townshend lost interest in the tale of adversity or bounty revealed in detailed accounting and looked only for the balance at account's end. Deteriorating descriptions of tenants' farms in the bailiwick accounts suggest as much: where once a farm had been described in careful terms, often including its acreage, it was sufficient in some accounts by the late 1710s—and universal after 1730—to speak of this one's "farm" *tout court* or of that one's holdings "as per lease."

The streamlining of accounts was part cause and part effect of Townshend's diminished involvement with his lands. The time he had free from Whitehall in the 1710s and 1720s was devoted to broad decisions rather than to the estate details that had drawn his father's eye. Where the first viscount niggled over minutiae, the second viscount attended more to his leases and to the proper cultivation of his land than to every farthing of yield. Proper care here was better rewarded than quibbling over pennies, and he mounted a campaign of land purchases, land exchanges, and capital improvements which dramatically raised the value of his estate. In other words, despite the opportunity to devote himself only part-time to agricultural pursuits, Townshend was the model of an absentee landlord. The means by which he made a success of his farms, and the other factors that materially eased his way in the world, are the focus of this chapter.

If only because his name is associated with modern, improving agricultural methods, an effort to sort out "Turnip" Townshend's agricultural practices and policies is an important one. Recent work has put his activities in a far less dramatic context than was once the case. We know that Townshend did not pioneer the use of turnips or initiate the wide-scale practice of marling land, any more than he invented the Norfolk rotations.[3] Precisely what he did to earn his

---

3. Reevaluation of agricultural innovation in eighteenth-century Norfolk has shown seventeenth- and even sixteenth-century antecedents. See, for example, J. H. Plumb, "Sir Robert Walpole and Norfolk Husbandry," *Economic History Review*, 2nd ser., 5 (1952): 86–89; G. E. Fussell, "'Norfolk Improvers': Their Farms and Methods, A Reassessment," *Norfolk Archaeology* 33 (1964): 332–44; B. Holderness, "East Anglia and the Fens," *AHEW*, V, 1:220–25; E. Kerridge, *The Agricultural Revolution* (London, 1967), 268–76; H. W. Saunders, "Estate Management at Rainham in the Years 1661–1686, and

nickname in fact remains tantalizingly obscure.[4] It is not impossible that he came up to London as a young aristocrat full of farming talk: we have seen already his deep engagement with the estate during his first years on the public stage. Presumably, knowledge of his agrarian interests brought the seemingly inappropriate presents of "bockwheat" and turnip seed from Hanoverian favorites when he was secretary of state.[5] Yet it may be that Townshend's reputation grew less from his conversation (or priority of practice) than from the inevitable prominence that attached to the steps he took.[6] He was the epitome in Norfolk of a county's "natural leader," and his agricultural endeavors may have attracted the county squirearchy's notice as much as did Sir Robert Walpole's political bacchanals. While Thomas Coke at Holkham pursued a line in farming roughly parallel to Townshend's, the future Earl of Leicester was nearly twenty years the viscount's junior and, until well into the reign of George II, his inferior in social profile as well. Townshend's actions were early and uniquely visible.[7]

If leadership was a key to the dissemination and propagation of new farming techniques, then Townshend was perfectly placed to serve as an advocate. One observer believed that the marling he gave his land was aimed at "enriching his tenants," and in retirement he apparently helped them to market their corn.[8] He personally received the rents of tenants at Raynham in the 1730s (a practice unknown to his father), occasions that encouraged the exchange of ideas as well as cash. Although he wrote no treatises and gave no learned papers on agriculture (even though he was a fellow of the

---

1706," *Norfolk Archaeology* 19 (1915–17): 41–46; N. Riches, *The Agricultural Revolution in Norfolk*, 2nd ed. (New York, 1967), 79, 82, 85.

4. Lord Cathcart testified to CT's interest in Scottish improvers and claimed CT learned about turnips in Hanover with George I: *DNB*, "Charles Townshend"; *AHEW*, V, 2:575. Alexander Pope in his imitations of Horace assumed that Townshend's alliteratively apt turnips would be familiar to his readers: J. Butt, ed., *The Poems of Alexander Pope* (New York, 1946), 4:185. Yet William Marshall's *Rural Economy of Norfolk* (2 vols., London, 1787) omitted any specific reference to Townshend, even in the section on "turneps" (256–300).

5. Payment to Count Bothmer's servant for turnip seed, 26 June 1721, household extraordinary a/cs 1719–23, RUBV; entries of 10 February 1724, London household a/cs 1723–25, RUBV, and 5–12 August 1727, extraordinary a/cs 1726–32, RUBV.

6. On the limited effect of the improving landowner, see P. Horn, "The Contribution of the Propagandist to Eighteenth-Century Agricultural Improvement," *Historical Journal* 29 (1982): 313–17.

7. Plumb, *Walpole*, 2:88–90; R. A. C. Parker, *Coke of Norfolk: A Financial and Agricultural Study, 1707–1842* (Oxford, 1975), chap. 4. Coke was made Knight of the Garter in 1725, created Baron Lovel in 1728, joint postmaster general in 1733, and Viscount Coke and Earl of Leicester in 1744: GEC, *Peerage*, "Leicester."

8. *Gentleman's Magazine* 22 (October 1752): 453; CT to S. Buckley, 21 December [1730], Sydney Papers, Clements Library, University of Michigan.

Royal Society from 1706), he quietly spent the last eight years of his life on his estate, making his influence felt by instruction among his tenants and by example.[9]

A tiny fragment of published correspondence has hitherto provided our chief clues about Townshend the farmer.[10] Material now available—correspondence, individual bailiwick accounts, leases, household accounts, and files of bills and vouchers—affords an examination of his relations with tenants, his extensive enclosure and consolidation of landholdings, his attention to details of cultivation, and the financial calculus that underpinned all these dealings. What emerges is the complex picture of an aggressive landlord, served by competent employees, prospering as he pursued a model course of agricultural improvement and modernization on his estate. It is the profile of an engineer of agricultural change.

Income

The place to begin assessing Townshend's role as landlord and improving farmer is with the financial measure of his success and especially a notion of his income: in the final analysis, increased yields of rent brought Townshend much of the prosperity he enjoyed. He himself judged the changes he wrought on his estate in financial terms, bragging to the Earl of Oxford in 1732 that by enclosing, marling, and sowing turnips, he had increased his patrimony by £900 a year.[11] On the estate as a whole, the rise in rental value, aided by new purchases, was much greater.

Sources of nonrental estate income fluctuated from year to year and survive haphazardly in the accounts. Their extent is difficult to assess, but manorial fines and court profits averaged £100 each year until 1723; thereafter, when Townshend's heir Lord Lynn received the profits of the Suffolk and Shipdham estates upon his marriage, they dropped to £20. These low figures reflect the weakness of feudal obligations in Norfolk, which generated little income from a

---

9. N. Kent, *General View of the Agriculture of the County of Norfolk* . . . (London, 1796), 40, records the legend that CT introduced turnip cultivation from Hanover "and recommended it strongly to his own tenants"; from there the cultivation "gradually spread over this county." On the influence of good examples, see Riches, *Agricultural Revolution*, 32–34; J. Thirsk, "Agricultural Innovations and their Diffusion," *AHEW*, V, 2:560–81, especially 574–75; and A. Young, *Political Arithmetic. Containing Observations on the Present State of Great Britain* . . . (London, 1774; reprinted New York, 1907), 167–77.

10. Saunders, "Estate Management," 39–66.

11. HMC, *Portland MSS*, 6:159. Presumably he meant this was the increased value on the acreage left him by his father.

landlord's putative manorial rights.[12] Sales of grain, dairy produce, wool, and livestock averaged £58 a year between 1701 and 1730, bringing in over £100 only exceptionally; timber sales were more valuable sources of occasional income and topped £400 a year in 1725–26 and 1728–29. The average for such miscellaneous income between 1706 and 1730 came to £350, but this figure is inflated by unusual yields in the late 1720s.[13] Such sums were not negligible in Townshend's fiscal balance, but they show that casual profits and production for market were tangential elements of the Raynham farm economy. Despite references to Scots cattle and dairying that appear in the 1706 accounts,[14] the evidence of significant market-farming is thin. The cattle grazed on the park were meant primarily for the table at Raynham, and as the steward William Prestland noted in 1719, "the produce of the dairy [was] applyed to the use of the family."[15]

Up to 1723, then, the nominal rents of Table 4.1 were augmented by nearly £500 a year,[16] thereafter by about £325, but Charles Townshend's actual receipts only indirectly reflected putative rents. All sorts of accidents intervened to prevent him from receiving full rent, yet the rental itself remained the only guide he had to estimate revenues or plan budgets: little had changed in this respect since the 1650s. The absence of realistic forecasts of income—the absence of any apparent concern to *determine* real income—is a reminder of how far from modern the accounting procedures of landowners remained. Even Edward Laurence's *Duty and Office of a Land Steward*,[17] which spelled out proper methods for making estate surveys, valuing individual farms, and accounting with tenants, nonetheless omitted any mention of how to calculate the real return on one's land. Ironically, the sole evidence of efforts to discover real returns

12. See Parker, *Coke*, 37. Townshend's annual fines from Suffolk averaged £26, those at Shipham £54. Norfolk's six other bailiwicks averaged £22: RUEA and RUEA[S], 1700–23.

13. This miscellaneous income is recorded in the 21 general a/cs and 13 annual household a/cs that survive for these years: RUEA. Running household a/cs from January 1731 to March 1737, RUBV, record only £330 received in miscellaneous income; more was probably accounted for in the missing steward's a/cs.

14. These signaled CT's forwardness to N. Riches: *Agricultural Revolution*, 32, citing Saunders, "Estate Management."

15. Household a/cs in RBF/CT Warde 1704, RBF/CT 1702–19, RUEA 1719 (Prestland's quotation) and 1724. Sales of dairy products for £3 in 1704 and five "old cows" for £14 in 1709 scarely constitute large-scale activity. See Stone, *Crisis*, 298, on consumption of meat by a noble household.

16. The total averaged £465 p.a., £90 from Suffolk, and £375 from Norfolk, the latter sum made up of £75 in fines (£50 p.a. from Shipdham) and £300 in miscellaneous sales.

17. 2nd ed., London, 1731; reprinted New York, 1979.

TABLE 4.1
Norfolk Rentals, 1701–1737

Bailiwick	1701	1704	1716	1723	1730	1731	1737
Raynham	£1,658	£1,653	£2,163	£2,597	£2,729	£2,895	£3,328
South Creake	303	303	493	522	562	559	562
Stiffkey	424	414	410	412	412	402	474
Langham and Morston	440	437	447	568	585	583	609
East and West Rudham	796	798	933	1,074	1,164	1,184	1,258
Stibbard and Ryburgh	104	105	104	151	160	160	160
Shipdham (bought 1704; to Lord Lynn in 1723)	—	305	401	—	—	—	—
Suffolk lands (to Lord Lynn in 1723)	1,222	1,200	[1,200]	—	—	—	—
TOTAL	£4,947	£5,215	£6,151	£5,324	£5,612	£5,783	£6,391

SOURCES: "An Account of the Estate ... in ... 1701 and ... 1730," RUE; "An Account of the Estate ... in ... 1701 and ... 1737," ibid.; bailiff's a/cs, RUEA 1704, 1716, 1723, 1731; RUEA[S] 1701, 1704.

on the Townshend estate dates from the indebted period in the first viscount's life.

While a landlord could ignore calculations meant to discover real returns, he still had to consider the impact of rent arrears and legitimate tenant allowances on disposable income. On the first score, the second viscount encountered less delinquency than his father. Information on defaulting tenants in the eighteenth century is sparse, but where it survives it shows that delinquency posed a relatively small problem from year to year.[18] Starting in 1732, annual accounts recorded each tenant's arrears still unpaid after a full year (Table 4.2). Arrears of 10 percent of the annual rental (as recorded in 1736 and 1737) are not to be dismissed lightly, but they do not compare in extent with the respites, valued at a full year's rental, which the first viscount encountered in the late seventeenth century. Moreover, arrears on the second viscount's accounts were short-lived, and only a minority of late-paying tenants ran behind with their payments in consecutive

18. RUEA 1708; RBF/CT 1702–19 for 1709 and 1713 lists. Unfortunately, the decade 1713–23, identified as one of rising arrears, is not well covered by the Townshend acounts: *AHEW*, V, 2:80.

TABLE 4.2
Rent Outstanding One Year after Due, 1732–1738

Year	Farm rents due	Previous year's arrears	Arrears as percent of rent
1732	£5,921	£155	3%
1733	6,184	156	3
1734	6,171	293	5
1735	6,230	487	8
1736[a]	4,450	479	11
1737	6,382	641	10
1738	6,978	373	5

SOURCE: RUEA 1732–38, and RUEA [1988] 1730–78.
[a] Only one of the two compendium accounts of tenants survives for this year.

years. While many farmers were months late with rent, there was no endemic delinquency among the Townshend tenants in the 1730s.[19]

Arrears in any event might only delay the receipt of a landlord's income, but allowances to tenants ate permanently into cash receipts. Of these deductions, by far the most significant in the first third of the eighteenth century were those made for taxes and repairs, as Table 4.3 shows.[20] Because the amount of the deductions varies according to the number of surviving bailiwick accounts, the percentage of gross rent consumed by these allowances is more significant than the absolute sums expended.

In the aggregate, the allowance figures show that one-fourth of the rental was allowed to tenants for taxes, repairs, and other expenditures between 1701 and 1730.[21] In the 1700s and 1710s, however, allowances often exceeded 30 percent, while after 1730 they fell well under 20 percent. The former levels are exceptionally high when compared with other eighteenth-century estates, where figures under 15 percent

19. When accounts were taken at March audits in the early 1670s, half or more of the rent was often unpaid. By the 1730s the audit occurred in January, and payment by tenants was more timely. For example, in January 1733, of £4,160 in rent due, £3,455 had been paid, and £380 allowed for taxes and repairs, while £325 remained in arrears: Raynham "collection" a/c, RUEA 1732. Nationally, arrears seem to have been rising in the 1730s: *AHEW*, V, 2:80–81.

20. It must be stressed that "repairs" extended beyond buildings to upkeep in the fields. Tenants made most repairs and took the cost as a deduction from rent, except as custom and lease covenants otherwise dictated. All tenants usually bore the cost of carrying materials and maintaining hedges, fences, and ditches; larger tenants usually paid for a specified number of days' work of thatchers and plasterers around their buildings. Local rates were universally borne by tenants, parliamentary taxes by the landlord. Cf. *AHEW*, V, 2:224–27.

21. Obviously, this conclusion assumes that surviving accounts are representative of the entire estate.

TABLE 4.3
Farm Rents and Tenant Allowances, 1701–1738

Year	Nominal farm rents[a]	Taxes Amount	Taxes Percent	Repairs Amount	Repairs Percent	Other Amount	Other Percent
1701	£3,709	£549	15%	£800	21%	£18	0%
1702	2,702	526	19	482	18	10	0
1703	2,918	474	16	434	15	22	1
1704	4,075	790	19	782	19	87	2
1705	4,042	841	21	489	12	23	1
1706	2,864	477	17	285	10	63	2
1707	504	155	31	84	17	50	10
1708	—	—	—	—	—	—	—
1709	1,396	287	20	186	13	8	1
1710	—	—	—	—	—	—	—
1711	1,743	367	21	346	20	153	9
1712	3,743	495	13	512	14	186	5
1713	3,347	153	5	279	8	286	9
1714	813	54	7	134	16	105	13
1715	—	—	—	—	—	—	—
1716	4,951	598	12	777	16	93	2
1717	917	116	13	135	15	55	6
1718	448	64	14	16	4	—	—
1719	4,092	517	13	391	10	140	3
1720	4,647	530	11	666	14	158	3
1721	2,507	298	12	499	20	63	2
1722	2,707	282	10	445	16	43	2
1723	4,912	385	8	1,028	21	151	3
1724	2,217	157	7	395	18	55	2
1725	584	40	7	109	19	—	—
1726	1,105	79	7	206	19	7	1
1727	1,517	171	11	256	17	5	0
1728	3,571	437	12	526	15	151	4
1729	582	62	11	30	5	—	—
1730	5,647	481	8	579	10	186	3
1731	5,783	380	7	666	11	102	2
1732	5,921	258	4	583	10	—	—
1733	6,184	191	3	471	8	252	4
1734	6,171	286	5	847	14	107	2
1735	6,230	431	7	559	9	112	2
1736	4,450	254	6	371	8	57	1
1737	6,382	394	6	536	8	179	3
1738	6,978	417	6	381	5	141	2

SOURCE: RUEA, passim. Accounts are also found in RUEA [fragile]; RBF, 17C a/cs 1606–86; RBF/CT 1702–19; RBF/CT Warde's a/cs 1690, 1695–96; RBF/CT Warde's a/cs 1692–93; RBF/CT Warde's a/cs 1697; RBF/CT Warde's a/cs 1704; RBF/CT Manning's a/cs 1697; RBF/CT Manning's a/cs 1698; RBF/CT Manning's a/cs 1699; RL drawer 69, 70, 74, 100, 102, 108, 109, 111

[a] Rentals represent nominal rents on bailiwicks where accounts survive in a given year; allowance totals are only for these bailiwicks.

are more usual.[22] Part of the elevation might be explained by the fact that in areas relatively near London (like Norfolk) the land tax at 4s. on the pound actually represented a 20 percent levy,[23] but even so, Townshend's tax burden clearly exceeds that on the Cokes' Norfolk estate.[24] From 1701 through 1711 taxes fluctuated between 15 and 21 percent of gross rental; with the end of the continental war, burdens fell, but (with three exceptions) remained above 10 percent of gross from 1716 to 1729. Thereafter they diminished, as tax assessments did not change to reflect an increasing rental. Still, the payments amply demonstrate the continuing heavy burden of taxation imposed on early-eighteenth-century landowners.

Taxes were not the only significant source of tenant allowances, however, and the magnitude of allowances on Townshend's estates is also attributable to generous deductions for tenant repairs.[25] Outlays here were highest in the nine years from 1720 to 1728, when they stayed above 14 percent of gross rent, but before 1720 there were many years when repairs ran as high. After 1728 these expenditures dropped, partly because Townshend in retirement could keep close check on them. It may also be that earlier major repairs (and new building) allowed maintenance of tenants' premises without substantial cost. The significance of these allowances remains clear, reflecting an acceptance by Townshend of the wisdom and ultimate benefit to the landowner of encouraging in tenants a conscientious approach to their farms. To allow nearly 13 percent of gross rental in the form of deductions for repairs was a generous and farsighted policy.[26]

In the end, it was this kind of encouragement that ultimately increased the landlord's income. Precise calculations of disposable net income are as elusive in Charles Townshend's estate history as in his father's, so the rental values of the estate are the best gauge of the son's success as well. They show decisively that the rent of his entire estate rose over one-third between 1701 and 1723, and that of his Norfolk land by 70 percent between 1701 and 1737. The sources of this increase must now be examined.

22. Beckett, *Aristocracy*, 201–3.
23. *AHEW*, V, 2:177–78.
24. There taxes amounted to 17 percent of gross rent in 1708–10, and 9 percent in 1722: R. A. C. Parker, "Direct Taxation on the Coke Estates in the Eighteenth Century," *English Historical Review* 71 (1956): 247–48.
25. Outlays for repairs have been calculated only from sums specified as such in the bailiwick accounts; payments for new building and other work that constituted improvement have been excluded. Thus the figures here are minimums.
26. By way of comparison, Thomas Coke at Holkham laid out 8 percent of gross rent between 1722 and 1759 on capital improvements and about the same amount on "running repairs": *AHEW*, V, 2:249.

TOWNSHEND THE ACQUIRER

There are obstacles to any effort to reconstruct Townshend's acquisitions. The absence of maps and the patchwork survival of accounts and leases make it difficult to delineate the role new acreage played in augmenting the estate's worth. The changing descriptive character of the accounts also raises difficulties. In seventeenth and early-eighteenth-century bailiwick accounts, each entry gave an idea of a particular farm's history, describing its acreage and the names of current and previous tenants and even previous owners. After about 1710 the descriptions omitted the acreage held, and by the 1720s they recorded only the rent of such a one's farm "as per lease," a formula that underlines the growing importance of written leases but frustrates delineation of specific farms. After 1730 the ability to identify tenants' holdings diminishes further, because each year's six separate bailiwick accounts were replaced by two compendium accounts, which merely listed tenants by name and recorded their rent, arrears, taxes, and the cash payments they had made. The accounts follow a roughly geographic arrangement, but the records themselves no longer claim to be the artifacts of a territorial unit like the manor or bailiwick; rather, they describe a fiscal and administrative unit denominated a "collection."

The new arrangement of accounts coincided with Townshend's presence in retirement on his estate, where he began personally to receive tenants' rent. Knowing his lands well, perhaps he needed no description of particular tenants' holdings. Yet the shift in terminology and procedure surely also reflects a broader development and reveals the increasingly bureaucratic and commercially rational cast taken on by estate management at Raynham. The fact that farms were described by reference to leases presumes that these documents were normal features of estate management and were available for easy reference; the impersonality of the records suggests an increasing distance between landlord or manager and tenant. These changes signal a new function for the accounts, which were no longer intended to enable a paternalist landlord to keep in touch with his multitude of tenants and exercise his influence in the countryside. Instead, the accounts allowed a businesslike landlord to keep track of improvement, experiment, and profit and loss. So much at least is suggested by the fact that, after 1730, one column of the "collection" accounts kept track specifically of "cash payd"; a designated "cash account" (the first among the Raynham manuscripts) survives for 1732.[27]

27. RUEA 1730, 1732. See similar cash accounts in RUEA 1734. One problem for the historian is that these accounts, significant though their very existence is, contain much less detail than the earlier ones.

TABLE 4.4
Sources of Increase in Rental Value on Norfolk Bailiwicks, 1701–1737

Bailiwick	Total	By purchase	By improvement	Newly leased[a]	Unknown
Creake	£255	£255	£—	£—	£—
Langham	170	50	120	—	—
Raynham	1,670	600	700	190	180
Rudham	460	80	280	100	—
Stibbard	55	—	55	—	—
Stiffkey	50	—	—	—	50

SOURCE: As for Table 4.3
[a] Lands once farmed directly and now rented out.

Even in the absence of clinically precise measures, it is clear that the growth in the value of Townshend's estate is the result of expanded acreage and improved productivity together. Merely a glance at the estate records reveals the inaccuracy of the Earl of Chesterfield's claim (meant as a paean to Townshend's rectitude in office) that he "did not add one acre to his estate."[28] A step-by-step examination of the six Norfolk bailiwicks Townshend held through his entire adult life goes beyond exposing Chesterfield's *blague;* it charts the estate's complex and dynamic growth (see Table 4.4).

The contribution to a rising rental made by purchases, improvement, and a shift from direct farming to leasing land varied from bailiwick to bailiwick.[29] At Langham and Morston there was nearly a 30 percent increase in rents, from 7s. to 9s. an acre, around 1720. At Stibbard a 50 percent jump in the rent there from £105 to £160 resulted from improvements made after Townshend failed to obtain a commons enclosure agreement.[30] The most spectacular increase took place on the East Raynham lands, where the rental grew by £1,000 from 1701 to 1730 and doubled in value from 1701 to 1737. Here, between 1701 and 1720, the rise in rent from £1,600 to £2,200 is almost equally attributable to purchase and improvement (some rents rose by 4s. an acre), although some land previously held in hand was

---

28. BL, Stowe 308, f. 14.

29. For purchases see indentures, 3 December 1707, RUEM/CT; 11/12 November 1707. 26/27 September and 28/29 September 1720, RUE deeds; 15/16 January 1717, 6/7 January 1729, 23/24 July 1730, RL drawer 93; 27/28 January 1718, RL drawer 117; mortgage assignments, 2 January and 15 December 1719, RL drawer 116; June 1706 Rudham great ground a/c, RUEA 1706; 1709 Rudham a/c, RBF/CT 1702–19; Rudham a/cs, RUEA 1721 and after; Langham a/cs, RUEA 1723, 1729; entry, 26 July 1707, general a/c, RUEA 1707. For improvements and direct farming, see RUEA, passim.

30. Langham and Morston rentals, RUEA 1718, 1720; Stibbard agreement, 18 November 1719, RL drawer 118; lease with J. Lee, 3 April 1729, RL drawer 117.

now farmed out.³¹ After 1720, meadow lands that had been improved to yield 10s. per acre further raised the total rent,³² and between 1723 and 1737 it rose from £2,300 to £3,300 per annum. Most of the final growth derived from rent increases, attendant upon consolidation of farms (occasionally through purchase) and otherwise justified by improvements. It is a sign of the landlord's potent role as direct manager that the bulk of this improvement took place when Townshend was at Raynham in retirement.³³

Improvement and subsequent rent hikes constitute the most important factor in enhancing rental values on the entire estate from 1701, contributing over 40 percent of the growth. New acquisitions accounted for nearly as much of the rise, costing upwards of £20,000 between Townshend's coming of age and his death.³⁴ Such an outlay, and the estimated annual yield of £980 from the new lands, compare favorably with the £1,070 in yearly value that Thomas Coke added to his Norfolk estate by purchase between 1718 and 1746.³⁵ Townshend was not the only large landowner in Norfolk adding to his rent roll.

Among Townshend's purchases, two large ones (for the manor of Shipdham and for the manor of Castleacre in South Creake), as well as a group made around 1720 in Shereford near Raynham, stand out most of all. Each provides a different object lesson about the motives to buy. At Shipdham Townshend bought a rather distant property, at odds with his normal propensity to consolidate nearby holdings. Nonetheless, the lands there lay together and were farmed by a single large tenant, which clearly recommended them. The tenant, John Stagg, who stayed on under Townshend, turned out to be a man given to procrastination, broken promises, and slow payment of rent.³⁶ The Shipdham estate even so proved a worthwhile

---

31. Conveyances, 16 October 1706, RUE deeds [NRO], and 3 December 1712, RL drawer 92. A comment that 260 new acres was yielding "full rent" of 10s. an acre in 1712 suggests it was first leased at a concessionary rent, with an increase after improvement: Raynham a/c, RUEA 1712, 1713, 1716.

32. Cf. Raynham a/cs for 1720 and 1723, RUEA.

33. Increases include that of Hammond at East Raynham from £68 to £131 (1731–33); Stringer at West Raynham from £111 to £161 (1730–32); and Clement at Helhoughton from £111 to £148 (1731–33). Consolidating purchases are noted in the 1723 general a/c, RUEA; indentures, 6 March 1731, RL drawer 77, and 16 September 1731, RUEM/CT; Raynham household a/cs, 1730–37, RUBV.

34. This figure ignores CT's willingness in 1729 to pay £17,000 for Henry Kelsall's lands in Colkirk, Gately, and Hempton. The deal was not concluded before CT's death and hung in the offing as late as 1740: indenture, 22 May 1729, RUE deeds [NRO], and Colkirk rentals, n.d., 1735, 1737, 1740, RL drawer 92.

35. Coke spent at least £22,800 (my calculation): Parker, *Coke*, 27, 38–39. Parker figures that Coke by improvement increased rents some 44 percent from 1718 to 1759.

36. Stagg was later replaced by five tenants who collectively paid £20 less than his £400 rent: Shipdham a/c, RUEA 1716.

if expensive investment, financed by the marriage portion brought to Townshend by his first wife and meant to provide, as it later did, a compact estate for his son Charles's use during Townshend's life.[37] In 1706, Townshend made a second major purchase, securing for £2,700 Castleacre manor in South Creake, where he already possessed a sizable estate he wanted to expand. As with the Shipdham lands, this new acreage lay consolidated within the parish, so it was a logical purchase. Under the previous owner it had been in the hands of a single farmer, who continued as tenant under Townshend, creating in Creake a substantial farm that sustained large tenant farmers in ensuing years.[38]

Purchasing discrete farms, large or small, provided freestanding elements for one's estate. Nevertheless, buying separate parcels of land to consolidate one's own holdings was perhaps even more necessary for an improving landlord than acquiring farms,[39] as Townshend's campaign at Shereford revealed. A series of consolidating purchases improved efficiency and might please tenants, but it was usually a prolonged matter.[40] In the early 1720s Townshend benefited from the unusually active land market generated by the South Sea Bubble and moved rapidly. Robert Britiffe, his legal advisor, reported in the summer of 1720 that "every thing sell[s] now, little as well as great estates," although the volatile land market offered no bargains. As Britiffe cautioned another client, "people make such demands for estates that purchasers must be very sanguine to buy."[41] Sanguine Townshend was, spending over £3,100 in twenty different purchases from 1720 to 1723, as he began a campaign to unify lands in Shereford and West Raynham, parishes neighboring his hall and park. The rental at Shereford, £15 a year

---

37. CT spent £8,500 in 1703 on lands of £395 p.a., 21½ years' purchase, and £500 the next year for lands worth £35 p.a. Deeds, 18, 25–26 October 1703, RBF/CT 1700–40; articles of agreement, 18 October 1704, RUE; recovery of Shipdham manor, 29 November [1704], RU, Norfolk deeds [NRO]. Indenture, 27 February 1705, RUS, indicates that the marriage portion paid for this land and land costing £1,150 in Suffolk.

38. Deeds, 2–4 December 1707, RUE; W. Watts to TW, 16 December [1707], RUC [NRO]; R. Donne's lease with W. Dove, 1 April 1700, RL drawer 99; Creake a/cs, RUEA 1709, 1711, and for 1712, RL drawer 70.

39. See *AHEW*, V, 2:177–86.

40. W. Prestland to R. Britiffe, 10, 17, and 20 December 1716; E. Rolfe to same, 12 January 1717, RBF/CT 1700–40; S. Poyntz to [?], n.d. [December 1716], RBF/CT 1705–20s.

41. R. Britiffe to CT, 18 July 1720, RBF/LL, Britiffe; Plumb, *Walpole*, 1:310. On the elevated land prices, see P. G. M. Dickson, *The Financial Revolution in England* (London, 1967), 146, n. 5; *AHEW*, V, 2:173; and C. Clay, "The Price of Freehold Land in the Later Seventeenth and Eighteenth Centuries," *Economic History Review*, 2nd ser., 27 (1974): 173–89. The last identifies an explosion of prices after 1720.

in 1720, rose to £354 in 1723, and as a consequence of consolidation, the bulk of the land there was brought into just four farms, charged with over 90 percent of the rent.[42] The Shereford purchases showed the wisdom of building on existing Townshend holdings.[43] Townshend also showed flexibility in acquiring the lands he sought. One yeoman sold a house, yards, and 3½ acres in Shereford field for £110 and the promise that his widowed mother could remain in the house until her death. A Shereford carpenter sold his land but retained the right to his house while he and his wife were living. Other sellers delayed taking the purchase money from Townshend, receiving the interest on it as a pension in the meantime.[44]

Purchase of land, in whatever amount or shape, provided one means to consolidate holdings and create compact farms; exchanges of land between one owner and another offered another. Townshend's father had employed exchanges in a limited fashion when expanding his park in the 1660s, an example the second viscount followed, exchanging lands in parishes near the hall rather than further afield.[45] Despite occasional altercations over the boundaries of lands involved,[46] exchanges served several useful functions for the landlord. Facilitating enclosure was a primary one, as exchanged land was almost invariably "intermixed" with what Townshend already possessed. In the late 1720s and early 1730s he also made exchanges in return for acreage he had appropriated "for makeing the roads" in his landscaping scheme.[47] Consolidation also appears to have been "connected with . . . psychological satisfaction and a desire for neatness and order."[48] For Townshend, both exchanges and purchases helped to create a more impressive, manageable, and profitable estate. Without a well-examined, carefully controlled policy for leases, however, consolidation would have gone for naught.

42. Improvement accounted for some of the increase, too. See Raynham a/cs, RUEA 1720, 1722, 1723 for rentals; the next surviving a/c after 1723 notes Shereford rentals of £447: RUEA 1728. Most of the consolidation took place in 1720: RUE deeds.

43. The descriptions of the conveyed land show how interspersed it was with CT's land, e.g., Henry Mallett's 14½ acres were contained in twenty-one scattered holdings dispersed in the open field: indenture, 29 September 1720, RUE deeds.

44. Conveyances, 29, 27/28, 26/27 September 1720, respectively, RUE deeds; interest payments in 1723 and 1724 general a/cs, RUEA.

45. Thirty of thirty-one exchanges made in 1702–36 involved land in the Raynham bailiwick accounts.

46. See problems with P. Stringer: exchange, 8 June 1703, and n.d. paper, RBF/CT 1696–1735; TW to CT, 31 January 1707, RBF/CT 1705–20s.

47. Sir F. Andrews to CT, 18 September 1711, RBF/CT 1705–20s, offered to exchange intermixed lands. Note in hand of R. Britiffe, n.d. [1720s–30s], RL drawer 118, refers to the roads.

48. *AHEW*, V, 2:179.

TOWNSHEND THE LEASER

Townshend's energetic application to business in his early adulthood has been explored amply in the last chapter. He did not suddenly become indifferent to estate business in 1709; there was no sharp break with past practice. Cultivation on the home farm and on lands temporarily untenanted shows particular signs of Townshend's continuing influence. In these lands, he had a laboratory in which to follow a course of agricultural improvement, although it was not especially profitable.[49] Elsewhere, Townshend's rocketing political career nonetheless left its mark on estate business. Changes that streamlined the accounts (and provided less detail for whoever perused them) point to a more remote control by the landlord than had previously been the case. The deaths of Thomas Warde, bailiff and steward, in 1710, of the auditor Edward L'Estrange in 1715, and of James Calthorpe in 1717 broke connections with the past. After the death of Warde, the depth and detail of communication between landowner and subsequent stewards diminished. During his politically active years, Townshend necessarily deputed to employees the authority to act independently on all sorts of small decisions, although they still had guidelines to follow. The one area where his attention remained sharp, however, was the all-important one of leasing.

Here a number of changes occurred, significant not just for Townshend's own agricultural regime but for the broad course of agrarian change in England. The emergence of innovative and productive schemes of cultivation is explored in detail below, but just as notable as the changes in what tenants were doing were changes in the character of the tenants themselves. First of all, the number of small tenants, those with farms under £20 annual rent, diminished even more strikingly than under the first viscount. At Rudham, where there were 35 minor farmers in the 1660s, a steady diminution occurred in the eighteenth century: 14 small tenants in 1701, 10 in 1716, only 3 in 1732. On lands in Langham and Morston, 40 minor tenants in 1677 fell to 18 by 1687, a figure that further declined to 12 in 1713 and to 6 by 1731. Nine small tenants at Stiffkey in 1701 fell to 3 in 1731. Even at Raynham, where frequent small purchases of land increased tenant numbers until new farms were consolidated with existing ones, minor tenants were far fewer than under the first viscount. At Stibbard they shrank by half from the mid-1690s to only 6 in the 1710s and none at all in 1731. Twelve small farmers at South Creake during the 1690s,

49. See accounts of Uphill farm in hand, RUEA fragile (to June 1702) and RUEA 1703 (to June 1703); accounts of Mill Ollands farm in hand, RUEA 1716, 1717, 1719, 1720; Stibbard a/c 1712, RL drawer 70; Stibbard a/c 1713, RBF/CT 1702–19.

when most land there was farmed in hand, were replaced by a solitary minor tenant of £3 per annum in 1701.[50]

As with the first viscount, there is no evidence in his son's time that the disappearance from Townshend's rent rolls of marginally significant farmers masked a policy of subleasing by his large tenants. If it had been profitable for large tenants to sublet, then why would Townshend himself not keep on these smaller farmers? The attrition of smallholders, long identified as a characteristic development of late-seventeenth and early-eighteenth-century land ownership,[51] is plainly evident on the Townshend estates, and the number of large tenants farming under the second viscount rose in a contrastingly great proportion. In part, the increase reflects the augmentation of the estate's overall value, since the benchmark used to identify "large farmers" can only be rental values, not acreage. As noted before, the rent of lands on many farms rose from 7s. to as high as 10s. an acre in the course of only a few years as a result of improvements. Still, the disappearance of small tenants contributed to the rising number of large rentals. In 1690 the Townshend holdings in Norfolk included only 18 farms valued at a rent of £40 or more; only 6 were worth in excess of £100. Eleven years later, 22 farms exceeded the £40 rent, and 5 rented at £200 or more.[52] In 1716, 31 rented for more than £40 and 17 for over £100. This trend meant that by 1735, tenants who farmed lands worth £200 or more accounted for 55 percent of the Norfolk estate's total value; more strikingly, farms renting under £100 a year made up only 8 percent of the entire rental.[53]

The increase in large farms made feasible the imposition of lease provisions that presupposed or required capital improvement by tenants. By analyzing the leases in four chronological groups, the evolution of Townshend's leasing policy, its growing sophistication and system, become apparent. For no other landlord of similar substance has such analysis been made. This is not to deny that leases are uncertain documents to decode. They were not to every landlord's liking, and their virtual absence from the Leveson-Gower estates from 1690 to the 1750s was highly beneficial there.[54] But the agricultural writer Edward Laurence endorsed the value of leases "for 15 or 21 years,"

50. RUEA, passim.
51. H. J. Habakkuk, "English Landownership, 1680–1740," *Economic History Review* 10 (1940), 2–17; *AHEW*, V, 2:170–74.
52. It should be noted that the Stiffkey bailiwick was in hand in 1690; in 1701 it provided two tenants with farms over £100 p.a.
53. Total rental was £6,240; tenants over £100 made up £5,749; those over £200 made up £3,419.
54. J. R. Wordie, *Estate Management in Eighteenth-Century England: The Building of the Leveson-Gower Fortune* (London, 1982), 23, 29, 39, 44–45.

bolstered by penalty clauses for nonperformance of the "proper covenants."[55] Long terms provided tenants with incentive to abide by lease conditions, secure in the prospect of enjoying the benefit of their investments. The longevity of many major farmers on the Townshend lands, especially in the 1720s and 1730s, demonstrates the acceptability of detailed lease provisions, which themselves bear close scrutiny.

A group of eighteen leases, entirely the work of the executors, predate Townshend's return from abroad in 1697. On the whole, they spanned brief terms of years and contained common provisions of the day, restricting the number of crops that could successively be taken on the land and requiring tenants to maintain the premises in good repair, to refrain from unauthorized subletting, and to fell no timber and remove no straw, hay, or dung from the premises.[56] Mostly the leases are notable for what they do not specify. There is no reference to sown grasses, only one mention of root crops, no level set to the amount of fertilizer to be placed on summerley (summer fallow) lands—all matters receiving much attention in later leases.[57] Concessionary lease provisions were rare before 1697 and restricted in scope: during these times of high average grain prices, tenants were available and incentives to attract them were largely unnecessary.[58]

In the second group, comprising twenty-four covenants from 1698 to 1706, incentives (often material) were far more commonly provided. Perhaps the concerted effort to end direct management of foldcourses and farms long in hand made these necessary, but Townshend also made concessions to persuade tenants to adopt progressive practices. One who took on a sixteen-year lease at £300 a year received livestock, wool, and hay valued at £200 "for his encouragement"; another tenant was given a low-interest loan; several obtained life leases. Others were promised that the landlord would enclose some of their lands, part of Townshend's plan of common field enclosures.[59]

55. Ibid., 30–31 and n. 20. Wordie cites Laurence's *Duty of a Steward to His Lord . . .* (London, 1727), of which *Duty and Office of a Land Steward* (London, 1731) is a verbatim reprint. Wordie's citation of Laurence seems somewhat tendentious: see *Duty and Office,* 14–15, 86–87, 159–79.
56. On common provisions, see *AHEW*, V, 2:214–24, and Riches, *Agricultural Revolution,* 72–73. Only four of these eighteen leases extended twelve years or more.
57. Leases 28 September and 29 October 1691, RL drawer 99; 14 August 1694, RUEM/CT; 30 July 1697, RL drawer 79.
58. For annual and decennial prices, see *AHEW*, V, 2:829–30 and 851. See leases of 29 October 1691, RL drawer 99; [?] July 1695, RBF/CT 1700–40; 7 July 1697, RL drawer 79; 9 [?November] 1697, RU household/estate [NRO].
59. Leases 14 October 1699, RL drawer 109; 14 October 1699 and 20 April 1700, RL drawer 99; 18 October 1701, RBF/CT 1700–40; 20 October 1701, RL drawer 96; 10 August 1703, RL drawer 117; 20 September 1696 (with renewal of August 1702), RL drawer 79; 30 July 1706, RBF/CT 1696–1735; 19 November 1703, RL drawer 93.

Of these leases, eighteen were for terms of years, at an average of 10.3 years, two years more than the preceding group of leases.[60] Adding five life-leases from the second period, one sees that Townshend's tenants were clearly obtaining longer terms from the landlord in the early 1700s than from his guardians in the 1690s, a policy which indicates a desire for long-term, steady tenants, especially on larger farms and lands previously farmed directly.[61] Longer leases were not the only characteristic of Townshend as a progressive leaser: the specified cultivation of clover and turnips, along with the use of sophisticated rotations, also grew more common.[62] The variety in these leases indicates that lease conditions were open to bargaining. Depending on the size of the farms leased, for example, the tenants' responsibility to make repairs varied greatly, and whether the farmer paid for labor was negotiable.[63] In general, there was a drift in the farm leases away from the compendious ones common under the first viscount toward more cut-and-dried and more narrowly conceived terms. Matters not directly related to cultivation and upkeep of the premises were omitted, like the care of dogs or carriage of coals. This change seems to reflect a more rigid calculus operating between tenants and landlord, and even Townshend's flexibility appears more in negotiating rent abatements, plain and simple, than in discussing extraneous duties and requirements. Thus, in a lease anticipating common future practice, sliding rent payments were specified, while in another instance total rent was unmentioned and only the rent per acre appeared, 8s. the first year, 9s. the second, and 10s. thereafter.[64]

After 1708, a third group of nineteen leases spans the twenty-odd years up to 1730, when Townshend retired to the country;[65] they provide a natural grouping to contrast with earlier and later leases, since they embrace the years of Townshend's politically prominent

---

60. This excludes Uphill farm, long in hand, leased for only a year, probably to see what could be got for it, and two leases pertaining to CT's water mills and windmills.

61. In general the period from the 1690s into the 1730s seems to have been one of increasing lease terms: *AHEW*, V, 2:213–14; Beckett, *Aristocracy*, 187.

62. Leases of 20 August 1698, 20 April and 6 August 1700, RL drawer 99; 18 October 1701 and 30 July 1706, RBF/CT 1700–40; Grannohill a/c to June 1699, RBF/CT Manning 1699. In one instance, on land newly cultivated, two crops of turnips were to be followed by four crops of corn; the land was then to be laid to clover for the remainder of an eighteen-year term: lease, 23 July 1701, RL drawer 77. This practice corresponds with the course of cultivation common on weak soils of East Anglia, where "a semi-permanent ley" was put in "after the common sequence of grains and roots": *AHEW*, V, 1:213.

63. Leases of 14 October 1699 and 20 April 1700, RL drawer 99; 18 October 1701, RBF/CT 1700–40 [two leases]; 20 October 1701, RL drawer 96; 23 July 1701, RL drawer 77; 10 August 1703, RL drawer 117; 19 November 1703, RL drawer 92.

64. Leases of 14 October 1699, RL drawer 99 and 30 July 1706, RBF/CT 1696–1735.

65. No leases dating from 1706–08 have survived.

career. One striking feature they share is their long duration, averaging just under seventeen years; eight were for the classic term of twenty-one years.[66] Significantly, these leases of the 1710s and 1720s nearly all pertain to Townshend's major farms. Either leases were not preserved as carefully for lesser holdings or were not drawn up at all. If, as Christopher Clay says, leases were not a critical factor in the relationship between landlord and tenant, but only "a loose framework" within which the two could work, and if conditions set out in leases usually reflected "locally accepted agricultural usage," then the absence of leases for minor Townshend tenants is not necessarily surprising and may not mean that large tenants farmed under unique conditions.[67] On the other hand, the fact remains that leases were commonly drawn up for Townshend's major tenants, a practice endorsed by agricultural writers at the end of the eighteenth century but far from universally accepted at its beginning. The survival of so many leases for the Townshend estate is in itself highly unusual and indicates that, here at least, the role of written leases was more significant than Clay suggests. A document like the note of "Leases and Surveys" found in the closet of Townshend's late steward, Thomas Warde, in December 1710 shows the widespread use of leases at a very early date.[68] Two dozen are listed, fourteen with tenants who rented farms worth £40 a year or more.[69] Eight of the remaining leases pertained to small farms on the bailiwick most remote from Raynham Hall, Langham and Morston, where distance probably encouraged the use of leases as a means of control over faraway tenants.[70]

Whatever the practice in 1710, nearly two decades later Townshend sought indiscriminately to bind his tenants to him with written leases. In a memorandum to his steward William Fenn, Townshend in 1728 ordered that the tenants "of all my farmes in . . . East & West Rudhams, Hellrington [Helhoughton], East, West & South Rainhams, Toftrees & Sherford take leases." He added the parenthetical caveat "(if they think fitt)" but believed most would do so, as he demonstrated by providing his bailiff with special instructions for the tenants *until* they "shall take leases." Townshend's intention to apply covenants uniformly and "for any number of years not exceeding twenty-one" are

66. Two make no mention of the term and three were effectively lifetime leases: leases of 2 May 1719, RL drawer 93; 3 April 1729, RL drawer 117; 16 February 1725, RL drawer 119.
67. *AHEW*, V, 2:228–29.
68. "A Note of Leases and Surveys left with Mr. Smyth found in Mr. Ward's closett," 21 December 1710, RBF/CT 1705–20s.
69. There were twenty-two such farms in all.
70. The other distant holding, at Stiffkey, had only six small tenants to Langham and Morston's fifteen: RUEA 1711.

the salient features of the instructions to Fenn, which strongly show the landlord's belief in the utility and wisdom of leases. Lease-based control over tenant practices was an essential element of Townshend's successful managerial regime and begins to explain his reputation as an innovative agriculturalist. It also testifies to the fundamentally commercial conception he had of the ties between landlord and tenant.[71] Offering long leases to major tenants reflected a strategy to involve tenants in capital improvements. The same was true with levying rents initially fixed low but escalating after farm improvements.[72]

Beyond assessing flexible rents, the leases of the 1710s and 1720s show increasing turnip and clover cultivation and the integration of these crops into the regime of husbandry. References to large acreages of turnips (over 20 percent of one farmer's holding) demonstrate that the crop was being consciously employed in a restorative crop rotation (and not just to feed livestock), an unusual practice at this date.[73] An extensive set of lease articles bears out this view. In 1717 John Money leased from Townshend for twenty-one years the Grange Farm in West Rudham, premises in the process of improvement.[74] Townshend and Money spelled out specific terms for cultivating this land, perhaps an indication of the novelty of the arrangements. The 460-acre farm included 90 acres set aside from the sheep foldcourse as arable "breaks"—temporary conversions of foldcourse land, probably made here with an eye to permanent enclosure.[75] The landlord designated 30 acres of breaks for cultivation annually, of which Money promised to marl 20 acres at his expense with "60 good loads of marl upon every acre," enjoying deductions from his rent for marling the other 10 acres. In addition, Money leased the Marl Closes, which Townshend was marling at his own cost and which would encompass 176 acres when finished. Both breaks and closes leased for the high rent of 10s. per acre.

Landlord and tenant further agreed on closely circumscribed terms of cultivation:

> Item, the said John Money covenants to use the said marled brecks in this manner. The first year of every breck is to be summerly [i.e. fallow], the second year rye, the 3rd year summerly & marled; the fourth year wheat; the fifth year barly; & the sixth year oats; & at the same time laid down with Clover

---

71. "Directions about the leases to be made," 18 April 1728, RL drawer 118.
72. Leases of 2 July 1711, RU [NRO] and 16 April 1722, filed with Butler's 1697 lease, RL drawer 79.
73. Leases of 1 August 1728, RL drawer 121; 18 April 1728, RL drawer 118; 16 April 1722, filed with Butler's 1697 lease, RL drawer 79. *AHEW*, V, 2:95, notes that until 1750 turnips were largely grown for fodder; see ibid., 1:212.
74. Lease, May 1717, RUEM/CT.
75. For breaks, see Parker, *Coke*, 204.

&c. But if it be found that this method be not convenient for the said marled brecks, then it is agreed that some other method shall be taken as shall be settled between . . . Lord . . . Townshend and . . . John Money.

Item, the said John Money agrees to use the 176 acres of marled ground in the closes . . . after this manner. The first year when the ground is marled is to be turneps, the second year barley, the third year wheat & the fourth year barley & [then?] laid down with Clover &c.

The precise character of these conditions indicates a desire to have a conforming tenant, and Townshend's liking for artificial grasses is evident. The first paragraph suggests he may have intended his tenant to use the breaks as semipermanent leys, undergoing a short term of intense cultivation followed by reversion to grass (albeit sown grass). But the application of marl seems more to speak of a long-term reclamation process on these Rudham heaths, and the increasing value of other farms in Rudham further suggests he was embarked on a program to convert hitherto temporary foldcourse breaks like those rented by Money into permanent arable.[76] On the Marl Closes, the name and the specified arable regime together show that conversion to arable was well advanced, since the soil was expected to bear three successive corn crops, an unusual but not unknown sequence. Clover might then have been laid down for two years, perhaps for as many as four, but on land that Townshend had both enclosed and marled, arable cultivation would surely have been resumed thereafter.[77]

Money's lease may have been exceptional, yet it reveals the full integration of clover into the arable regime in an era when its use was not yet widespread. Moreover the prescribed husbandry on the Marl Closes, although odd in its barley-wheat-barley sequence according to Brian Holderness, nonetheless anticipates by thirty years, with its specific reference to turnips *and* clover, similar prescriptions in this part of Norfolk. In sum, the lease terms outstrip in precision any known Norfolk leases of this date and show Townshend as already unmistakably in the vanguard of agricultural improvement.[78]

The fourth group of leases, those made after 1730, continued the provisions of preceding years, as a lease covenant book reveals in detail.[79] Including leases noted there and elsewhere, provisions survive

76. On the conversion of foldcourses, see *AHEW*, V, 1:212–13, 228–31.

77. Ibid., 1:224–25. It is unlikely that any land described as "Marl Closes" would have been the temporary breaks which Brian Holderness identifies as the occasional object of more than two successive corn crops: ibid., 1:213.

78. Christopher Clay says that "explicit prescription of any of the more advanced husbandry courses is exceedingly rare" in leases before 1775: ibid., 2:218, citing Parker, *Coke*, 55, for an example from 1751.

79. "Covenant Book," endorsed "Edward Case His Book," RLBV, containing lease abstracts, 1730s–50s, and field rotations, 1755–71.

for thirty-one leases between 1730 and 1738.[80] Five ran for nine-, ten-, or eleven-year terms; the twenty-five others were all for twenty-one years and included farms worth as much as £370 and as little as £8 annually.[81] With both large tenants and small, Townshend laid down ever more precise terms, which signaled growing confidence about agricultural practices that time had borne out. As he came to understand better what worked on his estates, he demanded of his tenants careful adherence to these methods. He required specifically and innovatively that his tenants lay their land to "clover, nonsuch[82] or other grasses" after two or four successive crops, depending on the soil. He dictated the amount of manure to be put on summerlaid grounds, the number of plowings to be given land, the acreage of sown grass to be left at the lease's expiration, and the volume of seed to be sown per acre.[83]

Most significant, however, is the appearance amid the cropping covenants of the allowance that "turnips [were] not to be accounted a crop" when counting the successive crops of corn planted on a given parcel of land. Here is striking, early, and unambiguous evidence of inducement for regular turnip cultivation in the arable rotation, since tenants could extract an extra grain crop from their land by planting the root. Tenants in effect employed a seven-year rotation, inserting a year of turnips among four of field crops, then laying the land down for a two-year clover ley. The implication of a similarly constructed six-course rotation has been found on the Coke estates, but only in a lease of 1751; at Raynham, the turnip-oriented rotation first appears in 1732.[84] This priority on its own may explain Townshend's nickname; it clearly justifies placing him among agrarian modernizers of an early date.

None of these lease covenants were merely for show; two compelling reasons encouraged tenant performance of lease covenants beyond what was already common practice. First, certain tenant practices, above all summer tilling of fallow lands more than once, were re-

80. These exclude one for a rabbit warren being improved, made 3 January 1737, Add. 41655, f. 197.
81. For example, leases of 26 March 1737, RL drawer 121; n.d. NRO, MS 3484, 4C2; 1 November 1734, "Covenant Book," RLBV.
82. "Nonsuch" was the Norfolk name for black medic, i.e., alfalfa: *AHEW*, V, 1:223.
83. Leases 6 August 1731, RBF/CT 1700–40; 26 March 1737, RL drawer 121; 31 October 1730, RL drawer 121; and "Covenant Book," RLBV, passim. CT occasionally provided tenants with seed: entries for 20 January 1731, 13 January 1733, 21 April and 16 May 1735, household a/cs 1730–37, RUBV.
84. Turnips are mentioned as not counting as a crop in leases with S. Frost, 10 February 1732, "Covenant Book," RLBV; W. Fenn, Sr., same date, W. Fenn, Jr., same date, E. Gooding, same date, B. and R. Leary, 17 February 1732, RL drawer 119. Cf. Parker, *Coke*, 55.

warded by annual per-acre abatements of rent, as well as by deduction at the expiration of a lease. Second, Townshend protected himself from tenants who defiantly overcropped his premises just before their leases expired by covenants reserving his right to enter the lands in the last year of the lease, typically to sow either turnips or clover. While one year of such cultivation would not restore badly abused land, it set that land on the road to recovery a season or year earlier than otherwise.

The preceding analysis of lease practices illustrates one way by which Townshend improved his Norfolk lands. It is all the more important because early evidence for other agriculturalists is lacking.[85] Townshend's turnip and grass cultivation and his marling were not in themselves novel, but they were not yet universal practices, and his reliance on leases to bring tenants to his view of husbandry was indeed a farsighted, innovative, and effective strategy. That action alone should account for the reputation he acquired as innovator and reformer.

CAPITAL IMPROVEMENTS

The capital expenditures Townshend made to enhance the value of his lands support the image of improving landlord. Ditching and hedging, the accompaniments to enclosure, played an essential role in augmenting landed value, especially of new acreage. The logic of acquiring small pieces by purchase and exchange was to create discrete closes that were both easier to crop than strips in old open fields and more readily manipulated to fit an appropriate course of husbandry. Unlike marling, making hedges and ditches usually remained a charge upon the landlord, although tenants were obliged by lease to maintain and repair them. It is therefore not surprising that Townshend's ditching charges outstrip those for marling, at least where the two were specifically entered in the estate accounts. Unfortunately, the full range of these outlays is irrecoverable, but an idea of the dimension of improvements and outlays is nonetheless obtainable.[86] In 1706–07, marling and ditching cost £230 a year, but nearly £250 in 1716; ditching alone ran to £389 in 1711.[87] The outlays on ditching and hedging

---

85. Ibid.; Parker, "Coke of Norfolk and the Agrarian Revolution," *Economic History Review*, 2nd ser., 8 (1955–56): 159; *AHEW*, V, 2:218.

86. Until 1715, the landlord's capital outlays on marling and ditching appear in the general account; from 1716, they are recorded in the bailiwick accounts, which survive spottily. The general account for 1729 implies that a separate set of ditching accounts once existed, but they do not survive. In the Raynham household accounts, laborers' expenses are not divided between labor on improvements and on other tasks; given the labor-intensive nature of any improvement, this murkiness inevitably masks the cost involved.

87. RUEA 1706, 1707, 1711, 1716.

correspond with Townshend's claims about how he improved his land[88] and with the pattern of consolidation outlined in the discussion of his purchases. It is after 1720, and in the Raynham bailiwick accounts, that the bills for expenses related to enclosure are sustained at the highest levels.[89]

The costs of marling were sometimes thrown onto tenants' shoulders, but whoever bore the burden, much labor was entailed in digging, carting, and spreading the claylike substance, since even the best soils required at least twenty-five loads per acre and often twice that much.[90] Still, the increased value of marled land must rapidly have paid for itself. Marling undertaken after 1733 by a tenant to Thomas Coke, Lord Lovel, was expected to raise farm rent from a level of 6s. to 8s. 6d. per acre. Similar examples can be found on Townshend lands: at Rudham the difference between untreated and "clay'd" land was 3s. per acre.[91] Applying marl helped bring into permanent cultivation lands previously included in the foldcourse breaks, which land in that context had been infrequently cropped and then returned to grazing. Marginal lands not embraced by the sheepwalks could also be converted to arable by this means.

Townshend's willingness actually to pay for improvements from his own pocket is worthy of attention. The calculus involved in determining whether landlord or tenant made the investment in improvements was not solely an economic one, although underlying any decision was the assumption that the tenant farmer (or the landlord for that matter) possessed the necessary capital. If the tenant invested, the landlord abated his rent a corresponding amount to cover the sum, but the landlord did not have to divert funds from other uses to this particular end. On the other hand, if the landlord directly undertook capital improvement, any inconvenience he encountered in paying for it was offset by his ability to initiate, supervise, and guarantee the quality of the work. That Townshend chose the latter course over the former confirms the image of him as a landlord directly involved with his estate.[92]

Work at East and West Rudham in the 1710s and 1720s shows the impact of improvement. In 1714 alone, 3,700 loads of marl and 800 of "waste mould" were spread; the cost that year was £58, but the

---

88. In 1732 CT bragged that he had increased his patrimony by £900 a year by sowing turnips, applying marl, and enclosing land: HMC, *Portland MSS*, 6:159.
89. In 1722 and 1723, £216 and £148 respectively were spent on "fences" in the Raynham a/cs (those for 1721 and 1724–27 are missing): RUEA.
90. Riches, *Agricultural Revolution*, 79–81.
91. Parker, *Coke*, 41; a/c to Michaelmas 1730, RUEA.
92. See Parker, *Coke*, 56–57, and Wordie, *Estate Management*, 36–37, 42–44.

investment brought rapid returns.[93] References to farm rents "advanct" over their previous level "for marling" show the direct correlation between marling and enhanced rent. Nor was this the only activity at Rudham: the six surviving accounts for 1716–24 show £531 spent on ditching, £120 on marling, nearly £800 in renovating farm buildings, almost £200 in tenant allowances, and over £700 in normal, unexceptional repairs. The impact of the process speaks for itself: Rudham "infield" land, once part of the open fields but now enclosed and marled, brought 10s. an acre by the mid-1720s, instead of 7s. as previously. By 1730, a 497-acre farm was fully enclosed and renting at 10s. per acre. Rudham's rental shot up accordingly: assessed at £834 in 1709, it had risen to £933 in 1716, £1,074 in 1723, and £1,147 in 1730.[94] Rudham was a bailiwick upon which Townshend lavished much attention,[95] but throughout his estate there is evidence of his initiative in agricultural improvement. "Farmers," Christopher Clay reminds us, "especially small farmers, tended to be suspicious of unfamiliar methods unless their own eyes convinced them that they were worth while, and innovations undoubtedly spread more rapidly where they had an example to copy."[96] Townshend provided such an example for his tenants, to some extent by the practices he employed on his home farm and farms in hand, to a far greater extent by the lease covenants he insisted upon and by the capital investment he made in improvements. Together these endeavors improved the estate's value and enabled the second viscount to rely upon his agrarian income in a way his father never could. He also had resources that his father lacked.

NONAGRICULTURAL INCOME

Derived from a variety of sources—public office, investments, marriage portions—the nonagricultural income that came to the second viscount substantially exceeded in amount and proportion of total income the sums his father derived by similar means. Although the first viscount garnered £2,100 annually out of his coal farm, his indebtedness and the burden of portions and jointures precluded the kind of investments his son was able to make. Charles Townshend not only

---

93. W. Prestland to CT, 17 and 26 February, 12 March, and 14 April 1714, RBF/CT 1700–40; Prestland's marling a/c, filed with 1713 general a/c supplement, RUEA 1713.

94. Rudham a/cs, RUEA 1716, 1719, 1720–21, 1723–24, 1730; lease of 16 April 1722 and "Particulars of Thos Howard," n.d., both filed with Butler's 1697 lease, RL drawer 79. Howard's "particulars" contain a comment that "these are now the settled rents . . . the marling being all done."

95. See CT's autograph "A proposall for the improvement of the Warren Farm, the warren being to be destroyed," n.d., RUM [1988] misc. box 1.

96. *AHEW*, V, 2:235.

began life with a substantial surplus provided by his executors, but his marriage to Elizabeth Pelham immediately brought him £12,000. The younger Townshend's account with Joseph Wilson, a London merchant banker, for the years 1709–20 provides a measure of his nonagricultural, nonofficial income.[97] Wilson's receipts came to £60,000 over eleven years, with rent remittances making up one-third of the total; income from investments brought in nearly £10,000; sales of financial instruments brought in £20,000 (an amount that was immediately reinvested); miscellaneous sources made up the balance.[98] Dividend income appears to have been Wilson's investment aim, and accordingly Townshend's involvement in the financial markets was generally conservative. His largest holdings lay in Bank stock and then annuities. Other investments—subsidy and tin orders, navy bills—were equally safe. Unlike many of his fellows, Townshend was not much of a financial gambler.[99] In June 1716 he bought into the South Sea Company, acquiring £1,500 in stock which he sold for 9 percent profit two years later. He also purchased £1,700 of trust South Sea stock, but its fate is unknown after Wilson's account breaks off in the third week of September 1720, at a time when the price was collapsing. There is no reason to think Townshend got out ahead of the market.

With the end of the account with Joseph Wilson, Townshend's high finances fall into shadows.[100] In 1730, when track of Townshend's investments can be resumed, South Sea stock made up a large portion of his holdings in the hands of John Selwyn, whose positions as controller of customs, treasurer of the queen's household, and treasurer to the Prince of Wales are testimony to his financial acumen.[101] These holdings, when the accounts begin, amount to some £4,700 held on Townshend's behalf and another £6,000 of his late wife's commercial paper. Selwyn's accounts with Townshend, extant for the years between May 1730 and the viscount's death, reveal disengagement from London life and a diminishing recourse to metropolitan financial mar-

97. "Mr. Wilson's Account," RUBV.
98. Ibid. Of these last sources, £5,100 at most may have come from profits of office, but there is no proof that this was so.
99. CT's known speculations were in fairly reputable projects: Ram's Insurance (later the London Assurance) and the York Buildings Company, a water company bought by a speculator hoping to use its charter to acquire forfeited Scottish lands. For these ventures see W. R. Scott, *The Constitution and Finance of English, Scottish and Irish Joint-Stock Companies to 1720*, 3 vols. (London, 1912; reprinted Gloucester, Mass., 1968), 3:399–403, 418–34; Dickson, *Financial Revolution*, 60, 76–77, 145.
100. He took part in the South Sea Company's third and fourth "money" subscriptions to the tune of £2,500: Dickson, *Financial Revolution*, 108–11, 123–29; CT to C. de Gols, 20 April 1721, Sydney Papers, Clements Library, University of Michigan.
101. *HP 1715–54*, 2:416; Selwyn from 1730 was father-in-law of CT's second son, Thomas. Nineteen letters or accounts from Selwyn survive.

kets. If an improving landlord, which Townshend clearly was, could actually obtain "more than four times [the return] available to the investor in government securities,"[102] it is no wonder he shifted money out of London. Concerned with his children's future, Townshend bought in the fee farm rents due to the crown from that part of his estate settled for their benefit, and he probably had his posterity in mind when, after looking for a safe investment, he took advice against putting money into 3-percent annuities and took refuge in Bank stock.[103] This caution was typical—but so too was the range of investment prospects before him, themselves a product of England's growing commercial sophistication.[104]

To settle his London accounts and obtain capital for his architectural renovations and his estate, Townshend applied the money he had invested with Selwyn, who disbursed over £6,000 on the viscount's behalf between June 1730 and June 1732. By early 1732, Townshend's retirement from metropolitan life was profound and permanent, and by 1734 the statesman had liquidated most of his paper investments, all but closing the books on the London financial world.[105] By the measure of many aristocrats, Townshend's fortune in his later years was small. This was partly the result of cautious actions—paralleling his father's—to leave his estate relatively unburdened at his death. By 1730 his Suffolk lands and part of his Norfolk income were settled on his eldest son; his only surviving daughter by his first wife had married; his daughters by his second marriage had been partly looked after by their mother; and other Norfolk lands were settled by Townshend to raise £25,000 for his younger children.[106]

In assessing Townshend's fortune, it is doubtful whether office supplied him a source of extensive riches. Unlike a paymaster general, lord treasurer, or secretary of war,[107] he had no access to public funds

102. *AHEW*, V, 2:83.
103. J. Selwyn to CT, 1 July 1732, RUEM/CT, and enclosed memo.
104. C. Wilson, *England's Apprenticeship, 1603–1763*, 2nd ed. (London, 1984), 221–25.
105. Selwyn's a/cs 1730–38, RUEM/CT. Selwyn paid under £300 p.a. for CT in the last five years of the viscount's life; dividend income (earned on Bank and South Sea stock, bonds and annuities) was under £450 p.a.
106. Settlement of Lord Lynn, 20 May 1723, RUS; "Instructions for the Lord Townshend's Settlement," n.d. [c. 1723], RUEM/CT. Elizabeth Townshend married Charles Lord Cornwallis in November 1722: GEC, *Peerage*, "Cornwallis." Lady Townshend probably left £5,000 to her daughters: will, dated 18 May 1725, proved 1 February 1732, RBF, Norfolk wills (ii); CT's will, 1 February 1737, proved 10 July 1738, RBF, Norfolk wills (iv); memorandum concerning CT's legacies, ibid.
107. Sir Stephen Fox used his office as paymaster general to become "the richest commoner in three kingdoms": C. Clay, *Public Finance and Private Wealth: The Career of Sir Stephen Fox, 1627–1716* (Oxford, 1978). Robert Walpole did not do badly for himself as paymaster either: Plumb, *Walpole*, 1:204–9.

to manipulate for personal gain. His fiscal rectitude was legendary, and even Lord Hervey, critical in virtually every way, had no charges of impropriety to level at him.[108] J. H. Plumb straightforwardly asserts that he "lost rather than made money through his service to the Crown,"[109] but the materials upon which this study is based do not admit of such assurance. Office nominally provided him substantial income; even set at its lowest realistic value, central government office gave the second viscount perhaps twice as much as the £2,100 his father had annually received from his coal farm. As secretary of state, Townshend's secret service money each year came to £3,000, his salaries to £1,950; both were augmented by a per diem payment totaling nearly £750 and by his share of office fees, which latter fluctuated dramatically but averaged perhaps £2,000–£2,500 a year.[110] Townshend's gross income from office ran to £8,000 a year, significantly more than his rental, but his net was far less. Fees, taxes, salaries and office expenses alone amounted to nearly £3,000 per annum, and of the remainder, only that assigned over to Jonathan Heyman, his London steward, can be confidently assumed to have gone for the viscount's personal use; many personal expenditures bore directly on his exercise of office anyway. His position entailed expenditures beyond those required to maintain the staff, and money directed to Townshend's undersecretaries should not necessarily be looked upon as part of his private income.[111] Office in fact had its own costs. In Townshend's case, accompanying the monarch on four different trips to Hanover cost him nearly £13,000, although part of the expense was defrayed from official sources;[112] prolonged stays at Windsor were also costly.[113] The return on these ventures was nonetheless never

108. BL, Stowe 308, f. 14; Gilbert Burnet, *History of His Own Time*, ed. M. J. Routh, 2nd ed. (Oxford, 1833; reprinted Hildesheim, 1969), 5:416; W. Coxe, *Memoirs of the Life and Administration of Sir Robert Walpole, Earl of Orford*, 3 vols. (London, 1798), 1:64; John Lord Hervey, *Some Materials towards Memoirs of the Reign of King George II*, ed. R. Sedgwick, 3 vols. (London, 1931), 1:80–85.

109. Plumb, *Walpole*, 2:133.

110. See various official a/cs in RL drawer 74, RBF/CT 1721–26, RBF/CT 1700–40, RUM [1988] misc. box 1, and Yale University, Osborn shelves, Townshend box 6. In the years when a new monarch took the throne and the secretary's office issued scores of new commissions, CT received as much as £1,700 in a single month as his share of office fees.

111. According to R. Kelch, "it is likely that official salary and perquisites were only a supplement and not the mainstay in the incomes of those who held office" at this time: *Newcastle, a Duke without Money: Thomas Pelham-Holles, 1693–1768* (Berkeley, 1974), 2.

112. "An account of the Charges of the 4 Journys from England to Hannover," NRO, MS 553, T142B. CT to C. Delafaye, 22 June/3 July 1725, PRO SP 43/6, notes £1,000 in expense money ordered to CT by the king.

113. CT spent over £100 a week there in 1728 simply supplying his household needs: see Table 4.6.

supposed to be financial: political advancement and exigency equally demanded Townshend's presence. He never forgot the lesson of 1716, when his absence from Hanover helped enable James Stanhope to secure his dismissal from the secretaryship: only proximity to the king could guard the interest he had worked to create,[114] just as proximity to his estates was crucial in maintaining his agricultural interests there.

Expenditure

Townshend's shifts of career, first into public life and then out of it, affected his expenditure as well as his income. The 1720s marked the peak of his expenditure on lavish living and the remodeling of Raynham Hall, although this latter activity carried into the 1730s. Even outside these years Townshend lived on a scale exceeding that of his father, although not one of extravagance by comparison with other statesmen of his position. Unlike Walpole, he had no mistress, no great collection of pictures; unlike Newcastle, he had no debts.[115] Calculation of Townshend's expenditures is plagued by incomplete and variant accounts. Whereas income was received from relatively few sources and by relatively few hands, expenditures were made by butler and cook, private secretary, steward, and banker, as well as the viscount and viscountess themselves.[116] The absence of sources, their overlap, and changes in accounting cloud the exact measure of expenditure, but the outlines of disbursement are evident, fluctuating with the size and age of Townshend's family and with his status as married man or widower, officeholder or outcast.

In the early 1700s Townshend's total London and Raynham expenditures exhibited little discrepancy, largely because he spent substantial time in Norfolk with his family. London costs were greater than the expenses of the countryside, but construction and remodeling in the country balanced many of the costs of coachmaker and tailor, draper and wigmaker, grocer and wine merchant in the

114. See CT's ebullient letter from Hanover in 1723, expressing his self-satisfaction when affairs went smoothly with the king: CT to R. Walpole, 6 August 1723 (NS), PRO, SP 43/4.
115. Plumb, *Walpole*, 2:196, notes that "the Walpoles lived with a profusion that Townshend could never have emulated had he wished to do so."
116. For example, the "household" accounts of William Watts, CT's secretary in London and Norfolk, were a hodgepodge of outlays. There were, moreover, three different "household" accounts in London: kitchen and housekeeping, nursery, and "extraordinaries" such as wages, rent, and quarterly bills. The Raynham bailiff kept an account partly for the household and partly for the estate; before 1710 and after 1730, when CT was regularly in the country, a separate Raynham household account was kept. CT also had transactions with his London agent and banker.

TABLE 4.5
Monthly Rates of Household Expenditure, 1704–1724

London, 1704–11	£ 90	Raynham, 1719	£ 29
London, 1714–16	242	London, 1721–23	135
Raynham, 1717	133	London, 1723–24	472

SOURCES: London household a/cs 1704–16, RUBV; 1717 London and Raynham household a/cs, RUBV; household extraordinary a/cs 1719–23, RUBV; household and extraordinary a/cs 1723–25, RUBV.

capital.[117] With Townshend's accession to positions of power and authority, however, the pattern of expenditure altered significantly. He shortened his country sojourns and treated them as vacations from court and parliamentary life, and not meant for expensive entertaining at political "congresses" like those Robert Walpole held at Houghton.[118] Instead, London became the focus of his life and expenditure. Tables 4.5, 4.6, and 4.7 provide an indication of the expense involved; the fact that expenses were reduced in the country because of the provision of consumables without the expenditure of cash only underlines, as Beckett suggests, how draining metropolitan living could be on cash income.[119]

London outlays (including the expenses incurred while with the king elsewhere) amounted to £6,600 per annum over six and a half years; expenditure at Raynham ran about £3,600 annually between 1730 and 1736, and that figure includes between £500 and £1,000 a year on estate business. By retiring to the country, Townshend substantially reduced the drain on his greatly diminished income.

Provision for his children, which could easily drain aristocratic resources, especially for a man with eleven surviving offspring, was largely accomplished either after Townshend's death or by relatively inexpensive means. From his first marriage, he married off the sole surviving daughter in 1722, just six months before his eldest son Charles took a wife, but the size of her dowry is unknown. As for the other children by his first wife, four surviving boys, they received allowances, assistance into marriage, and generous boosts into office or positions of reward. But their advancement was paid for by expenditure more of Townshend's social and political credit than of his fiscal credit. Three sons were helped into parliamentary seats almost as soon as they came of age and through their father's influence enjoyed

117. This is evident from W. Watts's household a/cs 1703–16, RUBV, which focus on London expenditure. For Norfolk they record only extraordinary expenditures on the household (not housekeeping) and then only for 1703–07.
118. Watts's household a/cs 1703–16 and London household a/cs 1704–16, RUBV.
119. Beckett, *Aristocracy*, 366–67.

TABLE 4.6
London and Related Expenses, 1724–1730

	1724	1725	1726	1727	1728	1729	1730[a]
Household expenses, quarterly bills	£2,868	£1,118[d]	£2,477	£2,360	£1,552[f]	£1,323[i]	£885[k]
Extraordinary expenses	2,228[c]	763	2,721	3,252	2,090	1,949	2,082
Servants' wages	304	—	187	575	200	230	118
Children[b]	75	135	567	—	420	422	373
London house rent	—	—	300	300	300	300	300
Travel to Hanover	—	1,527	—	882	—	596	—
At Hanover	—	3,728[e]	—	—	—	1,551[j]	—
At Windsor	541	—	—	—	673[g]	—	—
At Hampton Court	—	—	—	—	530[h]	—	—
TOTAL	£6,016	£7,271	£6,252	£7,369	£5,765	£6,371	£3,758

SOURCE: "An account of money received and disbursements," 1723–32, RUEM/CT; London household a/cs 1726–30, RUBV; household extraordinary a/cs 1726–32, RUBV.

[a] CT left London when he resigned on 15 May 1730.
[b] Expenses for schooling, children's allowances, and the nursery.
[c] This figure excludes £1,382 spent for Townshend's installation as Knight of the Garter.
[d] 23 weeks [f] 35 weeks [h] 10 weeks [j] 17 weeks
[e] 28 weeks [g] 7 weeks   [i] 35 weeks [k] 20 weeks

TABLE 4.7
Raynham Household Expenditures, 1730–1736

	1730[a]	1731	1732	1733	1734	1735	1736
Household expenses	£227	£630	£721	£739	£412	£762	£847
Servants' wages	—	75	161	257	330	395	467
For the children	14	410	234	226	480	200	319
Paid to Lord Townshend	—	154	75	69	75	31	159
Sent to London	—	1,046	684	611	821	645	314
Land purchases	—	70	239	—	—	—	—
Other[b]	1,065	2,777	1,664	2,202	1,859	2,963	2,345
TOTAL	£1,306	£5,162	£3,778	£4,104	£3,977	£4,996	£4,451

SOURCE: Raynham household a/cs 1730–37, RUBV.
[a] From May 1730.
[b] Includes household extraordinaries and payments for estate business.

numerous plums. Charles experienced the signal honor of elevation to the House of Lords during his father's lifetime (he entered as Lord Lynn in May 1723) and was appointed lord of the bedchamber to George I the same year. Thomas served his father as undersecretary of state for six years after 1724 and was made a teller of the exchequer in 1727, an office ultimately worth £7,000 a year to him. William served as aide-de-camp to George II and as groom of the bedchamber to his son the Prince of Wales, while Roger enjoyed somewhat more modest military employment and promotion.[120]

Matters proved different with the children by the viscount's thirteen-year second marriage to Dorothy Walpole, which began in 1713. None of the six surviving offspring were infants at Townshend's death, but only one was old enough during Townshend's years of political influence to be launched on a career or into marriage. This exception was the eldest, George, who in 1729 at age fourteen began a naval career that would culminate in his appointment as admiral.[121] For the rest, it is clear that Townshend fully met their material needs (although about their emotional requirements little can be said). During his second wife's lifetime this meant seeing her supplied with sufficient

---

120. Charles, elected at Great Yarmouth in 1722, was succeeded there on 11 June 1723 by William, just two days past his twenty-first birthday. Thomas was MP for Winchelsea, 1722–27, and for Cambridge University, 1727–74. For the elections and honors, see *DNB*, "Charles Townshend"; *HP 1715–54*, 2:471–74. The election of CT's sons corresponds with a dramatic increase in the number of peers' sons who sat as MPs during the eighteenth century: J. Cannon, *Aristocratic Century: The Peerage of Eighteenth-Century England* (Cambridge, 1984), 112–13.

121. *DNB*, "George Townshend" (1715–69). At CT's death in 1738, his eldest child by his second wife was only twenty-four, his youngest not quite eighteen.

funds to care for her own infants and the more grown stepchildren.[122] As early as 1714 Stephen Poyntz, later Townshend's personal secretary, was employed to school the "young masters," the sons by Townshend's first marriage, boarding them out separately from the family and receiving a substantial salary for his pains.[123] Childrearing for the younger children entailed separate households, because the house in Albemarle Street and then in Cleveland Court could not accommodate them—or because the parents wanted them kept apart. Rented houses in Greenwich and Chelsea housed the children at different times, and they went to Raynham in the summer, often without their parents.[124]

The income from office undoubtedly helped Townshend to defray the expense of his growing family. A more serious problem than expense was presented in 1726, when he had to cope with the demands of a motherless household after his wife died in early March, not yet forty years old. By 1730, when Townshend retired to Raynham, his eldest unmarried daughter, Dorothy, was able at sixteen to supervise the household. In the hectic four years in between, six children, aged from six to twelve in 1726, required close attention during the most active and dislocated years of the secretary's career. In 1727 he made a trip to the continent, cut short by George I's death en route to Hanover and followed by his own serious illness. The next year Townshend spent five full months at Hampton Court and Windsor, apart from his children; seven months after returning to London, he departed again, in May 1729, for a five-month sojourn in Hanover with George II.[125] Small wonder that the presence of Mrs. Johnson, the housekeeper, was felt everywhere; small wonder too that the busy politician in part solved the problem of what to do with his children by throwing money at it and escaping from it.[126]

Townshend's personal expenses present few surprises. Payments

---

122. The household steward received his money from Lady Townshend, and she examined and passed the accounts: see a/c of "money received and disbursed" 1723–32, and household a/cs 1717, 1719–23, RUBV.

123. Household a/c book 1703–16, RUBV, passim.

124. The children were at Chelsea in 1721–22 at least, and the "nursery" was at Greenwich in 1722 and 1724: a/c of extraordinaries 1719–23, and household and extraordinary a/cs 1723–25, RUBV. After the second Lady Townshend's death the elder boys stayed in Kensington, the infants at Twickenham: entries at the end of 1726, extraordinary a/cs 1726–32, RUBV.

125. "An account of the charges of the 4 journys from England to Hannover," NRO, MS 553, T142B.

126. Such at least is the impression from the household accounts, which document CT's absences, the continuing delegation of the youngest children to a separate household, and a level of payments on their behalf that ranged above 10 percent of the household budget. This figure omits the hire of their servants. In Table 4.6 the figures for children's expenses are lower than 10 percent because they exclude extraneous bills sometimes left unspecified, sometimes accounted for separately.

show none of the dramatic adjustment to circumstances that characterized the newly ennobled Horatio Townshend's outlays. Raised as a nobleman, Charles Townshend lived as one from the beginning of his adult life. His transactions with bankers Joseph Wilson and John Selwyn might have been expected to reveal any unusual directions in which money went, but in fact the bulk of the sums disbursed went to stewards, secretaries, and his wife or daughter-as-agent. Lady Townshend, Jonathan Heyman, Stephen Poyntz, and other "employees and agents" received nearly 40 percent of the £62,000 disbursed by Wilson from 1709 to 1720. Over 25 percent was spent on paper investments, and another £8,000 went to interest and principal payments, a paltry sum compared to the debt payments made on the first viscount's behalf. Legacies, allowances, and lump sums to children and other relatives ate up £6,000, and the remaining disbursements (about £7,000) went in unknown outlays, perhaps some for land. If the sums presumably subsumed in the other accounts, and the money reinvested in commercial paper, are excluded, Wilson appears to have been expending about £1,900 a year on the viscount's behalf.[127]

Similar accounts are lacking for the decade from 1720 to 1730, when Townshend presumably sustained or exceeded this level of expenditure: these were the years of his remodeling work at Raynham, the decade when he went abroad with the king four times, the period when four of his children—and his only eligible daughter—found marriage partners. Only some of the costs attendant upon these events can be estimated; those related to Raynham Hall are discussed in the next chapter. But by the time Townshend's account with John Selwyn picks up in 1730, the viscount had retired to Norfolk. From there the significance of his London agent's business transactions diminished quickly. Over eight years Selwyn disbursed under £9,000 for the viscount, more than half in the first year of Townshend's retirement. He paid £3,000 to employees, about £1,500 to Townshend's children, and about £1,800 on some final expenses for the renovations at Raynham Hall; a few small loans were repaid and legal fees settled.[128] During Townshend's last years, Selwyn's payments (again excluding those that reemerged as receipts in other employees' accounts) amounted to just £750 per annum, about two-fifths the rate of such expenditures by Wilson.[129]

The reduced level of expenditure after the residue of metropolitan

127. "Mr Wilson's Accounts," RUBV.
128. J. Selwyn's accounts 1730–38, RUEM/CT.
129. In the first two years of CT's retirement, however, expenditures ran to £1,880 a year, almost exactly Wilson's annual average payments (excluding investments) down to 1720.

living was paid for accords well with the image of the statesman in repose. Townshend's latter years at Raynham illuminate the boundaries of life for an eighteenth-century aristocrat away from the limelight. He reverted to his former close involvement with estate business and agriculture, resuming activities that the press of business—and ambition—had forced him to push aside. His career suggests that politics and business in some sense did not mix. It was possible, as Townshend had, to make farming profitable while an absentee, but not truly to be a full-time agriculturalist. The careers of improving farmer and national politician tended to be mutually exclusive: the time demanded by one had to be stolen from the other. In retirement Townshend undertook activities that went beyond enjoyment: within a year he had put himself into the corn trade, as he called it, acting as factor for local farmers whose corn he marketed.[130] He even took over some of his steward's tasks, receiving in person the tenants' rent as it fell due.[131] One can imagine the questions Townshend must have addressed to his farmers and others from the neighborhood on these occasions, urging the former to keep to their lease terms and exchanging information about agricultural practices with both. These were undoubted instances when the instructive example of an aristocratic landowner might have great diffusive force.

Beyond the renewed satisfactions of his life as an agriculturalist, Townshend found his "heart's content" in "enjoying [Raynham] in the utmost perfection."[132] Busy with a life that provided (at least for one guest) a "delightful situation . . . perfect liberty . . . & improving conversation," it is no wonder that Townshend had no need for the fripperies of London life or the expense of the cosmopolitan world.[133] As the next chapter observes, the fashion in which Townshend made over his house at Raynham helps to account for his contentment in rural retirement.

130. CT to S. Buckley, 21 December [1730], Sydney Papers, Clements Library, University of Michigan. See also payments, 14 August 1736, for insurance and commission "on the tenants' corn," household a/cs 1730–37, RUBV.
131. See entries for money received by Dolly Townshend, ibid., which make it clear she received from CT the rent that tenants had personally given him.
132. CT to [Lord Lynn], 1 June [1730], RBF/LL family.
133. R. Gale to W. Stukeley, 24 June 1736, *The Family Memoirs of the Rev. William Stukeley . . . and other Correspondence . . .*, ed. W. C. Lukis, Surtees Society, 73 (1880), 289.

∗ Chapter 5 ∗

The Renovation of Raynham Hall
A Study in Cultural Change

As the dominant building of the rural scene, after the parish church, the English country house stood out as visible evidence of the power, wealth, and social preeminence of the landed order. The house's social functions were manifold: it served as administrative center for a landed estate, as the headquarters of power for a political ruling class, as a locus for dispensing hospitality and partaking in sport and other pleasures. Considering the weight that attached to country seats, it is understandable that building and remodeling them was a predominant occupation for many landowners. In this respect, the first two Viscounts Townshend were like their peers.[1] Yet if the functions, demands, and attractions of the country house provided a constant element in elite life, the country seat has its own changing history as well. Time that aristocrats spent in residence varied from century to century, affected by the calendar and especially by the growing attraction of London and resorts. Taste changed too, as classical styles and the growing elite desire for detachment came to dominate the later seventeenth and eighteenth centuries. The siting of houses, their views, the interior arrangements, which increasingly served to preserve and create privacy, all altered over time.[2]

The place of Raynham Hall in the two Townshends' lives bears

---
1. This chapter takes as its point of departure L. Stone and J. Stone, *An Open Elite? England 1540–1880* (Oxford, 1984), part III, especially 295–358.
2. The local and regional economic impact of country-house building should not be ignored, although it is not of immediate note here.

out these developments and also mirrors the contrasting worlds of each. Both men used the hall in similar ways, yet some of the functions Raynham served for the first viscount were simply irrelevant to his eighteenth-century successor. Because Horatio Townshend's career was grounded in social and political arrangements themselves firmly fixed in the provinces, the hall operated as a literal base of power. In an era when Whig and Tory parties had little organization and uncertain meaning, his country house provided a focus for political activity that was more oriented around competition for local honor and reputation than around partisan ideological goals. Perhaps also because of his own nonnoble origins, the first viscount seems to have viewed his house almost as did a country gentleman, for whom it was "the only means of exercising authority and making himself useful . . . an essential element of his existence, and a prime justification for his claim to deference."[3] Charles, the second viscount, saw Raynham Hall far more clearly as a retreat than as a locus for building and sustaining "an interest." He entertained few strictly political visitors and set himself apart from the county when in the country, rejecting his father's practice, which was to use the hall as a base of operations from which to spread influence throughout Norfolk.

There should be no mistaking: for both father and son the hall took on tremendous importance in the way they presented themselves to the world. But for the father, the world was largely that of Norfolk, while for the son it was the kingdom at large. Although residence at Raynham and the assumption of the duties of landlord went hand in hand for both men, the distinction is once again clear between the outlooks each adopted toward his tenants and locales: one was effectively focused on the immediate community that gave him sustenance, whereas the other looked toward a larger world and conspicuously the London metropolis.[4]

Horatio Townshend and Raynham Hall

It is not surprising that a man so caught up with securing his social position as Horatio Townshend should turn his attention to finishing the grand house at Raynham that his father had begun.[5]

3. Stone and Stone, *An Open Elite?* 300.
4. See N. Landau, *The Justices of the Peace, 1679–1760* (Berkeley, 1984), 3–5, for her corresponding distinction between "patriarchal" and "patrician" attitudes among the elite.
5. The sale of construction materials after Sir Roger's death indicates that work was going on when he died: executors a/cs 1637–43, NRO, Bradfer-Lawrence, V x 24.

By the summer of 1656 Townshend shifted residence from Stiffkey, where he had been born and had for some time lived, to Raynham, despite the rough state of its interior.[6] The precise timing and progress of renovation cannot be fully reconstructed, but its scale is clear.[7] Major work may have waited several years after 1656, until Townshend had taken steps to pay his three unmarried sisters' dowries; the fundamental improvement he made in 1659 by hiring a London engineer to supply water to the hall is the kind of project with which one would have begun a final fitting out. The need for this work in any case shows how far conditions had decayed since Sir Roger Townshend's death.[8] Sale of lands in Essex may have helped finance completion of the hall, the known cost of which between 1659 and 1662 came to at least £3,000 and probably a good deal more. At a time when Townshend had just committed his fortune to restoring and serving the Stuart line in England, it is easy to see that his resources might have been stretched—and that the remodeling meant much to him.[9]

Structurally, Townshend left his father's work unaltered, either because he found it essentially pleasing or because he could not afford to change it. The house was a double pile, that is, a rectangular plan, two rooms deep and two full stories high. (Figures 5.1, 5.2, 5.5, 5.7) At this point, however, its layout was somewhat old-fashioned: it had double entrances (rather than a central one) on the west front, with doorways that led into screens passages on either side of the great hall, "a duplication of the traditional medieval arrangement."[10] The interior was no more than roughly finished and in its completion the architect Roger Pratt probably had a hand. Toward the end of September 1661 he dined at Raynham and his testimony from about 1663 demonstrates

6. HT was described as "of Stiffkey" and "of Raynham" in the 1650s, but expenditures made at the "New Hall" in Raynham point to his residence there: bills, Raynham and "New purchased lands" a/cs, RUEA 1656, including a letter of 6 January 1657 to P. Stringer at "Sir H Tounson . . . Raymun Hall." J. Harris, "Raynham Hall, Norfolk," *The Archaeological Journal* 118 (1963): 181–82, argues that HT completed Raynham in the 1650s, an assessment that corresponds with evidence of completion in 1661–62.

7. Raynham bailiwick a/cs for 1657–59 and household a/cs before January 1659 are missing.

8. TF to HT, 4 April 1659, Add. 41655, ff. 121–22. The engineer proposed a fountain that was never built.

9. R. Reade's a/c records money received "for and towardes the finishing of Reynham," but beginning only in January 1661: receivers' a/cs 1658–87, RUBV. Household a/cs 1659–70, RUBV, note outlays of £3,100 from January 1660 to October 1662.

10. Harris, "Raynham Hall, Norfolk," 182. The "screens passage" was "a passageway separated from a medieval hall by a decorative screen, above which was often constructed a gallery"; the front entrance of many houses opened into this passage, and the screen thus prevented drafts from entering the hall: D. Yarwood, *Encyclopedia of Architecture* (New York, 1986), 325.

an intimate knowledge—and approval—of the layout.[11] For the work itself, Townshend relied upon a London carpenter as the equivalent of a modern contractor. Unfortunately, the carpenter proved troublesome and slow, threatening to leave when denied a constant supply of money. The work was also disruptive enough to force Townshend and his wife to stay with his brother-in-law, Sir Ralph Hare, at Stowbardolph for four months in 1661. It was not until 1663 that the last paint had been applied to the impressive array of black and white, green, blue, yellow, "wrought," and damask rooms.[12]

Despite Roger Pratt's enthusiasm, another East Anglian, Roger North, who disliked compact Neopalladian houses like Raynham, had little time for the interior. The formal hall, he thought, had "great prerogative of room, to the damage of the rest of the house." He complained that the staircases were ill lit and the east front's small rooms "lumpish," yet he acknowledged that the house as a whole was "noble and pleasant." Thomas Browne concurred, asserting that Raynham was the "noblest pyle among us," and it was easily the most impressive residence in west Norfolk. It stood out in its surroundings much as Townshend hoped to do in the county community.[13]

His work on the grounds was also extensive. Already in 1656 workmen had erected rails around the hall, fenced in the oak yard and "burch walk," and sowed acorns and walnuts. Now, new outbuildings and stables were erected and a walled orchard was created, to be stocked with trees and grafts from London. The existing bowling green was reflagged and fenced, and landscaping of a formal nature continued throughout the 1660s.[14] Beyond his formal gardens and

11. R. Reade records mutton left after "Mr Chitsley and Mr Pratt was here": a/c of money received, January–October 1661, receivers' a/cs 1658–87, RUBV; entry, 25 September 1661, household a/cs 1659–70, RUBV; R. T. Gunther, ed., *The Architecture of Sir Roger Pratt* . . . (Oxford, 1928), 9, 132–34.

12. R. Reade to C. Spelman, 20 January 1662, Add. 41655, f. 130; J. Scott's acquittances, 4 May 1661, RL box 74, and 16 January 1663, RUFP [NRO]; household a/cs 1659–70, RUBV for whereabouts; sweep's bill, 19 January 1665, and laborer's bills, RUEA 1665, for description of rooms. Note that one of the rooms at Stowbardolph was called "My Lord Townshend's chamber" in an inventory of 1672: NRO, Hare 5644, 224x5.

13. H. Colvin and J. Newman, eds., *Of Building: Roger North's Writings on Architecture* (Oxford, 1981), 55, 76; T. Browne, dedication to "Hydriotaphia," in *The Religio Medici & Other Writings of Sir Thomas Browne* (London, 1931), 93. See Stone and Stone, *An Open Elite?* 341–42 on North's dislike of the Neopalladian style. HT apparently also undertook work in Raynham church, since his will instructed that he be buried in "the new dormitory there made by me": PRO, PROB 11/389, f. 196. Unfortunately, the original church was replaced in the mid-nineteenth century.

14. Exterior work can be reconstructed from Raynham a/c, RUEA 1656; entries of February 1659 to May 1661, household a/cs 1659–70, RUBV; Philips's gross sums, RUEA 1663, 1665; R. Reade to C. Spelman, 20 January 1662, Add. 41655, f. 130; bill, 25 November 1667, NRO, MS 20446, 127x1. Sir E. Harley's servant brought fruit trees from Herefordshire: Spelman's gross sums, RUEA 1663.

bowling green, Townshend turned to his park. Here, concern with profitable estate management mixed with his desire for a suitable environment for the dominating house. The scale of the work suggests that years of neglect had taken a toll: to make a proper deer park required over three years and then took unceasing effort to maintain. But the importance of setting as a testimony to status justified the effort: when seeking preferment around 1664, Townshend by his own admission sought "some monnie some way or other, if it be no more then to make up my parke."[15] His intention to keep a herd of five hundred deer was a way for a status-conscious new nobleman to bolster his position, and not just because its presence bespoke his wealth. Like his eighteenth-century counterparts, the first viscount bestowed the deer on relatives, allies, and friends as neatly calculated gifts meant to acknowledge one and reward another.[16] Remaking the park had practical and symbolic, political and social dimensions to it.

For his park project, Townshend converted some of the "new purchased lands" acquired during the 1640s and 1650s. This and other acreage around Raynham was held in hand, and leases on adjacent lands were not renewed as they fell in. By the time work began in 1664, Townshend already directly controlled much of the land involved.[17] He had simultaneously bought up freehold land and bought out copyhold tenants living inside the projected new park; he exchanged land with others from whom he rented, to consolidate his holdings further.[18] Townshend spent over £2,100 on lands in and around East Raynham from 1660 through 1667, mostly after late 1665.[19] Because part of the new park had been common land, new provision of common (or rent abatement compensating for loss) was offered to the affected tenants. Upon resurvey of other farms in 1666, tenants and landlord made a "devision of the farmes

15. HT's draft, c. 1664, "When I was last in towne," RBF/HT misc.
16. HT to Sir E. Harley, 24 January 1678, BL, Loan 29/182, f. 259. TW to HT, 30 January 1687, RL drawer 69, for deer given away in 1686; "bucks given away," 20 July 1687, RUM/HT [NRO]. CT kept up the custom: CT to his keeper, A. Field, 28 October 1703, RBF/CT 1700–40; J. Calthorpe to TW, 20 and 29 June 1710, and S. Poyntz to TW, 18 June [1709] and 11 November 1710 (NS), RBF/CT 1705–20s; list of "Bucks 1711," Add. 41656, f. 69; B. Nuthall to CT, 10 July 1721, PRO, SP 35/27, no. 75. See E. P. Thompson, *Whigs and Hunters: The Origin of the Black Act* (New York, 1975), 158–60, on the practice in the eighteenth century.
17. East Raynham a/cs for 1656, 1660, 1662, 1665–67 (the only surviving a/cs to 1667), RUEA.
18. HT had to confirm an exchange with the rector of East Raynham legislatively: C. Robbins, ed., *The Diary of John Milward, Esq.* . . . (Cambridge, 1938), 90, 96, 104; *LJ*, 12:127–29, 144, 178–79.
19. See deeds in RL drawers 63, 64, 94, 103, 106, and RUE deeds, lists in RL drawer 110, and note in Add. 41655, f. 120. Most purchases over the period can be identified as relating to the park.

in East Raynham on [the] new enclosing" to establish these changes formally.[20]

After buying land and drawing boundaries, Townshend began physical alterations. He built fences and walls with brick that came to King's Lynn in the summer of 1666, roads were altered, and workmen came from Suffolk to help, laboring into the following year before finishing the job.[21] His deer could not be contained within the old park while the new work was in hand, so Townshend sent many out to friends for safekeeping, exploiting his wide contacts among the gentry.[22] By the summer of 1667 the expansion was over. At a cost of £4,000–£5,000, the old park of 450 acres had been replaced by a new one of over eight hundred.[23]

Townshend made good use of his country seat, and not just by overawing antagonists like Owen Hughes, who was lured to a meeting at "stately Raineham" and then literally forced out the door by Townshend. The viscount dined his militia troop and even held formal lieutenancy meetings there; in 1679 the leading Whig gentry came to confer for several days about parliamentary choices.[24] To put it most plainly, Horatio Townshend's Raynham was an extension of his power and authority. There was a steady and varied flow of guests in and out of Raynham to which this image was presented. The most frequent visitors were relatives, Norfolk Whigs, and a group of local men of slight status, but some were of great stature. The king himself came in 1671, and Townshend entertained political guests of national note: the Earl of Arlington, Sir Samuel Barnardiston and Sir Robert Carr, and Sir Edward Turnor, speaker of the House of Commons.[25] When at Raynham, Townshend significantly retained old forms of entertain-

20. "1666 Devision of the Farmes," Add. 41655, ff. 137–38; "A note of the severall houses," RL drawer 110; surveying bill, 25 January 1667, filed with East Raynham a/c, RUEA 1667. Three tenants had allowance for "want of common" in 1666.

21. P. Lowke's book of gross sums, 1666–87, RUBV; receivers' a/c book 1658–87, RUBV; allowances to tenants on W. Clerke's sheep reeve's a/c, RUEA 1667, and on sheep reeve's a/c 1667–69, RL drawer 74. Payments and allowances amounted to over £1,250.

22. P. Lowke's 1667 payments concerning deer and ditching, RUEM/HT, and his book of gross sums 1666–87, RUBV.

23. "This paper concernes my wifes 3000 pounds," RL drawer 100. Settlement indenture, 25 November 1673, RUS, says the park was 812 acres. The estimated cost is extrapolated from known purchases (£2,100) and labor and allowances (£1,250); legal fees for the parliamentary act are unknown, as is the cost of additional material, labor, and purchases.

24. O. Hughes to Sir R. Southwell, 12 July 1675, Folger Library, Bacon-Townshend, V.b.305, f. 36; household a/cs 1659–70 and 1671–86, RUBV, passim; Sir J. Hobart to J. Hobart, 14 and 16 July 1679, Bodl., MS Tanner 38, ff. 55, 58; *NLJ 1660–76*, 100, 129.

25. Household a/cs 1659–70, 1671–86, RUBV, passim, for marginal notes of guests.

ment, keeping occasional open house as lord lieutenant and reaffirming his personal and paternalist bonds with his tenants by feasting them at Christmas and on his son Charles's birthday. The sheer size and magnificence of Raynham was used to impress tenants on these occasions and also when they came to pay rent or when manor courts were held there.[26] In all these ways the hall served a function in conformity with a way of life, predicated on persistent interaction between the elite and the lower orders, which was dying out.

Charles Townshend and Raynham Hall

Beyond the 1660s, the first viscount appears to have made no other major effort to remodel and reshape around Raynham, perhaps for lack of money.[27] After he died in London in 1687, Raynham Hall was largely left unoccupied. Young Charles Townshend came occasionally while at university, but his visits were brief and ended altogether when he took his tour abroad from 1694 to 1697. It was only on the eve of his marriage, in early 1698, that he began to put the hall in habitable condition again. Happily, he faced less work than his father had when he came of age, and minor expenditure made the hall suitable for Charles Townshend and his new bride.[28] In spring 1699 Townshend was devoting himself from early morning until ten at night to remaking his grounds, ignoring his farm lands in the process.[29] He also began what became a seven-year campaign of piecemeal renovations in the house itself.[30] This work was altogether more haphazard than that of the first viscount in the early 1660s or his own in the 1720s and after, perhaps because it was much less extensive and financially burdensome. No indication of a guiding plan has survived, but the mason William Edge was paid £3 in 1698 "for drawing a model of the house."[31] Some of the second viscount's labors in the early 1700s in fact should be seen as capital repairs required after years of near vacancy, but the

26. Ibid.
27. HT's debt had been maintained around £12,000–£15,000 from 1660–66 but spiraled to £24,000 in 1667 and to £33,000 six years later. Because accounts survive in profusion for the 1670s and 1680s, it is unlikely that any renovation project has been missed.
28. J. Jephcott to CT, 23 May 1698, Add. 41656, f. 168; entries for 4 July 1698, receivers' a/cs 1693–1706, RUBV; *LJ*, 16:352. J. Jephcott to E. Mann, 13 February 1699, RL drawer 70, noted some things still "wanting here."
29. J. Calthorpe to E. Mann, 16 and 23 April 1699, RUC [NRO].
30. Entries for March–May 1699 in receivers' a/cs 1693–1706, RUBV; J. Calthorpe to E. Mann, 23 April 1699, and W. Manning to same, 17 April 1699, RUC [NRO]; 1698 household a/c, RBF/CT Manning 1698; joiner's bill, 5 July 1701, household a/cs, RUEA 1701.
31. Raynham 1698 household a/cs, RBF/CT Manning 1698.

remodeling was needed both because parts of the hall were structurally deficient and because its outward appearance and interior decor, especially the west front with its double entrance and the dated entry rooms, were not in line with contemporary taste.[32]

Townshend gave remodeling a high priority in the first decade of the new century. The absence of separate accounts hides the renovation's cost and precise nature, as does the fact that some of the labor was locally supplied, but none of this obscures the importance Townshend placed on the work.[33] His injunction to his bailiff to be "sparing in [tenants'] repairs" during 1704 shows his willingness to subordinate other estate matters to this one. Do nothing for tenants "but what must be done of necessity," he cautioned, "for I would be at as little expence as I can in all things till I have finished my house."[34] His close personal attention shows his desire to make the house once again a Norfolk showpiece of recent, London-oriented fashion. The use of non-Norfolk and London-based craftsmen on comparatively modest renovations was meant to ensure their competent and stylish execution. Local men could be trusted with rough work, and Townshend's mason was from the neighborhood. But Matthew May, who came from a job at the Earl of Nottingham's in Rutland, served as master carpenter. With his business centered in London, he was at Raynham only intermittently, and his absences proved a source of irritation and concern, but he knew his craft. The painters employed on the woodwork, and the stonecutter-pavier Miles Poemerroy, with his assistant William Lacey, also came from the capital.[35]

Often in London himself, Townshend kept well abreast of the work and made all substantive decisions: the stonecutter's agreement was originally drawn up in the metropolis and only later sent to Norfolk; the local mason, William Edge, sent designs to the city for Townshend's approval before proceeding with his brickwork. Townshend himself

32. N. Pevsner, *The Buildings of England: North-West and South Norfolk* (London, 1962), 150, notes that the double entrance was falling out of fashion even as it was being built by Sir Roger Townshend.

33. The dimensions of the remodeling are masked by the fact that normal repair charges were not distinguished from the expenses of renovation. Day-labor costs include work on the renovations and other activities, surviving mason's bills may not pertain to alterations, and accounts of payments to London-based artisans do not survive. Existing bills obviously related to renovation total £900, surely a vast underestimate of the actual cost: household a/cs, RBF/CT Manning 1698, 1699; RUE fragile [for 1700]; RUEA 1701, 1703, 1705–06; RBF/CT Warde 1704.

34. CT to TW, 16 May 1704, RBF/CT 1692–1704.

35. Correspondence in RBF/CT 1692–1704, passim. On May's previous job, see W. Watts to R. Leman, 19 and 30 April 1703, ibid. J. Calthorpe made the point to R. Leman that CT's renovation "fills us at present with London workmen and a great deal of dust": 21 June 1703, ibid.

arranged for the workmen who erected a great staircase and for the painters who followed them.[36] Because the remodelings caused commotion and disorder, they encouraged the viscount to remain away from Norfolk, whether in London or on extended visits to his Pelham in-laws at Halland in Sussex. He was not forced out of residence, as had happened to his father, but at Raynham the dust and chaos inhibited entertainment of guests.[37]

Much of the undertaking was more prosaic than grand—excavation in the basement, laying new drains, remaking the servants' quarters—but Townshend made a dramatic change in the house's external appearance. The only elevations and floor plans of the period that survive have been dated to the time of King Charles's visit in 1671. These portray the house with its double-entry west front, and what has been called "a very restless" east front, also with two doors.[38] (Figures 5.1, 5.2) To calm the east front, Townshend stopped up the ground-level doorways and replaced them and the Venetian windows on the first floor above with new windows, conforming to the rest of the façade. Unless he then cut no new door in this façade, which is hardly likely, Townshend must have now built the central door, although it would have been made in what apparently remained the chapel.[39] On the west front (the entrance front) the double entryways with external stairs up to the doors were also removed. As on the other side of the house, the doors were replaced by windows to match existing ones, and an ascending series of stone steps was built up to the new central doorway, flanked by Corinthian columns and topped by an open pediment. To the modern eye at least, the balance achieved is harmonious and pleasing.[40] (Figures 5.3, 5.4) It certainly was grander and in its symmetry more fashionable than the previous design. As for the interior, the rooms affected were mostly on the ground floor, where the outmoded screens passages flanking the great hall

---

36. W. Watts to TW, 25 March, 6 and 11 May, and CT to TW, 16 May and n.d. [postmarked 28 June] 1704, ibid.; W. Watts to TW, 13 January, and TW to CT, 16 January 1705, RBF/CT 1705–20s. In 1704 TW at Raynham was ordered to write every post to apprise CT of progress; some forty letters between the two survive for the first seven months of the year in RBF/CT 1692–1704.

37. CT to TW, 5 June 1704, and CT to R. Leman, postmarked 11 August [1703], RBF/CT 1692–1704.

38. Pevsner, *North-West and South Norfolk*, 150; plans of Raynham Hall, c. 1671, British Architectural Library, Royal Institute of British Architects.

39. M. May to J. Godby, 18 January 1705, mentions materials for pews and seats in the chapel: file of bills 1703–05, RBF/CT, TW's a/cs 1701–07.

40. The renovations of 1703–06 confirm J. Harris's impression that Kent had little hand in altering either front: Harris, "Raynham Hall, Norfolk," 182, where he notes that the changes appear in sketches of 1716.

were abandoned, and where changes in the basement necessitated the relocation of staircases and the leveling of floors.[41]

Through Thomas Warde, and in person when possible, Townshend badgered and cajoled the artisans to careful and thorough work. On-again, off-again activity was unfortunately encouraged in them by the continual disappearance and reappearance of the overseeing master craftsmen. Poemerroy the stonecutter failed to provide a steady supply of stone, and William Edge was particularly slow: only threats of dismissal put an end to his delays.[42] Threats were mixed with incentives like advance payments, but these inducements could backfire: "I doubt," Townshend wrote of Poemerroy, that "I have paid him too much money in hand, which makes him so careless in finishing his work."[43] Despite such problems, the work was accomplished. Sufficient order had been restored amid the carpenters' scaffolds for Townshend and his wife to return to Raynham from Sussex in August 1704. In fact, the disorder can never have been complete, considering that Townshend's three children (carefully segregated from the workmen), as well as twelve servants, were lodged in the hall while Lord and Lady Townshend were with her family at Halland.[44] Although the work in the courtyard and around the hall was not completed until 1706, the undertaking was still got through in relatively rapid order.[45]

These early renovations were not aimed at remaking Raynham Hall as the basis for Townshend's exercise of authority, since he was already demonstrating that London would be the source of his local power and reputation. Yet the work reveals his intention to reside in the country and a desire for direct involvement in estate affairs that was facilitated by his presence. Without suggesting an artificial distinction between the affairs of the country and those of the capital, it is clear that the second viscount used his country seat in a different way than did his father: not for him the heavy entertaining or the political gathering of allies. Raynham Hall was a place from which to supervise

41. This account of external and interior work is based on household a/cs RUEA 1703; on bills in RBF/CT, TW's a/cs 1701–07, RL drawer 74 and RUEM; and on TW's letters to CT from late 1703 to 1706, RBF/CT 1692–1704 and 1705–20s. I am currently preparing a full examination of the early-eighteenth-century renovation.

42. CT to TW, 17 June, 26 June, n.d. [c. 28 June 1704] and TW to CT, 3 July 1704: RBF/CT 1692–1704.

43. CT to TW, 24 May, 15 and 17 June, and 5 July [1704], ibid.

44. CT to TW, 25 April 1704, and TW to CT, 20 July 1704, ibid.

45. TW to CT, 10 January 1705; W. Watts to TW, 13 January, and TW to CT, 16 January 1705; TW to CT, 13 May 1706: RBF/CT 1705–20s. See also M. May to Mr. Godby, 18 January 1705, 1704–05 file of bills, RBF/CT TW's a/cs 1701–07. Some stonework was incomplete as late as 1709: M. Poemerroy to TW, 31 May 1709, RBF/CT 1705–20s.

his lands and "the farming part" of his business,[46] not a base of power but something of a retreat. It is no surprise that when Townshend was thrown into the consuming life of high politics around 1709, he gave up any thought of major projects at the hall for a decade and a half.

When Townshend next seriously turned his hand toward his house, the proud care (and money) he lavished on remaking Raynham Hall and its environs showed a more self-conscious attention than before to the symbolic display of status and power embodied in his physical surroundings. The hall still served no major socializing function: Townshend was no great sportsman, had little interest in or success with grand entertainment, but he cared for his house as a symbol, as physical evidence of his social eminence. Lord Hervey plausibly claimed that Raynham's displacement by Robert Walpole's Houghton Hall as the county's leading house figured prominently in the political quarrel between the two owners, since Townshend saw "every stone that augmented the splendour of Houghton as a diminution of the grandeur of Raynham."[47] That grandeur, however, remained unchallenged into the 1720s.

About the time when Thomas Coke of Holkham first dreamed of erecting a grand house and when Walpole was only breaking ground at Houghton, Townshend began extensive renovations at Raynham.[48] Prior to this major effort, minor work had been more or less continuous, in the house and out,[49] but when he began more thoroughgoing remodeling, the second viscount followed the example of father and grandfather to see that Raynham reflected modern fashion.[50] But while Roger served as his own designer and his son Horatio used local craftsmen extensively (although consulting the renowned local

46. The phrase is that of TW to CT, 27 April 1709, RBF/CT 1705–20s. Cf. CT to TW, n.d. [mid-July 1709, in reply to TW's of 21 June], RBF/CT 1705–20s.

47. Lord Hervey, *Memoirs*, 1:84–85. Hervey noted that in London Walpole's house "was crowded like a fair with all sorts of petitioners, whilst Lord Townshend's was only frequented by the narrow set of a few relations and particular flatterers": ibid., 1:83. In this light, it is significant that there is nonetheless much more evidence in CT's household accounts of entertainment in London than in the country.

48. Parker, *Coke*, 24, comments that Coke "developed designs for his house . . . for sixteen years after his return from Italy" in 1718. See also M. I. Wilson, *William Kent, Architect, Designer, Painter, Gardener, 1685–1748* (London, 1984), 173. The major work at Houghton began about 1722: Plumb, *Walpole*, 2:81–82.

49. Bills for new landscaping, April 1719, RL drawer 80; W. Prestland to CT, 5 September 1720, RBF/CT 1700–40; J. Pye's plumbing bill, RUEM/CT; entries August 1720–July 1721, a/c of extraordinaries 1719–23, RUBV.

50. J. Harris, "Inigo Jones and the Prince's Lodging at Newmarket," *Architectural History* 2 (1959): 38–40, has demonstrated the influence of Jones's new styles on Sir Roger's original building. CT himself subscribed to each of Colin Campbell's three volumes of *Vitruvius Britannicus or The British Architect* (London, 1715–25; reprinted New York, 1967).

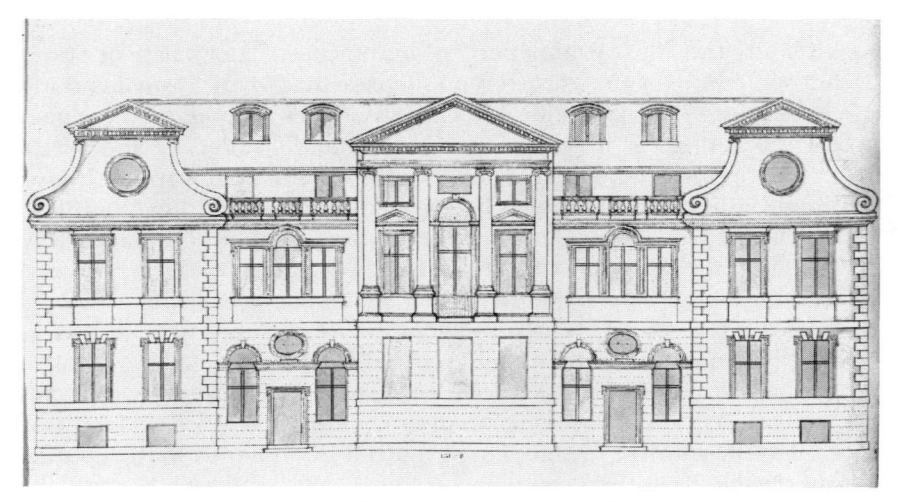

Figure 5.1. East façade of Raynham Hall, c. 1671
Courtesy, British Architectural Library/RIBA

Figure 5.2. West façade of Raynham Hall, c. 1671
Courtesy, British Architectural Library/RIBA

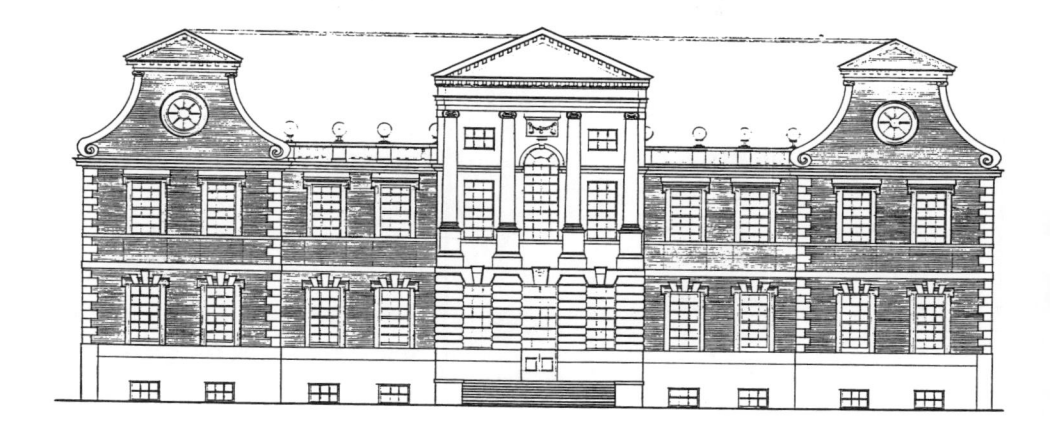

Figure 5.3. East façade at present
Drawing by Feilden and Mawson Architects

Figure 5.4. West façade at present
Drawing by Feilden and Mawson Architects

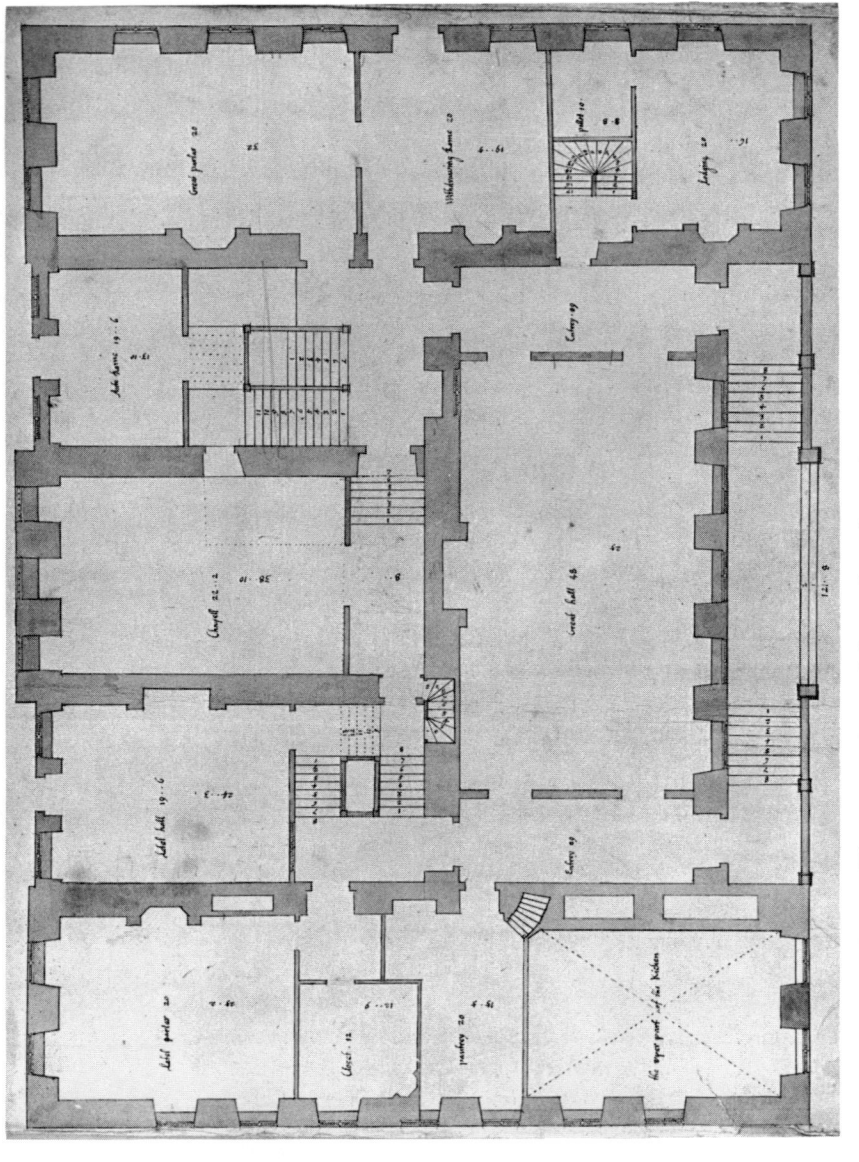

Figure 5.5. Ground-floor plan of Raynham Hall, c. 1671
Courtesy, British Architectural Library/RIBA

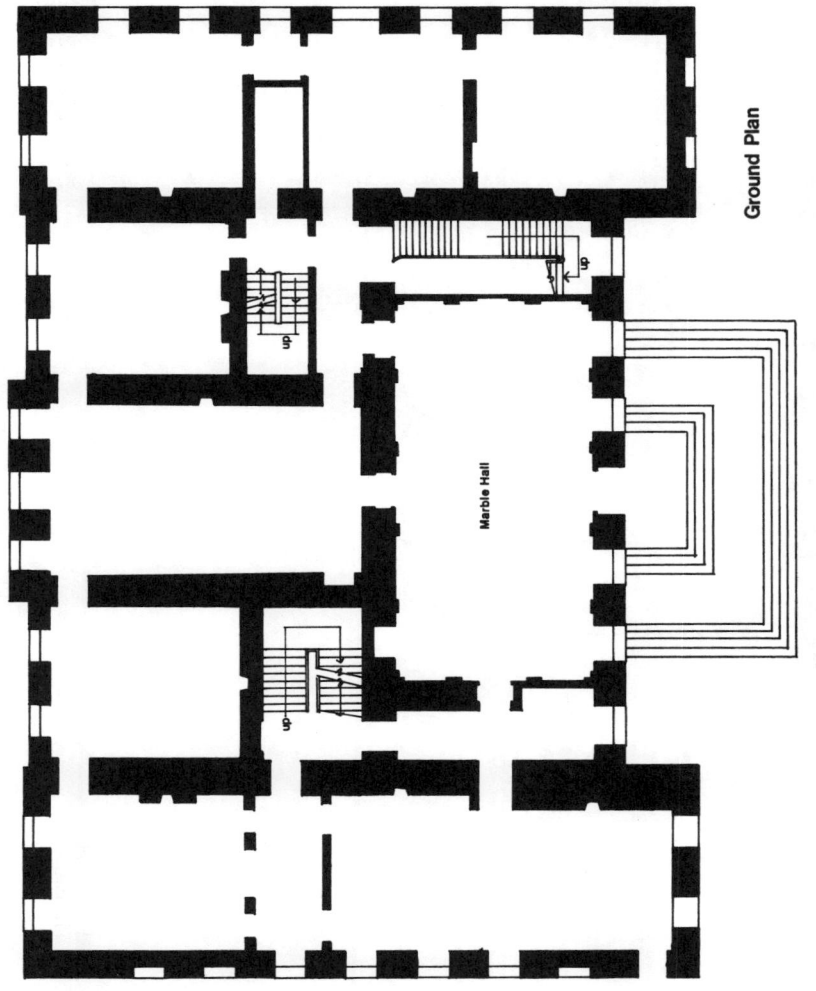

Figure 5.6. Ground-floor plan of Raynham Hall at present
Drawing by Brad Nass

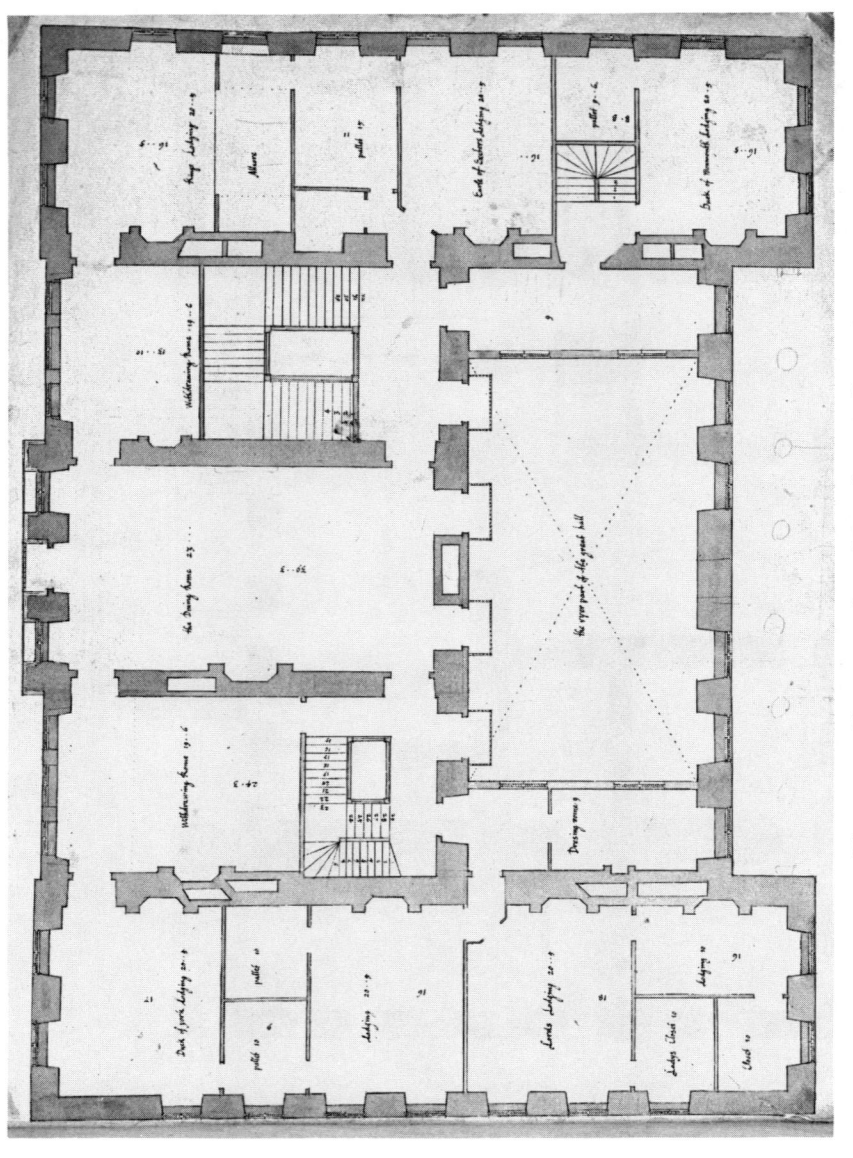

Figure 5.7. First-story plan of Raynham Hall, c. 1671
Courtesy, British Architectural Library/RIBA

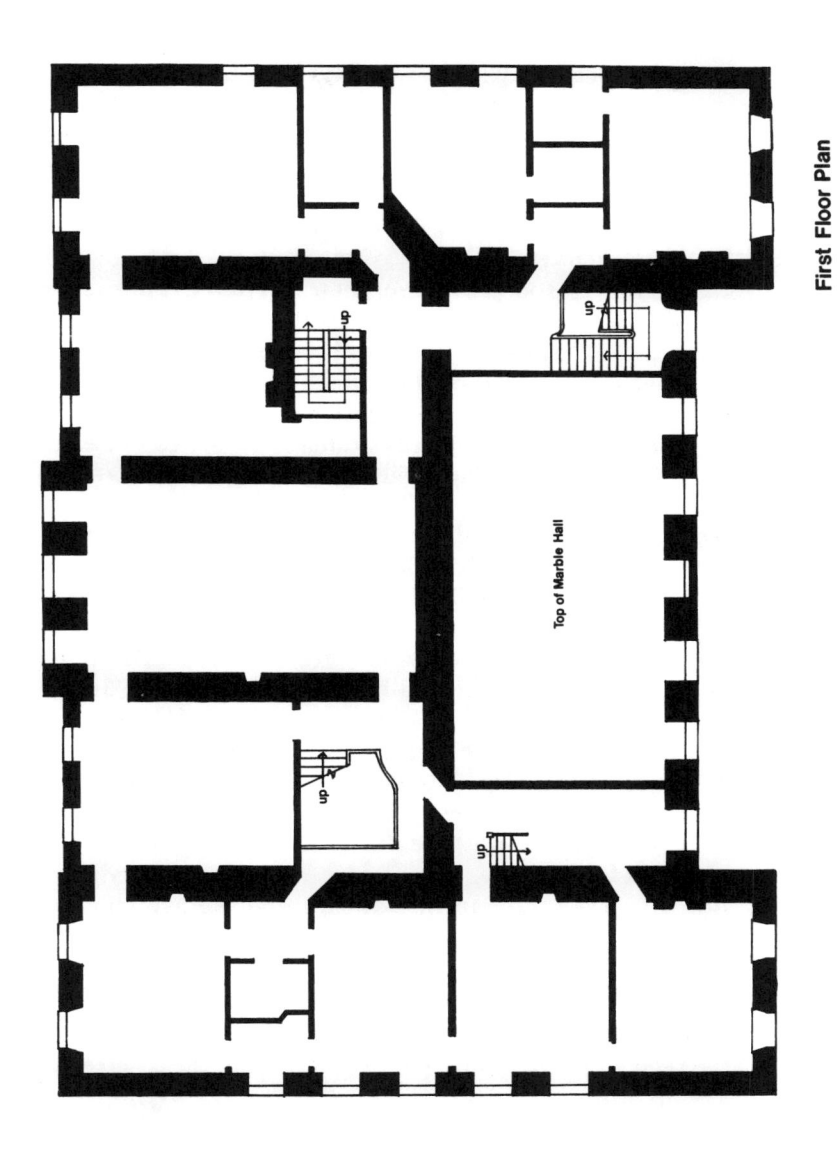

Figure 5.8. First-story plan of Raynham Hall at present
Drawing by Brad Nass

architect Sir Roger Pratt), Charles Townshend both used a nationally known designer in William Kent and engaged London and even foreign artisans to guide and assist local labor in executing Kent's plans. For an eighteenth-century aristocrat of Townshend's standing, nothing less would do.

After a survey of his lands in 1724, Townshend began the centerpiece for the new, open landscape by carving out a lake below the hall, contracted for at £1,100. The "pondmen" arrived in June, soon creating a "garden isleland" and an arch in the lake and probably finishing by early 1726.[51] Simultaneously with work at the lake, Townshend strove to make the hall's setting more naturalistic. In this he helped lead the shift in landscape that rejected formal plans, topiary, and symmetry and replaced them with dramatic views, expanses of grass, and irregular plantings. The grounds had long boasted a "Wilderness," but sometime after 1727 Townshend also abandoned the formal, walled garden and moved the kitchen garden and fruit trees out of sight of the hall. Margaret Jourdain has suggested that the "new spirit in the gardens" may be attributed to William Kent; if so, it is as early evidence as any of Kent's career as a landscape gardener.[52] The removal of the old garden laid the ground for further landscaping, including the creation of fosses (or ha-has), abandonment of an old road, and absorption of tenants' lands to open up vistas. Horace Walpole later described precisely such "destruction of walls . . . and . . . invention of fosses," along with "levelling, mowing and rolling," as features of the modern garden he so forcefully advocated. Where his father's garden at Houghton was one of the first created in the new "simple, though still formal style," Raynham is its contemporary if not its predecessor.[53] In 1732 the Earl of Oxford came to Raynham and found its setting "by much the finest in England that ever I saw."[54]

---

51. Household a/cs, RUEA 1725, 1726, 1728; W. Fenn's a/cs to March 1724 and January 1725, RUEM/CT; Fenn to Lady Townshend, 30 November 1724, ibid.

52. M. Jourdain, *The Work of William Kent* . . . (London, 1948), 74; Stone and Stone, *An Open Elite?* 333–39. Wilson, *Kent*, 191, believes it unlikely that Kent worked on gardens "much before 1730." On the grounds, see W. Fenn's a/cs April–October, November 1723, and September 1724, RUEM/CT; household a/c 1726, RUEA; Fenn to Lady Townshend, 7 September 1724, RL drawer 74, and 30 November 1724, RUEM/CT.

53. H. Walpole, *The Anecdotes of Painting in England*, ed. J. Dallaway and R. N. Wornum, 4 vols. (London, 1876; reprinted, 3 vols., New York, 1969), 3:80–81. A Raynham tenant was abated £2 rent for land "taken into the new road and [for] some layd into the vistoe [i.e., vista]": general a/c, RUEA 1729. A fosse was specifically mentioned at Houghton in 1731 (HMC, *Carlisle MSS*, 85), but the first signs at Raynham are entries of 22 June and 22 July 1727 in the household a/cs to Ladyday 1728, RUEA [1988] 1716–29.

54. HMC, *Portland MSS*, 6:159. CT continued to improve the grounds thereafter; Kent, in his only extant letter to CT, advised that "where you have made openings [in

As work on the landscape continued, so did renovation, remodeling, and repair inside the hall itself. In 1724 the tempo of work picked up, as Townshend employed a stonecutter and found it economical to erect two brick kilns, which produced half a million bricks in two years.[55] He also gave oversight of the proceedings to an outside party, a sign that the changes envisaged went beyond piecemeal improvement. Kent may have supervised the project, but the architect Thomas Ripley, a colleague of Kent's and "executant" of the designs for Houghton Hall, conducted day-to-day work and served as general contractor.[56] His accounts of money received commence in April 1724; fine work probably began in 1726, when outlays in January for "fraight with marble" signaled sure progress. Well before then, however, Ripley and his assistant had visited Raynham to report to Townshend in London on work in progress.[57]

Despite Ripley's supervision, the work of decoration did not start smoothly, and in his absence the Raynham steward William Fenn was a poor substitute, especially when dealing with the local craftsmen employed for part of the work. In November 1724 jealous competition between two local masons set back Townshend's plans, and so did a scarcity of ready money, forcing Fenn to scramble for cash to pay the workmen. Progress was further hindered by delays like those caused by the plumbers, who proved "neglegent in there work, being mostly at Houghton." If Townshend's growing coolness toward his brother-in-law Walpole arose partly from envy of the splendid edifice going up at Houghton, the fact that work there diverted men from Raynham could only irk the viscount even more.[58] Regardless of tensions, Townshend still borrowed craftsmen from Walpole, like "the Italian" and "Mr. Begutty," the latter identifiable as Giovanni Bagutti, collaborator with Giuseppe Artari, who designed the ceilings at Houghton. The carver, "Mr. Richards," may well be James Richards, Grinling Gibbons's successor as master carver to the crown; "Mr. Moor" may be one of two James Moores, elder and younger, cabinetmakers of the

---

the vista] & left two or three trees, they must be group'd with fine elms &c [so] that you may see your designes finishd con gusto": W. Kent to CT, 27 October 1735, RBF, 18th–20th century catalogues.

55. W. Fenn's a/cs February–December 1724, RUEM/CT (except May a/c, RL drawer 121); Fenn to Lady Townshend, 7 September 1724, RL drawer 74; bill of J. Fellows of Lynn, 1723–25, RL drawer 120.

56. H. Colvin, *A Biographical Dictionary of British Architects*, 2nd ed. (London, 1978), 694, and *DNB*, "Thomas Ripley." See Ripley's a/cs 15 and 26 January 1732, RUEM/CT.

57. W. Fenn to Lady Townshend, 9 October 1724, RUEM/CT; Ripley's a/cs 15 and 26 January 1732, ibid. Household a/c, RUEA 1725.

58. W. Fenn to Lady Townshend, 12 October and 30 November 1724, RUEM/CT.

TABLE 5.1

Thomas Ripley's Bills for Work at Raynham, 1724–1732

Payee	Dates of payments	Amount
Mr Parker, merchant	Feb. 1726	£93
Mr Allen, merchant	Mar. 1726	28
Mr Duvall, plumber	April 1724–May 1730	1,903
Mr Lawrence, joiner	July 1725–Sept. 1730	2,800
Mr Cash, mason	Feb. 1727–Mar. 1731	2,268
Mr Mansfield, plasterer	Dec. 1726–April 1731	743
Mr Richards, carver	Dec. 1727–Sept. 1730	760
Mr Fransom, ironmonger	Feb. 1726–Feb. 1728	203
Mr Phillips, founder	Oct. 1727–Jan. 1731	19
Mr Begutty, plasterer	Dec. 1727	47
Mr Kelham, pumpmaker	Dec. 1726–Mar. 1730	18
Mr Jones, for oil, colors, and gilding	April 1727–Jan. 1732	599
Mr Knott, painter	June 1728–Mar. 1729	112
Mr Minns, glazier	Mar. 1726–Aug. 1730	194
Mr Cleaver, smith	May 1729–April 1731	308
Others	Dec. 1728–Jan. 1732	303
TOTAL		£10,398

SOURCE: Paper headed "Paid for . . . Ld Visct Townshend," 15 January 1732, RUEM/CT.

period.[59] Begged, bought, or stolen, Townshend obtained the best possible craftsmen for this work.

Payments to Ripley (Table 5.1) show that the greatest building activity took place at Raynham between 1726 and early 1731, years that coincide with William Kent's traditional association with the house,[60] and also with the height and then decline of Townshend's power.

The renovations made were substantial, but the basic layout of rooms remained largely intact from an earlier date.[61] Some structural alterations were required, especially as the former chapel was now converted into the grand saloon; new floors were laid in several places,

---

59. Wilson, *Kent*, 99–100, 108, 129, 132; *The Treasure Houses of Britain: Five Hundred Years of Private Patronage and Art Collection*, ed. G. Jackson-Stops (London and New Haven, 1985), 233.

60. Wilson, *Kent*, 102, assigns this period to 1725–32; Ripley's accounts began in 1724.

61. See Harris, "Raynham Hall, Norfolk," 182. Pevsner distinguishes between Kent's structural and decorative contributions: *North-West and South Norfolk*, 151. Wilson, *Kent*, 101, seems mistaken in attributing the layout of the central hall to Kent. The absence of eighteenth-century floor plans obscures what Kent did to the structure, as opposed to the decoration. Still, as previously noted, the new doorways were probably not cut nor the old ones blocked up by Kent; rather, that was done when the central entrance in the west front was created in 1704–06.

excavations in the basement affected the ground floor above, and the introduction of a much-criticized archway into the ground-floor dining room required work on the walls.[62] (Figures 5.5, 5.6, 5.7, 5.8) The house was never gutted or wholly renewed, but the remodeling changed its internal look. The marble entrance hall became a showpiece of black and white classical elegance. Elsewhere gilt was laid on generously, and typically Kentian carved doorways and molding were introduced. Kent adorned the "Belisarius Room," then housing Salvator Rosa's eponymous painting, with a striking painted mosaic, and he introduced into the ground-floor dining room a miniature Arch of Severus that attracted critical comment but usefully separated the room's service alcove from the diners gathered round the table.[63] In addition to these changes inside the hall, the erection of the office and servant block went on at the same time. A direct connection with Kent as designer of these outbuildings is difficult to establish but seems likely.[64]

Despite the survival of Thomas Ripley's accounts, the absence of household records for 1727 and their lack of detail after 1730 render the total cost of the renovations irrecoverable. As usual, the cost of local labor is obscured among payments to "workmen" whose precise tasks are not laid out. Discernible expenditures between 1724 and 1732 nonetheless probably omit little of great substance. Digging the lake was probably the most expensive element of landscaping, and its cost is known. Ripley evidently directed the bulk of the renovations, presumably covered by his accounts, and separate observers agreed that work had been largely completed when they visited in late 1731 and 1732.[65] Between 1724 and 1731 Townshend seems to have spent about £15,000 on his renovations, an average approaching £2,000 a year, most of it incurred while Townshend enjoyed income from office.[66] (Table 5.2)

At this rate, current income provided for Townshend's architectural and decorative ambitions. His manifestly affordable expenditures are,

62. W. Fenn to Lady Townshend, 12 October and 30 November 1724, RUEM/CT; "Joyners work ... att Rainham Hall," paid February 1734, RL drawer 74.
63. The arch was condemned explicitly by the Earl of Oxford (HMC, *Portland MSS*, 6:159–60) and implicitly by Horace Walpole (*Anecdotes*, 3:58).
64. Much of the cost was accounted on the steward's household books, but of £1,170 recorded there as expended on "the offices" or for "offices building," nearly half was "settled" or "allowed" by Kent's colleague Ripley. The workmen employed on the offices nonetheless seem to have been local: household a/c, RUEA 1729. The buildings are known to this day as "the Kent wing."
65. HMC, *Portland MSS*, 6:158; HMC, *Carlisle MSS*, 86.
66. Ripley received over £10,000 in 1725–32, mostly from CT's London banker John Selwyn. Only £650 was paid after CT resigned in 1730. Raynham household accounts 1730–37, RUBV, record just £400 related to the renovation.

TABLE 5.2
Expenditures on Raynham Renovations, 1724–1731

The lake	£1,690
Other landscaping	205
The offices	1,168
The hall (Thomas Ripley's account)	10,398
Miscellaneous (from household accounts)	1,577
TOTAL	£15,038

SOURCE: T. Ripley's account, 26 January 1732, RUEM/CT; W. Fenn's monthly accounts April 1723–March 1725, RUEM/CT (except May 1724, RL drawer 121); household accounts, RUEA 1724–26, 1728–29; household accounts 1730–37, RUBV.

as averages rather than as total expenses, in line with those of men of comparable stature who were building from scratch rather than renovating.[67] On the other hand, the cessation of work at Raynham shortly after Townshend left public office suggests that the lack of official income made further work unaffordable. If this is the case, it testifies again to the relative modesty of his means, when compared with men of really great fortune in his era.

The renovations Townshend undertook at Raynham in the end speak eloquently of the man. They were stylish, even in the vanguard of fashion, where the viscount had long sought to place himself.[68] At the same time, however elegant the work at Raynham, it lacks the opulence and outrageous splendors of nearby Houghton and Holkham. Whatever Townshend's resentment of the former's grandeur, he never suffered the kind of doubt about why he built that beset Holkham's lonely owner, the Earl of Leicester.[69] Something in the second viscount's character corresponded much better with the temperate comfort of Raynham than with the gaudy display of Houghton. He was a man of ambition, to be sure, a power-seeker and public figure, yet a private man, not one given to political "congresses" like Walpole's at Houghton or to medieval Christmas feasts for tenants and neighbors. Little austerity appears in him, but there is reserve.

67. Five noble builders in the first half of the eighteenth century laid out £1,800 to £2,800 annually, although these averages conceal massive outlays concentrated at particular points in the process: Beckett, *Aristocracy*, 331–33. See also H. J. Habakkuk, "Daniel Finch, 2nd Earl of Nottingham: His House and Estate," in *Studies in Social History*, ed. J. H. Plumb (London, 1955), 153.

68. See CT's desire for a new kind of chair and for mourning "exactly to the fashion" in W. Watts to R. Leman, 4 June and 8 December 1704, RBF/CT 1692–1704, and his concern to wear the prescribed riding clothes expressed in G. Tilson to C. Delafaye, 10/21 September 1725, PRO SP 43/7.

69. Wilson, *Kent*, 182.

Born to his title and estate, secure in them both in ways his Norfolk rivals could never be, Townshend did not require the ostentation that served social and political functions for the come-lately Coke and Walpole. Nor did he need the hospitable gestures, the (often unsuccessful) displays of political influence, the elaborate and hectic socializing and taking of pulses in which his father engaged. In these ways the son was not simply different in character from his father; his life and therefore his country seat reflected the temper of a different age. It was one when an aristocrat could rest in his country seat, removed from quotidian pursuits, guarded behind the palings of a park across which no one wandered, with generous vistas that were the artificial creations of a protected social stratum, creations made possible by and symbolic of both isolation and security.[70] The son was different from the father in taste and in involvement with his local surroundings, but he also lived in times that had changed. The story of the second viscount's political career is the final and best indication of how and even why that change had occurred.

70. Stone and Stone, *An Open Elite?* 335–40; J. Bassin, "The English Landscape Garden in the Eighteenth Century: The Cultural Importance of an English Institution," *Albion* 11 (1979): 15–32.

❋ Chapter 6 ❋

Charles Townshend
National Reputation and Local Politics

The political career of the second Viscount Townshend contrasts with that of his father in many ways, not the least in the traditional measures of success. Yet in addition to his achievements—the embassy to the Netherlands, membership on the Privy Council, appointment as secretary of state, the honor of the Garter—Charles Townshend's energies were directed into a political world in which partisanship had become an inevitable feature of the scramble for office and reward. Where the first viscount easily trimmed his loyalties, his son adhered to one group; more tellingly, where the father displayed discomfort with the very idea of party, clinging to beliefs that confrontational politics were unnecessary, the second viscount accepted party conflict as a cardinal feature of political life. These representatives of two different generations demonstrate in their attitudes toward party politics a fundamental shift that had occurred in the political world since 1660: the emergence of party.[1] In their differing political successes, too, father and son exemplify just how far the locus of power had begun to shift out of the county by the early eighteenth century. Horatio Townshend's political failures can be attributed largely to the vexed, factious, and insecure temper of Norfolk politics during his day, yet county affairs fade in significance for interpreting Charles Townshend's accomplishments. Although county government drew the second viscount's attention (especially in his role as Norfolk's lord lieutenant), it never preoccu-

---

1. J. R. Jones, "Parties and Parliament," in J. R. Jones, ed., *The Restored Monarchy, 1660–1688* (Totowa, N.J., 1979), 48–70.

pied him. Nor was his value to the central government and the monarch calculated by them in terms of his local authority. In large part, this state indifference to Townshend's local role grew from the more peaceable circumstances of his day, when even fears of Jacobite plots extended only marginally to Norfolk and had little impact on county life.

Tensions among the elite of Augustan and early Hanoverian Norfolk derived much less from apparent challenges to basic structures of county life (whether in the form of republicanism, possible Dutch invasion, or religious nonconformity), and far more from the local resonances of party-labeled national issues.[2] Perhaps as a result of the growth of ideological quarrels, Charles Townshend's profile as county figurehead was less pronounced than that of his father. The second viscount consorted with gentry less parochial than their Restoration predecessors, relatively removed from county administration.[3] The expansion of central government bureaucracy into the provinces in the early eighteenth century, notably in the persons of numerous excise collectors and customs agents in the war-mobilized society of Augustan England, eroded provincial insulation from central government direction. Anthony Fletcher persuasively talks of a successful "assertion of the primacy of county institutions" in the struggle between central and local authority after 1660,[4] but it seems less likely that local institutions retained effective primacy much after 1700, as the counties began to fill with central government agents as military and taxing institutions expanded. The mediating role of the lord lieutenant between the province and center remained, but it was diminished in importance. Of growing consequence to the county's landed interest were those, MPs notably among them, who could open the doors to patronage at Whitehall and provide access to the more than 12,000 permanent positions that England's "corps of public servants" occupied in the 1720s.[5] The receipt of such plums helped draw the sting from land tax at 4s. on the pound. In the absence of office itself, the best way to lessen the impact of government agencies on the country gentry

2. For a view from other areas, see G. S. De Krey, *A Fractured Society: The Politics of London in the First Age of Party, 1688–1715* (Oxford, 1985), and P. Jenkins, *The Making of a Ruling Class: The Glamorgan Gentry, 1640–1790* (Cambridge, 1983), especially chaps. 6 and 9.

3. On this removal see J. M. Rosenheim, "County Governance and Elite Withdrawal in Norfolk, 1660–1720," in A. L. Beier et al., eds., *The First Modern Society: Essays in English History in Honour of Lawrence Stone* (Cambridge, 1989).

4. *Reform in the Provinces: The Government of Stuart England* (Cambridge, 1986), 367.

5. G. Holmes, *Augustan England: Professions, State and Society, 1680–1730* (London, 1982), 255 and chap. 8, passim.

was to move as close to the source of authority as possible. A word in the lord lieutenant's ear or a place on the commission of the peace might no longer suffice.

Aware of the constricted nature of his power in county society, Charles Townshend devoted to county business no more energy than it recompensed. How much he expended varied according to the electoral seasons and the course of his career, but his involvement in the day-to-day competitions of county business never approached that of his father. With success, in fact, the second viscount absented himself from Norfolk entirely during the mid-1710s and during four trips to Hanover in the 1720s, as well as during parliamentary sessions each year.[6] There is no better indication that neither his reputation nor his power was grounded in the county.

The Making of a Young Statesman

Despite the advantages he enjoyed in making his way in the world, the second Viscount Townshend began his career without fanfare and, with respect to partisan allegiance, somewhat tentatively. In his first years of adulthood, perhaps out of deference to the seventh Duke of Norfolk, current lord lieutenant, he stood apart from county affairs. His delay in entering local politics may be a sign he did not consider the establishment of a local base as a prerequisite for attaining a position of political substance. Instead, having taken his seat in the House of Lords in December 1697, he frequently attended there.[7] Raised under the moderate Tory influence of James Calthorpe in the 1690s, and exposed to the Whiggish one of the senior Robert Walpole, Townshend found his political direction slowly. Between 1699 and 1701 he joined Tories in several Lords' protests, and in April 1701 showed hostility to the Whig Junto lords, including his future mentor, Lord Somers. By the time Somers was acquitted at his impeachment, however, Townshend was beginning to come around to the Whigs.[8]

---

6. CT was apparently not in Norfolk between the death of Queen Anne and April 1717: household a/cs 1703–16 and 1717, RUBV; London household a/cs 1704–16, RLBV. He was abroad June–December 1723, June 1725–January 1726, June 1727 (a trip cut short by George I's death), and June–September 1729: "An account of the Charges of the 4 Journys from England to Hannover," NRO, MS 553, T142B.

7. *LJ*, 16:174–350, passim. Still, his approaching wedding in July cut into attendance in 1698, and he did not speak in the House until May 1701: C. T[urner] to [R. Walpole], 15 May 1701, CUL, C(H) corr. #142.

8. *LJ*, 16:377, 655, 756; A. S. Turberville, *The House of Lords in the Reign of William III* (Oxford, 1913; reprinted Westport, Conn., 1970), 220. W. Coxe, *Memoirs of the Life and Administration of Sir Robert Walpole, Earl of Orford*, 3 vols. (London, 1798), 1:63, notes CT's early Tory inclination; *DNB* misstates his position on Somers's impeachment. For

His father-in-law, Thomas Pelham, was an active politician who could introduce Townshend to the intricacies of Williamite politics and whose government service tempered a Whiggishness never so immoderate as to lose him the esteem of "the other side of the House."[9] Pelham's influence may account for Townshend's growing identification with the court, which coincided with his appointment as lord lieutenant in Norfolk upon the incumbent's death in early 1701.

In Norfolk the absenteeism of the previous lieutenant, the Duke of Norfolk, and the aging and death of an older generation of party men, helped to lower political temperatures. The elections of 1695, for example, had lacked contests for all six county constituencies, in defiance of recent precedent, and the choices for knight of the shire apparently represented an agreement between Whig and Tory to share the seats.[10] By 1698, however, the echoes of the plot to assassinate the king helped engender more contentious elections: the Norfolk county seats were disputed, with two Tories victorious. Townshend nonetheless took no part in the elections, the first of his adult life, even though Sir Henry Hobart, standing in the Whig interest, went to great pains to secure the support of the viscount's former guardian, the elder Robert Walpole.[11] In fact, in the aftermath of the contest, when Hobart was slain in a duel with the Tory squire Oliver Le Neve, who was rumored to have questioned Sir Henry's military valor, Townshend helped save Le Neve from outlawry and prosecution for murder. Townshend's modest aid in procuring an amenable sheriff was his most energetic intervention in Norfolk affairs to date.[12]

Hobart's death opened the door for Townshend to mediate be-

CT's ties to Somers see W. Sachse, *Lord Somers: A Political Portrait* (Madison, 1975), 260, 278.

9. *HP 1660–90*, 3:218–21; H. Horwitz, *Parliament, Policy and Politics in the Reign of William III* (Newark, Del., 1977), 227, 229, 248, 258, 352, 364. Pelham had a country streak in him and was an opponent of the standing army in January 1699: D. Hayton, "The 'Country' Interest and the Party System, 1689–c. 1720," in C. Jones, ed., *Party and Management in Parliament, 1660–1784* (New York, 1984), 77.

10. Rosenheim, "Oligarchy," 307–8, 411–12.

11. CT's steward Thomas Warde, reproved by CT for meddling in this election, denied he had done so and expressed pleasure "to heare as I formerly have, that your lordship would not consern yourselfe therein": [draft] TW to CT, 10 June 1698, RBF/CT 1700–40. CT's caution may have led HT's friend, the aged Sir John Holland, to compliment the "prudent conduct of your selfe & affaires": Sir J. Holland to CT, 10 September 1698, RBF/HT Felton. See also W. B. Gurdon, ed., "The Gurdon Papers, no. 7," *The East Anglian . . .*, n.s., 5 (1893–94): 67.

12. CT also significantly promised to intervene for Le Neve "att the cabinet councel of London," if the trial went badly. M. Knyvett to O. Le Neve, 4 April [1700], NRO, KNY 926, 372x6; H. Rippingall to [O. Le Neve], 31 July 1699, BL, Egerton 2719, f. 96. R. W. Ketton-Cremer, *Norfolk Portraits* (London, 1944), 58–68; N. Luttrell, *A Brief Historical Relation of State Affairs . . .*, 6 vols. (Oxford, 1857), 4:418–19; Rosenheim, "Oligarchy," 311–12; *Prideaux letters*, 192–93.

tween county partisans, since it removed a factious and largely unmourned character from among them. An analysis of county politics, made by Humphrey Prideaux, Dean of Norwich, before Le Neve's acquittal, suggests that the opportunity was there for Townshend to seize. Reflecting in January 1700, when the Duke of Norfolk's ill health gave reason to consider the future, Prideaux discerned in Norfolk two groupings, the composition of which transcended party labels. The faction "which now prevails" was identified with the Duke of Norfolk, while the "opposit faction" revolved around Robert Walpole the elder. Yet both men belonged in the Whig parliamentary camp under William III, a national allegiance suggesting both the uncertainty of contemporary party loyalties, and the likelihood that Norfolk disputes in this era were distinguished by local more than national issues.[13] In spite of current factionalism, however, the future looked calm to Prideaux. He justifiably assumed that only Townshend would succeed as lord lieutenant on the duke's death, itself a near prospect: "nothing else," he asserted, "can be acceptable to the countey, or, in truth, doe the king any service in it." Townshend would carry all the duke's supporters, Prideaux predicted, as well as his erstwhile guardian Walpole, the only one of "any parts or interest in all that [opposing] party." Thus the choice of Townshend as lord lieutenant would "remove all manner of divisions out of this countrey . . . [which] for now 25 years hath been continually harassed with them."[14]

Others similarly looked to Townshend as the natural future leader of Norfolk, not because of anything he had done, but because of who he was. Rumors that Lord Orford would replace the Duke of Norfolk upset the county, "for all the gent[ry] are zealous for my good Lord Townshend." One gentleman reiterated that it was in "the interest of the county that the king do make [Townshend] his leiueftenant . . . rather than . . . a forrenor or some other person whose power it can never be in to unite this coun[ty]." The viscount's appointment at the end of April 1701 gave a "generall satisfaccon to all friends with us," an ally happily reported.[15]

That Townshend would impose a somewhat partisan unity was not impossible, as three months prior to his appointment he had

13. Ibid., 194–95; Horwitz, *Parliament, Policy and Politics,* appendices B and C; Horwitz, "The Structure of Parliamentary Politics," in G. Holmes, ed., *Britain after the Glorious Revolution* (London, 1969), 96–114.
14. *Prideaux letters,* 195.
15. C. Turner to R. Walpole, 9 April and 5 May 1701, CUL, C(H) corr. #120, 135; J. Lovell to same, 15 April and 13 May 1701, ibid., #124, 140. For the commission, see *CSPD 1700–02,* 310; commission as *custos rotulorum,* 31 May, and as lieutenant, 26 June 1701, RU commissions.

abandoned electoral neutrality by supporting his younger brother Roger for knight of the shire in the Whig interest in January 1701. Roger paired with Robert Walpole the younger, whose father had died in November 1700, but only the young Townshend proved successful, being elected with a veteran Tory MP, Sir Jacob Astley. Lord Townshend was in the country at election time and, campaigning enthusiastically for his brother, had his tenants conveyed to the polls in Norwich. The decidedly poor showing of Walpole and of Astley's partner, Charles Paston, suggests that many voters may have supported the idea of splitting the representation as in 1695, though Townshend did not.[16] The campaign marked the viscount's first foray into county elections and provided a taste, in the Townshend-Walpole alliance, of things to come. Further, the poll and the change in the lord lieutenancy together symbolized the passing of an old guard and the removal of county leadership into new hands. Had young Walpole and Roger Townshend not stood as knights of the shire, Ashe Windham, the Townshends' young first cousin, wealthy and from a respected family, might have been a logical choice, too, while the sixty-two-year-old Astley's partner Paston, son of the second Earl of Yarmouth, was only twenty-seven.[17] In a society that still deferred to age, the eminence of such youths testified to the emergence of a new era, as did a contemporary roll of the aged and dead. Among the latter were Hobart, nonagenarian Sir John Holland (who died two years shy of his century in 1701), Robert Walpole the elder, the Duke of Norfolk, and Sir Peter Gleane. With the exception of Astley, other veteran campaigners from the battles of the 1670s and 1680s now bowed off the stage: Sir Robert Kemp, Sir John Turner, Sir Neville Catelyn—all of them sixty-five or older in 1700 and inactive in politics. Perhaps these men, with an uncomfortable history of infighting and feuding behind them, favored electoral accommodation, but not the younger men. For them the party fight was the legitimate focus of their personal aspirations.

Into this arena Townshend fully entered after the election in early 1701. In London, perhaps emboldened by his lieutenancy commission, he made his maiden speech in the Lords in May.[18] About the same time, back in the county he garnered honors intimating his growing stature: he became high steward of King's Lynn and of Norwich cathedral, received the freedom of Norwich,

---

16. W. Manning's general a/c vouchers for 1700 and "An account of the money disbursed att Norwich eleccon," RUEA fragile; list of 13 freeholders' votes: RL drawer 74; NRO, Rye MSS 9, Norris's Collections, vol. 2 for vote totals.
17. *Prideaux letters,* 193; GEC, *Peerage,* "Yarmouth."
18. C. T[urner] to [R. Walpole], 15 May 1701, CUL, C(H) corr. #142.

and secured appointment as *custos rotulorum* for Norfolk.[19] As new lord lieutenant he used his military patronage in the county, rewarding old friends and making new with the distribution of militia posts.[20] He retained the lieutenancy virtually intact from the days of the Duke of Norfolk, and those he sought as deputies were almost unanimously willing to serve, echoing the "generall voice of the county" with their "rejoycing that your lordship is lord lieutenant of this county." Major Robert Houghton knew of no one who would "desert serving under the Lord Townshend, tho I found few willing to serve under any other, especially a stranger" to the county.[21] Although he had taken a partisan position in the county election of January 1701, Townshend made no attempt to create a party bastion in the lieutenancy (as he would in 1715), having no desire to factionalize the county by ill treatment of former deputies.[22] He found that, by adding his own men to those who had served under the duke, he could obtain an amenable mix, a strategy similar to that employed with the magistrates' bench in subsequent years, when opponents were not so often purged as they were overwhelmed by newly created, loyal justices.[23]

Townshend took these steps to constitute the lieutenancy and militia corps of officers without leaving London, an indication of his unwillingness to allow local affairs to break into his life in the capital. He made the point of coming down for the assizes in August 1701, however, to meet with his new deputies. He received generous civic receptions in the county,[24] entertained local company at Raynham (something he rarely did), and was heading back to the capital when

---

19. Lynn steward 21 April; Norwich cathedral steward 30 April; freedom of Norwich 15 August; appointment as *custos* 31 May 1701: RU commissions.

20. The deterioration of the lieutenancy journal after 1701 prevents accurate identification of all militia officers, but in 1697 they numbered 110 (ensigns and above) for four foot and one horse troop, and 35 for the borough militia: R. Hindry Mason, *The History of Norfolk* (London, 1884), 435–36. It should be noted, however, that regimental commanders usually appointed their lower officers.

21. Houghton's words were reported in E. L'Estrange to CT, 19 May 1701, RBF/CT 1696–1735.

22. Tory Sir Neville Catelyn was retained as deputy until his death, while Tory Sir John Wodehouse was offered a deputation, which he accepted in 1702: NLJ 1676–1715, NRO, NRS 27276, 372x7. CT singled out for nonrenewal only Sir Francis Guybon, a Tory whose failing lay not in his party but in blatant commercialization of his position: E. L'Estrange to CT, 19 and 26 May 1701, RBF/CT 1696–1735. See *HP 1660–90*, 2:455 on Guybon, mistakenly said to have kept his commission until his death.

23. Cf. the deputies of the Duke of Norfolk in March 1701, *CSPD 1700–02*, 249, with a list of 4 August 1702, *CSPD 1702–03*, 392, and with a list, July 1702–January 1704, found loose in the lieutenancy letterbook 1701–39, NRO, MS 503, T133A. CT added John Harbord and Sir John Holland, second baronet.

24. "Money expended at Norwich Assizes ... August 1701," RUEM/CT; W. Watts to R. Leman, 31 August 1701, RBF/CT 1696–1735.

the "sudden dissolution" of parliament stopped him.[25] Even so, he left Norfolk before the general meeting that chose Sir John Holland, second baronet (grandson of the first viscount's friend), and Roger Townshend as the consensus (Whig) candidates for knight of the shire.[26] Despite predictions that this choice by the "gent. of the county" would prevent opposition, the indefatigable Tory campaigner Sir Jacob Astley eventually put himself forward, although he lost at the poll.[27]

While he benefited from the reflected glory, Townshend exercised little influence on the election results countywide. Most of the Norfolk Whigs returned at this second general election of 1701, the first after Townshend became lieutenant, had displayed their party colors years before, and he carried no weight at Castle Rising, little at King's Lynn, and none for which there is evidence at Norwich.[28] The "very talented squadron" of Norfolk Whig MPs that emerged in Queen Anne's reign[29] was discernible in outline at the end of William III's, but what it owed specifically to the energies of Townshend (or Robert Walpole) was yet to be demonstrated.[30] Lord Townshend's own position, in county and in capital, was far from clear in the latter days of William's reign. One rumor in early 1702 had him considered as a replacement for the late Lord Tankerville as Lord Privy Seal,[31] but nothing came of it, and the analysis made by Robert Walpole's uncle Horatio (admittedly the views of a jaundiced Tory) suggests that Townshend enjoyed little influence at court.[32] Horatio Walpole's simultaneous account of a quarrel between himself and the Turner family nonetheless confirms that Townshend publicly identified himself as a party adherent, as

25. J. Calthorpe to R. Leman, 1 October and 18 November 1701, ibid. Parliament was dissolved 11 November 1701.

26. P. Le Neve to O. Le Neve, 22 November 1701, NRO, MC1/52, Le Neve correspondence; Sir W. Cooke to [R. Townshend], 26 November 1701, HMC, *Townshend MSS*, 329.

27. HMC, *Portland MSS*, 4:26–27; Sir W. Cooke to [R. Townshend], 26 November 1701, HMC, *Townshend MSS*, 329, and R. Hare to same, n.d., RBF/CT 1696–1735; S. Fuller to same, 12 December 1701, NRO, Sotheby purchase, 13.3.1980, S154D; election agreement, 6 December 1701, RBF/CT 1701–34; Rosenheim, "Oligarchy," 409–13.

28. On Norwich, see G. Guth, "Croakers, Tackers, and Other Citizens: Norwich Voters in the Early Eighteenth Century" (Ph.D. diss., Stanford University, 1985), 333–57.

29. G. Holmes, *British Politics in the Age of Anne* (London, 1967), 231.

30. Perhaps CT encouraged Sir John Holland to stand at this election, but Roger, who ran first in January 1701, was only second to Holland in December, apparently because Holland's voters did not support him. This suggests no strong alliance between the two: [R. Hare] to [unk.], n.d. [after July 1702], BL, Egerton 2720, f. 469; D. Hayton, "A Note on the Norfolk Election of 1702," *Norfolk Archaeology* 37 (1980): 321.

31. H. Bland to R. Walpole, 3 February 1702, CUL, C(H) corr. #173.

32. Even so, Horatio implied that CT had exercised considerable electoral influence at the last election: H. Walpole to R. Walpole, 14 February 1702, ibid. #184.

one might expect at a time when, and in a county where, political partisanship was the order of the day.[33]

Townshend's failure to gain government place in the early years of Anne's reign, and the dismal showing of the Whigs in Norfolk over the same period, exemplify the problems resulting from adherence to the party of the "outs." Yet Townshend's lack of promotion may also suggest that his qualities as a politician laid claim to significant attention only over time, and that a blunt, even abrasive, personality lengthened the period required.[34] Despite his political allegiance, Townshend—in the absence of a more qualified resident peer—was retained by Anne as lord lieutenant when William III died in March 1702, and he had no Tory deputy lieutenants thrust upon him. On the bench, however, it was a different matter: no displacements occurred at the queen's accession, but eighteen new men were made justices, mostly identifiable Tories. Purges of Whigs followed, adjustments to the commission that suggested the high fortune both of Norfolk Tories and of the party nationally.[35] The outcome of the elections to Anne's first parliament in the summer of 1702 emphasized the point.

In the light of later developments, it is possible to overestimate the ease with which a powerful and reliable Whig interest was erected in the county, allowing Daniel Defoe in 1712 to call Norfolk "the territories of King Walpole." The "small but influential group of Whigs . . . particularly associated . . . with young Robert Walpole" (fundamentally a local group) became visible only after 1705 and in parliament, not during 1702 in Norfolk.[36] The energy of Walpole as an electioneer must not be underestimated, but locally Townshend was credited with building up the group of Whig MPs, though in the elections of 1702 he took no active part. Townshend's low profile suggests his doubt about the electoral influence he exercised. He stayed away from the county before the poll in 1702, an absence that coincided with his brother's decision not to stand for knight of the shire. Without family claims to motivate him, the viscount may have reflected on his recent

33. Ibid. Cf. J. Hoste to same, 2 March 1702, ibid. #195, who comments that "the 2 names of Wigg and Tory [are] made a very jest everywhere and to all meetings."

34. The Earl of Chesterfield began his character of CT by explaining that "very long experience and unwearied application" made him "an able man of business": BL, Stowe 308, f. 14. Lord Hervey is unexceptionably harsh about CT's "slow, blundering capacity," but if there is any truth in Hervey's characterization, what he describes as the viscount's impatience, obstinacy, rashness, and natural insolence (among other traits) would not have urged his rapid promotion: John Lord Hervey, *Some Materials towards Memoirs of the Reign of King George II*, ed. R. Sedgwick, 3 vols. (London, 1931), 1:80–82.

35. List of JPs, c. April 1702, BL, Harleian MS 7512B; commission of the peace, 20 September 1702, NRO, T287A; L. K. J. Glassey, *Politics and the Appointment of Justices of the Peace, 1675–1720* (Oxford, 1979), 154–58.

36. Holmes, *Politics*, 230–231.

retention by the queen as lord lieutenant, deciding that discretion and gratitude dictated adoption of a neutral stance. He may also have been showing both awareness of the county's sensitivity to a lord lieutenant's interference and respect (albeit fleeting) for the House of Commons' resolution, passed in 1701, which condemned peers' involvement in parliamentary elections as an "infringement of the liberties and privileges of the Commons."[37] In any event, Townshend made explicit his wish "not to be concerned in the election."[38]

It is not clear why his brother Roger declined entering the lists. It may have been because he foresaw defeat (thinking his second-place finish in December 1701 signaled limited popularity), or because ill health had already begun to weaken him. Publicly he claimed that his not appearing would "contribute not only to my own ease but to the county's unanimity," and he took care that "the gentlemen shall know at their quarter sessions that I don't designe to stand for the county."[39] One historian sees the move as manipulative and argues that with Townshend's withdrawal the leading Whigs also aimed to discourage Sir John Holland (who had fallen in their esteem) from himself standing.[40] In either case, the announcement of Roger Townshend's decision brought disarray to a public meeting in Norwich in May 1702, which broke up without naming any candidates. Despite promptings not to stand, Holland persisted, linking with Sir Edward Ward, who had earlier been set forth as a compromise choice.[41] Astley and Sir William Cooke were set up as Tory nominees, and at the election not only did Astley run Holland a close second, but Cooke ran a strong third. In a poll of nearly 11,000 votes, only 173 separated top from bottom, but the result was a split representation, part of a strong Tory showing that returned eight of the twelve MPs for the county's constituencies.[42]

In April 1702 one observer had predicted that a united Whig party would be victorious in these elections; the story in July and August

37. Quoted in J. Cannon, *Aristocratic Century: The Peerage of Eighteenth-Century England* (Cambridge, 1984), 104.
38. R. Townshend to R. Walpole, n.d. [c. 11 April 1702], CUL, C(H) corr. #590. This letter is dated 1708 in CUL but clearly comes from 1702: although electoral circumstances in 1702 and 1708 were similar, Roger in 1708 had made his decision not to run by January: W. Watts to TW, 13 January 1708, RBF/CT 1705–20s.
39. R. Townshend to R. Walpole, n.d. [c. 11 April 1702]; CUL, C(H) corr. #590. That the use of the word "unanimity" here implies nonpartisanship may be doubted, but see M. Kishlansky, *Parliamentary Selection: Social and Political Choice in Early Modern England* (Cambridge, 1986), 128–29 and 144–46, on the persistent search for unanimity in a partisan world.
40. Hayton, "The Norfolk Election of 1702," 320–24.
41. [Sir C. Turner] to R. Walpole, 7 May 1702, CUL, C(H) corr. #214.
42. R. Hare to [unk.], n.d. [after July 1702], BL Egerton 2720, f. 469.

was entirely different, because unity had not been preserved.[43] The dominance of Tories at Great Yarmouth (where they stood unopposed for the second time running), their decisive victory at Norwich, and the capture of one of the county places by Astley, all marked a shift in county opinion, and the evidence of particular influences (apparently that of the Earl of Nottingham among them) was alarming to the Whigs.[44] Moreover, signs at King's Lynn indicated that the Whig interest as embodied by the Turner, Walpole, and Townshend families would face future electoral challenges even there. This was an especially significant development, since the borough was geographically proximate to Walpole at Houghton and to Townshend at Raynham. If the collective political strength of these grandees could not secure seats in King's Lynn, identifiably in their neighborhood, then there was little chance of shepherding many west Norfolk voters to the county elections in Norwich without unacceptably large cash inducements. According to one Whig, the attempted imposition of Robert Walpole, a nonresident, led many King's Lynn voters to "grudge and repine at our governing here (as they are pleased to call it)," sentiment that boded ill for an effort to build a Whig party interest.[45] In the final analysis, however, Walpole's ability to provide convoys for the King's Lynn fleet (with Townshend's aid) and to help with legislation of local import secured him his seat unopposed. Access to the central government gave Walpole his influence in the provinces; the same could be said for Townshend. In each case, however, the election of 1702 showed that their electoral influence remained uncertain, because their access to the avenues of central government power was limited.[46]

The dismal Whig showing at the elections of 1702 prompts speculation about the means by which Townshend, Walpole, and friends elevated their interest in ensuing years to the point of making Norfolk their private fief. The outcome of further elections in Anne's reign clarifies the picture, documenting the slow spread of Whig electoral power from west Norfolk to Norwich and then to Great Yarmouth in the east. The Whigs' foothold at King's Lynn and Castle Rising pro-

43. R. Hare to R. Walpole, 1 April 1702, Add. 9092, ff. 1–2.
44. R. Walcott, *English Politics in the Early Eighteenth Century* (Oxford, 1956), 220; Mason, *History of Norfolk*, 434, n. 2; *CSPD 1702–03*, 237; Guth, "Croakers, Tackers," 413, 416.
45. J. Turner to R. Walpole, 8 May 1702, CUL, C(H), corr. 216; Rosenheim, "Oligarchy," 334–36; Plumb, *Walpole*, 1:102–4, who misconstrues Turner's reference to "Mr. Townshend," who is neither the fictitious uncle Horatio that Plumb invents, nor CT's brother Horatio—still under age at this time—but obviously Roger Townshend.
46. Sir C. Turner to R. Walpole, 11 May; C. Turner to same, same date; J. Turner to same, 18 May and 3 June 1702, CUL, C(H) corr. #222, 223, 227, 233.

vided a party base from which to grow, and Townshend's retention of his office as lord lieutenant, despite rumors of dismissal, contributed to his influence in the county.[47] Above all, the growing acknowledgment within the county community that Norfolk's affairs depended on its politicians' connections in London ultimately debased the importance of internal county politics and enhanced the local stature of the figure who enjoyed central government influence. Still, the future in 1702 did not look encouraging, if only because the Whigs' prospects as a national party were obviously clouded. When Queen Anne eventually yielded to the necessity of waging war energetically, and opened her ministerial ranks to allies of the Junto (and then its members as well), Townshend gained advancement; in the meantime, he faced an uncertain road.

In parliament Townshend demonstrated his taste for national politics. At the start of Anne's reign, when he helped draw up the address to the queen and figured on the committee that applauded her declaration of war, he gave the first sign of the support he later lent to England's overseas commitments. His attendance in the Lords was assiduous, and the house began to acknowledge his efforts. Signs of emerging stature appear in his regular appointment to major committees from 1702–03 on and in his active role in reports and conferences.[48] He was chosen to help investigate the "Scotch Plot" in 1703—and to lambaste Nottingham in a stormy session.[49] By Christmas of that year, the press of parliamentary business prevented Townshend from giving his estate its accustomed attention,[50] and he remained in London until the parliamentary session ended the following April, adhering to what became a pattern of life: half a year in London (October or November until April or May) and half a year in the country.[51] All the same, as long as the "Norfolk group"[52]—including its noble member—held no office and possessed no connection to the inner corridors of power, its influence in Norfolk remained confined to the northwest of the county. Even in the county the absence of local

---

47. J. Turner to R. Walpole, 3 June 1702, CUL, C(H) corr. #233, mentions such a "flying report" current at Lynn. See also H. Sorrell to R. Leman, 20 June 1702, RBF/CT 1696–1735. The foothold at Castle Rising was due to the Walpole family's interest there: see H. L. Bradfer-Lawrence, "Castle Rising and the Walpoles," in C. Ingleby, ed., *A Supplement to Blomefield's Norfolk* (London, 1929), 29–46.
48. *LJ*, 17:192–681, passim.
49. *The History and Proceedings of the House of Lords* . . ., vol. 7, *1697–1714* (London, 1742), 47–48; Holmes, *Politics*, 433; H. Horwitz, *Revolution Politicks: The Career of Daniel Finch, Second Earl of Nottingham, 1647–1730* (Cambridge, 1968), 191–96; Luttrell, *Relation*, 5:371.
50. CT to TW, 25 December [1703], RBF/CT 1692–1704.
51. Household a/cs 1703–16, RUBV, document the pattern.
52. The phrase is Holmes's: *Politics*, 233.

Whig MPs from quarter sessions in 1703 dismayed their adherents (especially from west Norfolk), who were vulnerable to partisan attacks reminiscent of those which generated regional squabbles within the magistracy in the 1680s. This time, however, the intercounty rivalries played off party divisions within Norfolk and elicited pleas for recognized local leaders like Robert Walpole to abandon the parliamentary session for the county.[53]

Townshend's place within this sociopolitical structure was ambiguous—*in* but not *of* it. He seems to have envisioned for himself no active role in the cycle of county administration, and his advisor James Calthorpe certainly saw no great advantage to be gained by diligence in mundane county affairs, among which he included even the once-meaningful assizes.[54] Yet if Townshend generally ignored assizes, spent little time politicking in the county's boroughs, and personally attended only eleven of 139 meetings of his lieutenancy (seven of these before 1709), he was not entirely an absentee lord lieutenant. Nor did he abdicate all the responsibilities that fell on him as the county's leading and brightest magnate. In part, he could avoid county activities in which his father had engaged, because his stature was guaranteed without them. He had no aristocratic rival in the county; as heir to, rather than recipient of, his noble title, he encountered little of the jealousy his father faced. In part, he neglected public occasions in the county because of a temperament that led him to forgo Walpole's political congresses at Houghton,[55] even when the two were staunch allies. Moreover, the ability to have his way in the magistrates' meetings, and the ability to direct county affairs through traditional channels, were less important in creating an interest in the county than was the carefully husbanded dispensing of inside knowledge, the promise of access at the center. As patron, as manipulator of bench, shrievalty, and lieutenancy, he still played his part in Norfolk.

Evidence of Townshend's role as dispenser of patronage ranges from the grant of ecclesiastical livings in his gift to the sale of his barley to his steward Thomas Warde's son-in-law, leaving aside the official positions that he later bestowed as secretary of state. Early in his career, above all Townshend spoke up for supplicants, whether he was trying to secure royal assistance after a fire at Great Yarmouth or helping

---

53. Sir J. Turner to R. Walpole, 5 February 1703, CUL, C(H) corr. #286; J. Hoste to same, 18 January 1703, ibid., #278; C. Turner to same, 28 February 1703, ibid., #295. See complaints about similar absences from a meeting of land tax commissioners: J. Wrott to R. Walpole, 7 and 21 May 1703, ibid., #305, 307.
54. J. Calthorpe to R. Leman, 17 July 1704, RBF/CT 1692–1704.
55. On these gatherings, see Plumb, *Walpole*, 2:88–89.

with a private member's bill on behalf of a down-at-heels Norfolk gentleman.[56] He had few places he could actually assign, and while his word went further in some arenas than in others (and in many went further than that of any other Norfolk man), as early as 1705 Robert Walpole, serving on the Admiralty Council, had effective patronage powers that the viscount did not gain even in 1707, when made Captain of the Yeomen of the Guard.[57]

Townshend directly influenced official appointments to the lieutenancy and militia; indirectly he helped with nominations to the bench and provided assistance in keeping men from appointment as sheriff. Yet even in these endeavors his power was limited—by the useful number of deputy lieutenants and the absolute number of militia officers; by the pliancy of successive lords chancellor in accepting recommendations for the bench; by the monarch's willingness to skip over Townshend's protégés as potential sheriffs. The employment of patronage was not an effortless exercise in power politics but rather a series of calculated advances and retreats, where favors begged balanced those granted. We have seen already how the provision of convoys for the fishing fleets of King's Lynn could affect borough elections.[58] The demands of family naturally figured in these calculations of patronage, and Townshend's position helped some, like his cousin William Windham, whose military pension was threatened, or the Pelham in-law who was brought to the Duke of Marlborough's "particular notice."[59] Some could not be assisted, and another cousin accused Townshend, "notwithstanding all his promises & protestations," of making no effort to secure him an equerry's place.[60] Townshend similarly rejected his own steward (who craved a militia place for a friend), and turned down an aspiring clerk for his Dutch embassy by arguing that "on the conclusion of a peace the young gentleman

56. S. Clarke to [CT], 24 April 1707, RBF/CT 1696–1735; R. Britiffe to [CT], 13 December 1708, RBF/LL Britiffe.

57. T. Saunders to TW, 7 and 16 September 1710, RBF/CT 1705–20s, claims that the "interposition of great men" prevented his receiving a place CT had promised him in the Guard; R. Mann to H. Walpole, 4 August 1709, similarly complained that the Duke of Leeds had "interfer'd in the last [Guard's] vacancy": HMC, *Townshend MSS*, 335.

58. CT helped provide similar protection for the fleet at Great Yarmouth, where his electoral interest was well established after 1715: see CT to the mayor of Great Yarmouth, 28 September 1721, PRO, SP 44/122, p. 169.

59. W. Windham to A. Windham, 20 May 1715, NRO, WKC 7/24, 404x2; A. Cardonnel to H. Walpole, 19 May and 5 June 1710 (NS), RUC [NRO]. See also F. Spelman to R. Leman, 27 April 1702, RBF/CT 1696–1735; same to same, 5 May 1702, Add. 41654, f. 46; G. Townshend to CT, 21 June 1721, PRO, SP 35/27, no. 32; E. Ashe to CT, 23 June 1721, PRO, SP 35/27, no. 35, and 30 May 1723, PRO, SP 35/43, no. 82.

60. J. Windham to A. Windham, 28 September 1714, 28 June 1715, NRO, WKC 7/28, 404x2; K. Windham to same, n.d., NRO, WKC 7/21, 404x1.

would again be adrift."[61] Yet when the patron could or would perform no service, the effort had to appear to have been made. When pressed to recommend a clerk to Robert Walpole in the Admiralty Office, Townshend admitted he could not be "very earnest" in the recommendation, but wanted Walpole to let the supplicant know of the attempt.[62]

Maneuverings around the commission of the peace and the shrievalty had deeper reverberations—administrative, political, and electoral. When Townshend in 1705 considered possible justices, "young Captain Buxton" received a recommendation because he had an influential Whig baronet for an uncle and because he came from southeast Norfolk, where another JP was "absolutely necessary " to provide administrative coverage. Sir Richard Allin, a Suffolk man, was recommended the same year because, as Sir Charles Turner told Robert Walpole in London, "now you are gone from amongst us I am sure you ought to give us who are left all possible assistance, to bear up against the common enemy."[63] Considerations of political geography could not lightly be dismissed. Townshend's efforts to have a benefice bestowed on an ally frankly aimed to do "good service to our interest in that part of the country" where the living was located.[64] A decline in local gentry involvement in the business of county life was a source of concern among the county's aristocratic leaders, too, although they set a poor example by "clearing [their] hands of county businesse," as Robert Walpole said in 1703. But the retreat of greater gentry justices simply mirrored, further down the social scale, a man like Townshend's disengagement from the county arena, except where electoral or other overtly partisan concerns were at stake.[65]

J. V. Beckett's view that the aristocracy saw itself as a "service elite which freely offered its time in administering the countryside" is in any event not sustained by an examination of Townshend's activities.[66] His limited local government presence demonstrates substantial preoccupation with party manipulations, less with his own reputation, and scarcely any with the daily conduct of county affairs. He showed little interest in the issues that engaged the JPs, except as they affected electoral politics, and his (limited) participation in county business

---

61. CT to TW, 6 February [1705], RBF/CT 1705–20s; HMC, *Townshend MSS*, 334–35.
62. CT to R. Walpole, 8 July 1705, CUL, C(H) corr. #422.
63. Sir C. Turner to R. Walpole, 2 July 1705, CUL, C(H) corr. #420; CT to R. Walpole, 8 July 1705, ibid., #422.
64. CT to R. Walpole, 23 September 1706, ibid., #535.
65. Plumb, *Walpole*, 1:116–17; R. Britiffe to [CT], 17 March 1707, RBF/LL Britiffe. See also Rosenheim, "County Governance and Elite Withdrawal."
66. Beckett, *Aristocracy*, 374.

before 1709 is most notable because it actually marked the peak of his engagement. He took an interest in a county address of 1704 and backed the petition of Norwich Whig voters in a 1705 electoral dispute.[67] He was present in Norwich during sessions week in the autumn of 1705 and 1706, and in the latter case he dined publicly with the justices and privately with some forty gentlemen, helping to draw a congratulatory address to the queen on the victory at Ramillies.[68] Later he found neither time nor energy for such activity when in Norfolk.[69]

Townshend focused carefully on the sheriff's office in early years. Influence over it, as over the commission of the peace, was immediately apparent and showed one's standing with central authority. Because of its burdens, because it disabled its holder from election to parliament, and because it provided control over the place and time of elections, the shrievalty remained an important local post; moreover, the business of appointment was confined to one season and took place in London, and to this degree was not a county matter. In 1704 the nomination of three men as possible sheriffs, all with claims on Townshend's energies to prevent their appointment, exposed the full range of considerations that might complicate county political life. With elections on the horizon, securing a trustworthy sheriff was essential, and electoral strategy entered the calculations Townshend furiously made. He and Walpole intended to promote Roger Townshend and the sitting county member, Sir John Holland, as Whig candidates for parliament, dropping the Whig loser of 1702, Sir Edward Ward, whom they nonetheless strove not to alienate as a political ally. Since Ward was among the three shrieval nominees this year, preventing his appointment might make up for passing him over as a county candidate. If he *were* chosen sheriff, however, he would surely assume he had been purposefully chosen to remove him as a parliamentary candidate, which conviction it was feared might dissuade him and his friends from supporting the eventual Whig nominees. Townshend worried that "any division [among Whigs] on that [eastern] side of the country" where Ward and his allies lived would make it "difficult to propose any thing in matters of election with any success," a concern revealing the limited circumference of Townshend's

---

67. J. Turner to R. Walpole, 10 October 1704, CUL, C(H) corr. #356; CT to same, 8 October 1705, ibid., #436.
68. Household a/cs 1703–16, RUBV; Sir C. Turner to R. Walpole, 11 October 1706, CUL, C(H) corr. #538; CT to same, n.d. [August] and 14 October 1706, ibid., #525, 540.
69. This is not to suggest that CT failed to advance borough interests from London and especially in parliament. See for example the letter from the Norwich corporation, 1 April 1721, with thanks for CT's role in the passage of beneficial legislation: PRO, SP 35/26, no. 3.

electoral influence and underscoring the urgency he felt to keep Ward from being made sheriff.[70] Committed to Ward, and having already promised to get off a cousin, Ashe Windham, Townshend could do nothing for the third candidate for sheriff, Robert Walpole's uncle, James Hoste, who desperately visited Raynham to see if he could avoid what he later came to call—after his efforts proved futile—"my damned new office."[71]

Whatever Hoste's dismay, it could not match Townshend's relief at delivering on his promises to Ward and Windham. He knew that successful manipulation of appointments was enhanced by the mystery the process held for the layman, and he appreciated the cachet attached to his ability to penetrate the maze of inner government affairs. His failure to do so would have rendered him "but a very indifferent figure in these parts."[72] The consequences of the choice of friends as sheriff continued to preoccupy Townshend. He made efforts to prevent those skipped over for 1705 from being chosen for 1706, suggesting the names of alternative nominees. He sought the Duke of Newcastle's assistance to keep men off, and he considered a direct approach to the assize justices, who themselves submitted a list of qualified gentlemen to the Exchequer and thus might "take care of our friends." He employed whatever means were at hand to prevent his allies' nomination.[73] Yet Townshend did not always desire to "take care" of friends. When forthcoming elections necessitated the appointment of a sympathetic Whig sheriff in 1707, Townshend mentioned a man of slight interest, insignificant as a marshaler of voters from the area where he lived, but useful as presiding officer at the county poll. The honor actually went to another gentleman, whose inclusion among the candidates Townshend had carefully hidden, lest the man's importunities to be let off interfere with the political necessity of appointing him.[74]

Underlying the manipulation of the sheriff's office lay electoral

70. CT to R. Walpole, 6 and 8 November 1704, CUL, C(H) corr. #370, 372. Ward lived at Bixley, just south of Norwich.
71. J. Hoste to R. Walpole, 8 November and 27 December 1704, University of Chicago, Regenstein Library, MSS 274. An effort was perhaps made to ease the financial burden of office for Hoste: see C. Turner to same, 29 January 1705, CUL, C(H) corr. #402.
72. CT to R. Walpole, 20 November 1704, CUL, C(H) corr. #377. J. Hoste admitted he was "wholly a stranger to all these affairs": J. Hoste to R. Walpole, 8 November 1704, University of Chicago, Regenstein Library, MSS 274. See Plumb, *Walpole*, 1:48, where this incident is confused with the next year's efforts.
73. CT to R. Walpole, 10 and 22 October 1705, CUL, C(H) corr. #441, 443 (the letter of 10 October is endorsed 26 October); CT to same, n.d. [but October/November 1705], ibid., #446; CT to same, 14 October 1706, ibid., #540.
74. CT to R. Walpole, 8 November 1707, ibid., #582.

considerations, and in this arena other tools could be brought to bear, tools of a sort the first Viscount Townshend either lacked or did not use. The changing process of selecting candidates was one of these. In the early seventeenth century, selection of candidates followed many channels; gentry meetings, when held, were apparently most often meant to arrive at consensus.[75] In Norfolk after the Restoration, and especially during the 1670s and 1680s, such gatherings often made the choice, but they were frequently restricted to the like-minded, who gathered almost invariably in Norwich to decide upon acceptable but partisan nominees as knights of the shire. In the eighteenth century the locus of decision-making shifted, so that the "Norfolk group," resident in London and dominated by the second viscount, caucused among themselves and transmitted their choice of candidate to the county. Selection was slipping from the local gentry's hands, although not without comment and resistance.[76]

Roger Townshend confessed in 1705 that he first broached his candidacy "at Soho Square [in Lord Townshend's house] in company with some . . . very good friends." This gathering acknowledged the need for local input, and "further advice" was solicited from the county, but only in choosing a partner for Roger, whose selection as the first candidate was a *fait accompli*. Despite the grandees' ostensible obeisance to county opinion, some local gentry objected to this pre-emptive way of nomination and became "very angry we [in London] did not stay in expectacon of a generall meeting" in Norfolk.[77] Roger Townshend argued that the delay entailed in such a meeting would have given the Whigs' enemies an opportunity to frustrate any "accommodation" and declare their candidates first: such were the imperatives imposed by party politics. More significantly, however, he showed a distaste for county meetings in themselves. "Such assemblys have never yet contributed to the peace of the county," he claimed, "nor have even those been thought by all sides to be generall enough, where there was the greatest appearance of gentlemen."[78] Whether the logistical problems of general meetings justified decisions made in exclusive conclaves is a matter for debate. Whatever face was put on it, decisions had been made in London that showed how far outside

---

75. Kishlansky, *Parliamentary Selection*, chaps. 1–2. See nonetheless an instance in 1621 when a prospective Norfolk nominee was approached by "the gentlemen of our county at London": ibid., 29.

76. Ibid., 142–46, presents evidence about preelectoral gatherings, mostly under Charles II, which were held in the county and sought to avoid contests. This is in contrast with Norfolk's partisan gatherings in London under Queen Anne.

77. [Draft] R. Townshend to [unk.], n.d. [1705], RBF/CT 1701–34.

78. [Draft] R. Townshend to [unk.], n.d. [1705], RBF/CT 1696–1735.

the county political power lay. The Tories seem to have met in Norwich to decide upon their candidates, but Whig followers apparently had to accept decisions made for them far away.[79]

Beyond using the mechanisms of selection to his advantage, Lord Townshend overtly enlisted his employees to canvass on his behalf. In 1705, when the parliamentary session kept him away from the county, Townshend relied on his steward, Thomas Warde, who in 1698 had been reproved for meddling in county elections.[80] Seven years later, however, Townshend encouraged Warde to solicit votes even before the sitting parliament dissolved, showing that the viscount now accepted as legitimate the party politicking which was generated by the predictability of elections under the provisions of the Triennial Act. By contrast, the first viscount had frowned upon campaigning that took place while parliament still sat. In 1705 no one registered such an objection, and following his master's instructions, Warde canvassed with "dilligence and care" on the lord lieutenant's behalf. He enlisted three of Townshend's largest tenants at Raynham and "15 of the cheife inhabitants & freeholders" in Shipdham, who promised forty votes. Since "but one" man in Shipdham had voted for the Whigs at the last election, this shift in the electoral balance justified Townshend's recent acquisition of land there.[81] The absence of declared Tory candidates for the county seats made most of these efforts superfluous, and Roger Townshend and Sir John Holland were returned with a "mighty appearance" that would have overborne any challengers. All the same, the Whigs had to maintain an effective political organization as long as their party remained, as Townshend's secretary William Watts put it, "an abomination to some people" in Norfolk.[82]

The elections of 1705 increased Whig representation for Norfolk's six constituencies from four to seven, including both seats for the city of Norwich, where municipal spilled over into parliamentary politics and where, despite his earlier separation from borough affairs, Lord Townshend had his prestige invested. His involvement began with city troubles that originated with the death of an alderman in August 1704. Despite the election of the Whig Thomas Dunch as new alder-

79. W. Watts to TW, with TW's draft reply, 13 February 1705, RBF/CT 1705–20s; J. Turner to R. Walpole, 19 February 1705, CUL, C(H) corr. #405; C. Turner to same, c. 21 February 1705, ibid., #406. See also CT to TW, 13 February 1705, RBF/CT 1705–20s.
80. [Draft] TW to CT, 10 June 1698, RBF/CT 1700–40.
81. [Draft] TW to CT, 21 February 1705, RBF/CT 1705–20s.
82. W. Watts to R. Leman, 4 April ("abomination"), 9 May 1705, RBF/CT 1705–20s; same to same, 30 April, 28 May, 1 June ("mighty appearance") 1705, RUC [NRO]; R. Britiffe to CT, 19 May 1705, RBF/CT 1705–20s.

man on two occasions, the Tory mayor William Blyth and his party in the court of aldermen, committed to returning High Churchmen, disallowed the voters' choice and ultimately swore in a Tory instead. Incensed, Dunch and his supporters sought outside help, from Townshend among others.[83] Amid this unresolved partisan struggle, the Norwich parliamentary elections were held in May 1705; they proved equally contentious, but Mayor Blyth's highhandedness cost his party the city's seats. His behavior alienated the voters, who gave Whigs Waller Bacon and John Chambers a clear majority as members of parliament. Blyth nonetheless prevailed on the sheriffs to make a double return, on the grounds that Chambers and Bacon were not freemen of the city and so could not be returned as MPs. This maneuver tossed the election into the House of Commons, where the Whig candidates were declared elected in December 1705.[84]

Townshend had interjected himself into the municipal controversy "upon the first notice" he received of the aldermanic debacle. He wrote "to the freemen" (by whom he presumably meant the Norwich Whigs) to promise his assistance and to urge them to avoid "all tumultuous heat & passion." The Norwich Whigs sought his advice on how to proceed, whether at law or by petition to the Council, and a letter he drafted to Mayor Blyth shows he had been well briefed on the affair. It is informative that Townshend cautiously "wou'd not take upon [him] to direct [the Whigs] in what manner they shou'd proceed," and he showed his lack of political experience by his admission to being "under some difficulty to know what person about the court it will be most proper to commend [the Whigs] to be introduced."[85] Undeterred by Townshend's caution, the Norwich Whigs drew up a petition, which Townshend and the Bishop of Norwich together endorsed. The Privy Council gave it a hearing but to Townshend's surprise rejected the petition. It took a legal writ to secure Thomas Dunch his place as alderman and required action by the Commons to bring Mayor Blyth to his knees at the House's bar, asking pardon for the irregularities he had committed. The Norwich parliamentary election was similarly decided in the Commons (where Robert Walpole was one of the tellers for the ayes) in December 1705, after Townshend had closeted in Norfolk with the two would-be members.[86]

83. Guth, "Croakers and Tackers," 363–85, provides a full account of the aldermanic election. See also W. Watts to R. Leman, 30 April 1705, RUC [NRO]; Sir T. Pelham to CT, 10 May 1705, NRO, Bradfer-Lawrence, VI a ii, Townshend MSS 17–18C.
84. Guth, "Croakers and Tackers," 385–404.
85. Two drafts, CT to "My Lord," n.d. [1705], Add. 63079, ff. 3–4; [draft] CT to [W. Blyth], n.d. [1705], RBF/CT 1696–1735.
86. Guth, "Croakers and Tackers," 404–8; CT to R. Walpole, 8 and 9 July, 8 October 1705, CUL, C(H) corr. #422, 423, 436; HMC, *Portland MSS*, 4:199–200.

Townshend's role in these Norwich fevers was strictly partisan. Gloria Guth has pointed out that county leaders in Norfolk "were extremely interested in the politicking going on at Norwich," but "they only played an indirect part in events."[87] Their assistance was essential for the success of the Norwich Whigs in this instance, but the city Whigs were nonetheless independent of outside control. Townshend had not approached them, but they him. In his effort to extend his county base, then, Townshend had only a measure of success at Norwich: he interceded on the city's behalf at the center but lacked great influence in the halls of power and could not be a fully effective champion. Moreover, he was not attentive enough to the local scene to build an effective interest in Norwich. As he declared in autumn 1704 from Raynham, when he asked Robert Walpole to keep him informed of news from London, "tho I am extremely fond of the country . . . I cannot keep my thoughts entirely from Westminster."[88]

Westminster and Norfolk thoughts, the interests of province and center, coincided in Townshend's effort between 1706 and 1709 (when he left as ambassador for The Hague) to create at Great Yarmouth the interest he could not build in Norwich. The first hint of his campaign came in the fall of 1706, when Townshend in the country and Walpole in London (now a member of Prince George's Admiralty Council) used the latter's new position to try to secure convoys for the Yarmouth fleet: the trick that earlier worked in west Norfolk at King's Lynn was now employed in east Norfolk. Townshend visited the borough personally, and the citizens there were promised a convoy for the winter months; by November the politicians had made good on their commitment, and despite the attempt of local Tory burgesses to claim credit, the town knew whom to thank for this favor.[89] Unfortunately, the convoy "fatally miscarried" before performing any escort service, and in the spring of 1707 delegations from Great Yarmouth, Norwich, and the county at large begged Townshend to help obtain "a standing convoy for our Holland trade." Even Great Yarmouth's Tories this time acknowledged Townshend's mediating role, indicating that municipal self-interest could override partisan wrangling.[90]

Townshend's increasing stature in the central government surely encouraged the men of Great Yarmouth to seek his aid. In 1706 he

---

87. Guth, "Croakers and Tackers," 404.
88. CT to R. Walpole, 27 October 1704, CUL, C(H) corr. #364.
89. Sir C. Turner to R. Walpole, 11 October 1706, CUL, C(H) corr. #538; CT to same, 14 October 1706, ibid., #540; F. Longe to [CT], 27 November 1706, RBF/CT 1696–1735.
90. R. Ferrier to CT, 14 March 1707, RBF/CT 1696–1735; R. Britiffe to CT, 17 March 1707, RBF/LL Britiffe.

was nominated among the commissioners to negotiate the Union with Scotland and took an active role thereafter; it is probably from this point that he began his association with Lord Somers.[91] In November 1707 he was made a member of the Privy Council, a position his father never achieved; in September 1707 he became Captain of the Yeomen of the Guard; he also had sufficient standing in the House of Lords to be elected one of seven peers constituting a committee to investigate accusations of treason against Sir Robert Harley's secretary, William Gregg.[92] Moreover, during 1707–08 his standing with the court was enhanced by his temporary break with the Junto over its attacks on both Marlborough and Godolphin, whom he defended. Undoubtedly this effort raised his credibility at court, allowing him to provide better for those in Norfolk who turned to him. In return, Townshend laid claim to the gratitude of Great Yarmouth in the most tangible possible way and forwarded his brother Roger, seriously ill and thus unfit to be knight of the shire, to stand for a seat there in the general election of 1708.[93]

Pushing his brother's candidacy at Great Yarmouth was a significant step for the viscount. Only three years previously, on the occasion of a struggle in the House of Commons over the choice of a speaker, he had confessed he had "no reason to think" he could influence the borough MP Benjamin England to vote for a Whig speaker, especially since England, "his nephew & all his friends in Yarmouth are very zealous another way."[94] In 1708, however, Townshend's political intervention succeeded; poor as Roger's health was, he ran second in a four-man poll, barely behind the Tory leader. His ability as the lord lieutenant's brother to win over Great Yarmouth voters enabled two other party men successfully to set up for the county, increasing Whig

91. G. Burnet, *History of His Own Times*, ed. M. J. Routh, 2nd ed., 6 vols. (Oxford, 1833; reprinted Hildesheim, Germany, 1969), 5:295; J. J. Cartwright, ed., *The Wentworth Papers, 1705–1739* (London, 1883), 154. Seventeen letter covers from CT to Somers, dated between July 1709 and March 1711, but not the letters, survive in Add. 4223, ff. 219–40.

92. GEC, *Peerage*, "Townshend"; HMC, *House of Lords MSS*, n.s., 7:548. CT missed only one of forty-five meetings of the Union commissioners: *The Minutes of the Proceedings of the Lords Commissioners of the Kingdoms of England and Scotland* . . . (London, 1706).

93. Holmes, *Politics*, 234. Roger Townshend, colonel of a foot regiment since 1706, had long been afflicted with the stone. In 1707 an observer noted that "he pisses perhaps 200 times in a day and night" and held little hope for his recovery. Roger died 23 May 1709 at Bath: C. Spelman to CT, 9 May 1698, RUC [NRO]; R. Townshend to CT, 30 November 1706, RBF/CT 1696–1735; W. Windham to A. Windham, 7/18 November 1707, NRO, WKC 7/24, 404x2; A. Windham to [CT], 24 May 1709, NRO, Bradfer-Lawrence, VI a ii, Townshend MSS 17–18C.

94. CT to R. Walpole, 10 October 1705, CUL, C(H) corr. #443; W. A. Speck, "The Choice of a Speaker in 1705," *Bulletin of the Institute for Historical Research*, 37 (1964): 20–35, 42.

representation for Norfolk by one. The party's inability even to nominate a candidate for the port constituency in 1710 and 1713, after Roger Townshend's death, suggests that only a man with his connections could have enjoyed success there in 1708. The next victorious Whig in the town was in fact the viscount's other brother, Horatio, in 1715.[95]

Great Yarmouth was not the only scene of party struggles involving Lord Townshend in the 1708 election. For the county, the Tories' failure to put forward a candidate in 1705 had motivated them to prepare for future elections well in advance. Edward Coke, wealthy and well-connected grandson of the Duke of Leeds, had proposed himself even in advance of the 1705 election as a possible county candidate at the next poll. Before then, however, illness weakened his local interest, and his death in 1707 removed the strongest potential Tory candidate and opened the doors for someone other than Roger Townshend to stand for the Whig party in 1708.[96] That other candidate proved to be Ashe Windham, the Townshend brothers' first cousin and a substantial landowner who had been proposed as a likely member as far back as 1699. The county learned of his candidacy, again hit upon by the grandees then resident in London, by letter rather than at a local meeting of the squirearchy. Townshend ordered his steward (enlisted once more in the campaign) to let him know in London if opposition arose to Windham and his proposed partner Sir John Holland, "for here [in London] there is no body named or thought of but these two at present." That the two Whigs ran unopposed demonstrates the authority of the London-based grandees, the efficacy of local electioneering, and the power of sitting members and the lord lieutenant to affect decisions at the polls—or to thwart polls altogether.[97]

What with other victories, including the unexpected one of Thomas De Grey (Windham's brother-in-law) at Thetford, the Whig party's cause in Norfolk grew strong in 1708.[98] After the polls, Dean

95. The Great Yarmouth poll of 1708 was Ferrier (T) 269; Townshend (W) 261; Samuel Fuller (W) 251; Benjamin England (T) 240: NRO, MSS 9, Norris's collections, vol. 2, separate sheet. After 1715 the Townshend interest became well entrenched in the borough; in 1723 Sir Charles Turner wrote CT about the election there that "there was no other contest in the town than who should show the greatest respect to your lordship": PRO, SP 35/43, no. 123.

96. W. Watts to R. Leman, 28 May 1705, RUC [NRO]; C. Turner to R. Walpole, 23 December 1706, CUL C(H) corr. #552; TW to CT, n.d. [late December 1706], RBF/CT 1705–20s; R. Britiffe to CT, 17 March 1707, RBF/LL Britiffe.

97. *Prideaux letters*, 193; W. Watts to TW, 13, 20 and 22 January, and c. 11 March 1708, RBF/CT 1705–20s; T. Townshend to same, 29 January 1708, ibid. On Windham, see R. W. Ketton-Cremer, *Felbrigg: The Story of a House* (London, 1982; paperback ed.), 81–100.

98. Rosenheim, "Oligarchy," 415; Guth, "Croakers and Tackers," 419–21; W. A. Speck, *Tory & Whig: The Struggle in the Constituencies, 1701–1715* (London, 1970), 34.

Prideaux surveyed the county scene as he had done in 1699. He commented on the popularity of the new Bishop of Norwich, Charles Trimnel, and on the low fortunes of the second Earl of Yarmouth and of the county's farmers. "But the Lord Townshend florisheth much among us," he happily concluded, "for the whole countey is absolutely at his beck, and he hath got such an ascendant here over everybody by his courteous carriage that he may doe anything among us what he will, and that not only in the countey, but alsoe in all the corporations, except at Thetford, where all is sould."[99] This sanguine appraisal is not entirely borne out by the facts: it takes no account of the energies of Robert Walpole and in any event would not apply a mere two years down the road, after Tory victories in another round of elections. Yet it approximated to reality: the influence of the viscount—attained, if not effortlessly, then with an ease his father would have envied—seemed likely to dominate the county for the future foreseeable from 1708.

The Statesman Made, 1709–1715

Prideaux and the whole world could not know that Townshend would soon remove, not just from the county, where he had shown signs of withdrawal, but from England altogether. In early May 1709, the Duke of Marlborough had arrived in London from the Continent, disconcerted by his negotiations with the Dutch, which were meant to pave the way for talks with the French to end the current wars, and seeking a partner for further talks. After Lord Halifax bowed out and the Earl of Sunderland's appointment was rejected, the choice as Marlborough's colleague fell on Townshend, "the most shining person of all our young nobility," Bishop Burnet noted, and one who had improved his "great parts . . . by travelling." Townshend, whose name had been advanced as plenipotentiary two years before, was already favorably regarded by the Dutch. Joining him with the intractable Marlborough showed the ministry's willingness to make concessions to Dutch claims for a defensive barrier against the French.[100]

Marlborough conceded that Townshend was an honest man but thought him one who did "not understand the temper of the Dutch,"

---

99. *Prideaux letters*, 200.
100. Burnet, *History*, 5:416; D. Coombs, *The Conduct of the Dutch: British Opinion and the Dutch Alliance during the War of Spanish Succession* (The Hague, 1958), 199; R. Geikie and I. A. Montgomery, *The Dutch Barrier, 1705–1719* (Cambridge, 1930; reprinted New York, 1968), 121–23.

a judgment that seems misguided, given Townshend's notably easy working relationship with the Dutch in 1709–11 and later.[101] Whatever Marlborough's original design in seeking a partner (and Halifax assumed that he sought someone to blame for what he foresaw as an unpopular treaty), the Duke and Townshend soon differed on the approach to take. Ultimately, Marlborough dissociated himself from the Barrier Treaty, and Townshend alone garnered the little credit and greater censure that accrued to it. His appointment nonetheless initially represented a victory for the Junto forces in the government and was for Townshend an obvious step up the ladder to office.[102]

Protracted wranglings with the Dutch (made worse by their discovery of England's duplicitous separate negotiations with the Spanish for Minorca), lack of cooperation from the Duke of Marlborough, and uninstructive advice from home combined to complicate Townshend's task in the Netherlands. By September 1709, however, he had received authority to make the commercial concessions needed to secure Dutch agreement to the treaty, which was signed and sent to London by the end of October. Although two separate articles outside the treaty's original ambit caused some consternation in the English ministry, by the middle of December 1709 they too had been ratified and the full treaty concluded.[103] Townshend stayed on for more than a year thereafter as ambassador to the Dutch, watching hopefully for the treaty's effects on the war. In June 1710 he wished "with all my heart we were got safely & honourably out of this war"; later in the summer the lack of progress in negotiations with the French at Gertruydenberg and "our madness at home" (that is, the collapsing interest of the Whig Junto) left him "almost distracted."[104] Robert Walpole's dismissal as secretary of war in September and "great jealousies" between Marlborough and Townshend led the latter to look for his recall, but his willingness to work for peace, his forthrightness,

101. W. Coxe, *Memoirs of the Duke of Marlborough, with His Original Correspondence . . .*, new ed., revised, 3 vols. (London, 1847–48) 2 (1847): 414. J. Drummond commented on CT's high reputation with the Dutch: Drummond to [Sir R. Harley], 10 October 1710 (NS), BL, Loan 29/196, ff. 194–95, and same to same, 7/18 August 1713, BL, Loan 29/201, f. 125. See also Hatton, *George I*, 124–25, on the Dutch welcome to CT's appointment as secretary in 1714, and note the respect shown CT at an extraordinary meeting of the Estates of Holland in 1725: CT to the Duke of Newcastle, 21 December 1725–1 January 1726, PRO, SP 43/8.

102. Geikie, *The Dutch Barrier*, 122, 139–45. It was reported that Marlborough was jealous of CT's close ties with the Dutch: J. Drummond to [Sir Robert Harley], 10 October 1710 (NS), BL, Loan 29/196, ff. 194–95.

103. Geikie, *The Dutch Barrier*, 135–64.

104. CT to Marlborough, 11 June 1710 (NS), Add. 61116, f. 9; CT to same, 21 [?August] 1710 (NS), Add. 61148, f. 206. See generally CT's correspondence to Marlborough, 1708–11, ibid., ff. 146–227, passim.

and "his personall respect for the Queen" spared him until early 1711.[105]

The uncertain duration of Townshend's stay abroad posed logistical problems for family, estate management, and county politics, but by the summer of 1709 Townshend solved one difficulty by bringing his family over to join him in the Netherlands.[106] At the same time, he faced from long distance the melancholy necessity of seeing to his brother's replacement as member of parliament for Great Yarmouth, for Roger Townshend died shortly after his brother went abroad. The Whigs optimistically sought to retain the seat they had picked up under the Townshend family aegis in 1708. This desire to promote their own man at Great Yarmouth unfortunately was at odds with the goal of preventing the outspoken Tory, Benjamin England, from gaining the seat. The Whigs also ran afoul of local Tories' strenuous efforts to end the city's internal turmoil by uniting to exclude any outsider as MP.

Eager to put in his nominee, the viscount took at face value the offer of Samuel Fuller the elder to defer to Townshend's choice of candidate. Ostensibly, the ambassador's influence had risen this high. Perhaps disingenuously, Townshend embraced Fuller's throwaway suggestion that Horatio Walpole the younger, Robert's brother and Townshend's secretary at The Hague, was suitable for the by-election, but Fuller clearly hoped his son would have the nomination.[107] Ashe Windham exposed the elder Fuller's letter "only as a compliment" to Townshend and explained that, stuck abroad as he was, Horatio Walpole could not win the seat unless he had "one fit to be a manager" for him at Great Yarmouth (a deficiency of which Roger Townshend had often complained). Moreover, only young Fuller seemed likely to defeat the Tory Benjamin England, and since Fuller's father had promised an alliance with Townshend's nominee at the next poll, Fuller *fils* seemed the safe bet. Yet all these calculations went for naught, as the unopposed return in November 1709 of a compromise candidate, Nathaniel Symonds, former bailiff and senior alderman, marked an accommodation between the borough's partisan groups and a rejection of outside interference. Townshend's inability to per-

105. J. Drummond to [Sir R. Harley], 10 October 1710 (NS), BL, Loan 29/196, ff. 194–95; Plumb, *Walpole*, 159–60. CT tried to obtain Marlborough's good offices upon his recall from The Hague: CT to Marlborough, 16 and 20 January 1711 (NS), Add. 61148, ff. 222, 225.
106. [Draft] TW to Lady Townshend, 22 July 1709, RBF/CT 1705–20s; John Bishop of Ely to [CT], 12 August 1709, NRO, Bradfer-Lawrence, VI a ii, Townshend MSS 17–18C.
107. S. Fuller to CT, 27 May 1709; CT to Fuller and H. Walpole to same, both 18 June 1709 (NS), NRO, Sotheby purchase, 13.3.80, S154D.

suade the French to abate their duties on imported fish (a proposal Samuel Fuller had urged on him) further led Great Yarmouth's voters to spurn the ambassador's man. The next year, any obligations created by Townshend's previous good offices on the city's behalf had been entirely forgotten; the Whig interest in the borough faded as badly at the election of 1710 as it did anywhere in the county—or country.[108]

Townshend had the good fortune to be abroad during the fiasco of the 1710 general election. Voter disenchantment with the war, royal disillusionment with the Whig ministers, and fallout from Dr. Sacheverell's trial meant that the elections in the autumn could scarcely have come at a worse time for Whigs. Townshend followed the changes from abroad and had no reason to assume his own embassy remained safe, but it was not until January 1711 that his supersession seemed certain.[109] In the meantime he watched helplessly as Whigs fell from office, and as the gains made by the party in Norfolk and nationally diminished almost to nothing. The confident predictions of a group of the county's Whig MPs gathered in London in June 1710 proved empty ones in the fall. They nonetheless present an informative view of the county, reflecting again the removal of political decisions from the local arena to the metropolis, from the hands of the many to the well-connected few. Especially in Townshend's absence abroad (since his presence otherwise helps explain meetings held under his auspices in London), the abandonment of the county forum is particularly noteworthy.

Presuming as far as any local politicians had ever dared, and superciliously ignoring the possibility that voters might exercise an informed and independent voice, Ashe Windham, Sir Charles Turner, and Robert Walpole met in London and proposed candidates for all Norfolk's constituencies.[110] They picked the incumbents for Norwich, and for Great Yarmouth the triumvirate suggested Samuel Fuller (Roger

108. A. Windham to CT, 7 and 14 June, 1709, NRO, Bradfer-Lawrence, VI a ii, Townshend MSS 17–18C; S. Fuller to same, 27 May 1709, ibid; Le Strange, *Lists*, 163, 182.

109. J. Taylor to H. Walpole younger, 5 January 1711, RUC [NRO].

110. The following account derives from A. Windham to CT, 8 June 1710, NRO, Bradfer-Lawrence VI a ii, Townshend MSS 17–18C. G. Guth, "Croakers and Tackers," 512–13 and n. 50, claims the meeting was among Windham, Turner, and *Horatio* Walpole the elder, Robert's uncle. Despite the confusing reference to "Colonel" Walpole in the letter, Robert also held the title and he is certainly meant, for Windham claims he presented an address to the queen with "Colonel Walpole," obviously Robert and not his Tory uncle. The political atmosphere of the day also argues against a meeting between leading Whigs and the Tory Horatio Walpole, and Guth herself notes Horatio's Tory energy: ibid., 514. "Mr T," identified by Guth as Mr. Turner, is clearly young Horatio Townshend. See the *Address Presented to the Queen at Kensington*, 1 June 1710, Harvard University, Houghton Library.

Townshend's former ally) and "Mr. T," that is, the viscount's merchant brother, Horatio, not long returned from his trading venture to Turkey. Since the only obstacle to Horatio's standing was financial, his brother was urged to commit himself to bearing the £300–£400 in anticipated costs.[111] As for Thetford, the borough that Humphrey Prideaux had dismissed because of its hopeless corruption, Robert Bayliss (a Whig incumbent) was named again, along with Sir Henry Furnese's son. The King's Lynn seats appeared likely to go to the incumbent Sir Charles Turner and, with luck, to young Horatio Walpole, in place of his brother Robert, who would stand with Windham for the county. Finally, the one seat controlled by the Walpole family at Castle Rising (where the other belonged to the Whig William Fielding) could ideally go to the current knight of the shire, Sir John Holland, who had lost standing with his Whig allies for his lukewarm support of an address to the queen and desired "to let the county alone" and sit for the pocket borough.[112] Only the claims of the Walpole uncle, crusty Horatio senior, and some feeling that Holland had no right to be so well served by those he had treated ill, were seen as deterrents to the last part of this scheme.

The plan so boldly laid out in London in June proved impossible to implement in the county, especially in the absence of Lord Townshend and in the presence of ideologically motivated electors. In Norwich it was the citizens, not the county grandees, who determined the outcome, if not the nominees.[113] Elsewhere, the choice of Whig candidates was not so easily resolved as the three MPs hoped, and the Tories refused to stand still in the face of their opponents' electioneering. Growing less certain of their prospects, the Whigs by late July sought an accommodation over the county seats, with the two parties splitting the representation. Within two weeks, the dismissal of Godolphin as Lord Treasurer so heartened the Norfolk Tories that their chief spokesman, uncle Horatio Walpole, saw the prospect of taking eight of the county's twelve seats and refused even to consider compromise.[114] His own efforts to make "an interest" in Norfolk played no little role in bringing about such bright opportunities, but the absence of Lord Townshend, and his brother's inadequacy as a substitute for him, proved equally damaging to the Whigs. Horatio Townshend,

111. Horatio was overseas, mostly in Turkey, from early 1706 until autumn 1709: W. Watts to R. Leman, 6 April 1706, RUC (NRO); J. Wilson to TW, 6 October 1709, RBF/CT 1705–20s.
112. Hayton, "Norfolk Election," 320–24.
113. Guth, "Croakers and Tackers," 514–20.
114. H. Walpole elder to R. Walpole, 27 July 1710, CUL, C(H) corr. #634; same to R. Harley, 11 August 1710, HMC, *Portland MSS*, 4:561–62.

who had been instructed to "goe down to Raynham and kill a sheep or two" to encourage the voters, was "nott the best manager in affairs of this nature," yet no matter how ineffectual, his efforts had publicly engaged the lord lieutenant's reputation in the outcome. That made it all the more necessary for Horatio to "go into the country, lay aside the merchant, and spend and speak like a gentlemen."[115]

Unfortunately, neither his nor the best efforts of others could retrieve a hopeless situation. The voters' opinion had swung away from Whigs, and the party in Norfolk managed to retain only three of the ten seats they had previously held. The absence of leading Norfolk figures for much of the election campaign was perhaps especially damaging. Sir John Holland displayed "strange remissness" in marshaling voters and apparently "came not into the countrye, till Friday before the election, and came on the [election] day into town with a very small appearance." One may speculate that Holland's demeanor would have been different, if Lord Townshend had been available to press him. Yet all the blame for failure did not fall on Holland, since the "carriage" of Townshend's own neighborhood proved disappointing. When James Calthorpe spoke to some of Townshend's neighbors, he found that "they would not believe I had any commission from your lordship" to promote the Whigs' candidacy. Ironically, a gentleman like Calthorpe carried less weight as the viscount's spokesman (when Townshend was abroad and had provided no visible evidence of his commission to Calthorpe) than did Townshend's mere steward in 1705, at least when directly empowered by a master who was only as far off as London. The lord lieutenant's proximity to the county obviously still affected his political influence there.[116]

The nationwide Tory electoral success in the fall of 1710 spelled change in the embassy where Townshend was engaged. His removal was delayed to assuage the Dutch (who liked Townshend and were alarmed by the ministry's temper) and to find a suitable successor in the person of Thomas Wentworth, Lord Raby (made Earl of Strafford in 1711), who arrived at The Hague in April, when Townshend came home.[117] It was to a changed political world that the viscount returned, one in which his friends and allies, so recently placed to determine events, now observed the shaping of policy from the outside. Robert

---

115. H. Walpole junior to R. Walpole, 9 September 1710, cited in Plumb, *Walpole*, 1:163–64.
116. S. Fuller to CT, 11 September 1710, Add. 38501, ff. 128–29; J. Calthorpe to CT, 20 October 1710, RUC [NRO]; Rosenheim, "Oligarchy," 343–46, for the election.
117. Geikie, *Dutch Barrier*, 201–2; Luttrell, *Historical Relation*, 6:664, 697; Coombs, *The Conduct of the Dutch*, 238–39; Cartwright, *The Wentworth Papers*, 181, 193; entry for 19 April 1711, 1703–16 household a/cs, RUBV.

Harley, the newly created Earl of Oxford, attempted negotiations with Whigs in the summer and fall of 1711, partly designed to bring Townshend and Robert Walpole back into the ministry, but considering the pair's loyal adherence to the Junto at this time, no arrangement could have been made based on these two alone. The Junto in turn managed in December to win over the Earl of Nottingham to the opposition, with Townshend taking a leading role.[118] The House of Lords remained under Whig control, and as shown in December 1711 with its vote against peace without Spain, business there had its bite. But events soon overran the Whigs generally and Townshend personally, when the conduct of the war—and of the allies—surfaced as an issue of fierce party conflict in the second session of this most Tory of Queen Anne's parliaments.

Jonathan Swift's *Conduct of the Allies,* published in late November 1711, set the stage for an aggressive condemnation of the late Whig ministry's dealings with the Dutch, and sparked the most hostile in a series of Tory-inspired parliamentary investigations that dated back to the previous session. The seriousness of Tory purpose was demonstrated by the queen's dismissal of Marlborough as captain-general and by the creation of twelve Tory peers in the wake of the Lords' attack on the policy of "Peace without Spain." In January 1712 Robert Walpole was accused of corruption as secretary at war and found himself committed to the Tower; the next month, Tory resentment at the Dutch "spilled over into a series of censure votes unbridled in their hostility."[119] The Dutch were quickly condemned for failing to meet their military obligations, and then the Commons turned to the Barrier Treaty that Townshend had negotiated. By massive votes, the commercial articles were attacked as harmful to British interests; Townshend and all who had advised ratification of the treaty were vilified as enemies of the monarch and the nation. Such was the judgment on nearly two years of effort.[120]

These trying times were made no easier for Townshend by any offsetting domestic or Norfolk triumphs after his recall from the Low Countries. Quite the opposite was the case; between April and June 1711, his newborn daughter, his wife Elizabeth, and his eldest son Horatio died in succession.[121] These "irreparable misfortunes" so af-

118. Plumb, *Walpole,* 1:174–76; Holmes, *Politics,* 242.
119. Holmes, *Politics,* 70.
120. *Cobbett's Parliamentary History of England* . . ., 6, *1702–1714* (1810): 1092–93; Coombs, *Conduct of the Dutch,* 290–91, 298–99; Plumb, *Walpole,* 1:177–82; G. M. Trevelyan, *England under Queen Anne,* 3 vols. (New York, 1930–34), 3 (1934): 195–201; Holmes, *Politics,* 70, 142.
121. GEC, *Peerage,* "Townshend"; East Raynham parish register 1627–1716, NRO, PD 369/1.

fected Townshend that he was "oblige[d] . . . to leave my house & family for some time" to recover.[122] Despite the claims of some, then and later, he did not rush into his second marriage with Robert Walpole's sister Dorothy.[123] Surviving correspondence between Townshend and his first wife reflects affection between the two.[124] Until her death it was only occasionally, as when Townshend first went to Holland, or when Lady Townshend visited Bath in 1707, that they were separated for more than a few days. Townshend's move to bring his family to The Hague as soon as he was settled indicated more than a conventional concern for them, especially considering the expense of maintaining a full household abroad.

Between the staggering blows of marital bereavement and public condemnation, it may have consoled Townshend to retain his position as lord lieutenant, especially considering the Tory nature of the ministry and the general climate of opinion after the election of 1710. Why he kept his place at a time of Tory dominance, when the Earl of Oxford was under pressure to put in Tories everywhere, is not entirely clear, especially as Townshend was removed as Captain of the Yeomen of the Guards. The absence of a logical replacement in Norfolk, and Oxford's reliance on moderate Whig Lords to save him from his high-flying Tory brethren in the Commons, best explain the retention of Townshend, but the viscount's votes were by no means at the government's service.[125] The Tory-inspired remodeling of Norfolk's commission of the peace did nothing to signal the ministry's favor toward Townshend as the county lieutenant. As early as February 1711, when he was still in Holland, a new commission added thirty-two justices; another nine came on in June. Along with marginally less partisan additions in early 1712, the augmentation of the bench was predominantly if not exclusively Tory. Moreover, the Whig connections of virtually all justices purged in 1711 and 1712 are clear, and the eighteen dropped included those whose dismissal was a blatant affront to the party's local leaders. Grandees like Robert Walpole

122. CT to [J. de Robethon], 9 July 1711, BL, Stowe 224, f. 103.
123. Plumb, *Walpole*, 1:125, says CT married Dorothy Walpole "as soon as his [first] wife died," whereas he in fact waited over two years. See also *The Letters and Works of Lady Mary Wortley Montagu*, ed. Lord Wharncliffe, 3rd ed., 2 vols. (London, 1861; reprinted New York, 1970), 1:71.
124. No letters from CT survive, but Lady Townshend mentions his "writing . . . constantly every post": c. 23 April [1707], RBF/CT 1696–1735.
125. Holmes, *Politics*, 371–72, 379–80; C. Jones, "'The Scheme Lords, the Necessitous Lords, and the Scots Lords': The Earl of Oxford's Management and the 'Party of the Crown' in the House of Lords, 1711–14," in Jones, ed., *Party and Management*, 158. Ties of cousinship between CT and Harley may have played a part in the retention: see CT to Oxford, 27 February, no year, BL, Loan 29/159.

and Sir Charles Turner were spared humiliation, but those dropped included one of Townshend's major tenants, a cousin of the Walpoles, Windhams, and Townshends, an in-law of the Turners of Lynn, and the fiery Whig John Turner, elected to replace the incarcerated Robert Walpole as MP for King's Lynn. These purges show that well before losing his lieutenancy in 1713, Townshend, as one might expect, had lost his power to effect local appointments or protect those he had earlier promoted.[126]

The hand of Horatio Walpole the elder, Norfolk's Tory leader, guided some of these alterations. Throughout 1711 and 1712 he peppered the Earl of Oxford with requests for central government reward. Other than the shuffling of the magistracy, however, the Tories endured disappointment. In May 1712 Horatio complained that the Tory party's interest in Norfolk was suffering, both because he had not been shown sufficient favor and because the purges of local government had not been thoroughgoing; in his dissatisfaction, Horatio Walpole joined a chorus of other unhappy and frustrated Tories.[127] By the autumn of 1712, Walpole's reports from Norfolk noted more than the alienation of unrewarded Tories. Emphasizing to Oxford the "stirring and treating" the Whigs were making, he foresaw the Tories losing all the advantage recently gained with the electorate. Some concrete government favor toward the party might counteract the voters' slide, he believed, but the Tories remained "very uneasey they have not a new lord leituenant." Those few who "dare look Lord Townshend in the face, who is now very active & very expensive," required encouragement. What they needed, Walpole argued, was "an assurance from [the Earl of Oxford] that they shall have a head to govern them; and it would be no small addition to there satisfaction to have the present severd."[128] Townshend's dismissal as lord lieutenant was the greatest service the Tory party in Norfolk could receive.

Under this pressure, Townshend could not protect his position, and in April 1713 James Butler, Duke of Ormonde, replaced him as Norfolk's lord lieutenant.[129] After his dismissal Townshend adopted

---

126. Fiats for Norfolk of 2 February and 8 June 1711, PRO, C 234/26; commissions of the peace, same dates and 12 March 1712, NRO, T287A. Cf. the generally Tory commission of sewers issued 26 February 1712, CUL C(H) papers, 91/7. On the Tory-inspired purges, see Glassey, *Justices*, 201–12; Plumb, *Walpole*, 1:181–82.

127. HMC, *Portland MSS*, 4:685; 5:24–25, 29, 137, 171–72, 192–93; Holmes, *Politics*, 342–43.

128. H. Walpole to Earl of Oxford, 29 September 1712, BL, Loan 29/200 (cf. HMC, *Portland MSS*, 5:228–29, which omits part of this letter); same to same, n.d. [January 1713], BL, Loan 29/160.

129. Le Strange, *Lists*, 4.

a low profile in the county, which he in some sense never raised, since his return to the highest county office in 1714 coincided with his elevation as one of George I's leading ministers, a promotion that distracted him from county business thereafter. In 1713 the parliamentary session and his impending wedding with Dorothy Walpole in July kept Townshend from the local maneuvers surrounding the elections slated for the autumn.[130] The Bishop of Norwich in August commented on the quiet life Townshend was pursuing in the country early in his marriage, and added that it was "better than stirring to no purpose."[131] The results of the elections bore out Bishop Trimnel, for Tories won the county and Great Yarmouth seats unopposed. At Norwich the Whigs ate into the Tory vote total, but the latter gained both seats anyway. Only at King's Lynn and at Castle Rising, where uncle Horatio Walpole had lost any claim to his nephew's interest, did the Whigs obtain a victory. They were left outnumbered eight to four in the county's constituencies, an increase for them of one seat, but no great advance. Townshend was perhaps wise to remain outside the fray.[132]

Then again, the reception in Norfolk of his dismissal from the lieutenancy may have persuaded Townshend that his circle of Norfolk friends and allies was smaller than he thought. It was rumored that his deputies would either "all . . . continue or all lay down" their commissions under Ormonde,[133] presumably staying on if Townshend urged it as their duty, or stepping down in loyalty to him. In the event, however, his deputies split: six of nine accepted new commissions and included among them the most active deputies during Ormonde's fifteen-month tenure. Here was an indication to Townshend to look for his allies outside the county.[134]

Beyond these suggestions, the declining volume of Townshend's correspondence around 1712 makes it difficult to assess his reactions to displacement from the lieutenancy. His actions can be followed, however, in the House of Lords, where he displayed an unsurprising animus toward the Tory ministry and where his political profile rose steadily if not spectacularly, overshadowed still by the remaining Junto

---

130. R. Walpole to A. Windham, 21 April 1713, NRO, WKC 7/33, 404x2; K. Windham to same, "Sunday" [April–July 1713], NRO, WKC 7/21, 404x1. But see Guth, "Croakers and Tackers," 423–24, for CT's involvement at Norwich this year.

131. Charles, Bishop of Norwich to [CT], 18 August 1713, Add. 38507, f. 84.

132. Rosenheim, "Oligarchy," 416–17; Guth, "Croakers and Tackers," 423–27.

133. K. Windham to A. Windham, "Sunday" [April–July 1713], NRO, WKC 7/21, 404x1.

134. NLJ 1676–1715, NRO, NRS 27276, 372x7, for attendance and list of Ormonde's deputies, c. 13 July 1713. CT's three appointees who did not serve Ormonde were Robert Walpole, Ashe Windham, and Thomas De Grey.

lords. In debate he followed the lead of Halifax, Wharton, and Nottingham.[135] On occasions when Townshend took the point on some parliamentary maneuver, he met with mixed results. His attempts to embarrass the ministry in April 1714, by moving to investigate the subsidies being paid to Highland clans, backfired badly when attention was drawn to the previous ministry's much larger payments.[136] Whig efforts to make similar political capital of the Scots' growing dissatisfaction with the terms of the Union led Townshend and his colleagues cynically to associate themselves with the Scottish peers' attempts in June 1713 to dissolve it. Such behavior adds no luster to Townshend's parliamentary career.[137]

Operating from such positions (and in the shadow of men like Wharton and Halifax), it is no surprise that Townshend cut a modest figure in the history of the Lords at the end of Anne's reign. Lord Somers, who had helped him to rise, could offer little assistance now as he neared the end of his life, diminished in energy and influence.[138] Townshend's personality did not help either, for to be "impatient of contradiction" and possessed of "invincible firmness, not to say obstinacy," was scarcely to possess traits that recommend a man for political office.[139] And if Townshend was, as Lord Hervey put it far more unpleasantly, "rash in his undertakings, violent in his proceedings, haughty in his carriage, brutal in his expressions, and cruel in his disposition," these posed a nearly insuperable set of characteristics for an aspiring politician to overcome.[140]

Moreover, where Townshend's personality was abrasive, no compensating parliamentary skills redeemed it. Admittedly he worked hard, but some questioned his judgment[141]; he spoke often but to

135. *Wentworth Papers*, 363, 397; *History and Proceedings of the Lords*, 7:425.
136. *Wentworth Papers*, 373–74; *History and Proceedings of the Lords*, 7:415–16.
137. Ibid., 7:398; Holmes, *Politics*, 113; Sachse, *Somers*, 308–9.
138. Sachse, *Somers*, chap. 15.
139. Thus the Earl of Chesterfield, BL, Stowe 308, f. 14. Note, for example, CT's imperious tone when writing from Hanover to the Duke of Newcastle, 29 June 1725 (NS), Add. 32687, f. 87, about sheriffs' elections in London: "I can't help imagining that Claremont [Newcastle's country home] and Norfolk take up a large share of your grace's and my brother Walpole's thoughts; and if it should happen that we cannot be able to carry but one sheriff in the City, I question whether your administration in that point would make the figure I desire it should, notwithstanding all the pains you promise to take in it."
140. Hervey, *Memoirs*, 1:80. There is some corroboration of this judgment from CT's allies. Robert Walpole wrote Newcastle, 25 July 1723, Add. 32686, ff. 284–85, about his fear "of displeasing Lord Townshend . . . in a point where I do not know his thinking" by stating his own case too fully. Walpole also complained of intemperate remarks in one of CT's letters, "tis hard that the villany of his adversaries is still imputed to the indiscretion of his friends": 31 August 1723, Add. 32686, f. 320.
141. See, for example, Mr. Wortley Montagu's comments: *Works of Lady Montagu*, 1:139.

little effect. The hostile Hervey thought him entirely unimproved by practice and claimed that even friends admitted that "he talked ill," although making "a much better figure in private deliberations than public debates."[142] If this was an unsympathetic view, even Lord Chesterfield found his friend's oratory "ungraceful and confused . . . perplexed in his arguments." Townshend, he explained, "spoke materially, with argument and knowledge, but never pleased. His diction was not only inelegant, but frequently ungrammatical, always vulgar; his cadences false, his voice unharmonious, and his action ungraceful. Nobody heard him with patience; and the young fellows used to joke upon him, and repeat his inaccuracies."[143]

If these are credible assessments of Townshend's parliamentary presence, how then can his rise be explained? The contrast with Walpole's gifts could scarcely be greater; Sir Robert's most notable modern biographer produces again and again instances when oratory helped him triumph.[144] Townshend with his seat in the Lords needed less of the political skill that Walpole possessed, but how he overtook the peers who were his colleagues is another matter. Burnet credited him with "great parts"; others thought him ingratiating.[145] These qualities may have helped him, as well as his generous approach to employees, friends, and adversaries such as the Earl of Oxford, Lord Bolingbroke, and Francis Atterbury, Bishop of Rochester.[146] But his success is also the tale of hard work and determination;[147] of fortuitous influence with one of George I's advisors, Jean de Robethon;[148] and of plain luck in the deaths of Viscount Stanhope and the Earl of Sunderland in

142. Hervey, *Memoirs*, 1:81.
143. BL, Stowe 308, f. 14; Philip Dormer Stanhope, Earl of Chesterfield, *The Letters of . . . Lord Chesterfield*, ed. B. Dobrée, 6 vols. (London, 1932; reprinted New York 1968), 4:1454.
144. Plumb, *Walpole*, 1:203–4, 261–64, 280, 371. See also E. Cruickshanks, "The Political Management of Sir Robert Walpole, 1720–42," in J. Black, ed., *Britain in the Age of Walpole* (London, 1984), 24–25.
145. Burnet, *History*, 5:416; *Works of Lady Montagu*, 1:124–25; *Diary of Mary Countess Cowper, Lady of the Bedchamber to the Princess of Wales, 1714–20*, ed. Hon. S. Compton, 2nd. ed. (London, 1865), 113–14.
146. CT's generosity with employees comes through in his estate correspondence. See also professions of loyalty in G. Tilson to C. Delafaye, 22 August–2 September 1729, PRO, SP43/10. CT advised the Duke of Newcastle: Newcastle to [Bishop of Chichester] 6–7 June 1723, Add. 32686, ff. 251–58, and Chichester to Newcastle, 12 June 1723, Add. 33064, ff. 218–23. He gave Chesterfield "many unasked and unequivocal proofs of his friendship": BL, Stowe 308, f. 14. Generosity to adversaries appears in CT to the Earl of Oxford, 20 December 1714, BL, Loan 29/204; Bishop of Rochester to CT, 25 September 1722, PRO, SP 35/33, no. 92; and [copy] Lord Bolingbroke to CT, 28 June and 17 September 1723, BL, Stowe 242, ff. 212b, 213.
147. "Lord Townshend . . . works too hard as usuall": E. Harrison to [Lord Lynn], 23 July 1728, RBF/LL family.
148. *Works of Lady Montagu*, 1:125.

1721–22, which removed obstacles to Townshend's ascendancy. The success of the second viscount's career after 1714 presents a contrast at nearly every turn with the failures of his father, a contrast that reflects not just the differences in their personal makeup but in the temper of the age as well. Horatio Townshend, most particularly, drew sustenance and authority from his base in Norfolk. Ironically, the acceleration of his son's career was characterized by a release, not from the "country" of Norfolk per se, but from the political community of the county. Charles Townshend's career ladder was set firmly on the streets of London, rather than in the sandy loams of west Norfolk.

Secretary and Statesman

A full appraisal of the second Viscount Townshend's career after 1714 is outside the scope of this study and could well fill another volume. His eventual displacement by Sir Robert Walpole has long led to an implicit disparagement of his own role in formulating policy. Yet, as Jeremy Black has recently made clear, historians' emphasis on parliamentary politics and domestic issues in the first third of the eighteenth century (justified and understandable though it is) has prevented a full assessment of the interaction of foreign policy with domestic affairs. Moreover, historians have perhaps disregarded the politics of the court, a forum for the determination of policy on a par with parliament itself.[149] In another light, Townshend might be assessed more favorably. His career as statesman and diplomat, however, is a measure of the success that this book seeks to explain rather than to chronicle. The forces behind his advance (especially the changed circumstances of eighteenth- as against seventeenth-century politics and the triumph of party over faction), rather than the nature of the advance, have been the chief concern in this telling of the Townshend story.

The accession of George I heralded dramatic changes in Townshend's fortunes; as a result, the Whig success in the election of 1715 marked the end of his need to manipulate closely the county polity. County politics after 1715 presented generally smooth sailing for

---

149. J. Black, "Fresh Light on the Fall of Townshend," *Historical Journal* 29 (1986): 41–64. See also J. Black, "British Foreign Policy in the Eighteenth Century," *Journal of British Studies* 26 (1987): 26–53, especially 33, 39, 41–42. D. Starkey and others remind us of the significance of the court in an earlier era, and despite the difference between the court's impact on politics in the period 1471–1642 from its impact thereafter, especially after 1688, access to the monarch still gave statesmen both prestige and power in the eighteenth century and beyond: D. Starkey et al., *The English Court: From the Wars of the Roses to the Civil War* (London, 1987).

Townshend—and Walpole. The elections of 1722 and 1727 between them saw only three contests, two of them token affairs at Great Yarmouth.[150] Quarter sessions engaged in relatively few disputes, and aside from dealing with handfuls of Jacobite sympathizers, the lieutenancy had little to do. The lord lieutenant obviously felt his lieutenancy warranted little close attention, since he came to only two meetings with his deputies between 1714 and his resignation in 1730, both of those in 1717 when he was temporarily out of national office.[151] It is noteworthy that Townshend spent his time away from the county yet with virtual impunity maintained his influence there. Both the earlier dismay of his steward at the news Townshend would not visit the country, and the various complaints when his colleague Walpole was delayed in the capital, fade away in later years. In the case of each man, the energy of Robert Britiffe, Norwich attorney-cum-politician, explains much; he did a great deal of the local work for which the brothers-in-law had no time. A man of some substance, Britiffe carried weight independently of his patrons, yet never so much as when he acted on their behalf. Britiffe was an accomplished attorney of modest gentry credentials, whose abilities brought him the nomination as one of two unsuccessful Whig candidates for the Norwich parliamentary seats in 1713 and victory for the same seat in 1715 and after. His assistance with county business in succeeding years proved invaluable.[152]

Britiffe's activities do not alone explain the Whig leaders' dominance in the county. Another obvious component lay in the increasing amount of patronage that Walpole and Townshend influenced and dispensed under George I and George II. The recruitment to the Whigs of Sir Jacob Astley, who had been a Tory knight of the shire, exemplifies the power of central government office. Splits in the Norfolk Tory ranks appeared as early as September 1714, as Astley spoke of finding a new partner at the next election; by November, he had grown so disenchanted with his colleagues that Walpole found him "very stout and resolute." After the Tories abandoned him, the prom-

150. *HP 1715–54*, 1:289–92.
151. NLJ 1676–1715, NRO, NRS 27276, 372x7. CT seems not to have set foot in Norfolk between the death of Anne in August 1714 and his dismissal from office in April 1717: household a/cs 1703–16, RUBV; London household a/cs 1704–16, RLBV; household a/cs January–December 1717, RUBV. CT's nonchalance is paralleled by Walpole's failure to visit his constituency before the election of 1722: R. Walpole to J. Rolfe, 17 March 1722, CUL, C(H) corr. #943.
152. Guth, "Croakers and Tackers," 423–24, provides evidence that CT encouraged Britiffe in his first parliamentary campaign. On Britiffe, who was recorder of King's Lynn from 1704, see *HP 1715–54*, 1:291, 488; *East Anglian Pedigrees*, ed. A. Campling, Norfolk Record Society, 13 (1940): 241–43; Plumb, *Walpole*, 1:310, 361.

ise of a place at the Board of Trade persuaded Astley to stand as a Whig for knight of the shire with Thomas De Grey, Thetford MP (and husband of Townshend's first cousin, Elizabeth Windham). The combination of moderate former Tory and "Townshend" Whig won the county poll with a margin of several hundred votes.[153]

Throughout the county, in fact, the Whig triumph in 1715 was nearly overwhelming, with the Tories retaining just three of their previous eight seats, one of those filled by a Hanoverian Tory, John Ward, who sat for Thetford.[154] In this thoroughgoing reversal of party strength, the Whig victory in Norfolk mirrored that in the nation at large. It is not clear whether locally it is attributable to the factors W. A. Speck has identified for the country in general, especially the influence in large constituencies of an early Whig victory in London and the greater fear among the electorate of a succession than of a church in danger.[155] For the Norfolk constituencies, surprisingly little information survives concerning this election; the only contests were for Norwich and for knight of the shire, although these were fierce.[156] The Tories' selection of two untested candidates for the county seat was perhaps an attempt to paper over internal divisions within the party, but it also had the virtue of advancing men untainted with the electorate by positions taken in former contests. By contrast, Robert Britiffe, one of the Whig victors at Norwich, where "an unusual recruiting effort" brought a 25 percent increase in the active electorate over 1710,[157] was presumably assisted by his connections to Walpole and Townshend.

The change in parliamentary personnel in Norfolk accompanied changes in local institutions. Two months after the death of Queen Anne, and only a week before Townshend won reinstatement as Norfolk's lord lieutenant, a new commission of the peace was issued for the county. Sixteen new JPs came on, and seven dismissed in Anne's reign now returned. By March 1716 another dozen had appeared in the commission, additions that swelled the justices' ranks less than otherwise because some twenty-five names were deleted over the same period. Still, no total purge of Tories took place, and Lord Chancellor Cowper's remodeled commissions generally advanced the Whig inter-

---

153. Coxe, *Walpole*, 2:49; J. Calthorpe to CT, 24 September 1714, RBF/CT 1696–1735; Ketton-Cremer, *Felbrigg*, 89; *HP 1715–54*, 1:423–24, 608; E. Earle to P. Le Neve, 25 November 1714, BL, Egerton 2721, f. 419; Rosenheim, "Oligarchy," 417.

154. *HP 1715–54*, 2:520; the two true Tories were Dudley North, also for Thetford, and George England at Great Yarmouth: ibid., 2:12, 299.

155. W. A. Speck, "The General Election of 1715," *English Historical Review* 90 (1975): 507–22.

156. Rosenheim, "Oligarchy," 359–62; Guth, "Croakers and Tackers," 524–30.

157. Ibid., 526, n. 85, and 530.

est in the magistracy without marking a "comprehensive reversal" of the changes made by his Tory predecessor, Harcourt.[158]

While shifts among the justices proved less than radical, they sent a message to the county, since the first new commission appeared long enough before the election of 1715 to signal Whig ascendancy. More extreme were the alterations Townshend made in the lieutenancy when he once more took command. Of Ormonde's fifteen deputies he retained only eight, four originally appointed by himself. He increased the size of the lieutenancy beyond its number under the duke to nineteen in all, although six never attended a meeting.[159] In fact, in the early days of George I's reign, none of the deputies proved particularly energetic, despite the rebellion in Scotland and the urgings of the lord lieutenant to muster the militia and prepare for danger. Seven deputies met to consider a Council order of July 1715 to disarm Catholics and nonjurors, but two months later Townshend had received no reply to instructions to ready the militia. The episode appears to show that he felt a residue of responsibility for Norfolk otherwise not much evident. In fact, his ostensible anxiety over the county's security was less than his worry "not [to] be the last who am enabled to acquaint the Council that . . . obedience is paid to their orders." Militia affairs still affected a lord lieutenant's reputation, but Townshend was more concerned with his standing among his fellow councillors than with the local community.[160]

After it dealt with threats to security raised by local Jacobites around 1715, the lieutenancy transacted essentially routine business over the next decade and a half, with only modest direction from Townshend. A handful of deputies managed affairs, most notably Sir Charles Turner, when he was in the county and not at Westminster; Sir John Hobart, who up to 1727 ignored the call of parliament (he sat for St. Ives) and attended an average of three lieutenancy meetings a year; and Harbord Harbord, who helped earn himself a later chance as knight of the shire through faithful lieutenancy service.[161] With such prominent men to help, it is small wonder that Townshend, even when in Norfolk, saw no need to attend lieutenancy meetings himself. The first viscount's personal and political credibility had been fostered by

158. Glassey, *Justices*, 243, 260–61, and chap. 8 in general; cf. N. Landau, *The Justices of the Peace, 1679–1760* (Berkeley, 1984), 86–92. Glassey notes that CT and Sir Charles Turner in early 1715 recommended "not especially remarkable changes" on the Norfolk bench: *Justices*, 261, n. 1. Changes can be followed in the fiats for Norfolk, PRO C234/26.
159. NLJ 1676–1715, NRO, NRS 27276, 372x7; NLJ 1715–50, NRO, NRS 27308, 447x.
160. Lieutenancy letter book 1702–39, entry of 24 September 1715, NRO, MS 503, T133A; entries for 1715, NLJ 1715–50, NRO, NRS 27308, 447x.
161. Ibid.

his intense involvement in lieutenancy affairs. This was partly the case because such activity counteracted his political weakness in the county and partly because in the 1660s and 1670s, when the state was less centralized than under George I, substantial authority was being channeled through the lord lieutenant. In the second viscount's day the position had begun its slide toward the almost entirely honorific post it became under the fourth Viscount Townshend, who was said, in the summer of 1764, to be away "at Dereham with his militia, playing at soldiers."[162]

The lack of local electioneering by Townshend after the Whig triumph of 1715 further illustrates his long-distance approach to maintain his standing in Norfolk. The Whig forces, to begin with, while not entirely without opposition in the county, so dominated the Tories that both county elections in the 1720s went uncontested, as did the two county by-elections of 1728 to fill places vacated when Thomas Coke and Sir John Hobart were elevated to the peerage.[163] It is not surprising, then, that Townshend invested little money, time, or political influence—beyond participating in the candidate-selection process—in these contests. Where his own family was involved and the outcome was less certain, he paid more attention, as in the election at Great Yarmouth in March 1722, where Sir John Holland (now a Whig defector, "full of disgust" toward Townshend) and a Great Yarmouth Tory, George England, challenged Townshend's eldest son, Charles, and Robert Walpole's brother Horatio.[164] The Whig pair's victory justified Townshend's outlay of £900, or about £2 per voter, and the expenditure had a lasting impact, for the election to replace Charles Townshend (newly created Lord Lynn) with his brother William the following year required only £40 for entertainment.[165]

The distance Townshend placed between himself and the county, while nonetheless retaining a strong interest there, reveals, as much as his rational and thoroughgoing approach to estate management, the change in outlook and habits that the making of a modern aristocracy

162. R. W. Ketton-Cremer, *Norfolk Assembly* (London, 1957), 192.
163. *HP 1715–54*, 1:289; political notes in the hand of R. Marsham, c. 1768, NRO, MS 10999, 34E1. Ironically, Sir E. Bacon of Garboldisham, chosen to succeed Hobart, proved to be an enemy in disguise, his support for a Whig in the Suffolk election of 1727 having made him appear safe. In parliament he sided with the opposition "in every recorded division" in which he participated: *HP 1715–54*, 1:322, 426.
164. Holland blamed CT for his not receiving "more than ordinary favour" at the Hanoverian succession: H[umphrey] P[rideaux] to CT, 22 June 1715, Add. 38507, f. 133.
165. *HP 1715–54*, 1:290, for elections and vote totals; bills for 1722, RL drawer 120; entries 10–24 March 1722, extraordinary a/cs 1719–23, RUBV; entry of 13 June 1723, Fenn's a/c April–October 1723, RUEM/CT.

entailed. Of course Townshend's aloofness from Norfolk should neither be exaggerated nor misunderstood. He remained attached to his estate and to a landowner's life; when he disengaged from Norfolk, it was because disengagement was more or less forced upon him by unfolding events. Townshend was a career statesman who could not advance himself by remaining isolated in the countryside. His career focused on the central government; his relative disregard of the provincial periphery must be seen in this light.

Townshend appears to have had an ambivalent attitude toward the demands of life at the center of public affairs. That he enjoyed the determination of policy and the work of statesmanship can scarcely be doubted, and Lord Chesterfield claimed that "business . . . was his only passion."[166] The intrigues of court life, however, were apparently less attractive, and Jeremy Black argues that he left office in part because of sheer frustration at having to operate in the face of constant opposition.[167] On his first trip to Hanover in 1723, he wrote privately to Robert Walpole with distaste that "if there be a place in the world where faction and intrigue are natural and in fashion, it is here, which makes it no easy task for a stranger to behave himself inoffensively. . . . [I]t is not a very agreeable situation to be eternally upon one's guard from all quarters."[168]

He nonetheless at least understood the need to keep abreast of affairs, and one of his secretaries reported from abroad in 1725 that, although Townshend would readily "excuse a letter of business, . . . he is earnest for tittle tattle." Yet whether he enjoyed such stories or viewed them instrumentally is less clear, for the same writer noted that Townshend sought the information because without it "he look[ed] mysterious at court in not knowing such little details sometimes."[169]

Whatever his later attitude, Townshend must confidently have awaited office during the days following the queen's death, since he had been included among the eighteen regents who governed until the arrival of George I. His appointment as secretary of state has traditionally been attributed to acquaintance with Jean de Robethon, whom he encountered at The Hague when negotiating the Barrier Treaty, and to Robethon's influence with George I's minister, Baron Bothmer, but Townshend had been "marked for future promotion"

166. BL, Stowe 308, f. 14. Late in CT's career, his secretary commented from Hanover that CT had "vigour and spirit" and went through "conferences, dispatches & what is worse feasting and entertaining with . . . much health & gayety": G. Tilson to C. Delafaye, 22 July 1729 (NS), PRO, SP 43/9.
167. Black, "Fresh Light," 63.
168. CT to R. Walpole, 6 August 1723 (NS), PRO, SP 43/4.
169. G. Tilson to C. Delafaye, 28 August 1725 (NS), PRO, SP43/6.

ever since the treaty with the Dutch had been signed. The office was one for which he was well suited as a result of the diplomatic experience of his Dutch embassy; as secretary, he became a member of the king's inner circle of advisors and was thrust immediately and regularly into the heart of government.[170]

Townshend's tenure in high government office began successfully. In 1715 he helped suppress the Jacobite threat at home and from abroad, and he furthered British and Hanoverian interests in the Baltic against Sweden. The next year, however, a number of circumstances worked to bring him into disfavor with the king. Above all, Ragnhild Hatton has argued, the two men experienced "a divergence of views on the balance of power" in the north of Europe,[171] and it was this split, rather than domestic intrigues and betrayal by enemies, that led to the departure from the ministry of Townshend and his brother-in-law, Walpole. Townshend was dismissed as secretary of state in December 1716, ostensibly because he had obstructed completion of the Anglo-French alliance on which James Stanhope had been laboring. Just as important, the viscount's desire to reestablish and preserve a balance of power in the north, especially between Sweden and Russia, ran counter to George I's more pressing concern to gain the French as allies against what the king saw as immediate threats to the safety of Hanover.[172]

Yet the king retained respect and affection for Townshend and sought to keep him in the ministry. Appointment to the lieutenancy of Ireland after demotion from the secretaryship meant that he remained within the inner cabinet circle, since he was allowed to reside in England for the duration of an appointment the king promised would be brief. Townshend accepted the lieutenancy and acknowledged a willingness to be reconciled with Stanhope and even the Earl of Sunderland, whom he blamed as architects of his disgrace.[173] The attempt to patch up relations failed. In early 1717 dinners among the

---

170. R. Hatton, *George I, Elector and King* (Cambridge, Mass., 1978), 105, 120–21, 123–24. See also L. Melville, *The First George in Hanover and England*, 2 vols. (New York, 1909), 1:241; W. Michael, *England under George I: The Beginnings of the Hanoverian Dynasty* (London, 1936; reprinted New York, 1970), 96–97; Coxe, *Walpole*, 1:80, 83; *Works of Lady Montagu*, 1:125.

171. Hatton, *George I*, 193.

172. This paragraph largely follows Hatton, *George I*, 174–93, but see also B. Williams, *Stanhope: A Study in Eighteenth-Century War and Diplomacy* (Oxford, 1932; reprinted 1968), 198–99, 211–25; and J. J. Murray, *George I, the Baltic and the Whig Split of 1717* (Chicago, 1969), 329–34.

173. [Copy] CT to the king, 11 December 1716, RBF/CT 1716; Hatton, *George I*, 193–202; Plumb, *Walpole*, 1:222–42. Sunderland had been irked when CT rather than he was made secretary in 1714: Earl of Oxford to his son, 18 September 1714, BL, Loan 29/204.

warring ministers, and the king's personal efforts, proved of no avail. Disputes within the royal family between the king and the Prince of Wales were injected into the ministerial conflict, which aggravated the situation beyond repair. Townshend and his friends made common cause with supporters of the Prince of Wales, and the viscount in April "clearly worked against the king in the Lords."[174]

Townshend's obstruction was spurred not by policy disputes, but by his personal determination to force the king to accede to a demand for Sunderland's dismissal. George I ultimately would not allow Townshend to dictate the composition of his administration and turned him out as lord lieutenant of Ireland in April 1717.[175] Dismissed, but determined to show the muscle he retained, the viscount "threw himself unequivocally" into defense of the Tory Earl of Oxford against the ministry's charges of treason, when the parliamentary session resumed in May 1717. A temporary alliance between Tories and Townshend's Whig faction in the Lords, bolstered by Whigs who thought Oxford was being unjustly pursued, sent the Earl of Sunderland to crashing defeat. By the time the parliamentary session ended in July, the ministry had reason to fear serious future disruption.[176]

In fact, neither Townshend nor Walpole threw in uncritically with the Tories, and when the rupture between the Prince of Wales and his father became open in November and December 1717, it allowed the Townshend/Walpole Whigs to rely on the Prince's supporters in their intraparty struggle against Stanhope and Sunderland. On the other hand, the Tories' strength was great enough for rumors to circulate at the end of 1717 that some among them would be brought into the ministry, and Jeremy Black has recently argued that the alliance between opposition Whigs and Tories "had more success than is sometimes recognized."[177] Stanhope's introduction in the session of 1718 of a bill to repeal the Occasional Conformity Act, anathema to the Tories, may have destroyed all prospect of "Tory assimilation into the administration," but the Whig split persisted nonetheless. Knowing

---

174. Hatton, *George I*, 199. Walpole and CT signaled their intentions when both failed to attend a ministerial meeting in early March which agreed in principle to repeal the Occasional Conformity and Schism Acts: C. Jones and G. Holmes, eds., *The London Diaries of William Nicolson, Bishop of Carlisle, 1702–1718* (Oxford, 1985), 640–41.

175. Hatton, *George I*, 197–201, 212–13; Plumb, *Walpole*, 240–41; [copy] Stanhope to CT, 9 April 1717, RBF/CT 1716.

176. C. Jones, "The Impeachment of the Earl of Oxford and the Whig Schism of 1717: Four New Lists," *Bulletin of the Institute for Historical Research* 55 (1982): 71–77, 85.

177. J. Black, "Parliament and the Political and Diplomatic Crisis of 1717–18," *Parliamentary History* 3 (1984): 91, 94.

that Stanhope could not now find support among Tories in the Commons, Walpole and Townshend demonstrated with their tactical opposition to Stanhope's bill just how much difficulty they could create for the ministry, unless a reconciliation among the Whigs occurred.[178]

In the end, the mutual recognition of Stanhope's success as a diplomat, and of Walpole's capacities as a parliamentary manager (revealed in the defeat he orchestrated of the ministry's Peerage Bill in 1719), helped bring an end to the overt Whig divisions. So did the unwillingness of even moderate Tories to come into the ministry one at a time.[179] George I was reconciled, at least publicly, with the Prince of Wales in April 1720; Walpole and Townshend made their peace with the king the next month, and in June both were back in office, the one as paymaster general (until the treasury office opened), the other as president of the Council. In February 1721, following the discrediting of Sunderland during the South Sea Bubble crisis and after Stanhope's death, Townshend left the presidency and returned as secretary of state. When he next gave up the office, in May 1730, he did so voluntarily.[180]

For the next nine years Townshend stood at the center of the English government. Yet the background against which his rehabilitation took place in 1720 opened the way for the shift in preeminence between him and his brother-in-law, which eventually undermined his position in the ministry. The South Sea crisis, which saw the collapse of stocks from the summer of 1720 and threatened the financial structure of the nation, was not miraculously solved by Robert Walpole; as J. H. Plumb points out, "none of his financial measures was constructive." Yet Walpole received much of the public credit for coping with the crisis and took the lead in the Commons to pass necessary legislation. The resolution of the South Sea matter was a turning point in the partnership of Townshend and Walpole, making it clear, if it had not been before, that Walpole was the dominant of the two.[181] There

178. L. Colley, *In Defiance of Oligarchy: The Tory Party, 1714–60* (Cambridge, 1982), 192–93; Black, "Parliament and the Crisis of 1717–18," 86–90. CT's behavior in urging the Prince of Wales to oppose repeal of the Schism Act confirms the contemporary opinion that his commitment to dissent was based "more upon politic views than any principle . . . to loose [dissenters] of their burdens": *The Diary of Dudley Ryder, 1715–1716*, ed. W. Matthews (London, 1939), 153–54.
179. Black, "Parliament and the Crisis of 1717–18," 93.
180. On healing the breach in the Whig ranks, see Plumb, *Walpole*, 1:285–92; Hatton, *George I*, 211–16, 244–46; Colley, *Oligarchy*, 193–98; W. Michael, *England under George I: The Quadruple Alliance* (London, 1939; reprinted New York, 1970), 302–8.
181. Plumb, *Walpole*, 1:357–58. Coxe, *Walpole*, 1:339, cites Walpole himself for the maxim, "as long as the firm of the house was Townshend and Walpole, the utmost harmony prevailed; but it no sooner became Walpole and Townshend, than things went wrong, and a separation ensued." It is ironic that the scheme of Robert Jacombe, which

was no reason at first to notice the shifting balance; Townshend's immediate concern was to put into effect the lessons brought home to him by his period out of office.[182] This meant a continuation by subtler means of the struggle to gain full ascendancy in the counsels of the king.

The resolution of the Whig split in 1720 may have meant, as Ragnhild Hatton says, that the king understood his government would "no longer tolerate Hanoverians as the king's advisers in any matter that touched British interests," but it did not mean that the monarch would simply allow one Whig faction to dominate him. The campaign against Sunderland and his adherents was therefore undertaken quietly and indirectly, as when the promotion of James Stanhope's brother was delayed at the behest of Walpole.[183] Neither he nor Townshend could prevent the appointment of Sunderland's ally Carteret as the other secretary of state in March 1721, proving that the subtle approach might not be successful, but the death of Sunderland in April 1722 cast adrift the remaining members of the Sunderland-Stanhope faction. The brothers-in-law Walpole and Townshend took advantage as they could, detaching the Duke of Newcastle from the faction, obtaining peerages for their respective eldest sons, and engineering Carteret's dismissal in 1724. Newcastle, now at one with the dominant pair, came in as the secretarial replacement.[184]

From his period in the political wilderness, Townshend had learned the crucial importance of taking into account the king's "prejudices and principles" when trying to formulate policy.[185] He also learned the value of proximity to the king. Failure to accompany the monarch to Hanover in 1716 contributed to his dismissal as secretary of state, because misunderstandings which arose between monarch and minister could not be clarified. Townshend would not repeat the error, no matter how much his attachment to home might be stretched. So in 1723, 1725, and again in 1727—the first time in Carteret's company, the latter times as the king's sole English minister—Townshend traveled to Hanover with his master; he did the same with George II in 1729.[186] He found Hanover in 1723 rather uncongenial, but he

---

Walpole embraced as the solution to the South Sea crisis, was first laid out to CT: ibid., 2:193.

182. Hatton, *George I*, 256, 260.

183. Ibid., 246; Plumb, *Walpole*, 1:366; Lord Carteret to the Duke of Newcastle, 27 August 1721, Add. 32689, f. 193.

184. R. Browning, *The Duke of Newcastle* (New Haven, 1975), 24–25; Hatton, *George I*, 256–57, 274–75; Plumb, *Walpole*, 2, chap. 2; GEC, *Peerage*, "Townshend" and "Walpole."

185. Hatton, *George I*, 213.

186. "An account of the charges of the 4 Journys from England to Hannover," NRO, MS 553, T142B. The trip in 1727 was interrupted by the king's death.

survived.[187] Present on the scene, he could interpret for the king Walpole's communications from London and counteract what he saw as malign foreign influences; soon he found himself "to be every day gaining an interest."[188] Norfolk was left far behind in this strategy. Where his father had created an interest (such as it was) in the county or, more exotically, in London, the second viscount created his miles away and across the sea.

By means of his increasing interest with George I, Townshend most persistently sought to spell out for the king what Hatton has called "a specifically British point of view" in foreign policy, although under George II Townshend was also careful in looking out for Hanoverian interests.[189] His was a "specialized, if geographically limited, knowledge" of foreign affairs, one largely confined to northern regions and informed by a modest, noninterventionist view of Britain's role in Europe.[190] A primary concern he had under George I was to keep England out of Baltic embroilments by maintaining the balance of power there.[191] Under George II his own inclination was to seek reconciliation and alliance with Austria, largely as a counterweight to France, but his views were ultimately "subordinated to royal policy," and that meant protection of Hanoverian interests.[192] On balance, Townshend achieved his goals, even if the treaty with Austria waited until after his resignation. He did not stamp his imprint on foreign affairs as fully as he might have wished, and in this sense his career is evidence of the continuing power of the monarch to shape English policy. But all the same, Townshend's cautious activity as secretary was in its way a perfect complement to the prosperity encouraged by Robert Walpole's policies at home.

The later years of George I's reign brought Townshend increasing success and honor. In July 1724 he received the Garter and spent nearly £1,400 for the investiture.[193] The next year, he and George I concluded the alliance of Hanover to counteract successfully the Austro-Spanish treaty of Vienna, which had been signed in April 1725. Despite the somewhat bellicose response that the alliance evoked on the continent (especially from Spain), an international crisis in 1726 and early 1727 never broke out into open war. Townshend retained

187. CT to R. Walpole, 6 August 1723, PRO, SP 43/4.
188. [Copy] Duke of Newcastle to R. Walpole, 24 October 1723, Add. 32686, f. 361.
189. Hatton, *George I*, 213; Black, "Fresh Light," 62–63.
190. Hatton, *George I*, 260, who also notes CT's hope "to avoid entanglements in Italy" in 1716 (183); Black, "Fresh Light," 45–46, 56.
191. Hatton, *George I*, 189.
192. Black, "Fresh Light," 45, 50, 59.
193. GEC, *Peerage*, 2:563 (Appendix B); household and extraordinary a/cs, 1723–25, RUBV.

influence with the king and had little reason to doubt that the continued exercise of power would be his. The unexpected death of George I, however, and Townshend's own life-threatening illness later in 1727, raised serious questions about the likelihood of his persisting in public life.[194] Some historians have identified a movement of foreign policy decisions from Townshend to Walpole and Newcastle during the 1720s, which George II's accession was seen to accelerate. After all, George II as Prince of Wales never displayed admiration for the viscount, and as king he apparently thought him a "choleric blockhead." It was Walpole who assiduously courted the queen, made every attempt to spend time alone with the king, and successfully won the latter's trust.[195] Yet Jeremy Black has recently shown that after an initial bad patch, Townshend and the new king worked together well, whatever the monarch's personal feelings, and that as late as a month before his resignation in 1730, the secretary still controlled important negotiations then in hand. Townshend and his brother-in-law had come close to a parting of the ways by 1727, but it was not certain that their differences would drive one man from office, nor was it clear in that event who might go.[196]

The rift between Walpole and Townshend was perhaps inevitable, given their different backgrounds and personalities, but circumstances combined to make it worse. The defeat of early, mutual enemies in London and Norfolk reduced the need to make common cause and paper over differences. The death of Lady Townshend, Walpole's beloved sister Dorothy, in March 1726, further attenuated the link between the two men and removed the one person who could mediate between them.[197] Walpole's anxiety over foreign policy and his growing ambition to have a say in its implementation clashed with Townshend's unbending faith in his own opinions and projects, even if the brothers-in-law generally agreed on the direction of policy itself. As early as 1723, Walpole was proffering his own "sudden & possibly very

194. J. F. Chance, *The Alliance of Hanover* (London, 1923); G. C. Gibbs, "Britain and the Alliance of Hanover, April 1725–February 1726," *English Historical Review* 73 (1958): 404–30; Plumb, *Walpole*, 2:116–22; Hatton, *George I*, 274–79; Browning, *Newcastle*, 47–50. CT fell ill in the late summer or early fall and was slow in recovering: H. Walpole to [G. Tilson], 3 October 1727 (NS), Add. 48982, f. 86; T. Windham to A. Windham, 2 and 21 November [1727,] NRO, WKC 7/25, 404x2; [copy] CT to H. Walpole, 13 December 1727, Add. 48982, ff. 117–22; G. Tilson to J. Dayrolle, 19 December 1727, Add. 15867, f. 246; H. Walpole to CT, 2 January 1728 (NS), NRO, Bradfer-Lawrence, I c, Townshend State Papers, vol. 1; Coxe, *Walpole*, 2:240, 544–45.

195. Hervey, *Memoirs*, 1:29 ("choleric blockhead"), 82–83; Browning, *Newcastle*, 54; Plumb, *Walpole*, 2:2–3, 162–72, 175–76; Black, "Fresh Light," 43, n.7; *Diary of Mary Countess Cowper*, 65, 80, 113–14.

196. Black, "Fresh Light," 50–51, 62.

197. Coxe, *Walpole*, 1:334–35; Plumb, *Walpole*, 2:132–33.

improper thoughts upon a subject that I am but little acquainted with." He subsequently became better acquainted with diplomacy and overseas affairs, a familiarity and growing interest that did not sit well with his brother-in-law Townshend. The quarrel of the two, when it came, took foreign affairs as its spark, but it was "a struggle for power rather than a dispute over policy."[198] Townshend did not well endure the rise (visible in the stones of Houghton and the crowded gatherings at Walpole's London home) of his commoner schoolmate to a prominence rivaling—even exceeding—his own. The two ministers' relationship was complex, and its dissolution grew from multiple causes, as even Walpole's first biographer knew.[199]

Beyond the sources of personal conflict between the men, Townshend's illness in 1727 had sparked speculation about a successor. Those who envisaged a government without Townshend, and with their friends in his place, did not dismiss this image once the viscount recovered.[200] Yet as long as Townshend enjoyed the king's backing, no one suggested his dismissal; even Walpole attacked indirectly, fearing the damage that would ensue if Townshend took others with him out of office. The prime minister could not afford a frontal assault, because the king had no major policy dispute with his secretary and had no obvious replacement for him. The quarrel over foreign affairs between Walpole and Townshend, Jeremy Black suggests, was "a matter of diplomatic tactics, rather than strategy." What divided them was a question of who would prevail, and as the Earl of Chesterfield said, Townshend "was not of a temper to act a second part, after having acted a first."[201] Since George II would not allow Townshend unquestioned dominance, the imperious, impatient viscount may have wondered by the late 1720s whether the continuing struggle to maintain the influence he had was worth the effort it cost him, aging and increasingly ill. He was considering resignation in the autumn of 1729[202] and by the following spring had made up his mind. Far from belying the claim of ill health with which Townshend explained his resignation, the seven further years of life he enjoyed in retreat at

---

198. [Copy] R. Walpole to CT, 23 July 1723, PRO, SP 43/4; Black, "Fresh Light," 59. Hatton notes Walpole's interest in foreign affairs "bearing on parliament and the treasury": *George I*, 276. See also Plumb, *Walpole*, 2:38–39, 114–15, 132–33, 139 for Walpole's changing attitude to foreign policy.

199. Coxe, *Walpole*, 1:332–33.

200. Coxe, *Walpole*, 1:332, 2:544; Hervey, *Memoirs*, 1:82–87; Plumb, *Walpole*, 2:195–96; Black, "Fresh Light," 60–61.

201. Black, "Fresh Light," 57–58; BL, Stowe 308, f. 14; Plumb, *Walpole*, 2:196–97.

202. S. Poyntz to CT, 11 October 1729 (NS), Yale University, Beinecke Library, Osborn shelves, c.201, letter 12; same to [T. Townshend], 5 November 1729 (NS), ibid., letter 13.

Raynham testify to the rejuvenation that withdrawal from public life gave. After nearly thirty years in the public eye, the tired statesman sought relief.[203]

With his retirement to Raynham in May 1730, Townshend left political life behind him, freely admitting that, although his health since his major illness "n'a jamais été parfaitement rétablie," his resolve to resign had been strengthened by the "mésintelligence . . . entre le chevalier Walpole et moy."[204] Yet he made no party against Walpole, then or later; they were apparently on civil enough terms to visit formally immediately after Townshend left office.[205] He was as good as his resolution, announced explicitly in 1733, to avoid political contests, and his only slip was to solicit votes that year for his son Thomas as MP for Cambridge University. Even then he acknowledged "how improper it is for me, who has so far renounced all publick business as not to concern myself in any of the elections in the county where I live, to be solliciting others," but his fondness for his son won out.[206] He claimed at one point over these years "never [to] write any thing but what I desire the ministry may see." Admittedly he gave his proxy to Richard, Earl of Scarbrough, for three years (a vote of which the earl made use in opposition to the ministry), but Townshend's failure to grant the proxy after January 1734 (the last session of George II's first parliament) demonstrates his unwillingness to provoke the ministry further.[207]

In the elections of 1734, the first after Townshend's retirement, the Whigs' diminished showing in Norfolk, where the Tories shockingly won both the county seats, could not in any way be laid at Townshend's feet, for the voters he sent from Raynham to the county poll in Norwich proved strictly loyal to the party.[208] Townshend outlined his position on politics in reply to a friend who solicited his intervention with Walpole to secure a favor. Writing from Raynham,

203. His intended resignation at the end of the parliamentary session was well known in early 1730: same to T. Townshend, 19 April 1730 (NS), ibid., letter 20; HMC, *Carlisle MSS*, 71, 73.
204. CT to the Pensionary Slingelandt, n.d. [May 1730], Add. 48982, f. 242. Cf. CT to Mons. Stein, ibid., f. 240, and to Mons. de Bousset, ibid., f. 244, all three reprinted in Coxe, *Walpole*, 2:698–700.
205. R. Walpole to the Duke of Newcastle, 3 July 1730, Add. 32687, f. 376, seems to describe a visit to CT, where "the conversation was civil, formal, grave & insignificant."
206. Coxe, *Walpole*, 1:338; CT to the Earl of Oxford, 22 November [1733], Add. 4291, f. 231.
207. CT to S. Buckley, 16 September [no year], Bodl., MS Eng. lett. c.144, f. 267; House of Lords Record Office, Proxy Books 1730–34; HMC, *Carlisle MSS*, 118; Plumb, *Walpole*, 2:266–67, 277–78.
208. Plumb, *Walpole*, 2:320–22; notes on Norfolk politics, c. 1768, NRO, MS 10999, 34E1.

National Reputation and Local Politics 239

the viscount explained that he had "made it a rule with me never to ask a favour of Sir Robert Walpole since he & I parted." He went on:

> You must know that I never go near Houghton during what they call the Congress but content myself with a visit to Sir Robert at his coming down in the summer, & with sending a civil message at this season [he wrote in November] to excuse my not waiting upon him, upon the account of my going into Suffolk, whither I always remove at this time to pay a visit to Lady Cornwallis [his daughter Elizabeth]. . . . In these circumstances you see it is impossible for me to comply with what you desire. . . . I think my speaking wou'd hurt you in your pretentions, Sir Robert & his friends having taken the utmost care to possess every body that applying to me was the sure way not to succeed. This precaution they thought necessary towards preventing my forming a party against them here. The same jealousie still continues and is, I believe, rather increased than abated by the loss of the last election, tho' they cou'd not reasonably object anything to my conduct upon that occasion, my tenants having all of them voted on their side.[209]

When Townshend had said that his departure from office would bring no change in ministerial policy, he was not simply reassuring his foreign colleagues about his and Walpole's general agreement on that policy, but also indicating that his own future posture would be one of loyalty to the Whig party, if not to the ministers.[210]

In local affairs Townshend was nearly as quiet. He had few visitors and traveled rarely, except to see his family. He retained eminence, but it was not something at which he worked.[211] He gave up his lord lieutenancy when he resigned but must have been gratified that his son was named to succeed him.[212] He contributed £20 to the new sessions building at Fakenham in 1731 and took a minor part in a controversy over legal fees charged by the chief constable of his hundred, probably because it affected parishes where he had tenants.[213] In the last month of his life, he acted in his capacity as JP and personally interrogated parties in a local theft, but otherwise he apparently had little public life.[214] Indeed, the relief Townshend expressed on his departure from that life gives the impression of one who had willingly

---

209. CT to S. Buckley, 9 November [1735], Bodleian, MS Eng. lett. c.144, f. 269.
210. CT to Mons. de Bousset, Mons. Stein, and Pensionary Slingelandt, May 1730, Add. 48982, ff. 240–44.
211. H. Harbord deferred advancing parliamentary candidates until he knew "none of Lord Townshends sons woud have *his* [consent] to appear for the county": H. Harbord to Lord Lynn, 2 June 1733, RBF/LL 1723–63; emphasis in the original.
212. Le Strange, *Lists*, 5; note of deputies' commissions, 1730–31, RU, Lord Lynn [NRO]; E. Weston to Lord Lynn, 27 and 30 October 1730, RBF/LL 1723–63.
213. Entry for 10 October 1731, Raynham household a/cs 1730–37, RUBV; [copy] CT to Captain Wilson, 3 March 1735, RBF/CT 1696–1735.
214. Examinations of 7 and 9 June 1738, PRO, ASSI 35/178/16.

quit the world. Three weeks after coming to the country in 1730, he wrote his heir that he had found Raynham "in the greatest beauty" and "the utmost perfection." After six months his mood had mellowed further, and he reflected upon the changes his retirement brought. "I look upon it as great good fortune," he explained to his friend Samuel Buckley, "that I left the world before I had any reason to be angry with it, having therefore no malice. . . . I read . . . accounts of publick transactions . . . wishing ill to no man, but best to my own country." He was, he said, "very happy at home & much more sociable to the people amongst whom I live." Twice daily rides (a luxury London could not afford) added to his fine spirits. With a host in such a mood, it is not surprising that a visitor to Raynham shortly after Townshend quit found it difficult to leave.[215]

Later glimpses indicate that Townshend remained content. Family affairs were largely harmonious, and affection flowed both ways, as did visits between the father and those of his children who had married and set up on their own.[216] Others who visited Raynham found the viscount growing lazy by his own admission and occupied with his house and estate.[217] He looked carefully to provisions for his young children. By the settlement made on his eldest son's marriage, he was allowed to charge his estate with £25,000 for his offspring, and because his second wife, Dorothy Townshend, had left legacies for the two daughters she bore him, he provided disproportionately for his sons.[218] Townshend also worked closely with his heir, Lord Lynn, on estate affairs, encouraging him to improve his own son's patrimony with a major purchase of land. "I must own to you," Townshend confessed,

---

215. CT to Lord Lynn, 1 June [1730], RBF/LL family; CT to S. Buckley, 21 December [1730], University of Michigan, Clements Library, Sydney papers; R. Gale to W. Stukeley, 13 June 1730, in *The Family Memoirs of the Rev. William Stukeley . . .*, ed. W. C. Lukis, Surtees Society, 73 (1880): 234.

216. T. Townshend to S. Poyntz, 30 July 1732, RL, Poyntz letters (photocopies); A. Townshend to CT, 20 December [1730–34], Add. 63095, f. 234. See Raynham household a/cs 1730–37, RUBV, passim, for gifts from CT to his grandchildren.

217. CT to S. Buckley, 27 December 1732, Add. 63101, f. 53. Visitors included Sir T. Robinson in 1731 (HMC, *Carlisle MSS*, 85); R. Gale in 1730 and 1736 (*William Stukeley's Memoirs*, 234, 289); the Earl of Oxford in 1732 (HMC, *Portland MSS*, 6:158–60); and former employees in the secretary's office (household a/cs).

218. Settlement indentures of 20 May 1723 and 16/17 March 1727, RUS and RL drawers 116, 118. CT provided for only nine children in the end, because Elizabeth had married Lord Cornwallis in 1722 and William predeceased CT by four months: a note of CT's legacies, Add. 63095, f. 238. CT left £5,000 to Roger but had paid £1,473 on it before he died; Lord Lynn agreed to pay £527, charging the estate with the remaining £3,000. Of the other children, Thomas received £6,000; Edward, Augustus, George, and Horatio £3,000 each; Dorothy and Mary £2,000 apiece. Lady Townshend's will, dated 18 May 1725, proved 1 February 1732, RBF, Norfolk wills (ii), specifies payment to her two daughters of money arising from her stocks, annuities, and lotteries. This may have amounted to £3,000 apiece: see J. Selwyn's a/cs 1730–38, RUEM/CT.

"it will break my heart if this opportunity sh'd be lost of securing that estate to our friend little George."[219] The absence of family, which causes sorrow to many elderly parents, took its toll. However busy and well occupied Townshend was at Raynham, there must have been times of loneliness in a mansion largely empty, void of house guests, inhabited by an aging former statesman and his two unmarried daughters. He looked forward eagerly to family visits.[220] He missed his grandchildren, "the dear little ones," and bragged of the praise heaped on young George by Dr. Graham at Eton. A note of wistfulness crept into his letters: "I heartily wish I cou'd see you here, were it but for a day," he wrote Lord Lynn in the late 1730s.[221] The death in January 1738 of his son William, MP and Groom of the Bedchamber to the Prince of Wales, compounded these feelings. It may thus have been at a time of comfort, with his son Thomas present on a visit, and having "been very chearfull all the evening," that he died suddenly toward the end of June 1738.[222]

219. D. Jones to Lord Lynn, 3 May 1732, RBF/LL 1720–39; C. Carter to same, 12 and 17 April, RUC [NRO], and 12 July and 24 August 1736, RBF/LL Carter; R. Neve to same, 4 September 1736, RUC [NRO]; CT to Lord Lynn, 11 April [1737], RBF/LL family. See *DNB*, "Charles Townshend," for the boys' later careers.
220. CT to Lord Lynn, 17 May [no year], Add. 63095, f. 236. Lord Lynn's cash book, December 1730–July 1733, RUBV, records five visits to Raynham, but they were bunched together between June 1731 and April 1732.
221. CT to Lord Lynn, 27 November 1736 and 11 April [1737], RBF/LL family.
222. T. Townshend to S. Poyntz, 22 June 1738, University of Michigan, Clements Library, Sydney papers.

Conclusion

There is something ironic about the second viscount's quiet retirement to Raynham in the 1730s, for he looks very much like the prosperous baronet that his father was until Charles II launched him into the peerage. That Charles Townshend could find satisfaction in the county is partly the measure of a different personality from that of his father. But it was also the legacy of a political career formed in circumstances far different from those of his father, who made his way at a time when "urgent public issues" still provided "a convenient front for the pursuit of private rivalries."[1] The second viscount was born into the age of party, a fact which provided for the independence from the county community that allowed him to return to it freely and willingly when he resigned from office. The county for him was not an arena in which he had been balked, so it comforted him in ways it had not comforted his father, who until his death haunted London, trying somehow to reinsert himself into political life, occupying himself when in Norfolk with petty affairs that engaged his sense of honor and reputation.

Charles Townshend, the Earl of Chesterfield said, was "an able man of business," a man, he meant, of public affairs.[2] So was his father, but unlike him, the second viscount stood firmly on a political, economic, and psychological foundation that allowed him to walk on a national stage. Horatio was consigned to the county. His ambition was to be a great man there, as a stepping stone to further greatness: unable to

---

1. A. Fletcher, "Honour, Reputation and Local Officeholding in Elizabethan and Stuart England," in A. Fletcher and J. Stevenson, eds., *Order and Disorder in Early Modern England* (Cambridge, 1985), 103.
2. Business was "his only passion," said Chesterfield with some exaggeration: BL, Stowe 308, f. 14.

achieve the first step, he had no chance at the second. His son, on the other hand, applied his talents to the central stage from early in his career, assuming that the vehicles of partisanship, the unity and organization of like-minded, ideologically bound allies and friends would enable him to fight off challenges in the county and provide him with support (if and when he needed it) to demonstrate his local credit with the ministry.

In his public life wealth did not urge the second viscount on—"[m]ere domestic economy was his only care as to money," said Chesterfield; pursuit of pleasure left him cold; dominance—the ability to dictate, to arrange the world to his content—is what he sought.[3] The arrogant self-assurance, the stubbornness that even his friends disliked, the brusque, impatient manner, the propensity of a poor orator to speak often and at length, these characteristics combine to create a picture that is far from appealing. It is the picture of a man determined to have his way, who will not compromise. And it was party, and especially the exploitation of party machinery, which gained him that way, just as retirement, complete and irreversible, freed him from it. Would that his father could have been so happily released.

This father and son, born forty-five years apart, lived overtly parallel lives: each made two good marriages, raised families, profited by their estates, served as lord lieutenant, and became involved in national politics. Their respective failure and success nonetheless mark them decidedly as men of different ages, in much the way that J. H. Plumb demonstrated was the case with the Walpoles, father and son.[4] This latter Norfolk pair consisted of a rustic father, Robert Walpole senior, and a more urbane son, Sir Robert, the prime minister. The elder did not lack sophistication and was himself an MP, but he remained very much a man of the country. To the extent that the same may be said of Horatio Townshend, we have a critical clue to the nature of his career; there is much to suggest that the first viscount never transcended his origins among the country gentry. His anxious insistence on outdated manorial privileges, his sensitivity to his local reputation, the supreme value he placed on his service as lord lieutenant, all these and much else mark him as a man whose roots were inextricably planted in county society.

The parallels between Robert Walpole the younger and the second Viscount Townshend are rather less clear, in part because Walpole was in many ways a unique figure of his age. Moreover, Walpole's

---

3. Ibid. Chesterfield said "he only loved power for the sake of power."
4. "The Walpoles: Father and Son," in J. H. Plumb, ed., *Studies in Social History* (London, 1955), 179–207.

career as what Plumb calls "the last royal favorite" in some measure defines him not as a man even of this age but as one belonging to "earlier centuries than his own."[5] Certainly this is not the case with Charles Townshend. All the same, both men were to some extent born to power, the one to a family seat in the House of Commons, the other to a peerage. Both men were party politicians who accepted the legitimacy of political conflict and who understood the significant role of parliament in the exercise of power. And for all the attraction that his seat at Raynham held for the secretary of state, he like the younger Walpole was a man not of the provinces but of London, of the center.

In many ways, the observation of another father-and-son chronicler seems to hold true of father and son here, whether Townshend or Walpole, that "one was born to fly backward, the other could not help being carried forward."[6] Yet in other ways, those things which persist between the generations are as remarkable as the differences: when Edmund Gosse depicted the conflict of eras in his family's late-Victorian clash of minds, he perhaps could not see much that overlapped between his father's day and his own. This study of the Townshends has identified both that which persisted and that which changed in the transformation of an early modern into a modern aristocracy.

The world in which Horatio Townshend came of age in 1651 and gained a peerage ten years later was perhaps no simpler than that in which his son Charles attained majority in 1696, but by the time Charles died in 1738—or even when his heir became an adult in 1721—the shape of elite society in England was beginning to be transformed. The forty-five-year gap in age between Townshend father and son emphasizes the changing relations between peerage and gentry; the increasingly complex role of peers at the center of their local societies of tenants, dependents, allies, and employees; the challenges posed by modern estate management.[7] This story, effectively leaping over an entire generation (whereas the Walpoles' story does not) presents the two men's lives in sharp contrast. The second viscount let to tenants the land Horatio Townshend farmed directly; the son ignored the minute financial details of estate management that absorbed his father; the first viscount's political world was broken up by partisan channels he found unnavigable but through which his son moved smoothly. Where the county of Norfolk was the locus of exhausting power struggles for the elder Townshend, for the younger it was a

---

5. Plumb, "Walpoles," 205–6.
6. E. Gosse, *Father and Son: A Study of Two Temperaments* (1907; New York, 1963), 9.
7. See M. L. Bush's review of J. Cannon, *Aristocratic Century* in *Albion* 17 (1985): 332–34.

venue in which to exercise the influence and patronage he derived from office and connection in central government. For one occupant, the family seat at Raynham Hall was the premier symbol of his status and reputation; for his successor, it was far more a rural retreat and a true home.

By contrast with his father's case, Norfolk was not the environment to provide Charles Townshend the success he enjoyed, nor did it nurture his self-image or give him social stature. Norfolk meant the protected, cared-for, stylish surroundings of Raynham, removed from the energetic roil of the metropolis that the second Viscount Townshend voluntarily gave up late in life. For his father, country life had a potency and resonance that were being redefined in the eighteenth century. Between them, the Townshends illustrate the impact on provincial life of what Philip Jenkins identified among the Glamorgan gentry as the spread of "metropolitan standards,"[8] whether in party politics, investment practices, or cultural values. Their lives reveal the growing influence of the metropolis and of the state on the aristocracy's actions, self-perception, and relationship with the surrounding community. Perhaps inevitably, the influence of new standards altered notions of honor and reputation even among the nobility: the exquisite sensitivity to county reputation that Horatio Townshend frequently demonstrated is rarely if ever found in his son's more confident demeanor. The world of the capital, of Westminster politics and cosmopolitan values, may ultimately have satiated Charles Townshend, but he was very much the product of it, as his father was the product of a more provincially oriented society. For neither man was province or center an arena to ignore; the interplay of the two lay at the heart of their careers and lives, as it lay behind the shaping of English society as a whole.

8. P. Jenkins, *The Making of a Ruling Class: The Glamorgan Gentry, 1640–1790* (Cambridge, 1983), chap. 9.

❊ Selected Bibliography ❊

Printed Materials

PRIMARY SOURCES

Browning, A., ed. *Memoirs of Sir John Reresby.* Glasgow, 1936.
Burnet, G. *History of His Own Time*, ed. M. J. Routh. 2nd ed., 6 vols. Oxford, 1833; reprinted Hildesheim, Germany, 1969.
Calendar of State Papers, Domestic Series.
Calendar of Treasury Books.
Cartwright, J. J., ed. *The Wentworth Papers, 1705–1739.* London, 1883.
Causton, H. K. S. *The Howard Papers.* London, n.d.
Colvin, H., and Newman, J., eds. *Of Building: Roger North's Writings on Architecture.* Oxford, 1981.
Coxe, W. *Memoirs of the Life and Administration of Sir Robert Walpole, Earl of Orford.* 3 vols. London, 1798.
——. *Memoirs of the Duke of Marlborough, with His Original Correspondence.* New ed., revised. 3 vols. London, 1847–48.
Cozens-Hardy, B. *Norfolk Lieutenancy Journal, 1676–1701.* Norfolk Record Society, vol. 30 (1961).
Dunn, R. M., ed. *Norfolk Lieutenancy Journal, 1660–1676.* Norfolk Record Society, vol. 45 (1977).
Firth, C. H., and Rait, R. S. *Acts and Ordinances of the Interregnum, 1642–1660.* 3 vols. London, 1911.
Fuller, T. *The History of the Worthies of England.* 3 vols. London, 1840; reprinted New York, 1965.
Gunther, R. T., ed. *The Architecture of Sir Roger Pratt. . . .* Oxford, 1928.
Gurdon, W. B., ed. "The Gurdon Papers," nos. 6 and 7, *The East Anglian*, n.s., 5 (1893–94): 33–35, 65–68.
Hervey, John Lord. *Some Materials towards Memoirs of the Reign of King George II*, ed. R. Sedgwick. 3 vols. London, 1931.
Hill, R. H., ed. *The Correspondence of Thomas Corie, Town Clerk of Norwich, 1664–1687.* Norfolk Record Society, vol. 27 (1956): 7–58.
Historical Manuscripts Commission, *10th Report, appendix, pt. vi.*
——. *Carlisle MSS.*
——. *House of Lords MSS.*
——. *Portland MSS.*
——. *Townshend MSS.*
House of Commons *Journals.*
House of Lords *Journals.*
Hyde, Edward, Earl of Clarendon. *The History of the Rebellion and Civil Wars in England*, ed. W. D. Macray. 6 vols. Oxford, 1888.

Jones, C., and Holmes, G., eds. *The London Diaries of William Nicolson, Bishop of Carlisle, 1702–1718.* Oxford, 1985.
Kent, N. *General View of the Agriculture of the County of Norfolk.* . . . London, 1796.
Keynes, G., ed. *The Works of Sir Thomas Browne.* New ed., 4 vols. Chicago, 1964.
Laurence, E. *Duty and Office of a Land Steward.* London, 1731; reprinted New York, 1979.
Le Strange, H. *Norfolk Official Lists.* Norwich, 1890.
Lukis, W. C., ed. *The Family Memoirs of the Rev. William Stukeley.* . . . Surtees Society, vol. 73 (1880).
Luttrell, N. *A Brief Historical Relation of State Affairs.* . . . 6 vols. Oxford, 1857.
North, R. *The Lives of the Norths,* ed. A. Jessopp. 3 vols. London, 1890; reprinted 1972.
Palmer, C. J., ed. *The History of Great Yarmouth by Henry Manship.* . . . Great Yarmouth, 1854.
Robbins, C., ed. *The Diary of John Milward, Esq.* . . . Cambridge, 1938.
Rutt, J. T., ed. *Diary of Thomas Burton, Esq., Member in the Parliaments of Oliver and Richard Cromwell, 1656 to 1659.* 4 vols. London, 1828; reprinted New York, 1974.
Saunders, H. W., ed. *The Official Papers of Sir Nathaniel Bacon of Stiffkey . . . 1580–1620.* Camden Society, 3rd ser., vol. 26 (1915).
Schofield, B., ed. *The Knyvett Letters (1620–1644).* Norfolk Record Society, vol. 20 (1949).
Smith, A. H., ed. *The Papers of Nathaniel Bacon of Stiffkey,* vol. 1, *1556–1577,* and vol. 2, *1577–1585.* Norfolk Record Society, vol. 46 (1978–79) and 49 (1982–83).
Snyder, H. L. *The Marlborough-Godolphin Correspondence.* 3 vols. Oxford, 1975.
The History and Proceedings of the House of Lords . . ., vol. 7, *1697–1714.* London, 1742.
Thompson, E. M., ed. *Letters of Humphrey Prideaux . . . to John Ellis . . ., 1674–1722.* Camden Society, n.s., vol. 15 (1875).
Walpole, H. *The Anecdotes of Painting in England,* ed. J. Dallaway and R. N. Wornum. 4 vols. London, 1876; reprinted in 3 vols., New York, 1969.

SECONDARY SOURCES

Abernethy, G. R., Jr. "The English Presbyterians and the Stuart Restoration, 1648–1663." *Transactions of the American Philosophical Society,* n.s., 55, pt. 2. Philadelphia, 1965.
Aylmer, G. E. "Crisis and Regrouping in the Political Elites: England from the 1630s to the 1660s." In J. G. A. Pocock, ed., *Three British Revolutions: 1641, 1688, 1776.* Princeton, 1980.
Barnes, T. G. *Somerset, 1625–1640: A County's Government during the "Personal Rule."* Cambridge, Mass., 1961; reprinted Chicago, 1982.
Bassin, J. "The English Landscape Garden in the Eighteenth Century: The Cultural Importance of an English Institution." *Albion* 11 (1979): 15–32.
Beckett, J. V. *Coal and Tobacco: The Lowthers and the Economic Development of West Cumberland, 1660–1760.* Cambridge, 1981.
———. *The Aristocracy in England, 1660–1914.* Oxford, 1986.
Black, J. "British Foreign Policy in the Eighteenth Century." *Journal of British Studies* 26 (1987): 26–53.

———. "Foreign Policy in the Age of Walpole." In J. Black, ed., *Britain in the Age of Walpole*, 145–69. London, 1984.
———. "Fresh Light on the Fall of Townshend." *Historical Journal* 29 (1986): 41–64.
———. "Introduction" to J. Black, ed., *Britain in the Age of Walpole*, 1–22. London, 1984.
———. "Parliament and the Political and Diplomatic Crisis of 1717–18." *Parliamentary History* 3 (1984): 77–101.
Blomefield, F. *An Essay towards a Topographical History of the County of Norfolk*. 11 vols. London, 1805–11.
Bradfer-Lawrence, H. L. "Castle Rising and the Walpoles." In C. Ingleby, ed., *A Supplement to Blomefield's Norfolk*, 29–46. London, 1929.
———. "The Merchants of Lynn." In C. Ingleby, ed., *A Supplement to Blomefield's Norfolk*, 143–203. London, 1929.
Broad, J. "Sir John Verney and Buckinghamshire Elections, 1696–1715." *Bulletin of the Institute for Historical Research* 56 (1983): 195–204.
Browning, A. *Thomas Osborne, Earl of Danby and Duke of Leeds*. 3 vols. London, 1944–51.
Browning, R. *The Duke of Newcastle*. New Haven, 1975.
Cannon, J. *Aristocratic Century: The Peerage of Eighteenth-Century England*. Cambridge, 1984.
Carruthers, S. W. "Norfolk Presbyterianism in the Seventeenth Century." *Norfolk Archaeology* 30 (1952): 89–100.
Chance, J. F. *The Alliance of Hanover*. London, 1923.
Clark, J. C. D. *English Society, 1688–1832: Ideology, Social Structure and Political Practice during the Ancien Regime*. Cambridge, 1985.
Clay, C. "The Price of Freehold Land in the Later Seventeenth and Eighteenth Centuries." *Economic History Review*, 2nd ser., 27 (1974): 173–89.
———. "Property Settlements, Financial Provisions for the Family, and Sale of Land by the Greater Landowners, 1660–1790." *Journal of British Studies* 21 (1981): 18–38.
———. *Public Finance and Private Wealth: The Career of Sir Stephen Fox, 1627–1716*. Oxford, 1978.
C[okayne], G. E. *The Complete Peerage*. . . . New ed., 12 vols. London, 1910–59.
Coleby, A. M. *Central Government and the Localities: Hampshire, 1649–1689*. Cambridge, 1987.
Coleman, D. C. "London Scriveners and the Estate Market in the Later Seventeenth Century." *Economic History Review*, 2nd ser., 4 (1951–52): 221–30.
Colley, L. *In Defiance of Oligarchy: The Tory Party, 1714–60*. Cambridge, 1982.
Colvin, H. *A Biographical Dictionary of British Architects*. 2nd ed. London, 1978.
Coombs, D. *The Conduct of the Dutch: British Opinion and the Dutch Alliance during the War of Spanish Succession*. The Hague, 1958.
Coward, B. *The Stanleys, Lords Stanley and Earls of Derby*. Chetham Society, 3rd ser., vol. 30 (1983).
Cruickshanks, E. "The Political Management of Sir Robert Walpole, 1720–42." In J. Black, ed., *Britain in the Age of Walpole*, 23–43. London, 1984.
Davies, G. *The Restoration of Charles II, 1658–1660*. San Marino, 1955.
Davies, M. G. "Country Gentry and Payments to London, 1650–1714." *Economic History Review*, 2nd ser., 24 (1971): 15–36.
Davis, R. "The 'Presbyterian' Opposition and the Emergence of Party in the

House of Lords in the Reign of Charles II." In C. Jones, ed., *Party and Management in Parliament, 1660–1784.* New York, 1984.

De Krey, G. S. *A Fractured Society: The Politics of London in the First Age of Party, 1688–1715.* Oxford, 1985.

Dickson, P. G. M. *The Financial Revolution in England.* London, 1967.

Durham, J. *The Townshends of Raynham, Part I: 1398–1600.* Cambridge, 1922.

Evans, J. T. *Seventeenth Century Norwich.* Oxford, 1979.

Ezell, M. J. M. *The Patriarch's Wife: Literary Evidence and the History of the Family.* Chapel Hill, 1987.

Fletcher, A. "Honour, Reputation and Local Officeholding in Elizabethan and Stuart England." In A. Fletcher and J. Stevenson, eds., *Order and Disorder in Early Modern England,* 92–115. Cambridge, 1985.

———. *Reform in the Provinces: The Government of Stuart England.* New Haven, 1986.

Fussell, G. E. "'Norfolk Improvers': Their Farms and Methods, A Reassessment." *Norfolk Archaeology* 33 (1964): 332–44.

Geikie, R., and Montgomery, I. A. *The Dutch Barrier, 1705–1719.* Cambridge, 1930; reprinted New York, 1968.

Gibbs, G. C. "Britain and the Alliance of Hanover, April 1725–February 1726." *English Historical Review* 73 (1958): 404–30.

Girouard, M. *Life in the English Country House.* New Haven and London, 1978.

Glassey, L. K. J. *Politics and the Appointment of Justices of the Peace, 1675–1720.* Oxford, 1979.

Guth, G. "Croakers, Tackers, and Other Citizens: Norwich Voters in the Early Eighteenth Century." Ph.D. diss., Stanford University, 1985.

Habakkuk, H. J. "Daniel Finch, 2nd Earl of Nottingham: His House and Estate." In *Studies in Social History,* ed. J. H. Plumb, 141–78. London, 1955.

———. "English Landownership, 1680–1740." *Economic History Review* 10 (1940): 2–17.

Haley, K. H. D. *The First Earl of Shaftesbury.* Oxford, 1968.

Harris, J. "Inigo Jones and the Prince's Lodging at Newmarket." *Architectural History* 2 (1959): 26–40.

———. "Raynham Hall, Norfolk." *The Archaeological Journal* 118 (1963): 180–87.

Hatton, R. *George I, Elector and King.* Cambridge, Mass., 1978.

Hayton, D. "A Note on the Norfolk Election of 1702." *Norfolk Archaeology* 37 (1980): 320–24.

Henning, B. D. *The History of Parliament: The House of Commons, 1660–90.* 3 vols. London, 1983.

Holmes, C. *Seventeenth-Century Lincolnshire.* Lincoln, 1980.

———. *The Eastern Association in the English Civil War.* Cambridge, 1974.

Holmes, G. *Augustan England: Professions, State and Society, 1680–1730.* London, 1982.

———. *British Politics in the Age of Anne.* London, 1967.

———. "The Achievement of Stability: The Social Context of Politics from the 1680s to the Age of Walpole." In J. Cannon, ed., *The Whig Ascendancy: Colloquies on Hanoverian England,* 1–27. London, 1981.

———. *The Electorate and the National Will in the First Age of Party.* Kendal, 1976.

Horn, P. "The Contribution of the Propagandist to Eighteenth-Century Agricultural Improvement." *Historical Journal* 25 (1982): 313–29.

Selected Bibliography

Horwitz, H. *Parliament, Policy and Politics in the Reign of William III.* Newark, Del., 1977.
———. *Revolution Politicks: The Career of Daniel Finch, Second Earl of Nottingham, 1647–1730.* Cambridge, 1968.
———. "The Structure of Parliamentary Politics." In G. Holmes, ed., *Britain after the Glorious Revolution,* 96–114. London, 1969.
Hughes, E. "The Eighteenth-Century Estate Agent." In H. A. Cronne et al., eds., *Essays in British and Irish History in Honour of James Eadie Todd,* 185–99. London, 1949.
Hutton, R. *The Restoration: A Political and Religious History of England and Wales, 1658–1667.* Oxford, 1985.
Jenkins, P. *The Making of a Ruling Class: The Glamorgan Gentry, 1640–1790.* Cambridge, 1983.
Jones, C. "The Impeachment of the Earl of Oxford and the Whig Schism of 1717: Four New Lists." *Bulletin of the Institute for Historical Research* 55 (1982): 66–87.
———. "'The Scheme Lords, the Necessitous Lords, and the Scots Lords': The Earl of Oxford's Management and the 'Party of the Crown' in the House of Lords, 1711–14." In C. Jones, ed., *Party and Management in Parliament, 1660–1784.* New York, 1984.
Jones, G. F. T. "The Composition and Leadership of the Presbyterian Party in the Convention." *English Historical Review* 79 (1964): 307–54.
Jones, J. R. *Charles II, Royal Politician.* London, 1987.
———. "Parties and Parliament." In J. R. Jones, ed., *The Restored Monarchy 1660–1688,* 48–70. Totowa, N.J., 1979.
———. "Restoration Election Petitions." *Durham University Journal,* n.s., 22 (1961): 45–57.
———. "The First Whig Party in Norfolk." *Durham University Journal,* n.s., 15 (1953): 13–21.
———. *The First Whigs.* Rev. ed. London, 1970.
Jourdain, M. *The Work of William Kent. . . .* London, 1948.
Kelch, R. *Newcastle, a Duke without Money: Thomas Pelham-Holles, 1693–1768.* Berkeley, 1974.
Kerridge, E. *The Agricultural Revolution.* London, 1967.
Ketton-Cremer, R. W. *A Norfolk Gallery.* London, 1948.
———. *Felbrigg: The Story of a House.* Paperback ed. London, 1982.
———. *Forty Norfolk Essays.* Norwich, 1961.
———. *Norfolk Assembly.* London, 1957.
———. *Norfolk in the Civil War.* London, 1969.
———. *Norfolk Portraits.* London, 1944.
Kishlansky, M. *Parliamentary Selection: Social and Political Choice in Early Modern England.* Cambridge, 1986.
Lacey, D. R. *Dissent and Parliamentary Politics in England, 1661–1689.* New Brunswick, N.J., 1969.
Landau, N. "Independence, Deference, and Voter Participation: The Behaviour of the Electorate in Early-Eighteenth-Century Kent." *Historical Journal* 22 (1979): 561–83.
———. *The Justices of the Peace, 1679–1760.* Berkeley, 1984.
Markham, C. R. *The Fighting Veres: Lives of Sir Francis Vere . . . and Sir Horace Vere. . . .* Boston and New York, 1888.
Mason, R. Hindry. *The History of Norfolk.* London, 1884.

Michael, W. *England under George I: The Beginnings of the Hanoverian Dynasty.* London, 1936; reprinted New York, 1970.
———. *England under George I: The Quadruple Alliance.* London, 1939; reprinted New York, 1970.
Moore, A. W. *Norfolk & the Grand Tour: Eighteenth-Century Travellers Abroad and Their Souvenirs.* Fakenham, 1985.
Murray, J. J. *George I, the Baltic and the Whig Split of 1717.* Chicago, 1969.
Owens, G. "Norfolk, 1620–41: Local Government and Central Authority in an East Anglian County." Ph.D. diss., University of Wisconsin, 1970.
Parker, R. A. C. *Coke of Norfolk: A Financial and Agricultural Study, 1707–1842.* Oxford, 1975.
———. "Coke of Norfolk and the Agrarian Revolution." *Economic History Review,* 2nd ser., 8 (1955–56): 156–66.
———. "Direct Taxation on the Coke Estates in the Eighteenth Century." *English Historical Review* 71 (1956): 247–48.
Pevsner, N. *The Buildings of England: North-West and South Norfolk.* London, 1962.
Plumb, J. H. *Sir Robert Walpole,* vol. 1, *The Making of a Statesman,* and vol. 2, *The King's Minister.* London, 1972.
———. "Sir Robert Walpole and Norfolk Husbandry." *Economic History Review,* 2nd ser., 5 (1952): 86–89.
———. "The Walpoles: Father and Son." In J. H. Plumb, ed., *Studies in Social History,* 179–207. London, 1955.
Power, M. J. "The East and West in Early-Modern London." In E. W. Ives et al., eds., *Wealth and Power in Tudor England: Essays Presented to S. T. Bindoff,* 168–85. London, 1978.
Reinmuth, H. S., Jr. "A Mysterious Dispute Demystified: Sir George Fletcher vs. the Howards." *Historical Journal* 27 (1984): 289–307.
Riches, N. *The Agricultural Revolution in Norfolk.* 2nd ed. New York, 1967.
Roberts, C. *Schemes & Undertakings: A Study of English Politics in the Seventeenth Century.* Columbus, 1985.
Roebuck, P. "Post-Restoration Landownership: The Impact of the Abolition of Wardship." *Journal of British Studies* 18 (1978): 67–85.
Rosenheim, J. M. "An Early Appreciation of *Paradise Lost.*" *Modern Philology* 75 (1978): 280–82.
———. "An Examination of Oligarchy: The Gentry of Restoration Norfolk, 1660–1720." Ph.D. diss., Princeton University, 1981.
———. "County Governance and Elite Withdrawal in Norfolk, 1660–1720." In A. L. Beier et al., eds., *The First Modern Society: Essays in English History in Honour of Lawrence Stone.* Cambridge, 1989.
———. "Party Organization at the Local Level: The Norfolk Sheriff's Subscription of 1676." *Historical Journal* 29 (1986): 713–22.
Sachse, W. *Lord Somers: A Political Portrait.* Madison, 1975.
Sacret, J. H. "The Restoration Government and Municipal Corporations." *English Historical Review* 45 (1930): 232–59.
Saunders, H. W. "Estate Management at Rainham in the Years 1661–1686, and 1706." *Norfolk Archaeology* 19 (1915–17): 41–46.
Schwoerer, L. G. *Lady Rachel Russell, "One of the Best of Women."* Baltimore, 1988.
Scott, W. R. *The Constitution and Finance of English, Scottish and Irish Joint-Stock Companies to 1720.* 3 vols. London, 1912; reprinted Gloucester, Mass., 1968.

Selected Bibliography

Sedgwick, R. *The History of Parliament: The House of Commons, 1715–1754.* 2 vols. London, 1970.
Sharpe, K. "Crown, Parliament and Locality: Government and Communication in Early Stuart England." *English Historical Review* 101 (1986): 312–50.
Smith, A. H. *County and Court: Government and Politics in Norfolk, 1558–1603.* Oxford, 1974.
Speck, W. A. "The General Election of 1715." *English Historical Review* 90 (1975): 507–22.
———. *Tory & Whig: The Struggle in the Constituencies, 1701–1715.* London, 1970.
Stone, L. *Family and Fortune: Studies in Aristocratic Finance in the Sixteenth and Seventeenth Centuries.* Oxford, 1973.
———. *The Crisis of the Aristocracy 1558–1641.* Oxford, 1965.
———. "The Residential Development of the West End of London in the Seventeenth Century." In B. C. Malament, ed., *After the Reformation*, 167–212. Philadelphia, 1980.
———. "The Results of the English Revolutions of the Seventeenth Century." In J. G. A. Pocock, ed., *Three British Revolutions: 1641, 1688, 1776*, 63–100. Princeton, 1980.
Stone, L., and J. C. F. *An Open Elite? England 1540–1880.* Oxford, 1984.
Thirsk, J., ed. *The Agrarian History of England and Wales*, vol. 5: *1640–1750*, part 1: *Regional Farming Systems.* Cambridge, 1984. Part 2: *Agrarian Change.* Cambridge, 1985.
Townshend, C. H. *The Townshend Family of Lynn, in Old and New England.* . . . 4th ed. New Haven, 1884.
Trevelyan, G. M. *England under Queen Anne.* 3 vols. New York, 1930–34.
Turberville, A. S. *The House of Lords in the XVIIIth Century.* Oxford, 1927; reprinted Westport, Conn., 1970.
Underdown, D. "Community and Class: Theories of Local Politics in the English Revolution." In B. C. Malament, ed., *After the Reformation: Essays in Honor of J. H. Hexter*, 147–62. Philadelphia, 1980.
———. *Royalist Conspiracy in England, 1649–1660.* New Haven, 1960.
Walcott, R. *English Politics in the Early Eighteenth Century.* Oxford, 1956.
Williams, B. *Stanhope: A Study in Eighteenth-Century War and Diplomacy.* Oxford, 1932; reprinted 1968.
Wilson, C. *England's Apprenticeship, 1603–1763.* 2nd ed. London, 1984.
Wilson, M. I. *William Kent, Architect, Designer, Painter, Gardener, 1685–1748.* London, 1984.
Wordie, J. R. *Estate Management in Eighteenth-Century England: The Building of the Leveson-Gower Fortune.* London, 1982.

Manuscript Sources

MANUSCRIPTS AT RAYNHAM HALL

My work at Raynham Hall was largely undertaken before completion of the list of manuscripts recently compiled by the Norfolk Record Office for the Historical Manuscripts Commission (*Report on the Family and Estate Papers of the Townshend Family, Marquesses Townshend, 14th–20th Century*, London, 1986). As a result, the references used in this study are of my devising, but they correspond with those of the Norfolk Record Office's *Report* in almost all instances. I am grateful to the Norfolk Record Office for generously supplying me with a copy of this list.

Material from the trunks in the attic at Raynham, sorted and boxed by the record office (*Report*, 162–69), has been specified herein by the designation "[NRO]". Because I originally examined this material while it was in the record office for sorting and not yet boxed under the scheme recorded in the report, my references are necessarily general, as for instance to "correspondence" and "state-lieutenancy papers." The date, description of document, author and recipient of correspondence, and comparison with the report should make identification of individual pieces possible.

All manuscripts are located in the Raynham Hall attics unless otherwise noted. Manuscripts have generally been identified as follows:

    RBF: box files, mostly arranged by T. S. Blakeney, late honorary archivist
    RL: Raynham Hall library
    RLBV: bound volumes in the library
    RU: uncatalogued papers not otherwise sorted
    RUBV: bound volumes
    RUC: uncatalogued correspondence extracted from the attic trunks
    RUEA: uncatalogued estate accounts, sorted from the attic trunks and arranged chronologically; accounts for Suffolk lands are noted as RUEA[S]
    RUEM: uncatalogued estate manuscripts (not accounts), sorted from the attic trunks and arranged chronologically
    RUFP: uncatalogued family and personal papers
    RUM: uncatalogued miscellaneous manuscripts
    RUS: uncatalogued marriage and estate settlements
    RUSL: uncatalogued state and lieutenancy papers

Following the practice of the Norfolk Record Office, the boxes built into the library's closets have been referred to as "drawers."

The box files in the attic were arranged in general chronological order by Blakeney, according to which family head the material pertained. These files have been designated as follows:

    RBF/HT for the first Viscount Townshend
    RBF/CT for the second Viscount Townshend
    RBF/LL for the third Viscount Townshend (Lord Lynn, 1723–38)

Further description of these box files is a shortened version of the sometimes lengthy labels given by Blakeney. Thus, for example, Blakeney's file labeled "Temp. 2nd Visct. Townshend Estate management c. 1705–1720s [a] Thomas Warde [b] Wm Watts [c] Rd Leman [d] misc." becomes simply "RBF/CT 1705–20s." Box files not assigned to a particular family head are given appropriate descriptions.

In March 1988, at a late stage in the preparation of this study, further papers were discovered at Raynham Hall and listed by the Norfolk Record Office. Those which I examined in June 1988 have been cited according to the scheme just noted and qualified by the addition "[1988]."

Selected Bibliography

OTHER MANUSCRIPTS

Bodleian Library:

    MS Ballard 4, 7, 26–27
    MS Carte 243
    MS Clarendon 60, 61, 64, 67, 70, 71, 72, 80, 83
    MS English letters c. 144
    MS Gough, Norfolk 33
    MS Rawlinson A174
    MS Tanner 36, 38, 42–43, 177, 259, 285, 305

British Library:

    Add. 4223: Biographical Anecdotes
    Add. 11601: Norfolk lieutenancy journal, 1661–76
    Add. 15867: Diplomatic correspondence
    Add. 22207: Strafford papers
    Add. 27447–48: Paston papers
    Add. 28621: Paston Papers
    Add. 32686–87, 32689: Newcastle papers
    Add. 33064: Newcastle papers
    Add. 33084: Pelham papers
    Add. 36540: Paston papers
    Add. 36988: Paston papers
    Add. 37634, 37636: Townshend papers
    Add. 37911: Windham papers
    Add. 38501, 38507: Townshend papers
    Add. 41140: Townshend papers
    Add. 41306, 41308: Townshend papers
    Add. 41654–56: Townshend papers
    Add. 46856: Horatio Walpole's correspondence
    Add. 61116, 61130, 61132, 61148, 61161: Blenheim papers
    Add. 63079–63109: Papers of T. S. Blakeney, including Townshend MSS
    Egerton 2719–21: Le Neve papers
    Egerton 3124: Diplomatic correspondence
    Loan 29: Portland papers
    Sloane 4037: Sir Hans Sloane's papers
    Stowe 142: State papers, 1375–1810
    Stowe 224–27: Hanover state papers, 1692–1719
    Stowe 242: Astle's Collections for English history, 1688–1744
    Stowe 247: Correspondence of James Craggs, senior and junior
    Stowe 251: State letters, 1723–48
    Stowe 256: Phelps correspondence, 1725–63
    Stowe 308: Chesterfield's Characters

Cambridge University Library:

    Cholmondeley (Houghton) Correspondence: Walpole papers
    Cholmondeley (Houghton) Papers 68: King's Lynn politics

Folger Library:

    Bacon-Townshend papers

256   *Selected Bibliography*

House of Lords Record Office:

　Proxy Books

Norfolk Record Office:

　Bradfer-Lawrence collection
　Bristow purchase 4.6.76, S187A
　Emmet & Tacon deposit, 29.7.74, T190A
　Hamond deposit, 21.8.75, S116C
　Hare collection
　Knyvett-Wilson collection
　Le Strange collection
　Minor Collections 1/52: Le Neve correspondence
　MS 503, T133A: lieutenancy letterbook, 1701–39
　MS 553, T142B: accounts of Lord Townshend's journeys to Hanover
　MS 10999, 34E1: papers on Norfolk politics
　MS 20446, 127x1: Townshend bills
　NRS 27276, 372x7: Norfolk lieutenancy journal, 1676–1715
　NRS 27308, 447x: Norfolk lieutenancy journal, 1715–50
　PD 369/1: East Raynham parish register, 1627–1716
　Rye MSS 9, Norris's Collections, vol. 2: election results
　Sotheby purchases, 23.12.76, R160B, and 13.3.80, S154D
　Stiffkey parish register 1, temporary loan, 25.4.78
　T287A: commissions of the peace
　Uncatalogued mss, Boxes D and M, P168C
　Windham/Ketton-Cremer collection

Public Record Office, London:

　ASSI 16, ASSI 35: Norfolk circuit assize records
　C231/7-10: Crown Office doquet books, 1660–1746
　C234/26: Fiats for commissions of the peace for Norfolk
　PROB 11: Probate records
　SP 35-36: State papers, George I
　SP 43/1-10: State papers, Regencies, 1716–29
　SP 44/116, 118, 122: State papers, letterbooks, 1714–34

University of Chicago, Regenstein Library:

　MSS 274: Walpole letters

University of Michigan, Clements Library:

　Sydney papers

Yale University, Beinecke Library:

　Osborn shelves, c.201
　Osborn files, "Walpole"
　Osborn shelves, Townshend box 6: office a/cs

* Index *

Note: The following abbreviations are used in this index: CT, for Charles Townshend; HT, for Horatio Townshend.

accounts:
    domestic and estate, 9, 11, 68–69, 74, 77–79, 81–82, 96, 98–104, 111, 119, 132–133, 135–138, 141–142, 155, 160
    of London agents, 73, 86, 118, 122, 157–158, 165
    methods for taking, 11, 64–65, 67–68, 96–104, 112, 122–123, 132–133, 136, 137, 141, 146
    of renovations at Raynham Hall, 109, 174, 185–188
agriculture:
    changes from 17th to 18th century, xiii–xiv, 11
    See also animal husbandry; clover cultivation; CT, agricultural policies of; direct farming; enclosure; HT, agricultural policies of; marling; sheep and sheep foldcoures; turnips
Allin, Sir Richard, 204
animal husbandry, 92, 128, 129, 136
    See also sheep and sheep foldcourses
Anne, Queen:
    CT's political career and, 120, 121, 215
    death of, 227, 230
    Junto and, 201
    Marlborough and, 219
aristocracy:
    agrarian policies of, 89–90
    changes from 16th to 17th century, 4–5
    country house and, 167, 173
    and debts during restoration, 83
    education of, 110–111
    as "service elite," 204, 245
    See also Beckett, J. V.; Raynham Hall
Arlington, first Earl of (Henry Bennet):
    enmity toward HT, 36
    entertained at Raynham, 172
    and reconciliation with HT, 47
Arundel, Earl of. *See* Norfolk, seventh Duke of
Ashe, Lady Mary (mother of Mary Ashe Townshend), 109
Ashe, Mary. *See* Townshend, Mary Ashe
Ashe, Sir Joseph (father-in-law of HT), 84

Astley, Sir Jacob:
    elected with Roger Townshend (1700), 195
    in election of 1702, 199, 200
    as executor of HT's will, 108
    recruited by Whigs, 226–227
    stands for knight of shire (1701), 197
    as Tory candidate (1685), 60
Atterbury, Francis, Bishop of Rochester, 224
Austria:
    alliance advanced by CT, 235
Austro-Spanish treaty of Vienna, 235

Bacon, Sir Nathaniel, 13
Bacon, Waller, 209
Bank of England, 105
    stock of, 157–158
Barnardiston, Sir Samuel, 47, 172
Barrier Treaty, 214, 219
    CT's involvement in, 230
Bayliss, Robert, 217
Beckett, J. V.:
    on debts of Restoration aristocrats, 83
    on expense of London living, 161
    on "service elite," 204
Bennet, Henry. *See* Arlington, Earl of
Berkeley House, 76
Berkeley, Jane Lady (HT's great-grandmother), 8–9, 13
Black, Jeremy:
    on alliance (1717) of Tories and Whigs, 232
    on CT and court of George I, 230
    on CT and George II, 236
    on dispute between CT and Robert Walpole, 237
    on foreign policy, 225
Blickling Hall, 38, 49
Blyth, William, 209
Bolingbroke, first Viscount (Henry St. John), 224
Booth, Sir George, 20
Bothmer, Baron, 230
Bower, Richard, 36
Britiffe, Robert:
    as adviser to CT, 144, 226

257

as Whig candidate from Norwich (1713, 1715), 226, 227
Browne, Sir Thomas, 170
Buckingham, second Duke of (George Villiers), 36
Buckley, Samuel, 240
Bullock, Thomas, 78
Burlington House, 76
Butler, James. *See* Ormonde, Duke of

Calthorpe, Sir Christopher, 51
Calthorpe, James:
 as adviser to CT, 109, 110, 111, 112, 113, 130, 192, 202
 as executor of HT's will, 108
 as spokesperson for CT (1710), 218
Cannon, John, 110
Carr, Sir Robert, 47, 172
Carteret, second Baron (John Carteret), 234
Castleacre manor, 143, 144
Castle Rising:
 by-elections of 1673 in, 38
 election of 1701 in, 197
 election of 1710 in, 217
 election of 1713 in, 222
Catelyn, Sir Neville, 42–43, 51, 195
Chambers, John, 209
Charles I, 40
Charles II:
 career of HT and, 6, 45, 57–58, 59, 71–75
 restoration of, 6, 22
 Rye House Plot and, 6
 and visits to Norfolk, 36, 39, 53–54
 and visits to Raynham, 75, 172
Chesterfield, fourth Earl of (Philip Dormer Stanhope):
 on CT as father, 120
 on CT as orator, 224
 on CT's personality, 142, 237, 242
 on CT's political career, 131, 230
Civil War, 27–30
Clarendon, first Earl of (Edward Hyde):
 as adviser and patron of HT, 25, 33, 71, 72
 fall of, 35, 36
 as high steward of Great Yarmouth, 27
 on HT, 19
Clarendon House, 76
Clay, Christopher, 150, 156
Clayton, Sir Robert, 86, 87
Clerke, William, 68
Clifton, Henry, 80
clover cultivation:
 under CT, 151–152, 154
Coke, Edward, 212
Coke, Robert:
 death of, 49–50
 in King's Lynn by-election (1675), 41–42, 48

Coke, Thomas (Baron Lovel and Earl of Leicester):
 elevated to peerage, 229
 farming practices of, 134, 153
 Holkham Hall and, 117, 143, 188, 189
 See also Holkham Hall
commission of the peace in Norfolk, 14, 36, 47–48, 57, 205, 226
 appointments to, 204
 and CT as justice of the peace, 239
 and HT as justice of the peace, 16
 manipulations of, 58, 196, 198, 220–221, 227–228
 and quarter sessions dispute (1685), 61–62
 for Thetford, 31
Conventicle Act of 1664, 34
Convention of 1660, 21–22
Cooke, Sir William, 199
Corporation Act, 26, 27
Council of State, 19, 20, 22
Cowper, William (first Earl Cowper), 227–228
Crew, Thomas (second Baron Crew), 109, 110, 117
Cromwell, Oliver, 17
Cromwell, Richard, 19

Danby, first Earl of (Thomas Osborne):
 enmity with HT, 45, 46, 47, 49, 84
 King's Lynn by-election (1675) and, 41, 50
 rise of, 35
 See also Paston, Sir Robert
Defoe, Daniel, 198
De Grey, Thomas, 212, 227
Dillingham, John, 22
direct farming by landlord, 90–91, 94, 102, 121, 128, 133, 149, 244
dissent and dissenters, 24, 27, 31–32, 34, 35–36, 39, 40, 44, 48, 49
Doyly, Sir William, 36
Dunch, Thomas, 208–209
Duncombe, Sir John, 72
Dutch:
 Tories' hostility to (1712), 219
 treaty with, 214–215
 See also CT; as ambassador to The Hague; CT, Dutch treaties and
Dutch Wars:
 HT and, 6, 25, 27, 32–33
 Sir Robert Paston and, 37
 See also Norfolk; Dutch threat to

Earle, John, 86
East Raynham. *See* Raynham, East
East Rudham. *See* Rudham, East and West
Edge, William (mason for Raynham Hall), 173, 174
 CT's difficulties with, 176
enclosure:
 under CT, 126–27, 148, 151

See also CT, estate and land management of
England, Benjamin, 211, 215
England, George, 229
Essex:
 HT's interests in, 67, 68–70, 169
estate management, 11–12, 64–65, 106
 See also CT, estate and land management of; HT, estate management of
Eton College, 108, 109, 110, 241
Ezell, Margaret, 9

Fairfax, Thomas (third Lord Fairfax of Cameron), 20, 22
Fakenham, 61, 239
Felbrigg Hall, 109
Felton, Timothy:
 HT's debts assessed by, 82–83, 86
 HT's land assessed by, 69
 as negotiator of leases, 92, 94, 100–101
 as ombudsman for HT, 97
Fenn, William, 150, 185
fertilization of land, 91
 in leases under CT, 148, 153, 155
 at Raynham, 127
 See also marling
Fielding, William, 217
Fleetwood, Charles, 17
Fletcher, Anthony, 191
Fowles, Sir Thomas, 113
Fuller, Samuel, 215, 216
Fuller, Thomas, 13

George I:
 CT's foreign policy and, 235–236
 CT's political career and, 222, 225–226, 230, 231–234
 death of, 164
 rupture with Prince of Wales, 232–233
George II:
 CT's favor with, 8, 164
 CT's foreign policy and, 235, 236, 237
 CT traveling with, 165, 234
 and view of CT, 236
Gertruydenberg:
 negotiations with French at, 214
Gleane, Sir Peter, 195
 as Whig candidate in 1679 election, 52
 Whig factionalism and, 55, 56, 58, 60
Godolphin, Sidney (first Earl of Godolphin), 217
Gosse, Edmund, 244
Grange Farm, West Rudham:
 plans for cultivation of, 151
Great Yarmouth, 27, 32, 210
 by-elections in, 215, 229
 corporation of, 26
 dissenters in, 27, 34–35
 dominance of Tories (1702) in, 200
 election of 1708 in, 211–212, 215–216
 election of 1710 in, 216
 election of 1713 in, 222
 elections of 1722 and 1727 in, 226, 229
 procurement of convoy (1706–1707) for, 210
 visit of Charles II to, 36
Gregg, William, 211

Halland, Sussex, 175, 176
Hanover:
 CT's travels in, 234–235
Harbord, Harbord, 226
Harcourt, Sir Simon, 228
Hare, Sir Ralph, 70, 170
Hare, Sir Thomas, 60
Harley, Sir Edward:
 as friend of HT, 17
Harley, Sir Edward (second Earl of Oxford):
 as friend of CT, 135
 and visit to Raynham, 184
Harley, Robert (1626–1673):
 and visit to Lord Fairfax with HT, 20–21
Harley, Sir Robert (first Earl of Oxford):
 as adversary of CT, 224
 as defended by CT, 232
 Horatio Walpole and, 221
 and negotiations with Whigs in 1711, 219, 220
 See also Gregg, William
Hatton, Ragnhild:
 on CT and Hanoverians, 231, 235
 on Whig split in 1720, 234
Hervey, John (Baron Hervey of Ickworth):
 on CT's fiscal integrity, 159
 on CT's public demeanor, 223, 224
 on Raynham and Houghton halls, 177
Heyman, Jonathan, 159, 165
Hobart, Sir Henry (fourth baronet), 193, 195
Hobart, Sir John (third baronet):
 death of, 60
 election of 1673 and, 37, 38–39, 42
 election of 1675 and, 42–43
 elections of 1679 and, 50, 51
 and partisan rifts with HT, 53–55, 56–57, 58, 59
 in Protectorate Parliaments, 17
Hobart, Sir John (fifth baronet, first Earl of Buckinghamshire), 228
Hobart, Lady Mary, 58
Holderness, Brian, 152
Holkham Hall:
 building of, 117
 contrasted to Raynham Hall, 134, 140, 177, 188
 See also Coke, Thomas
Holland, Sir John (first baronet):
 death of, 105, 195
 election of 1675 and, 42–43
 on HT in Norfolk, 49
 loan to HT, 87

nonpartisanship in Norfolk and, 59–60
quarrel on commission of peace and, 62
Holland, Sir John (second baronet), 195
  in election of 1701, 197
  in election of 1702, 199
  in election of 1704, 205
  in election of 1705, 208
  in election of 1708, 212
  in election of 1710, 217, 218
  in election of 1722, 229
Holles, Denzell (first Baron Holles), 47
Hoste, James, 206
Houghton Hall:
  design of, 185
  garden of, 184
  Raynham Hall and, 177, 185, 188, 237
  See also Walpole, Robert (prime minister)
Houghton, Robert, 196
Howard family. See Norfolk, dukes of
Hughes, Dr. Owen:
  enmity with HT, 47–49, 172
Huntington, Richard, 36

James II:
  coronation of, 61
  as Duke of York, 52, 59
Jenkins, Philip, 245
Johnson, James, 36
Johnson, Mrs. (housekeeper to CT), 164
Jones, Inigo, 14
Jones, J. R., 35, 58
Jones, Sir William, 117
Jourdain, Margaret, 184
Junto:
  CT and, 211, 214, 219

Kelly, Joan, 10
Kemp, Sir Robert, 55, 195
  HT's support of, 40–44, 48, 60
Kent, William:
  Raynham Hall renovations and, 184–187
Killigrew, Sir Peter, 86
King, Richard, 22
King's College, Cambridge, 110
King's Lynn, 29, 210
  by-election of 1675 and, 41
  and convoys for fishing fleet, 200, 203
  CT's influence in, 195, 197, 200
  election of 1679 and, 49–50
  election of 1713 and, 222
  HT's influence in, 21, 22, 30, 34, 38, 61
  Robert Walpole and, 221
  royalism (1643) in, 16, 19, 20
Kishlansky, Mark, 18

land exchanges, 79, 145, 169
land purchases:
  by CT, 124, 141–145, 165
  by executors of HT, 116

by executors of Sir Roger Townshend (first baronet), 66, 79–80, 171
  by HT, 79–81, 171
  by Jane Lady Berkeley, 8, 13
  by Sir Roger Townshend (HT's great-grandfather), 13
land sales:
  by HT, 69–70, 81, 169
  in Norfolk, 144
Landau, Norma, 5, 71
Langham:
  rents and leases in, 94, 124, 142
  small tenant farms in, 95, 146
Laurence, Edward, 136, 147–148
leasing policy:
  under CT, 145–154
  under HT, 90–96
Leicester, Earl of. See Coke, Thomas
Le Neve, Oliver, 193
  duel with Sir Henry Hobart, 193–194
L'Estrange, Edward:
  as auditor to CT, 112
  death of, 146
L'Estrange, Sir Nicholas, 117
Leveson-Gower estates, 147
Lewkenor, Edward, 6, 16, 67
Lewkenor, Mary. See Townshend, Mary Lewkenor
lieutenancy in Norfolk:
  declining significance of, 228–229
  and Duke of Ormonde, 221, 222, 228
  and Earl of Arundel (seventh Duke of Norfolk), 59, 60
  and Earl of Southampton, 22, 23, 25
  in elections, 43–44, 199
  mediating role of, 191–92
  and Viscount Yarmouth, 46, 49, 58
  See also CT, as lord lieutenants; HT, as lord lieutenant
Lindsey, first Earl of (Robert Bertie), 37
Little Yarmouth, 35
London, 10, 21, 33, 37, 46, 86, 103, 110–111, 113, 116, 122, 123, 129, 130, 132, 140, 157–158, 160, 166, 170, 176, 210, 227, 244–245
  craftsmen from, 170, 174, 184, 185
  and political direction of Norfolk Whigs, 207–208, 212, 216–218
  See also CT, and residence in London; HT, and residence in London
Lovel, Lord. See Coke, Thomas
Lowke, Philip, 97
Lynn, Lord. See Townshend, Charles, third Viscount

Mann, Sir Horace, 119
Marlborough, first Duke of (John Churchill), 203
  negotiations with the Dutch, 213–214
marling, under CT, 127, 151, 154, 155–156

Index

May, Matthew, 174
Medowe, Sir Thomas, 36
Monck, General George, 20
Money, John, 151–152
Monmouth, James (Duke of Monmouth), 47
Morris, John, 86
Morston:
  rents and leasing in, 94, 142, 150
  small tenant farms in, 95, 146

Newcastle, first Duke of (Thomas Pelham-Holles):
  as ally of CT, 206, 234, 236
  debts of, 160
  nonconformity of, see dissent and dissenters
Norfolk, fourth Duke of (Thomas Howard), 6
Norfolk, fifth Duke of (Thomas Howard), 23
Norfolk, sixth Duke of (Henry Howard):
  Catholicism of, 45
  and friendship with Sir Robert Paston, 37
  and influence in Norfolk, 23, 38
  and rivalry with HT, 30–33, 48, 59
Norfolk, seventh Duke of (Henry Howard, Earl of Arundel), 195
  as lord lieutenant, 59–60, 192, 193
  Whig factionalism and, 194
Norfolk, 28
  by-elections and, 38–39, 40, 41–43, 229
  clergy of, 42
  county addresses of, 21, 55, 58, 205
  Dutch threat to, 31, 32–34
  elections and, 17, 21, 23, 50–51, 52, 54, 60, 119, 193, 195, 197, 198–201, 207–209, 211–212, 216–218, 222, 225, 226, 227, 229, 238–239
  Howard family influence in, 31–32
  militia of, 6, 34, 43, 45
  opposition to Cromwell, 17
  partisan divisions in, 17, 23–24, 39, 40–44, 47–49, 50–51, 53, 55–57, 59–60, 190–191, 193–194, 195–196, 197–198, 199–200, 202, 209, 212, 217–218, 220–221, 226–228, 238–239, 244
  plague in, 31, 34
  political developments in, 6, 7, 14, 16–18, 105–106, 191, 194, 197, 198, 207
  projected royalist rising in, 19–20
  royalism of, 6, 16, 39, 58
  taxes in, 14
  Townshend family influence in, 13, 23, 140, 147, 158, 168–173
  visit of Charles II to, 36, 39, 53
  See also Raynham; CT; HT; Walpole, Robert (the elder); Whig party
North, Sir Francis, 38
North, Roger, 170

Norwich, 25, 34, 52, 58, 195, 199, 200, 207, 208, 210
  by-election of 1678 in, 49
  CT's activities in, 197, 208–210
  election of 1702 in, 200
  election of 1705 in, 208–209
  election of 1710 in, 216
  election of 1713 in, 222
  election of 1715 in, 227
  HT's activities in, 31–32, 42–43
  justices of the peace for division of, 61–62
  and municipal dispute of 1705, 205, 208–210
  as site of county elections, 21, 43, 200, 238
  See also Britiffe, Robert
Norwich, Bishop of. See Sparrow, Anthony; Trimnel, Charles
Nottingham, second Earl of (Daniel Finch), 200

Occasional Conformity Act, 232
Orford, Earl of (Edward Russell), 194
Ormonde, first Duke of (James Butler), 47, 53
Ormonde, second Duke of (James Butler, lord lieutenant of Norfolk), 1713–1714, 221, 222, 228
Osborne, Sir Thomas. See Danby, first Earl of
Oxford, earls of. See Harley

Palmer, Sir Geoffrey, 86
Parker, R. A. C., 11
Paston, Charles (Lord Paston), 195
Paston, Lady Rebecca (wife of Sir Robert), 37, 47
Paston, Sir Robert (first Viscount and first Earl of Yarmouth), 54
  campaign of Neville Catelyn and, 42, 45
  death of, 59
  influence in election of Jan., 1679, 51
  as rival to HT, 33, 36–37, 39, 40–41, 46, 50, 52, 57, 58
Peerage Bill (1719), 233
Pelham, Elizabeth. See Townshend, Elizabeth Pelham
Pelham, Thomas, (first Baron Pelham, CT's father-in-law), 7, 117
Pelham-Holles, Sir Thomas. See Newcastle, Duke of
Pell, John, 45
Philips, Samuel, 78
Piccadilly, 76, 77
Plumb, J. H.:
  CT's fiscal affairs and, 159
  on Robert Walpole, 233, 244
Poemerroy, Miles, 174
  inefficiency of, 176
Popish Plot, 39
Poyntz, Stephen, 165

as CT's secretary at The Hague, 129, 131
  as tutor to CT's sons, 164
Pratt, Roger, 169–170, 183–184
Prestland, William, 136
Prideaux, Humphrey:
  commentary on Norfolk politics, 194, 213, 217
Protectorate, 17, 38
  HT's expenditures under, 70

Quakers, 31

Raby, Lord. *See* Wentworth, Thomas
Raynham, East, 13, 92, 94, 99, 128, 137, 150, 155
  improvements at, 142–143
  purchases of land in, 79–80, 142, 171–172
  tenants in, 94–95, 146, 171–172, 208
Raynham Hall, 29, 38, 48, 49, 58, 81, 94, 107, 110, 114, 119, 124, 134, 146, 166, 200, 206, 218, 238, 240, 241, 242, 245
  building of, 14
  completion and renovations of under HT, 66, 75, 76, 82, 83, 168–169, 170–171, 177
  CT's children and, 164, 241
  deer park at, 74–75, 122, 171–172
  and entertainment under CT, 188–189, 196, 240–241
  and entertainment under HT, 74–75, 93
  exterior of, 175–176
  grounds of, 170–171, 184, 187
  household management at, 67–68, 74, 97, 111, 112, 119, 125, 128, 129, 132, 136, 160, 161, 163
  interior of, 170, 174, 175
  manuscripts at, 8–10, 104, 135, 141, 253–254
  political use of by HT, 47, 52, 54, 65, 75, 93, 168, 171–173
  renovations of under CT, 121, 125, 158, 160, 165, 173–178, 184–188
  and visit of Charles II, 36, 75, 172
  See also CT, estate and land management of; CT, retirement of; Kent, William; Poemerroy, Miles; Ripley, Thomas
Reading, Sir Robert, 53
rent arrears, 81, 97, 98–99, 100, 124, 137–138
Restoration, 65
  Norfolk royalists' attempt at, 6
  See also Charles II
Richardson, Thomas Lord (Baron Cramond), 23, 38, 40
Riches, Naomi, 127
Ripley, Thomas, 185, 186, 187
Robethon, Jean de, 224, 230
Rochester, Bishop of. *See* Atterbury, Francis
Rookewood, Nicholas, 22
Rosa, Salvator, 187

Rudham, East and West, 94, 95, 150
  agricultural improvements of under CT, 151–152, 155–156
  tenant farmers in, 146
  See also Grange Farm
Ruding, William, 80–81, 123
Russell, Lady Rachel, 9
Rye House Plot, 60

Sacheverell, Dr. Henry, trial of, 216
St. John's College, Cambridge, 15
Scarbrough, second Earl of (Richard Lumley), 238
Scarndale Closes, 124
Selwyn, John:
  accounts with CT, 157–158, 165
Shaftesbury, first Earl of (Anthony Ashley Cooper), 53
  HT caballing with, 45–46, 47, 52
sheep and sheep foldcourses, 81, 103, 116, 121, 122, 123, 136, 148, 151–152, 155
Sherard, Dr. William, 116–117
Shereford, 143, 144–145
  leases under CT in, 150
sheriff, office of in Norfolk, 14, 45, 48, 193, 203, 205–207
Shipdham, 123
  in election of 1705, 208
  inherited by Lord Lynn, 135
  purchased by CT, 124, 143–144
Smyth Samuel, 101–103
Snelling, Bartholomew, 101, 102
Somers, John (first Baron Somers), 192, 211
  influence on CT, 223
Southampton, fourth Earl of (Thomas Wriothesley), 22, 23, 25
South Creake, 95
  leases of under CT, 123, 125, 131
  minor tenants in, 146–147
  purchase of by CT in, 143, 144
South Sea Bubble, 144, 157, 233
Southwell, Sir Robert, 47
Sparrow, Anthony (Bishop of Norwich), 42
Speck, W. A., 227
Stagg, John, 123, 124, 143
Stanhoe, 80–81
Stanhope, James (first Viscount Stanhope), 160
  Anglo-French alliance and, 231
  death of, 224
  opposed by CT, 232–233
Stibbard, 142
  tenant farming and, 146
Stiffkey, 13, 169
  estate management and, 92, 95
  income from, 94, 96
  minor tenant farms and, 146
Stone, Lawrence, 68, 76
Stowbardolph, 170

Index 263

Suffolk:
  Dutch threat to, 32
  HT's land interests in, 67, 68–69, 108, 112
  and profits from CT's estates, 135, 158
Sunderland, third Earl of (Charles Spencer), 224–225
  and enmity with CT, 231, 232–234
Swift, Jonathan, 219
Symonds, Nathaniel, 215

Tankerville, Earl of (Ford Grey), 197
Taylor, Simon, 41
tenants and tenant farming:
  under CT, 121, 123, 124–125, 129–131, 137–140, 141, 145, 146–154, 155, 166
  under HT, 90–96, 146–147
Thetford, 30–31, 217
  See also DeGrey, Thomas; Ward, John
Thurisby, William:
  as CT's guardian, 109, 116
  as HT's executor, 108, 113
Toftrees, 80, 123, 125
  leases under CT, 150
Tories:
  in Norfolk, 53, 55, 59, 60–61, 108, 109, 193, 195, 199–200, 212, 213, 217, 220–221, 226–227, 229, 238
  in Norwich, 209, 222
  in parliament, 192, 218–219, 220, 222, 232–233
  See also Walpole, Horatio (the elder)
Townshend, Anne (HT's grandmother), 9, 13
Townshend, Charles (second Viscount):
  acquisition of land by, 79, 143, 144
  agricultural policies of, 11–12, 68, 97, 106–107, 116–117, 125–131, 140, 141–155
  as ambassador to The Hague, 105, 119, 120, 121, 123, 125, 129, 131, 132, 203, 213–218, 220
  aristocracy and, 4, 10, 110
  and campaign for brother Roger, 195, 197
  as captain of the Yeoman Guards, 211, 220
  censured by House of Commons, 7, 219
  childhood of, 75, 84–85, 97, 173
  as commissioner for union with Scotland, 121, 211, 223
  and commission of peace, 198, 203–205, 220, 228
  and court, *see* Anne, Queen; George I; George II
  Dutch treaties and, 214–215, 231
  and elections of 1705, 208–210
  and elections of 1710, 216–218
  estate and land management of, 141–145, 146, 149–151, 153–154, 155, 157–159, 166, 201, 229
  European tour of, 111, 116–117, 173
  expenses of, 140, 160, 164–165, 174, 186–188
  as father, 119–120, 163–165, 240; *see also* Townshend, Charles (third Viscount, Lord Lynn); Townshend, Dorothy (daughter of CT); Townshend, Thomas; Townshend, William
  and Henry Hobart, 193–194
  as high steward of King's Lynn, 192
  illness of, 164, 236, 237
  Junto and, 211, 219
  as lord lieutenant of Ireland, 231, 232
  as lord lieutenant of Norfolk, 7, 120, 121, 190, 194, 195, 196, 198–199, 201, 202, 220, 226, 227, 228
  and loss of favor of George I, 231
  and loss of lord lieutenancy, 221–222
  marriages of, 7, 106, 117–118, 119, 120, 157; *see also* Townshend, Elizabeth Pelham; Townshend, Dorothy Walpole
  as minister to George I, 222, 226, 234
  as orator, 224
  and order of the Garter, 8, 235
  origin of nickname, 133–134, 153
  parliamentary and government career of, 117, 120, 121, 129–130, 159, 190–192, 197, 201, 210, 211, 213–215, 218–220, 222–225, 230–238, 242–245
  personality of, 130–131, 223–224, 240; *see also* Black, Jeremy; Chesterfield, Earl of
  as privy councilor, 7, 211
  receipt of rent by, 137, 140, 141, 151, 166
  and residence in London, 109, 110, 118, 119, 130, 161, 164, 174, 196, 200, 207–208
  retirement of, 146, 158, 161, 164, 165, 166, 168, 238, 239–241
  Scotch plot and, 210
  as secretary of state, 8, 234
  support of Prince of Wales, 232
  supporter of Tories, 232–233; *see also* Stanhope, James; Sunderland, Earl of
Townshend, Charles (third Viscount, Lord Lynn, son of CT), 119, 135, 144
  elevation to House of Lords, 163
  elected for Great Yarmouth, 229
  estate affairs and, 240–241
  marriage of, 161
Townshend, Dorothy (daughter of CT), 132, 164
Townshend, Dorothy Walpole (second wife of CT):
  death of, 164, 236
  and domestic affairs, 119, 132
  expenses of, 163–164, 165
  legacy of, 158
  marriage of, 8, 9, 220, 222
Townshend, Elizabeth Pelham (first wife of CT), 106, 117, 118–119
  death of, 219–220
  marriage settlement of, 7, 144, 157
Townshend family papers, xiv, 253–254

Index

Townshend, George (fourth Viscount, grandson of CT), 240–241
Townshend, Horatio (first Viscount), 78
  agricultural policies of, 89–104
  and aristocracy, 4, 5, 16–17, 90
  birth of, 14
  Charles II and, 57–59, 71–72, 74–75
  childhood of, 6, 15
  as contrasted to CT, 165, 243–245
  and council of state, 19
  debts and expenses of, 65–66, 69, 71–79, 81–89, 116, 137, 165, 169; *see also* Felton, Timothy
  and Danby, 47, 49–50, 72, 84
  and dispute with Dr. Owen Hughes, 47–49
  and Dutch Wars, 32–33, 35, 72
  estate management of, 64, 66–73, 88, 156, 159
  government favor sought by, 32–33, 53, 58, 59, 71–72
  government favor toward, 6, 23, 36, 45, 59, 71–72, 159
  and Sir John Hobart, 53–57
  land purchases of, 79–81, 171
  as lord lieutenant, 6, 22, 24–25, 31, 32–34, 37, 38, 39, 40, 63, 70, 71, 75, 82, 89, 97, 173, 229
  loss of lord lieutenancy, 39, 41, 45, 85, 97
  and opposition to Oliver Cromwell, 17
  peerage of, 6, 23, 24, 70, 78, 97
  and political influence in Norfolk, 16–24, 47, 70–71, 168
  and religious dissenters, 34–36
  and residence in London, 51–52, 58, 75–79, 82, 173, 242
  Restoration and, 46
  and rivalry with Henry Howard, 30–32, 33, 38
  and rivalry with Sir Robert Paston, 37–41
  and support for Sir Robert Kemp, 42–44
  and Tory conversion, 57
  and Whig crisis in Norfolk, 51–57
Townshend, Horatio (third son of HT):
  apprenticeship of, 118
  inheritance of, 85, 107–108, 112
  as parliamentary candidate from Great Yarmouth, 212, 217
  upbringing of, 113–116
Townshend, Horatio (first son of CT), 119
  death of, 219
Townshend, Mary Ashe (second wife of HT), 58, 76
  death of, 61, 107
  marriage of, 7, 66, 80, 84–85
Townshend, Mary (sister of HT), 66–67
Townshend, Mary Lewkenor (first wife of HT), 6, 16
  death of, 66, 84
  marriage settlement of, 67

Townshend, Mary Vere (wife of Sir Roger), 14, 70
Townshend, Sir Roger (HT's great-grandfather), 13
Townshend, Sir Roger (first baronet, father of HT) 9, 13–15
  construction of Raynham Hall by, 14, 169
  death of, 6, 15, 66
  marriage of, 14
Townshend, Sir Roger (second baronet, brother of HT), 6, 15
Townshend, Roger (second son of HT), 121, 215
  death of, 215
  decline of political aspirations, 199
  inheritance of, 85, 107–109, 112
  upbringing of, 113–116
  as Whig candidate for parliament, 195, 197, 205, 207–208; *see also* Great Yarmouth, election of 1708 in
Townshend, Thomas (son of CT), 87, 241
  political career of, 163, 238
Townshend, Vere (sister of HT), 70, 73, 82
Townshend, William (son of CT), 229, 241
Triennial Act, 208
Trimnel, Charles (Bishop of Norwich), 213, 222
Tubbing, Peter, 123, 124–125
Tubbing, Philip, 96, 98–101, 102, 122
Turner, Sir Charles, 204, 216, 217, 228
Turner, Sir John (d. 1712), 195
Turner, John (later second baronet), 221
turnips, cultivation of, 126, 133, 135, 151, 152, 153, 154
Turnor, Sir Edward, 172
Twickenham, Middlesex, 110

Vere, Horace (Baron Vere of Tilbury), 14
Vere, Mary. *See* Townshend, Mary Vere

Walpole, Dorothy. *See* Townshend, Dorothy Walpole
Walpole, Horace (son of Robert, prime minister), 184
Walpole, Horatio (the elder), 217, 221, 222
  on CT, 197
Walpole, Horatio (brother of Robert, prime minister), 215
  elections of 1710, 217–218
  elections of 1722, 229
Walpole, Robert (the elder), 8, 108, 110, 113
  contrasted with son, 243
  death of, 195
  and influence on CT, 192, 193
  and political impact in Norfolk, 194
Walpole, Robert (prime minister), 110, 134, 189, 204, 216, 231
  on admiralty council, 203
  as ally of CT, 210, 219, 232–233, 235
  commission of peace and, 220–221

committed to Tower, 219
contrasted with father, 243
contrasted with CT, 224, 243–244
departure for ministry, 231
dismissal as secretary of war, 214
and elections of 1705, 209
George II and, 236
political impact in Norfolk of, 197–198, 200, 202, 205
recreational expenses of, 160, 161; *see also* Houghton Hall
and rivalry with CT, 177, 188, 225–226, 233, 236–237, 238–239
as Whig candidate with Roger Townshend, 195
Ward, Sir Edward, 199
as nominee to shrievalty (1704), 205–206
Ward, John, 227
Warde, Thomas (bailiff and steward to HT and CT), 68, 95, 103–104, 112, 121, 123, 124, 127, 128–131
death of, 146
leases and surveys of, 150
as ombudsman for CT, 208, 216, 226
renovations at Raynham Hall and, 176
Watts, William, 208
Wentworth, Thomas (Lord Raby, first Earl of Strafford), 218
Westmorland, Lady Mary. *See* Townshend, Mary Vere

Westmorland, Mildmay Fane, second Earl of, 15
West Raynham, 144, 150
West Rudham. *See* Rudham, East and West
Whig party:
  development of in Norfolk, 12, 51
  in elections in Norfolk (1679–1681), 52–57
  in elections of 1705, in Norfolk, 207, 208–209
  in elections of 1708 in Norfolk, 212–213
  in elections of 1710 in Norfolk, 216
  in elections of 1715 in Norfolk, 225–229
  in elections of 1734 in Norfolk, 238–239
  Tory alliance with, 1717, 232
William III, 4, 198
Wilson, Joseph, 122, 157
  as disburser of CT's funds, 165
Windham, Ashe, 195, 215, 216
  as Whig candidate in 1708, 212
  as Whig candidate in 1710, 217
Windham, Elizabeth, 227
Windham, William (brother-in-law of HT), 50, 51, 108–110
Windham, William (brother of Ashe Windham):
  as assisted by CT, 203, 206

Yarmouth, Earl of. *See* Paston, Sir Robert
Yarmouth, Great. *See* Great Yarmouth
Yarmouth, Lady. *See* Paston, Lady Rebecca
Yarmouth, Little. *See* Little Yarmouth
York, James, Duke of. *See* James II

ABOUT THE AUTHOR

In his visits to England, beginning with an NEH grant in 1983, James M. Rosenheim explored the attics and library at Raynham Hall in the county of Norfolk. The seventh Marquess Townshend had given him access to the unexplored and uncatalogued papers of the family going back to the seventeenth century.

Rosenheim's interest in the English nobility began with his doctoral dissertation at Princeton. He is a graduate of Harvard (B.A. 1972) and of Princeton (Ph.D. 1981). He is editor, with A. L. Beier and D. N. Cannadine, of *The First Modern Society: Essays in English History in Honour of Lawrence Stone*, also published in 1989. Rosenheim taught, from 1978 to 1982, in the arts and sciences department of Westminster Choir College, in Princeton. Now associate professor of history at Texas A & M University, he lives in College Station, Texas.

ABOUT THE BOOK

This book was composed on the Mergenthaler 202 in Baskerville, a contemporary rendering of a fine transitional typeface named for the eighteenth-century English printer John Baskerville. It was adapted for the 202 from the Linotype version by the Mergenthaler Corporation. The book was composed by WorldComp of Sterling, Virginia, and designed and produced by Kachergis Book Design of Pittsboro, North Carolina.

WESLEYAN UNIVERSITY PRESS, 1989